Seeking Security in an Insecure World

Seeking Security in an Insecure World

Third Edition

Dan Caldwell and Robert E. Williams Jr.

ROWMAN & LITTLEFIELD
Lanham • Boulder • New York • London

Published by Rowman & Littlefield
A wholly owned subsidiary of The Rowman & Littlefield Publishing Group, Inc.
4501 Forbes Boulevard, Suite 200, Lanham, Maryland 20706
www.rowman.com

Unit A, Whitacre Mews, 26-34 Stannary Street, London SE11 4AB

British Library Cataloguing in Publication Information Available

Library of Congress Cataloging-in-Publication Data

Caldwell, Dan. | Williams, Robert E., 1959–
Title: Seeking security in an insecure world / Dan Caldwell and Robert E. Williams Jr.
Description: Third edition. | Lanham, Maryland : Rowman & Littlefield, [2016] |
   Includes bibliographical references and index.
Identifiers: LCCN 2015036398| ISBN 9781442252134 (cloth : alk. paper) | ISBN
   9781442252141 (pbk. : alk. paper) | ISBN 9781442252158 (electronic)
Subjects: LCSH: Security, International. | National security. | Internal security. |
   Economic security. | Security (Psychology) | Threat (Psychology)
Classification: LCC JZ5588 .C35 2012 | DDC 363.1—dc23 LC record available at http://
   lccn.loc.gov/2015036398

Printed in the United States of America

Contents

**PART III: POLITICAL AND SOCIAL
CONDITIONS OF SECURITY**

Preface to the Third Edition

We began thinking about and discussing this book several years after the Berlin Wall fell and the Soviet Union disintegrated. At that time, states and military issues were the principal, if not exclusive, concern of most of those who focused on security studies. On September 11, 2001, a nonstate actor, Al Qaeda, attacked the United States and killed more Americans than in any single day since the Civil War. This event marked the beginning of what several scholars have called the "second nuclear age."[1]

Globalization has contributed to worldwide prosperity, communications, and commerce; it has also made the world a more dangerous place and contributed to the rise and increased power of nonstate actors—both good and bad—in international relations. Globalization has likewise contributed to the increased salience of nonmilitary issues.

In the first edition of this book, we presented a framework focusing on traditional subjects of security studies such as war, deterrence, and arms control as well as newer concerns on the security agenda, including cybersecurity, infectious disease, and environmental threats. Comments on the first edition of the book from students, fellow professors, and policy analysts caused us (and, importantly, our publisher) to think that we had written a useful book. We have now updated and expanded the book twice.

Much has happened since the publication of the first edition in 2006 and the second edition in 2012. The wars in Afghanistan and Iraq have wound down, but without decisive results; Osama bin Laden has been killed, but Al Qaeda and its successors—most notably the Islamic State—continue to threaten regional peace and stability; Russia under President Vladimir Putin has invaded and annexed the Crimea, previously a part of Ukraine; and China is growing in economic power and beginning to flex its military muscle. In this new edition of *Seeking Security in an Insecure World* we address these and other changes in the world within the framework developed in the first edition.

We owe a great deal to those who have assisted us. Our research assistants across all three editions have been Dalton Saunders, Stephen E. Williams, Natalie Gutierrez, Tearah Skie Osborn, Elizabeth Thompson, and Heather Odell. Lauren Berry also provided help in compiling the index for this edition. We are grateful to all of them.

A number of colleagues commented on previous editions, including Ellen Caldwell, Amy Eckert, Doug Becker, Caron Gentry, and Edward Laurance.

At Rowman & Littlefield, we have been fortunate to work with editors Susan McEachern on the first two editions and Marie-Claire Antoine on this edition. In addition, Renee Legatt, Pelham Boyer, Alden Perkins, Janice Braunstein, Monica Savaglia, and Patricia Stevenson were also helpful on the publishing and production end of things.

In our own department, Bob Escudero and Christopher Low provided much-valued technical assistance along the way, and we appreciate their help.

In the previous two editions of this book, we were very intentional about the cover photographs that we chose. We have done the same for this edition and are pleased to use a powerful photograph taken in Liberia during the Ebola crisis by a former student of ours, Morgana Wingard, who has produced many evocative photos for the U.S. Agency for International Development. We appreciate her artistic eye and ability to capture the human dimension of insecurity in her images.

The two authors equally shared the work for the first edition as well as this edition; Robert Williams revised the second edition primarily. The placement of the authors' names on the title page is simply alphabetical; both should share equally in any praise or criticism of this edition.

Robert Williams dedicates this book to his parents, Robert (Bob) and Carolyn Williams, whose love and support have provided security at the most important level. In addition, he would like to thank his wife and best friend, Sandy Harrison, for her love and support.

Dan Caldwell dedicates this book to Father Gregory Boyle, SJ, who has worked tirelessly to provide "jobs and not jail"—really basic security—for countless young people through Homeboy Industries of Los Angeles.

Dan Caldwell
Robert E. Williams Jr.
Malibu, California

Preface to the Second Edition

Things change, often rapidly and dramatically. As I write this preface, the death of Osama bin Laden is front-page news all over the world. The culmination of a manhunt that began during the Clinton administration is bound to have some impact on the future of religiously inspired terrorism, on American policy in the Middle East, or on other matters related to international security, but it is not immediately clear what that impact will be. The fundamental purpose of a second edition is to take account of the changes—in scholarship and in world events—that are germane to the subject matter of a book, knowing full well that the quest for understanding and the developments that must be understood will never remain static. One can never stay ahead of change; fortunately, that is not what is required for a book such as *Seeking Security in an Insecure World* to be considered useful.

What is required is an analytical framework that makes change easier to understand when it happens. Comments on the first edition of *Seeking Security in an Insecure World* from colleagues, students, and readers beyond the world of academia encouraged us to think that we had produced a useful book and that, with some updates and some improvements, might continue to be useful. Therefore, we were pleased to be given an opportunity to produce a second edition of *Seeking Security in an Insecure World*.

Because Dan Caldwell was deep into another major research project when the opportunity to revise this book arose, I have assumed primary responsibility for the new edition. Dan has, however, read every word, offered many helpful suggestions, and provided many forms of support for the project—all while writing an important new book on U.S. policy in Afghanistan, Iraq, and Pakistan. It is perhaps unusual for an author to acknowledge debts to a coauthor, but in this case it seems entirely appropriate, and so I begin by thanking Dan for his work in setting us on the right path in the first edition

ix

and for the confidence he demonstrated in turning the book over to me in this second edition.

Dan and I owe a great deal to many undergraduates who have read and commented on the first edition of the book or, more recently, drafts of the new edition. Two of them—Stephen E. Williams and Natalie Gutierrez—went above and beyond by offering research assistance. I am very grateful to both.

Amy Eckert of Metropolitan State College of Denver and Doug Becker of the University of Southern California were kind enough to comment on the first edition of the book for an "author meets critics" panel at the ISA-West annual meeting a few years ago. I thank both of them for the combination of encouragement and constructive criticism they offered on that occasion. Thanks are also due to Caron Gentry of the University of St. Andrews for arranging the panel.

At Rowman & Littlefield, this project has been patiently, graciously, and expertly directed by Susan McEachern. Janice Braunstein has very efficiently guided the manuscript through the production process. In my own academic department, Bob Escudero and Chris Low have provided many technical assists along the way.

The cover photo, of an aid distribution line in Darfur, was taken in 2007 by Voitek Asztabski for Doctors without Borders. We are grateful for permission to use the photo, which so perfectly illustrates much of what this book is about.

Finally, special thanks go to Sandy Harrison, my wife and best friend, for her love and support.

Robert E. Williams Jr.
Malibu, California

Preface to the First Edition

We began thinking about and discussing this book several years after the Berlin Wall fell and the Soviet Union disintegrated. Those of us in the field of security studies referred regularly to the "post–Cold War world," but it was not clear immediately what sort of threats this new world posed to individuals, states, or the international system. One especially dramatic threat appeared on September 11, 2001, when terrorists attacked the United States and killed more Americans than in any single day since the Civil War.

To be sure, terrorism is a clear and present danger to the United States and many other countries around the world, but terrorism is not the only threat that has emerged in the post–Cold War world. In the decade between the collapse of Soviet-style communism and the collapse of the World Trade Center, other threats—many of them associated with the shrinking of the world through processes associated with globalization—appeared to ensure the continuing necessity of seeking security in an insecure world.

This book is about security—both the sources of insecurity and the means to greater security—in a time of great change in the world. It offers an introduction to the meaning of security at a time when scholars, reflecting on changes in the world, are debating how we should understand the concept. We have written the book for interested nonspecialists—citizens who would like to gain a better understanding of what contributes to and threatens security in the modern world—as well as for students of international relations, political science, and global studies. Our approach is distinctive, if not unique, in that it presents an overview of security rather than focusing on one particular threat, such as nuclear, chemical, or biological weapons, environmental degradation, infectious disease, and so on.

In writing books, authors incur many debts along the way. Both authors would like to thank Dalton Saunders, who served as a researcher and critic for drafts of many of the chapters. Bob Escudero provided invaluable technical assistance at many different stages in the project.

In addition, the authors would like to thank David Baird and Chris Soper, both of whom are strong supporters of scholarship at Pepperdine University and, in various ways, have assisted this project. At Rowman & Littlefield, we gratefully acknowledge the editorial assistance of Jennifer Knerr, Alden Perkins, and Pelham Boyer. We especially thank Renée Legatt for answering our many questions throughout the process.

Intellectual debts, although no less real, are often more difficult to pinpoint. We have benefited greatly from our association over the years with a group of security studies scholars in the International Studies Association's International Security Studies Section and the American Political Science Association's section on International Security and Arms Control. The opportunity to present papers at conferences organized by these groups and to receive helpful comments on our work from their members has been indispensable. Some measure of what we owe these colleagues can be seen in our citations.

Dan Caldwell would like to thank his former teachers and professors who inspired and encouraged him: Beth McGrath, Cree Kofford, Virginia Pavelko, Carl Degler, and Alexander George.

Robert Williams would like to acknowledge his students, many of whom have read and commented on drafts of various chapters, and all of whom in recent semesters have waited a little longer than usual to get back their exams and papers. He also wishes to thank his sons, Daniel and Stephen, who have stepped up to the plate in many ways: checking facts in the library and online, making photocopies, and taking on extra household responsibilities (including cooking dinner on many occasions). They have also stepped up to the plate literally—offering their father an escape from writing to watch them play baseball.

The work for this book was shared equally by the authors, and the placement of their names on the title page is simply alphabetical; both should share equally in any acclaim or criticism of the book.

Robert Williams dedicates the book to his parents, Robert (Bob) and Carolyn Williams, whose love and support have provided security at the most important level. There would be far less insecurity in the world—at all levels—if all parents were like them.

Dan Caldwell dedicates the book to Father Gregory Boyle, SJ, who has worked tirelessly to decrease poverty and violence in East Los Angeles; he is an inspiration to all who know him.

Dan Caldwell
Robert E. Williams Jr.

Chapter One

The Meaning of Security Today

We know that happiness has many roots, but none is more important than
security.

—Edward R. Stettinius, U.S. Secretary of State, 1944–1945

We live in an insecure world. The sinister forces that make the world insecure, however, are not immutable. Humankind no longer lives in fear of
bubonic plague, one of history's deadliest killers. The prospect of another
war in Europe pitting French and German forces against one another appears
remote. We fear the possibility of a nuclear conflagration far less than our
parents and grandparents did; in fact, the yellow-and-black signs that directed
Americans to fallout shelters during the Cold War have almost entirely disappeared from the landscape.

On the other hand, a new and frightening form of mass-casualty terrorism
appeared on September 11, 2001. Subsequent terrorist attacks in Madrid, London, Bali, Mumbai, Nairobi, and Paris have spread insecurity around the globe.
Diseases unknown to earlier generations—SARS, avian flu, HIV/AIDS, and
Ebola—have emerged, while some old and well-known diseases—tuberculosis
and malaria, for example have reemerged in drug-resistant forms, raising
questions about whether modern medicine can provide protection against the
return of devastating pandemics. In place of the threats once posed by strong,
well-armed states, the world now confronts a variety of dangers related to
weak, ungovernable states: piracy on the high seas, transnational crime, terrorism, and humanitarian disasters that demand attention. But two threats that are
largely invisible may be the most serious: the rapidly developing cyberwar capabilities of both state and nonstate actors and the slow but steady accumulation
of carbon dioxide in the atmosphere from the use of fossil fuels. The former

threatens to wreak havoc on the industrial processes that create wealth while the latter threatens to wreak havoc on the natural processes that nurture life.

Insecurity reflects the state of the world, but it is also a state of mind. Consequently, the proximity, in both space and time, of a threat can affect its ability to produce insecurity. There also seems to be a "dread" factor in insecurity. Humans often dread the unknown and the uncontrollable event, such as a random bombing, out of all proportion to the actual threat such an event poses. The social dimension of insecurity—the creation and spread of collective fears—adds another element to our understanding of the subjective aspect of insecurity. Just as the conditions that produce insecurity change over time, so do collective understandings. Security—and insecurity—are socially constructed.

Much has changed since the Cold War, when tense standoffs between the United States and the Soviet Union over Berlin, Cuba, and the Middle East; a series of proxy wars; and major conflicts in Korea, Vietnam, and Afghanistan took place in the shadow of nuclear weapons. Perhaps even more has changed since the early days of the post–Cold War period, when it appeared to many in the West that the military establishments created to fight World War II and enhanced to prevent the spread of communism would remain relevant only if they could be adapted to the demands of peacekeeping and humanitarian intervention in the developing world. The shock of 9/11 and long, taxing wars in Iraq and Afghanistan ended whatever complacency about security may have developed in the aftermath of the Cold War. What they did not do, however, is erase the changes in the meaning of security that had developed during the 1990s. What we are left with is a quest for security that has become far more salient than it seemed to be during the early days of the post–Cold War period while also becoming far more complicated than it was during the Cold War itself.

The new security agenda is based in part on the recognition that most of the world's people are threatened by problems unrelated to weapons of mass destruction and terrorist networks. It is also based on the recognition that many of these problems ought to be concerns of those in the developed world who have generally focused only on threats of a military nature. The scope and gravity of the threats on the new security agenda can be shown with a few examples.

- In 2013, the most recent year for which data are available, approximately seventeen thousand children under the age of five died each day—most due to birth complications or disease. Undernutrition was a factor in almost half of these deaths.[1]

- Thirty-five million people worldwide are infected with HIV. Since HIV/ AIDS was first diagnosed, seventy-eight million people have been infected with HIV; half of those have succumbed to AIDS-related illnesses.[2]
- The International Labor Organization estimates that 20.9 million people are subjected to forced labor, of which over 2 million are being exploited by governments and rebel groups. Forced labor generates $150 billion in profits for criminals each year.[3]
- Cybercrime is estimated to cost the global economy over $400 billion each year, an amount that is certain to grow for the foreseeable future. Over eight hundred million individual records containing personal information were stolen in 2013 alone. The widespread theft of intellectual property means that losses of innovation must be reckoned among the costs of cybercrime.[4]

This very brief introduction to some contemporary sources of insecurity in the world suggests a few questions worth considering as we examine the meaning of security today. Major terrorist attacks in Europe, Asia, Africa, and North America have demonstrated that no matter where one lives, how much money one has, or how powerful one's country is, there is no such thing as absolute security. Nevertheless, although insecurity clearly transcends socioeconomic and geographic boundaries, the sources of insecurity differ considerably depending on whether one lives in North America or Western Europe, on the one hand, or sub-Saharan Africa or Southeast Asia, on the other. Therefore, the first question may well be: Whose security are we talking about?

Following hard on the heels of that question is one that shifts the focus from who to what: While terrorist attacks and civil wars may fit comfortably into our notions of what the study of security is (or should be) all about, where do disease and starvation fit in? If threats posed by famine and HIV/ AIDS are the proper subjects of a study of security (and if we have answered the "whose security" question in a way that forces those of us who don't face these threats to think about those who do), then how is the subject to be limited? Why is the threat posed by disease (or at least a particular pandemic) a fit subject for analysis while the threat posed in some parts of the world by wild animals or monsoons or earthquakes is not? These are certainly fair, and vexing, questions.

Answering these and similar questions requires that we examine the meaning of security with considerable care. Before we undertake that analysis, however, consider what a bit of historical perspective adds to our understanding.

Americans today live with the memory of 9/11 and the wars it spawned in Afghanistan and Iraq. National debates—about budget priorities, civil liberties, and, of course, electoral politics—are conducted within the context of a shared recognition of the threat that terrorists pose. For a different generation of Americans, "the Greatest Generation," life (or a part of it) was lived in the shadow of European fascism and Pearl Harbor. That same generation and the baby boom generation that followed lived in the shadow of the atomic bomb as well. For over four decades, most of the world lived in some measure of fear of nuclear war, a fear fed by recurrent crises, diplomatic saber rattling, and even popular culture (including movies like *Dr. Strangelove*, *On the Beach*, and *Fail Safe* in the 1960s and *The Day After* in the 1980s). These different experiences have shaped different understandings of security. This is perhaps the essential point with which to begin a discussion of the meaning of security: Our conception of security changes with the circumstances we face. Each generation and, for that matter, each community determines the meaning of security according to the threats it confronts in its time and place.

WHOSE SECURITY?

The question concerning whose security is at issue is one that could be answered in a number of ways. It is a question that, for students of international relations, raises familiar issues concerning levels of analysis. (Some of these issues will be addressed in the discussion below of the widening of our understanding of security.) It is also, however, a question that, for students of comparative politics, can prompt discussion of the widely divergent security interests of different states. To illustrate the point, Iceland, which has no standing military and spends just 0.13 percent of GDP on defense, operates in a security environment that is dramatically different from that of Iraq, which spends 8.70 percent of GDP on defense, or Israel (5.69 percent).[5]

Our focus in this book is on security as it is conceived in the developed world. We are, in other words, primarily concerned with the meaning of security for people in advanced market democracies, such as the United States, Canada, Japan, Australia, New Zealand, and the European Union. Our focus is, in part, a simple reflection of the fact that we ourselves live, and are writing primarily for an audience that lives, in the developed world. We hope, however, to avoid being overly parochial. The reasons for avoiding narrowness, although perhaps obvious, are worth stating as a means of articulating our principal assumptions about our subject.

First, at the risk of lending support for a strain of Western—and perhaps especially American—ethnocentrism that we believe is both unwarranted and unwise, we acknowledge that the security of the West is important not only to those who live there but also to much of the rest of the world. There is no better way to demonstrate this point than to examine, briefly, certain aspects of the American response to the 9/11 attacks. Since the American sense of security was shattered by the terrorist attacks on 9/11, the United States, in response, waged one war in Afghanistan and another in Iraq, ousting two regimes in the process; imposed significant costs and restrictions on immigration to the United States; looked the other way with respect to revelations concerning Pakistani nuclear technology transfers; imposed on other countries security requirements for airports and harbors as a condition for sending planes and ships to the United States; and underfunded many international aid programs as resources shifted into the "war on terrorism" and the reconstruction of Afghanistan and Iraq. Additionally, the terrorist attacks in Madrid on March 11, 2004—the deadliest terrorist attack in Spanish history—and in London on July 7, 2005, are widely believed to have been aimed at punishing the Spanish and British governments for their support of the American war in Iraq. The security of the United States and the methods used to defend it have a major impact on the rest of the world. As an old saying familiar to diplomats and businessmen everywhere puts it, "when the United States sneezes, the rest of the world catches a cold."

Against the temptation to adopt an insular focus, however, we must affirm a contrasting set of beliefs about security. First, security is, in many important respects, indivisible. Seeking security in an insecure world for one's state alone is a strategy doomed to failure. This is especially true in light of the increasing interconnectedness of the world's people and their problems, but it has been a fact of life throughout history. Bubonic plague (*Yersinia pestis*) originated in China but killed millions of Europeans in the Black Death of the fourteenth century. World War II, dramatic enough in its impact on Europe and Asia, led to revolutions in Africa that have convulsed that continent now for generations. These are but two of an almost limitless number of examples of security concerns that transcend boundaries.

Those of us in the West—particularly the United States—cannot act in the interest of our own security without having an impact on the security of others. Likewise, we cannot ignore the security of others without endangering our own. There is thus a very powerful consequentialist argument for thinking in terms of international, or global, security rather than of national security alone. To express the point as a paradox, a narrowly self-interested security policy cannot be narrowly self-interested.

Our view of security, however, is not grounded solely in utilitarian considerations. We believe that there are principled reasons for taking a broader view of security. A commitment to human rights—as well as broader humanitarian principles—demands that we give attention to many of the security concerns that are products of injustice in the world. We believe, to take but one example, that those living in the developed world should be exposed to, and should ultimately adopt as a matter of policy, a perspective on security that includes human trafficking as a security issue, because for millions of people worldwide it constitutes a serious threat to basic rights.

Viewed in this way, the question of "whose security" appears to be closely related to the question of what should be included among the things we define as security issues. This is as it should be. To define the boundaries of the contemporary security agenda is to specify what threats to the interests of which subjects ought to be given the priority associated with security issues. This can be a contentious issue.

Over sixty years ago, in the early days of the Cold War, Arnold Wolfers cautioned the realists who had put national security at the center of American foreign policy that "national security," like other commonly discussed terms, might mean different things to different people and, in fact, might have no precise meaning.[6] More recently, John Baylis has observed that the consensus among scholars is that "security is a 'contested concept.'"[7] While the concerns now being expressed about how we define security are both more widespread and more diverse in origin, it is remarkable how little things have changed since the 1950s. Today, as in Wolfers's day at the outset of the Cold War, the concept of security is in search of a definition that can command general assent.

What has changed in our understanding of security over the last six decades is this: Security can no longer be defined, if it ever could be, exclusively in terms of the ability of a state to defend its territory and its principal values against military threats. An ability to deal with other threats, including but not limited to transnational drug trafficking, international terrorism, resource scarcities, economic espionage, transboundary pollution, disease, climate change, and even cyberterrorism,[8] is now thought to be essential to the protection of national security.[9] The security agenda has expanded due to both a growing awareness of the limits of the traditional national security focus and the combined effect of increased interdependence and complexity in international relations.[10]

While expansion of the concept of security seems to have been unavoidable, given the limits of the traditional understanding and the challenges inherent in rapid globalization, the addition of so many different issues to the security agenda threatens to make the concept of security incoherent while making the study of international security indistinguishable from the broader field of international relations. When one adds to this concern the levels-of-analysis problem, with its implication that security can be seen in individual, state, and international terms (as well as in categories that lie between these), the task of providing a comprehensive account of the quest for security in the modern international system appears challenging, if not overwhelming.

Defining "Security"

The word *security* is derived from the Latin *securitas*, which, in turn, comes from *securus*—that is, "without a care." Security is a condition or state of being free from the threat of harm. There are both objective and subjective aspects of this condition, meaning that security involves material circumstances as well as the psychological state produced by those circumstances.

Security and peace have much in common. Psychologically, we often equate security with peace of mind. Politically, the traditional concept of security is commonly equated with an ability either to remain at peace (without having to sacrifice important values to do so) or, failing that, to restore peace quickly. Security and peace, in turn, are closely related to order and stability. The quest for international order is, fundamentally, nothing more than the quest for peace and security.[11]

The unmodified term *security* covers a broad terrain. It can encompass, at one extreme, the individual's perception of well-being when free of threats to his or her welfare and, at the other extreme, that state of order in the international system that is supposed to be the principal pursuit of the United Nations. No book yet written on the subject of security has even surveyed the entire range of meaning. Any book that attempted to do so would no doubt be unsatisfactory to both the psychologist, at one end of the spectrum, and the student of international relations, at the other. In order to make the concept manageable, social scientists have had to circumscribe it so that it conforms to what they perceive to be the primary subjects of their discipline. To the student of international relations, the subjects of security are generally defined in terms of levels of analysis. Consequently, it is possible to think in terms of *human* security, *national* security, and *international* security, as well as security at other, intermediate levels.

The Process of "Securitization"

Until recently, those who dealt with security issues, in both the academic and the policy realms, could think of the boundaries of their field as fixed and self-evident. Invasions by foreign armies, nuclear deterrence, and terrorist bombings were security issues; hurricanes, flu outbreaks, and computer crashes were not. Thinking about "national security" meant thinking about war or the threat of war. Military force, the means by which wars are waged (or deterred), was thought to be the primary, if not the sole, guarantor of the state's security.

Over time, the question of what should be considered a security issue took on a different aspect as more answers were accepted. New issues found places on the security agenda. Where once there had been only national security, which meant the security of the state against military threats, scholars and policymakers began discussing economic security, energy security, food security, health security, environmental security, and more. Public health experts, development specialists, and agronomists took their places alongside soldiers as critical actors in the quest for security. Our understanding of security had expanded.

But why? Were disease, famine, and resource scarcities new issues? Had those who used the new language of economic, food, and environmental security (among others) uncovered threats that had previously been unexamined? With a few exceptions, such as the emergence of the HIV/AIDS pandemic, the threats were not new, nor were they newly uncovered. What was new was the decision, made not by one individual but by many, to designate certain problems as threats to security. The process by which this occurs is called *securitization*.

According to what is called the Copenhagen School in security studies, a critical theory first articulated by Barry Buzan,[12] security is a socially constructed concept. The term has no fixed and self-evident meaning; instead, its meaning is a product of an intersubjective understanding. Essentially, security means what the members of a particular society mutually understand it to mean. That meaning is generated by a social process in which, from time to time, new understandings of security are proposed. For a problem to come to be regarded as a security issue, two things are required: First, someone in a position of authority must characterize the issue as a security concern—that is, as an existential threat. This, in the language used by the Copenhagen School, is the "speech act." Second, society must, on the whole, accept the new characterization. For example, if the president asserts that drug trafficking or illegal immigration or energy independence is a security issue and the assertion is met with general agreement, then the issue actually becomes a security issue as a result of this social process having created a new intersubjective understanding.

Securitization would mean very little if nothing more than a label were at stake. But to call an issue a matter of national security is to elevate its status so that efforts to deal with it typically take precedence over other, nonsecurity issues. Problems that have been securitized are generally exempted from the process of negotiation that yields the political compromises that are common in the search for solutions to lesser concerns. Thus, framing a problem as a security issue can help to ensure that more resources are devoted to solving the problem than might otherwise be the case.[13]

The Traditional Paradigm

Because the state was the focus of concern, at least in the dominant realist tradition, most of the attention given the subject of security among scholars of international relations during the Cold War centered on national security. Indeed, during the Cold War the mention of "security studies" suggested to the vast majority of scholars nothing more or less than "*national* security studies," which, in turn, was generally limited in common usage to matters relating to the use of military force. In that usage, "national security policy" and "defense policy" were generally regarded as interchangeable terms. While some regimes, particularly authoritarian dictatorships in Latin America, regarded internal threats as within the scope of national security policy,[14] advanced industrial democracies generally avoided the use of military force to promote internal order, preferring civilian police forces for that purpose. Since democracies have also avoided the use of military force in wars of aggression, the use of the term *defense policy* as a close substitute for *national security policy* is understandable in the context of the traditional paradigm.

There are, of course, a variety of purposes for which military force can be used. Within the state, the military may be used to assert the authority of the government over dissident portions of the population. This may include suppressing rebellions, harassing opponents of the regime, or fighting crime. These, as noted, are functions not normally undertaken by the military in most democracies. Looking outward, the military may be used to defend the state against attack, to defend other states (or nonstate actors) against attack, to perform police functions in other states, to punish other states (or nonstate actors) for the violation of international norms, or to attack other states.

The association in the traditional paradigm of security policy with the military is due to the nature of the assumptions underlying both the definition of security and the perception of corresponding threats. National security is fundamentally concerned with the preservation of sovereignty against external threats. It encompasses the state's efforts to control what happens to its territory, its citizens, its resources, and its political system. It is, in large measure, concerned with the defense of borders, so that outsiders may play a role within the state only on terms acceptable to the state. Historically, the most significant threat to the integrity of a state's borders and its ability to determine its own course came from the militaries of hostile states. Only armed forces, or so it was thought, could penetrate borders in such a way as to threaten seriously the sovereignty of the state. If the threat to sovereignty came from within, as in the case of insurrection, the military could be the guarantor of security in that instance as well. External threats not susceptible to military solutions were, until recently, virtually unknown.[15]

The traditional assumptions about the link between national security and territorial sovereignty, together with the limited types of threats that states experienced until recently, produced a narrow understanding of the concept of security that is still very much with us even though the landscape has changed significantly. Under the traditional paradigm, the state was considered the primary, if not the sole, subject of security studies. The primary threat to security was the threat of invasion (or, in some circumstances, blockade) by a hostile state and thus was perceived as a military threat. Consequently, preparing for war, either by arming itself or by enlisting allies, was the state's principal means of ensuring its own security.

The New Paradigm

To the extent that territorial states defended by military force remain central to human affairs, the traditional security paradigm continues to be serviceable. There are several factors, however, including the often-noted decline of the territorial state and the rise of new, nonmilitary threats, that suggest a need to think about security in new ways.[16] The late Richard Ullman argued that "defining national security merely in military terms conveys a profoundly false image of reality [and] causes states to concentrate on military threats and to ignore other and perhaps more harmful dangers." He suggested that a security threat be defined as "an action or sequence of events that (1) threatens drastically and over a relatively brief span of time to degrade the quality of life for the inhabitants of a state, or (2) threatens significantly to narrow the range of policy choices available to the government of a state or to private, non-governmental entities (persons, groups, corporations) within the state."[17]

The concept of security has been stretched in two directions: first, with respect to the issues to be included on the security agenda, and second, with respect to the subject (or what some scholars prefer to call the referent object) of security.[18] Richard Wyn Jones has suggested that the former move be labeled *broadening* and the latter *extending* in order to avoid the ambiguity of the single term—*widening*—often used to refer to both.[19] The effort to open up the concept in both directions began in the 1970s as analysts began to question the narrow focus within traditional security studies on Cold War defense issues as well as the problems associated with efforts to think exclusively in terms of *national* security. The interplay of military and economic issues that first attracted the serious attention of analysts in the 1970s, and the rise at about the same time of global environmental awareness, contributed significantly to efforts to challenge the traditional paradigm.[20] The end of the Cold War and the 9/11 attacks gave added impetus to supporters of a new security paradigm by diminishing the significance of the issues on the traditional security agenda while raising a host of new questions concerning both the proper subjects of security and the nature of threats to security.

To refer to a new security paradigm in the singular is, of course, an oversimplification, since in reality a variety of contenders for such a designation have emerged since the 1970s. In many instances, the new conceptions of security can be identified by their adjectives. From UN-sponsored discussions of the need to expand the concept of security have come proposals for a shift to *comprehensive* security (emphasizing the need for broadening) or *common* security (emphasizing the need for extending). The collective response to Iraq's invasion of Kuwait in 1990 renewed interest in the concept of *collective* security, which Woodrow Wilson popularized at the end of World War I. In 1993, Australian foreign minister Gareth Evans proposed what he called *cooperative* security.[21] Meanwhile, a move to extend the concept of security in the opposite direction (toward the individual rather than the international system as subject) came in 1994 when the United Nations Development Program put forth the idea of *human* security.[22]

These and other challenges to the traditional paradigm share a number of characteristics so that it may be reasonable, at least as a shorthand expression, to speak of a new paradigm. This new paradigm is characterized, first of all, by a willingness to consider a variety of possible subjects of security. Rather than focusing primarily on the state, new conceptions of security consider a wide range of possible subjects, from the individual through the international levels. Second, while under the traditional paradigm security was conceived primarily in terms of defense against military threats (with consideration occasionally being given to economic threats), under the new paradigm security involves defense against many different threats, including environmental problems, the collapse of currencies, human trafficking, and so on. A third difference between the paradigms is that the new conception of security is far more open to the possibility that the principal threat to the lives of citizens and other core values of a state may come from the state itself. In other words, the new paradigm recognizes the tremendous potential of states to generate insecurity both through direct threats against their own citizens and as an indirect consequence of the actions they take in the name of national security.

In general, these and other differences between the old and new paradigms may be reduced to one central point: The new paradigm expands the concept of security by broadening the agenda or extending the subjects. Strong arguments have been advanced for both moves, but important questions concerning the limits of these moves remain. In fact, the difficulties in circumscribing the concept of security under the new paradigm have left it, in the words of R. B. J. Walker, "embarrassingly limp and overextended."[23]

The Question of "Broadening"

How are we to limit the security agenda, given the fact that security, understood as the condition or state of being free from the threat of harm, involves so many different possible threats? Without even considering a range of threats associated specifically with individual security and international security (matters to be considered with respect to the question of "extending"), we can easily recall circumstances in which states have been concerned with threats posed by the military forces of neighboring states, terrorists, indigenous revolutionary movements, the possibility of an accidental nuclear launch, the collapse of national currencies, the collapse of commodity prices, monsoons, earthquakes, the spread of disease, famine, or overpopulation, to mention just a small number of threats on a very long list. Some island states even face the threat of gradual inundation by rising sea levels, as Maumoon Abdul Gayoom, president of the Maldives, noted in his speech at the United Nations Millennium Summit: "Our quest for progress must be sustainable. We have no right to destroy the earth. Ecological damage, including global warming, must be curbed. All low-lying countries must be saved: when the United Nations meets to usher in yet another century, will the Maldives and other low-lying island nations still be represented here?"[24] The inundation of the Maldives by the Indian Ocean tsunami in December 2004 made President Gayoom's question even more urgent than he could have imagined when he spoke in 2000.

Is climate change properly regarded as a threat to the national security of the Maldives and the Federated States of Micronesia, or does it belong in some other category? What about the threat from tsunamis, such as the one that inundated Japan's Fukushima nuclear power plant in March 2011 resulting in the meltdown of three of the plant's six nuclear reactors? Are the virus hunters of the Centers for Disease Control and Prevention in Atlanta properly regarded as part of the national security establishment? Is the Greek economic crisis a national security concern, either for Greece or for the other members of the European Union? Bangladesh suffers more death and destruction from natural disasters than from the military activities of its neighbors. Does this mean that protecting against the effects of monsoons should be the top national security priority of the Bangladeshi government? How, to restate the original question, are we to distinguish between threats that ought to be the concerns of a state's security policies and threats of other types?

Finding an answer to this question that is at once both direct and generally acceptable has proved impossible thus far. Scholars and policymakers occupy a wide range of positions regarding where the lines around their area of concern should be drawn. The best we can do is clarify the issues involved and offer some general principles as possible means of delimiting the field of security studies. The first step in doing this may well be to consider how we understand threats.

Under both the old paradigm and the new, the concept of security can be understood only in relation to threats. Indeed, the concept of threat is a necessary part of any intelligible definition of security and insecurity. Threats have traditionally been understood as the products of some combination of capabilities and intentions. A threat exists where a potential adversary has both the capability to do harm and malign intent. In the realist account, the potential adversaries are, of course, states, and their capability to do harm comes in the form of military power. The understanding that a threat must combine capability and intention conforms very well to what we see in the world. The United States perceives little or no threat from states with negligible capabilities, regardless of their level of hostility. Likewise, the existence of certain well-armed states in Western Europe, for example, poses little or no threat because the intent is benign. The value of this simple definition of threat is further demonstrated by the fact that it has been the foundation, at least implicitly, of two important concepts related to security: the security dilemma (in which threats are exacerbated because malign intent is assumed)[25] and the security community (in which threats are diminished because efforts have been made to provide assurances of benign intent).[26]

Consider the relationship of this formula to the security dilemma. Because military capabilities are, to some degree, out there for all to see while intentions are both largely unknowable and subject to rapid change, the prudent assessor of foreign threats must take what is known about the potential adversary's capabilities and combine this information with a worst-case reading of intentions. As a result of this better-safe-than-sorry approach, threats are inflated, measures are taken to counter the inflated threats, and the prudent assessor of threats on the other side is given evidence that seems to require a similar response.[27] This, more or less, is the problem of security and insecurity as seen by the realists. The point here, however, is not to deconstruct realism or even the notion of the security dilemma. It is, instead, to consider whether, under the new paradigm, we can still work with the understanding that threats involve a combination of capabilities and intentions.

First, we should acknowledge that the term *capabilities*, when used in this context, may conjure up thoughts of troops, tanks, ships, bombers, and perhaps even weapons of mass destruction, for those who remember security studies back in the days when life may have been "nasty, brutish, and short" but at least there was an easily identifiable enemy. Simply to avoid privileging the military view of security, we can substitute the phrase *potential to cause harm* for *capabilities* in the threat equation. But what are we to do with intentions?

The new paradigm in security studies appears to regard intentions as an unnecessary element of threat. Consider the addition of environmental threats or the rise of drug-resistant diseases to the list of security threats under the new paradigm. Except in cases of environmental warfare or biological warfare where the associated threats are wielded by human agents, what role can intentions play in assessments of these new security threats? It appears that the answer is none whatsoever. This might suggest, for those intent on defending the traditional paradigm against the broadening that has inevitably made security studies a much less focused discipline, that human agency might be the ticket to a return to coherence. This view would suggest that we should only consider as threats to security those possibilities that combine the potential to cause harm with an intent—that is, a human desire—to cause harm. Such an understanding would allow for the inclusion on the security agenda of some nontraditional threats, such as terrorism, the deliberate creation of refugee flows (as in Kosovo in the 1990s), and attacks on computer networks, while maintaining a familiar look to the field.

However tempting it may be to fight off the wideners on the grounds of intent, it is simply not possible without stipulating some counterintuitive limits. If a security threat, properly defined, can exist only where human intent is present, then President Gayoom of the Maldives, concerned about the possible inundation of his island state due to a rise in sea level produced by climate disruption, has a problem but not a security threat. If scientists determine that one of the thousands of asteroids in near-Earth orbits is destined to plow into our planet three revolutions around the sun from now, we have a problem but not a security threat.[28] This, some will no doubt argue, is too restrictive.

There are serious problems with the alternative of simply arguing that threat equals capability (or potential to cause harm). Most notably, the list of threats would quickly become unmanageable even for advocates of widening the security agenda. Such a formulation, left unmodified, also fails to discriminate between imminent and remote threats. Some of the problems, however, can be addressed by allowing for the operation of deterministic phenomena as a substitute for human intent. Threat, using the revised formula, becomes a product of the potential to cause harm and *either* intent or deterministic natural processes.

It is important to note that it may not always be possible to draw a hard-and-fast dividing line between human and natural threats. The interaction of humans with the environment means that threats to human well-being from such things as climate change, the spread of disease, population growth, and famine will generally have some combination of human and natural causes. However, the difficulty of drawing a line between human and natural agency in some cases does not negate the potential significance of such a distinction for our efforts to limit the scope of the security agenda.

Another distinction that needs to be examined in trying to delimit the proper concern of security policy is the distinction between threats that arise as a result of intentional behaviors and those that result from unintentional behaviors. Once again, the distinction is not absolute, as a number of examples will illustrate, but in assessing the proper concerns of security policy it nonetheless appears fitting that we should consider the extent to which threats emanate from deliberate actions. The more deliberate a threatening action appears to be, the more conclusively it merits consideration as a security issue. To illustrate, compare two threats to Western Europe emanating from the Soviet Union during the 1970s and 1980s, respectively. In 1977, the Soviet Union began deploying in Eastern Europe a new intermediate-range ballistic missile known as the SS-20. The deployment of SS-20s, aimed at targets in Western Europe, provoked antinuclear demonstrations and a counterdeployment by NATO of Pershing II missiles and ground-launched cruise missiles beginning in 1979. In 1986, an explosion at the nuclear power plant at Chernobyl resulted in the dispersal of radioactive material all over Europe. Although the effects of the Chernobyl blast on the well-being of the citizens of Western European states were more direct, more immediate, and more tangible than the effects of the earlier SS-20 deployment, the missile deployment was characterized as a security concern while the reactor accident was not. It is the absence of intentionality that accounts for this difference. Had the Soviet Union deliberately released radioactive material in order to cause panic in Western Europe, defense ministries would have been called upon to respond along with public health officials.

Some threats produced by human actions have a quasi-intentional character. The mismanagement of both agricultural policies and foreign assistance has been a factor in some of Africa's more devastating famines. It is unclear, however, that the production of famine was intentional in most of these cases. More troubling from the standpoint of our efforts to distinguish threats to national security from more "natural" threats is that category of activities involving deliberate actions with unintended consequences. On the one hand, there are action-reaction processes (arms races, for example) in which the behavior of one party is in some measure determined by the behavior of the other party. On the other hand, there are situations, such as the collapse of financial markets, in which the cumulative effect of rational individual decisions is unintended and sometimes dire.

One possible response to this distinction is to suggest that threats reflecting no underlying human intent ordinarily should not be the subjects of security policy. This has the effect of excluding all natural disasters (or "acts of God," in the parlance of theologians and insurance underwriters) from consideration. It also has the effect of excluding accidents and cases of mass hysteria from our list of security concerns. But is this as it should be? What about the classification of military accidents (e.g., accidental nuclear launches) as security issues? Nuclear accidents have been considered an important concern in U.S. national security policy since the late 1950s.[29]

It may seem that a definition of security that excludes threats that are "natural" or "unintentional" is simply a rationalization of the view that security policy cannot concern itself with threats against which no defense is possible. But there are defenses against currency crises, environmental degradation, and even, to some extent, natural disasters. This suggests that the effort to distinguish between threats to national security and other types of threats (that is, nonsecurity threats) must somehow focus on human agency and intentionality.

Those who are most interested in preserving traditional limits on the field of security studies often focus on the distinction between political and nonpolitical threats, arguing that only political threats are the proper concerns of government policies. A political threat is one involving human intent of a particular kind. A political threat targets the institutions and processes of a government. Using this distinction, cyberespionage aimed at stealing or altering data stored in military computers would constitute a security threat requiring a political response while similar actions intended to steal the trade secrets of a private corporation would not. While there are clearly dangers in giving governments authority to deal with an ever-expanding list of potential threats to security, we believe that complex linkages between political and nonpolitical, intentional and unintentional, or human and natural threats make it impossible to return to narrower, more traditional understandings of security.

The Question of "Extending"

Recognition that the national security of any given state cannot be meaningfully assessed in isolation from the national security of other states—that one state's quest for security may actually promote insecurity in other states—has led to calls for greater attention to *international* security or *global* security. Even in the quest for national security, such international measures as the establishment of international organizations, the progressive development of international law, and the negotiation of multilateral arms control agreements have long been regarded as indispensable.

As Barry Buzan has noted, the nature of states and the nature of the international system are so closely intertwined that it is impossible to address national security without considering international security, and vice versa. He writes,

> The political connection between states and system is so intimate that one is at risk of introducing serious misperception even by speaking of states *and* the international system as if they were distinct entities. Although they are distinguishable for some analytical purposes, states and the international system represent opposite ends of a continuous political phenomenon. The international political system is an anarchy, which is to say that its principal defining characteristic is the absence of overarching government. The principal defining feature of states is their sovereignty, or their refusal to acknowledge any political authority higher than themselves. The essential character of states thus defines the nature of the international political system, and the essential character of the political system reflects the nature of states. If units are sovereign, their system of association must be anarchy, and if the system is anarchic, its members must reject overarching government.[30]

Moving in the other direction, the recognition that the state, which is the subject of *national security*, is—or ought to be—merely an instrument for the promotion of the well-being of individuals has suggested a need to emphasize *individual* security or *human* security. The deference shown to states and the harm to the lives of individuals that resulted is widely regarded to have been one of the great evils of the twentieth century. One need only reflect on the terrible human rights abuses perpetrated in the Soviet Union by the KGB—the Committee for State Security—or the shameful U.S. record of nuclear tests involving military personnel to realize that national security has often threatened the security of people. As Richard Wyn Jones puts it, "In much of the world, states, far from fostering an atmosphere within which stability can be attained and prosperity created, are one of the major sources of insecurity for their citizens."[31]

It is also the case that, just as national security and international security are intimately linked, national security and human security are strongly connected. This is true even for those who reject the realist assumption that the security of the state guarantees the security of the individual. Robert Kaplan's concerns about the impact of international peace on domestic crime rates suggest one form that this interaction may take. A reduction in the size of the standing army, together with its gradual transformation into a better-educated and more elite force, means that large numbers of young males—a notoriously impulsive and violence-prone segment of any nation's population—will be released into society. This, Kaplan argues, portends "an increase in gang activity and other forms of violent behavior."[32] Of course, one need not range into controversial sociological conjectures to find circumstances in which national and human security concerns merge. The reverse of Kaplan's example—namely, the conscription of young men into the Army rather than their release from it—provides an obvious example.

From a liberal perspective, there are strong arguments for making the individual the primary subject of security. The state, according to this view, is valuable primarily as a means to the end of the well-being of the citizens who constitute the state. To concede primacy to the state is to risk making people instrumental agents in the service of the state rather than the reverse. The difference between a liberal state and an authoritarian state often turns on this distinction. Instead of providing security for their citizens, authoritarian regimes are often guilty of threatening the security of the individual in the name of national security. To state the difference bluntly, in democracies the state exists to protect the rights of individuals; in authoritarian states, individuals exist to serve the state. The suppression of political dissent by Latin American dictators operating under the so-called national security doctrine provides an example of this. As a result, there appears to be a strong case, at least from a liberal perspective, for bypassing the state in favor of the individual as the primary subject of security. However, human rights law, which is now well established in the international system, may offer a better means of protecting individuals by working with and through states.

What conclusions concerning efforts to broaden and extend the concept of security does this analysis suggest? The narrowness of the Cold War focus on security as a military matter could not help but provoke a reaction toward broadening the security agenda. Unless limits are established, however, broadening can create more problems than it solves, including, at the extreme, undermining the coherence of the discipline. Assessing whether threats merit inclusion on the security agenda on the basis of the extent to which they result from human agency rather than natural processes and on the degree of intentionality they exhibit offers a partial solution to the problem.

Extending the concept of security to include individuals may be useful as a corrective to the excessive focus on the state and its needs that characterized the Cold War. It is important, however, to ensure that notions of individual security are fully compatible (as the concept of human security is) with the well-established system of international human rights. Moving in the other direction to make groups of states (or the international system itself) the subjects of security appears unavoidable, given the reciprocal effects of states and the international system on each other. In fact, significant moves toward the concept of international security were part of the traditional security paradigm long before serious efforts to widen the scope of security studies began.

As an academic discipline, security studies can exist, and even thrive, indefinitely without achieving consensus on the limits of the concept of security. It is, arguably, very beneficial for a discipline to be populated with at least a vocal minority of scholars willing to push the boundaries of their field and question central assumptions.[33] Doing so can assist in the essential task of attempting to envision security threats that lie beyond the horizon.

Seeing Beyond the Horizon

As warfare has evolved from an activity in which the battlefield is small and killing occurs at the point of a sword to one in which the battlefield can embrace an entire continent or ocean and killing commonly occurs at long range, combatants have been forced to extend their range of vision in an effort to see threats as they develop at greater and greater distances. In the nineteenth century, observers were sometimes sent aloft in hot air balloons to see what enemy forces were doing beyond the ridgeline. The range of aerial reconnaissance was dramatically extended in the twentieth century as first airplanes and then satellites and drones gave military commanders the ability quite literally to see beyond the horizon. Since at least the time of Sun Tzu, it has been understood that the defender who knows what is coming is far more likely to succeed than the one who fails to anticipate an attack. The analysis of American intelligence failures prior to 9/11 and with regard to Iraqi weapons of mass destruction was widely reported in terms of its significance for the 2004 presidential campaign, but its more fundamental significance was related to the need to address a problem that left the United States inadequately equipped to defend itself in a dynamic threat environment.

Thinking tactically about security requires seeing over the horizon. Thinking strategically about security, on the other hand, requires seeing over the *years*. Technology cannot help us as much with strategic threat assessment as it does with tactical threat assessment. In order to plan for threats over the long term—that is, to see beyond the time horizon in the same way that soldiers now see beyond the terrestrial horizon—requires qualities that remain uniquely human and, consequently, imperfect. Strategic thinking about security requires all the knowledge we can assemble—of human nature, of history, of politics, of technology, and much more—but it also requires a great deal of imagination.

The effort to define security in a way that expands our ability to perceive the threats that are truly worth worrying about while avoiding the

self-defeating temptation to worry about everything has occupied the time
and talents of many scholars and policymakers. The outcome of that effort
remains contested. It is not an idle intellectual exercise, however; decisions
that are made on the basis of some definition of security about, for example,
whether to devote more resources to disease prevention and control rather
than ballistic-missile defense (or vice versa) are decisions that may determine
someday well beyond the time horizon whether people live or die. This, in
the final analysis, is what the study of security is all about: who lives, who
dies, how, and why.

We do not contend that our definition of security is the only one possible.
It offers, we believe, a necessary correction of the Cold War's myopic focus
on states and weapons without lapsing into inability to discriminate between
common threats, on the one hand, and significant (and thus security-worthy)
threats, on the other.

We also do not intend to suggest that our method of organizing the subject
in the pages that follow is the only possible method. Our starting point is
the assumption that the quest for security must begin with a thorough understanding of the sources of insecurity; solutions must always be grounded
in an understanding of the problems. We focus, as a result, on threats. Some
assessments of threat (especially those informed by the traditional paradigm)
have focused almost exclusively on the potential to cause harm, suggesting
that it is enough to know how many weapons of a certain type exist and what
their capabilities are. The crucial matter of intentions has often been left, un-
derstandably, to foreign-policy or comparative-politics analyses.

As we have noted, the traditional understanding of threats as the product of
capabilities and intentions is somewhat too simplistic for the new, widened
security agenda. In order to impose some order on our effort to describe a
broad range of security threats, we have divided the book into three parts. Part
I focuses on traditional threats—conventional weapons and war, weapons of
mass destruction, and proliferation issues. It is, in large measure, a survey
of technologies—the weapons that, combined with malign intent, threaten
lives—that advocates of the traditional paradigm should find completely
comprehensible. Part II addresses new sources of insecurity. To be more
precise, two of the three issues addressed—disease and trafficking—are not
new, but their inclusion in studies of international security is relatively new.
Part III moves away from instruments of insecurity toward the conditions
that engender threats. We examine the state (the traditional focus of security
studies) but also the role that ethnic conflict, economic conditions, environmental degradation, and the rise of new forms of terrorism play in generating
insecurity. The division is imperfect, but by the end of the book, we hope, the
underlying rationale for this approach will appear compelling.

ADDITIONAL RESOURCES

Books and Articles

Brown, Michael E., ed. *Grave New World: Security Challenges in the 21st Century.* Washington, DC: Georgetown University Press, 2003.

Buzan, Barry, Ole Waever, and Jaap de Wilde. *Security: A New Framework for Analysis.* Boulder, CO: Lynne Rienner, 1998.

Eckert, Amy, and Laura Sjoberg, eds. *Rethinking the 21st Century: "New" Problems, "Old" Solutions.* New York: Zed Books, 2009.

Fierke, K. M. *Critical Approaches to International Security.* Cambridge: Polity Press, 2007.

Kolodziej, Edward A. *Security and International Relations.* New York: Cambridge University Press, 2005.

Krause, Keith, and Michael C. Williams, eds. *Critical Security Studies: Concepts and Cases.* Cambridge: Polity, 2002.

Mathews, Jessica Tuchman. "Redefining Security." *Foreign Affairs* 68 (Spring 1989): 162–77.

Ullman, Richard H. "Redefining Security." *International Security* 8 (Summer 1983): 129–53.

Websites

Foreign Military Studies Office (Fort Leavenworth): fmso.leavenworth.army.mil/

GlobalSecurity.org: www.globalsecurity.org/index.html

International Crisis Group: www.crisisgroup.org/

Naval Postgraduate School, Center on Contemporary Conflict: http://www.nps.edu/ccc/

Part One

TRADITIONAL SOURCES
OF INSECURITY

Chapter Two

Conventional Weapons and War

It is important to remember that every defense dollar spent to over-insure against a remote or diminishing risk—or, in effect, to "run up the score" in a capability where the United States is already dominant—is a dollar not available to take care of our people, reset the force, win the wars we are in, and improve capabilities in areas where we are underinvested and potentially vulnerable.

—Robert M. Gates, U.S. Secretary of Defense, 2006–2011

Security studies, with its emphasis on threats of the worst kind imaginable, is generally a grim subject. There is, however, some good news. Both the incidence and the destructiveness of war are declining. Thus far, the twenty-first century looks nothing at all like the first half of the twentieth century, when two world wars resulted in casualties that numbered in the tens of millions. In fact, interstate war of any kind is, at present, quite rare. While terrible in their own right, the intrastate conflicts occurring today in Afghanistan, the Central African Republic, Iraq, Syria, Yemen, and elsewhere are not nearly as destructive as the great interstate conflicts of the past. Even taking a narrower view, looking only at the past quarter-century, there are some very positive trends.[1] During the 1990s, combat deaths averaged approximately one hundred thousand per year. Since the 1990s, that figure has been cut almost in half.[2]

War, nonetheless, remains a terrible scourge. Over 3.7 million Vietnamese were killed in Indochina's wars between 1954 and the fall of Saigon in 1975.[3] While the number of Americans who died in Southeast Asia (58,220)[4] pales in comparison, the Vietnam War nonetheless ranks as one of the most traumatic events in American history. In the civil war in Liberia between 1989 and 1996, two hundred thousand people died, and tens of thousands more were raped. In neighboring Sierra Leone, a civil war fought between 1991 and 2002 killed fifty thousand people, involved roughly five thousand child soldiers, and left thousands maimed by the machetes rebels often used against civilians.[5] A series of mortality surveys sponsored by the International Rescue Committee estimated that there were 5.4 million excess deaths—those above expected mortality—in the Democratic Republic of the Congo between 1998 and 2007. While less than 10 percent of these deaths can be directly attributed to combat, excess deaths due to starvation and disease were closely linked to the collapse of Congolese society that accompanied persistent intrastate warfare.[6] In the course of a quarter-century of conflict in Sudan, close to two million people have been killed by fighting, famine, and disease. And in another ongoing conflict that began in 2011 as part of the Arab Spring, over two hundred thousand people have been killed in Syria's civil war.

No nuclear weapons have been used in war since the bombing of Hiroshima and Nagasaki in 1945. While chemical weapons have been used sporadically in post–World War II conflicts, the vast majority of combat casualties have been caused by what are called (as a backhanded means of drawing attention to the grim potential inherent in weapons of mass destruction) "conventional weapons." It is important to devote attention to the threats posed by nuclear, biological, and chemical weapons, but it is equally important to note that conventional weapons and what are sometimes called "low-intensity conflicts"—those that proceed at a slow simmer rather than a rapid boil—have wrought enormous destruction. Long before the first nuclear bomb was tested in the New Mexico desert, long before the British and the Germans used chemical weapons against each other in World War I, conventional weapons were making warfare a nasty business.

They continue to do so. The deadliest wars of the post–Cold War era, most of them intrastate conflicts, have generally been fought with small and technologically unsophisticated weapons. And yet such weapons have been extraordinarily destructive. Weapons of mass destruction are unnecessary to achieve mass casualties. In fact, less than 1 percent of the fifteen million deaths in World War I and the sixty million deaths in World War II were caused by WMD. In contrast, a significant number of the eight hundred thousand people killed during the Rwandan genocide of 1994 were driven into confined areas by militants with guns and then hacked to death with machetes. These realities bring to mind Nobel Prize winner Thomas C. Schelling's observation in an influential book on strategy published in 1966. Acknowledging that "it is a grisly thing to talk about," Schelling wrote, "Against defenseless people there is not much that nuclear weapons can do that cannot be done with an ice pick."[7]

During the Cold War, security analysts tended to focus on issues related to nuclear weapons, including deterrence theory, proliferation, and arms control. In the post-9/11 world, many have focused on terrorism and forms of warfare involving nonstate actors. Both of these emphases reflect the common impulse to worry most about threats that are new and unfamiliar. But they also reflect an emphasis on the kinds of problems that seem most likely to affect the security of those living in the developed world. More and more, war seems to be a phenomenon confined largely to the developing world. Even when the world's advanced industrialized states go to war, they project their military power into the developing world and, typically, suffer far fewer casualties than the forces they fight.

Although war in the twenty-first century, as in the last half of the twentieth century, affects the world's poor far more than it affects the rich, conventional war remains a vitally important concern of the developed world, for a number of reasons. First, the militaries of the developed world are often involved in conventional wars in the developing world. Indeed, rich states are often responsible, whether directly or indirectly, for those conflicts. Even where they bear no responsibility, their interests are often affected as a consequence of refugee flows, threats to nationals, or resource supply interruptions. And then (although this should by no means be treated as an afterthought), there are humanitarian considerations. We cannot—or at least should not—be indifferent to the suffering and the deaths of millions of people, a majority of whom are innocents, in warfare, no matter where in the world it occurs.

It would be impossible to cover thoroughly in a single book, much less in one chapter of a book, conventional war and conventional weapons. Consequently, this chapter seeks merely to provide some sense of the big, seemingly intractable, issues associated with war and weapons, along with a brief look at a few of the problems, such as those associated with the use of private militaries and child soldiers, that are especially significant at present.

WAR AS COERCIVE VIOLENCE

A useful place to begin our consideration of conventional war and weapons is with a set of fundamental points concerning the objectives served by the use of force. In *Arms and Influence*, Thomas Schelling began by noting that force can be used to take what a country wants or to keep what it has: "Forcibly a country can repel and expel, penetrate and occupy, seize, exterminate, disarm and disable, confine, deny access, and directly frustrate intrusion or attack." But there is something else that force can accomplish: "Force can be used to hurt. In addition to taking and protecting things of value it can destroy value. In addition to weakening an enemy militarily it can cause an enemy plain suffering."[8]

With this insight, Schelling proceeded to explain the evolution of modern warfare from a point at which the ability to inflict punishment on an enemy depended on the ability to defeat that enemy in war to a point at which punishment could be inflicted *prior to* the military defeat of the enemy. Under the former circumstances, the conquest of a city or an entire state would enable the conqueror to seize economic assets and to enslave or kill the enemy's civilian population. The latter situation, in contrast, is one in which the destruction of noncombatants and property occurs in the course of the war. The aerial bombardment of cities in World War II offers the classic example.

The understanding that military force can be used to punish as well as to seize or defend leads to Schelling's most important observation: when punishment can be meted out before the military defeat of the enemy is achieved, it can be deliberately employed as a means of coercion. With weapons of mass destruction, the mere threat of such punishment can be used to coerce an adversary.[9]

Much of modern warfare has as its object seizing territory, overthrowing governments, or merely fending off the attacks of others. Superior military force is necessary to accomplish these ends. There is also, however, a great deal of fighting that occurs when one side has no hope of prevailing by brute force. Such warfare, far from being irrational, is based on the idea that one's objectives can often be accomplished merely by inflicting sufficient pain to make the adversary yield. It is this—the logic of coercive violence—that explains videotaped beheadings by the Islamic State and suicide bombings. It also explains the difficulty of defeating insurgencies in Algeria, Vietnam, Afghanistan, Chechnya, and Iraq. When a military contest becomes a matter of inflicting pain rather than demonstrating the superiority of one's weapons, matching the enemy's ability to endure pain is more important than matching the enemy's military power.

This understanding of coercive violence illuminates many important features of modern military strategy—from the desire of some states to acquire weapons of mass destruction (and the desire of others to prevent them from doing so) to the widespread use of terrorism and guerrilla warfare tactics. It also helps to explain why, in spite of a level of military dominance some believe to be unmatched in the history of the world, the United States does not enjoy a commensurate level of security at home or a commensurate ability to control events abroad. Paradoxically, the vulnerability of the United States and other developed countries may be a consequence of their military dominance. To see why this is the case, we need to examine the concept of asymmetric warfare and its relationship to (and perhaps even its dominance over) what was thought to be a "revolution in military affairs."

Asymmetric Warfare

During much of the modern period, war has been fought symmetrically—that is, contending armies have battled each other with comparable weapons, tactics, and organizational modes. The army that has prevailed has generally been the one with some measure of superiority, whether quantitative or qualitative, in these areas. Technological innovations have been decisive, but only for as long as it has taken other states to adopt the new weapons. Steam-powered ships defeated sailing ships on the high seas, armor defeated cavalry on land, and so on, but the advantages were fleeting.

On the whole, states have fought wars, if not exactly on equal terms, then at least in ways that were similar. Japan provides a dramatic example of the pressure to conform. Japan's arrival as a world power, signaled by its victory over Russia in the Russo-Japanese War of 1904–1905, came at the point at which a military culture dominated by the ideal of the samurai warrior was supplanted by Western ways of waging war. But what happens when states are unable to win on terms dictated by their adversaries?

World War II illustrates the tendency of states to move to asymmetric modes of waging war when they are unable to prevail in a symmetric war. Beginning with the attack on Poland in September 1939, Nazi Germany was able to sweep across Europe in large measure due to its Blitzkrieg tactics, which coordinated the actions of infantry, armor, artillery, and air forces. To fight on at all, conquered states were required to adopt guerrilla warfare tactics. The French Resistance, in other words, was engaged in asymmetric warfare. But the British and the Americans, while certainly not conquered, were also obliged to engage in asymmetric warfare initially. With most of Western Europe occupied by the Germans and no means available to mount a direct assault on German forces, the United Kingdom decided in 1940 to initiate a bombing campaign that targeted German cities. The United States joined beginning in 1942 and eventually extended the counter-city bombing strategy to Japan.[10] Michael Walzer, who accepts the necessity of the decision to bomb cities, nonetheless labels the bombing "Allied terrorism" and notes that over half a million civilians were killed by Allied bombs in Germany and Japan.[11] When the stakes are high enough, the prospect of defeat often compels the adoption of asymmetrical tactics.

Today, the U.S. military is so dominant that, with very few exceptions, any state (or nonstate actor) that finds itself at war with the United States must wage asymmetric warfare. This is true in part simply because the United States has retained a large military force since the end of World War II, but it also has much to do with what has been called the revolution in military affairs.

The revolution in military affairs (RMA) is the effect generated by the marriage of advanced communications and information-processing systems with state-of-the-art weapons-delivery systems. When information (including visual imagery) is collected from hundreds of sources, including satellites over the theater of operations, transmitted instantaneously to decision makers at all levels from the head of state to individual tank drivers on the battlefield, and immediately processed by computers into a readily usable form, the effect on the ability to wage war is indeed revolutionary. The RMA is, in essence, a means of overcoming the confusion and uncertainty—what the Prussian military thinker Carl von Clausewitz called "the fog of war"—that has been a constant feature of battle throughout history. The location of enemy forces, the speed and direction of moving targets, the success or failure of weapons in hitting their targets, and even the content of the enemy's communications can be monitored in real time by battlefield commanders, thanks to the existence of digital cameras (and other information sensors) and the ability to collect the information they provide from locations all over the theater of operations. To know and to be able to control what one's own forces are doing in the confusion of combat is a tremendous advantage; the advantage of knowing as well what enemy forces are doing is almost invariably decisive.

The effect of the RMA was most apparent in the first of the two wars fought by the United States in Iraq. In the 1991 Persian Gulf War, as it is known in the United States, the United States and its allies began by "blinding" the Iraqi military. Radar and communications facilities (pinpointed by prewar satellite surveillance) were destroyed with precision-guided munitions, including "smart bombs" dropped from airplanes and cruise missiles launched from destroyers and submarines located hundreds of miles from their targets. The success of the initial strike gave coalition forces the advantage throughout the war of owning the skies over Iraq. American generals were able to see virtually everything the Iraqis were doing, while the Iraqis themselves were, electronically speaking, operating in the dark.

The U.S. military's advantage was also apparent in the way distance factored in. During the war, the Pentagon frequently released cockpit-camera videos from American combat aircraft. Such videos invariably showed pinpoint strikes on targets from great distances. Even on the ground, the United States used its information dominance to direct tank movements and precision-guided weapons to defeat the Iraqi army, which in 1991 was thought to be the fourth-largest in the world and battle hardened from a long war with Iran. The advantage of distance allowed the United States to deliver devastating blows from positions in the air, at sea, and on the ground that the Iraqis simply could not reach in retaliation.

Two of the most significant impacts of these changes in warfare have been the dramatic reduction in casualties for military forces fighting at a distance and enjoying information dominance and the reduction of time needed to carry out large-scale military operations. In the Persian Gulf War, only 148 Americans were killed in combat.[12] A similar number (140) were killed in Operation Iraqi Freedom, the second invasion of Iraq by the United States, up to the end of major combat operations in 2003.[13] Perhaps even more remarkably, during a two-and-a-half-month period in 1999, NATO pilots flew over thirty-eight thousand sorties in Kosovo and Serbia, suffering no fatalities.[14] With respect to time, it is worth noting that the Afghan capital of Kabul was captured just over five weeks after the beginning of Operation Enduring Freedom in 2001 while Baghdad fell to Allied forces within three weeks of the beginning of Operation Iraqi Freedom in 2003. As retired major general Robert Scales put it in one of the official histories of the Iraq War, "A fundamental law of Newtonian physics applies also to military maneuver: one can achieve overwhelming force by substituting velocity for mass."[15]

Being able to fight shorter wars with fewer casualties makes the use of military force more tolerable to the citizens of a democracy. Consequently, many in the United States initially saw the revolution in military affairs as the means by which the ghosts of the long and costly war in Vietnam were exorcised. (At the end of the Persian Gulf War, President George H. W. Bush said, "By God, we've kicked the Vietnam syndrome once and for all!"[16]) But as the wars in Afghanistan and Iraq became more protracted and casualties mounted, comparisons with the Vietnam War began to appear with greater frequency. What were designed to be quick and decisive wars became long and indecisive counterinsurgencies. And when no decisive blow can be struck, the winner is the side that outlasts the other. Speaking of the Taliban in Afghanistan, Lt. Gen. David Barno said, "Americans have the watches, but they have the time."[17]

For the United States and its allies in Iraq and Afghanistan, the advantages associated with being able to fight at a distance largely disappeared when the military task shifted from the overthrow of a government to the occupation and stabilization of the defeated state. The need for "boots on the ground" to police neighborhoods, hunt down and disarm insurgents, and rebuild critical infrastructure meant that soldiers were forced to operate within range of the unsophisticated guns and bombs used by those wanting to defeat the occupations. As a result, casualty rates increased and the excitement evoked twenty years earlier by the revolution in military affairs waned.

Of course, when the stakes are life and death, military tactics and technology evolve quickly. The dangers associated with patrolling urban areas on

foot and disarming improvised explosive devices (IEDs), among other factors, have led the U.S. military to develop and deploy robots on a vast scale.

Today, iRobot, the maker of the Roomba robotic vacuum cleaner, supplies
a robot it calls the PackBot to the U.S. Army. Designed so that a variety of
modules can be connected to a single platform, the PackBot has been used
for bomb disposal, reconnaissance, and search and rescue. In fact, the first
operational use of the PackBot occurred on 9/11 at Ground Zero in New
York City. A rival manufacturer's robot, called Talon, has been outfitted
with weapons, making it the first armed robot (or warbot) to be deployed in
battle. In its SWORDS (for Special Weapons Observation Reconnaissance
Detection System) configuration, the Talon adds a .50-caliber machine gun, a
grenade launcher, or an antitank rocket launcher to the video cameras atop its
basic platform. A remote operator connected to the warbot by radio or fiber-
optic cable sees what its cameras see and can fire its weapons. With the right
applications attached, in some cases including a loudspeaker permitting the
operator to speak to the humans the robot encounters, SWORDS can "man" a
security checkpoint, search houses, or patrol the perimeter of a base in ways
that restore the advantages of distance to the soldiers controlling it.[18]

Taking technology a step further (as Google has done with self-driving
cars), it is possible not simply to place humans at a distance from robots
operating in harm's way but to take them out of the loop entirely. In 2012,
Human Rights Watch published a report arguing that "fully autonomous
weapons" should be banned on the grounds that their use would violate the
laws of war and that their mere existence might make war and repression by
authoritarian governments more likely.[19] Since the appearance of the report,
the Meeting of States Parties to the UN Convention on Certain Conventional
Weapons (CCW) has begun to examine the merits of a ban on what it terms
"lethal autonomous weapons systems," or LAWs, but thus far no consensus
has emerged. At present, the United States, the United Kingdom, Israel, and
South Korea have been identified as having operational autonomous weapons
systems; South Korea, in fact, uses a semiautonomous system to patrol its
border with North Korea.[20]

In the skies over Afghanistan, Pakistan, Iraq, Yemen, and elsewhere,
UAVs—unmanned aerial vehicles—are being used to collect intelligence and
attack militants. While the drones generally operate out of bases in combat
zones, their pilots control them remotely from offices at bases in the United
States. (Where UAVs—or, as the Air Force prefers, "remotely piloted vehicles"—are operated outside of countries with which the United States is
recognized to be at war—in Pakistan, for example—the CIA rather than the
Air Force is in charge of the program.) When combat missions are flown
from a cubicle in an office on a base in Nevada, a pilot can complete a mis-

sion over Afghanistan, perhaps launching a missile at a suspected insurgent in the process, then head home in time to have dinner with friends or family members. It is difficult to imagine how the advantages of distance in warfare could be increased beyond this. At the same time, the use of UAVs appears to be altering the culture of the Air Force, a service dominated in the past by fighter pilots who now must confront the fact that unmanned systems have capabilities that planes with human pilots do not, while raising fundamental questions about what it means to "go to war."[21]

Questions about the impact of UAVs on traditional understandings of how wars are fought have not translated into hesitation about their deployment and use. After early models of the Predator drone were used for surveillance in Bosnia and Kosovo in the 1990s, an armed version of the Predator was rushed into production after 9/11. The biggest jump in demand for UAVs, however, occurred in 2007 after the United States had shifted its tactics in Iraq to place greater emphasis on counterinsurgency operations. With troops on the ground searching for insurgents while trying to steer clear of IEDs, Predators—capable of streaming video images while staying aloft for up to twenty-four hours at a time—became very valuable commodities. In 2007 and 2008 alone, Predators and Reapers, another UAV, flew 10,949 missions in Iraq and Afghanistan. On 244 of those missions, missiles were fired from the UAV, most often at suspected insurgents.[22]

There are legal and moral questions that arise from the use of UAVs to kill suspected insurgents and terrorists, especially when such killings occur in countries that are not at war or under military occupation. American political and military leaders have argued that targeted killings in Pakistan provide the only means of dealing with groups seeking to destabilize Afghanistan from the sanctuary of a neighboring country that is either unwilling or unable to control such groups. Critics of the policy contend that drone attacks outside of Afghanistan and Iraq have undermined existing legal restraints on the use of force, opening up the possibility that as the use of armed UAVs spreads, many governments may feel legally entitled to attack suspected terrorists living in states with whom they are not at war.[23] In addition, missiles launched from drones often kill innocents. According to a study based on data gleaned from press reports, drone strikes in Pakistan's tribal regions had killed between 2,021 and 3,350 people between 2004 and early June 2013. Attacks became more frequent after President Obama took office in 2009. From 2004 to the end of George W. Bush's second term as president, there were forty-eight drone strikes reported in the region. From the time Barack Obama took office through January 2015, there were 456 drone strikes reported.[24]

In Pakistan, the number of drone strikes peaked in 2010. The U.S.-Pakistani relationship soured in 2011 due to the killing of Osama bin Laden on Pakistani

soil in May and the deaths of twenty-four Pakistani soldiers in a NATO bombing in November. Pakistani officials ordered the removal of CIA drones being
operated from a Pakistani air base; the number of drone strikes in Pakistan
dropped to seventy-three in 2012 and forty-eight in 2013.[25]

Even as the drone war in Pakistan diminished in intensity, a parallel
conflict in Yemen flared up. The first U.S. drone strike in Yemen, which
successfully targeted the mastermind of the attack on the USS *Cole* in 2000,
occurred on November 3, 2002. After a hiatus of seven-plus years, the program resumed in 2010 in response to terrorist plots against the United States
coming from Al Qaeda in the Arabian Peninsula (AQAP), which was based
in Yemen. There were at least forty-six U.S. drone strikes in Yemen in 2012,
according to data compiled by Peter Bergen and Jennifer Rowland for the
New America Foundation.[26]

New technologies clearly raise important questions about the changing
nature of warfare even as they open up new possibilities for waging war
more quickly and precisely with fewer casualties. They have also opened
up a tremendous gap between the military capabilities of those states able to
benefit from satellite guidance systems, precision weapons, real-time battlefield imaging, robots, and more, and states (and nonstate actors) unable to
afford high-tech military systems. And yet there are some respects in which
even the poorest and least sophisticated military forces are able to use new
technologies for military purposes. By now the extent to which Al Qaeda
was able to plan and coordinate a global campaign of terror via the Internet is
well known. The March 11, 2004, terrorist bombings in Madrid linked cheap
information technology to old-fashioned explosives with devastating effect.
Cell phones were wired to explosives in such a way that an incoming call
could trigger the bomb. However primitive such devices may seem in comparison to laser-guided bombs, the principle is the same: using communications and information technologies to make it possible to launch devastating
attacks from a distance.

Military dominance of the sort the United States has achieved is not without certain problems. We have already noted the possibility that the ability
to wage short wars with limited casualties may make the resort to war easier
than we might want it to be. There is also the enormous cost of high-tech
weaponry and the C[4]ISR (command, control, communications, computers,
intelligence, surveillance, and reconnaissance) that backs it up, a concern that
will be examined in the next section. But the most vexing problem associated
with American military dominance is that it forces most states or nonstate actors that might become involved in military conflicts with the United States
to fight using unconventional means only. Twice in Iraq and once in Afghanistan, the futility of fighting the United States in a conventional war has

been demonstrated, and yet the United States has been hurt by Al Qaeda, the Islamic State, and by insurgents in Iraq and Afghanistan fighting asymmetrically. As Sun Tzu stated 2,500 years ago in *The Art of War*, "In war, the way is to avoid what is strong and to strike at what is weak."[27] It is a lesson that is becoming increasingly familiar to America's adversaries. To put the point directly, the wider the gap in military capabilities between the strong and the weak, the more incentive there may be for the weak who feel compelled to attack the strong to resort to terrorism or guerrilla warfare.

The situation in the Iraq War before and after the end of major combat operations announced by President Bush on May 1, 2003, is instructive in this regard. As noted earlier, the initial phase was a conventional war dominated by coalition forces. There were relatively few coalition casualties. Between May 1, 2003, and May 22, 2015, however, there were 4,272 U.S. military personnel killed.[28] (In Operation Enduring Freedom in Afghanistan, there were 1,843 Americans killed in combat through June 1, 2015.[29]) In the Iraqi insurgency, coalition forces were attacked by individuals without uniforms who drove ordinary cars (sometimes laden with explosives) and who were capable of blending in with the civilian population. In both Afghanistan and Iraq, attacks came in the form of roadside bombs that were triggered remotely when coalition convoys passed. Targets on which American precision-guided munitions could be used largely faded into their surroundings, and efforts to locate them often alienated the population. Technology, in short, could not do for the United States in an insurgency what it had done in a more symmetrical conflict.

THE QUESTION OF COST

The military dominance in symmetrical conflicts that is made possible by technology comes at an enormous economic cost. But it isn't cheap to fight a low-tech war, either.

In 2014, the world's states spent almost $1.8 trillion for defense. The United States, at $610 billion, accounted for just over a third of the total.[30] The enormity of this figure can best be seen by comparing it to other global expenditures. For example, the total cost of UN peacekeeping operations from 1948 to 2010 is estimated to have been $69 billion. For the fiscal year ending in June 2015, $7.06 billion was allocated for the sixteen current UN peacekeeping operations.[31] The headquarters budget of the UN for 2012 to 2013 was $5.15 billion, or just under $2.6 billion per year.[32] (The peacekeeping budget is separate from the regular budget of the UN. Other programs, such as the World Food Program, are funded by voluntary contributions from member states.)

In reality, U.S. spending for national security is significantly understated when only the regular budget of the Department of Defense (DoD) is cited. The costs of the wars in Afghanistan and Iraq have been paid in large part through special appropriations, or "supplementals," that are not included in the DoD budget. The design, testing, production, and destruction of nuclear weapons is paid for through the Department of Energy. Benefits paid to military veterans are appropriated through the Department of Veterans' Affairs rather than DoD. Except for those expenditures related directly to military intelligence, intelligence gathering by the Central Intelligence Agency, the National Security Agency, and others falls outside the DoD budget. The costs of foreign military assistance—arms transfers—are generally included in the State Department budget, as are the costs of U.S. participation in regional security organizations, such as NATO, and U.S. contributions to UN peacekeeping operations. Finally, expenditures designed to protect the United States from terrorist attacks generally fall within the budgets of the Department of Homeland Security and the Federal Bureau of Investigation. Defense budgets topping $600 billion are worth pausing to contemplate, but they tell only part of the story. As Everett Dirksen, the long-time senator from Illinois, is supposed to have said, "A billion here, a billion there, and pretty soon you're talking real money."[33]

Defense spending must be considered in terms of opportunity costs: what is spent on the military is unavailable to be spent for other social needs. President Eisenhower stated the point eloquently in a speech to the American Society of Newspaper Editors in 1953:

> Every gun that is made, every warship launched, every rocket fired, signifies, in the final sense, a theft from those who hunger and are not fed, those who are cold and are not clothed. This world in arms is not spending money alone. It is spending the sweat of its laborers, the genius of its scientists, the hopes of its children. . . . We pay for a single fighter plane with a half million bushels of wheat. We pay for a single destroyer with new homes that could have housed more than 8,000 people.[34]

The issue associated with opportunity costs has become even more challenging since Eisenhower's day. With the cost of the U.S. Air Force's F-22 Raptor at $412 million per plane and wheat at roughly $5 per bushel,[35] a single fighter plane now costs the equivalent of over eighty-two million bushels of wheat.

Defense expenditures are even more vexing when one considers that money spent on weapons does not generally enhance productivity in other areas the way money spent for health care, education, transportation, or many other purposes does. Two-thirds of the money spent on research and development

(R&D) in the United States promotes military purposes. In contrast, only 35 percent of the total R&D budget in the United Kingdom goes toward the military rather than the civilian sector. To make the point differently, the United States spends 0.4 percent of its gross domestic product on military R&D, while Japan's military R&D budget consumes a mere 0.03 percent of GDP.[36]

The economic drain associated with defense spending is especially apparent in the developing world, where all too often corrupt governments ignore pressing social needs in order to spend limited state revenue on military forces. In 2014, there were twenty states in the world in which over 4 percent of GDP was spent on defense. Eleven were involved in armed conflict; only three were democracies. Topping the list, with military expenditures over 10 percent of GDP, were Oman and Saudi Arabia.[37]

Of course, the cost of preparing for war might be regarded as well worth whatever price is paid if military preparations were certain to prevent war, which has its own enormous costs, or at least to prevent defeat in war. But one can never be certain how much "security" is obtained for each dollar spent. Nor, for that matter, can one be certain in all circumstances that defense spending produces more good than harm.

In fact, the precise relationship between weapons and war has long been a matter of debate. Weapons are necessary to wage war, but they are also considered essential in order to promote peace and security. As a presidential candidate in 1960, John F. Kennedy said, "It is an unfortunate fact that we can only secure peace by preparing for war." Kennedy's observation, of course, was not new. The Romans were fond of the expression, "If you want peace, prepare for war." The opposite perspective was perhaps stated most cogently by Sir John Frederick Maurice in 1883: "I went into the British Army believing that if you want peace you must prepare for war. I now believe that if you prepare thoroughly for war you will get it."[38]

CONVENTIONAL WEAPONS AND WAR: HUMAN SECURITY CONCERNS

The traditional perspective on security pushes us to consider the impact of conventional weapons on national security and to ask questions such as those we have already noted: Are such weapons necessary to preserve the peace, or does their accumulation push states toward war? Are the costs of armaments justifiable, or does defense spending (at least beyond a certain point) jeopardize the state's ability to fulfill other important responsibilities? From a human security perspective, however, we must consider the ways that conventional weapons affect the well-being of individual human beings.

The welfare of individuals is, of course, commonly tied to the health of the states they inhabit. A country under the domination of another or constantly at war is unlikely to be in a position to promote human rights or human development to the fullest. Human security and national security are not alternatives. Instead, a focus on human security helps to protect against an extreme emphasis on national security in which the state and its defense are held, implicitly at least, to justify an indifference toward individuals. All too often, states have sacrificed human security for national security.

Here we wish to consider three of the issues related to human security that are presented by conventional weapons and war. Each is commonly ignored in studies focused solely on national security, and yet each is an issue attracting increasing attention from nongovernmental organizations (NGOs), international organizations, and a few states that perceive themselves to be "humanitarian great powers." The issues are small arms and light weapons (SALW), explosive remnants of war (ERW), and child soldiers.

Small Arms and Light Weapons

According to a recent report prepared for the Geneva Declaration, a group of states committed to reducing the negative impacts of weapons on development, an estimated average of 508,000 people died each year from 2007 to 2012 as a result of violence. This number includes intentional homicides (377,000), unintentional homicides (42,000), and deaths due to legal interventions (19,000), as well as conflict-related deaths (70,000). Small arms were used in almost half of the homicides and almost a third of the direct conflict deaths. In sum, firearms accounted for 197,000 deaths per year.[39] In a speech before the UN Security Council Ministerial on Small Arms on September 24, 1999, former Canadian foreign minister Lloyd Axworthy called them "small arms of mass destruction."[40] The impacts of small arms and light weapons are not new, but the end of the Cold War prompted an increased awareness of those impacts even as it exacerbated the problem in significant ways.

SALW have been the primary instruments of the intrastate conflicts that have plagued the Balkans, Sudan, the Congo, Sri Lanka, and other hotspots since the end of the Cold War. They are inexpensive and widely available, which makes it easy for aggrieved groups to take up arms against governments or other nonstate actors. These same characteristics facilitate illicit trade and make regulation more difficult to enforce. Their ease of use and small size make small arms ideal for untrained combatants and even child soldiers. Making the problem even worse, the end of the Cold War was accompanied by both a loss of superpower control over the SALW trade and the creation of a tremendous surplus of weapons. Furthermore, the existence of transnational criminal organizations trafficking in drugs and persons provided a ready-made network of dealers for the illicit weapons trade. In short, a broad convergence of factors brought the issue of small arms and light weapons to the fore during the 1990s.[41]

The issue of small arms and light weapons was added to the agenda of the United Nations through a resolution adopted by the General Assembly in 1991.[42] Little progress occurred, however, until the 1997 Ottawa Convention banning antipersonnel land mines was adopted. In an address to the UN General Assembly, Lloyd Axworthy pressed for UN action on small arms and light weapons just days after the text of the Ottawa Convention had been finalized at a conference in Oslo. Noting the spread of intrastate conflicts, Axworthy said, "As this type of war increasingly accounts for the great majority of all conflicts, the distinctions that once informed the work of international diplomacy—between military security concerns and humanitarian or civil concerns—break down." Consequently, Axworthy suggested, the concept of human security "takes on a growing relevance" and requires "addressing issues that cut across traditional boundaries between areas of concern." The issue of small arms, like the land mine issue, was, according to Axworthy, one such cross-cutting issue.[43]

NGOs and a few states constituting the Human Security Network pushed the small arms issue at the United Nations, and in July 2001 the UN Conference on the Illicit Trade in Small Arms and Light Weapons in All Its Aspects was held. In his speech on behalf of the United States on the opening day of the conference, Under Secretary of State John Bolton listed five broad areas of disagreement with the draft Program of Action being discussed at the session. Each point, from opposition to measures that would regulate arms manufacture and trade to opposition to any international threat to "the Constitutional right to bear arms," was significant.[44] The effect was to place the United States in a position of intransigence on the SALW issue rather than the more neutral position on the sidelines it had taken during the negotiations leading to the Ottawa Convention. U.S. opposition combined with a variety of structural and political obstacles (including the enormous profitability of the global trade in SALW) meant that no significant progress was made on the issue in 2001.

In 2003, a group of Nobel Peace laureates urged the international community to take action to curb the international trade in conventional arms. In 2006, the United Nations General Assembly adopted a resolution calling for the preparation of an Arms Trade Treaty (ATT) to deal with the SALW problem. The Group of Governmental Experts (GGE) reported its findings regarding the proposed treaty to the General Assembly in 2008, and, in 2012, the Conference on the Arms Trade Treaty was convened to negotiate the text of the agreement. The Arms Trade Treaty was opened for signature on June 3, 2013, and entered into force on December 24, 2014, ninety days after the deposit of the fiftieth ratification.[45]

While its predecessor, reflecting the interests of the progun lobby in the United States, opposed all efforts toward an agreement regulating trade in conventional arms, the Obama administration supported negotiations and signed the final agreement. There is little chance, given the requirement for a two-thirds majority vote in the Senate, that the United States will ratify the Arms Trade Treaty in the near future. Consequently, the United States will join Russia and China as major arms suppliers remaining outside the agreement's limitations. For the United States, Russia, and China in particular, the arms trade is a very lucrative business. In the period from 2010 to 2014, the United States controlled 31 percent of the world's legal arms trade. Russia, at 27 percent, was second, and China, at 5 percent, surpassed Germany for the first time to move into third place.[46] The total value of the legal trade in arms is estimated to be at least $178 billion a year.[47]

Explosive Remnants of War

An often overlooked aspect of armaments that must be thrown into the equation when considering the security implications of conventional weapons is their persistence. Many weapons are destroyed or expended in war, but not all of them. Some weapons are removed from service—and even destroyed—as a consequence of disarmament (most commonly when the victor forcibly disarms the vanquished). In many instances, however, weapons continue to be a factor in security (or insecurity) long after the conflict for which they were created and deployed has been resolved. This can be due to the circulation and reuse of weapons, as was noted in the discussion of SALW, but it can also be a consequence of the deadly residue that modern warfare often leaves behind.

Even weapons from wars far removed in time sometimes pose threats. In Belgium and France along World War I's Western Front, people refer to the "Iron Harvest," the collection of unexploded ordnance (UXO) by farmers plowing fields in the region. In the Ypres Salient, it is estimated that a third of the one billion shells expended by British and German forces failed to explode; most of the three hundred million unexploded shells have yet to be recovered.[48] World War II also generated large quantities of unexploded ordnance. In February 2004, thirty thousand people were evacuated in Sevastopol, a port city in Crimea, when a World War II–era mine weighing over a ton was dredged from the Black Sea. The mine was transported through a portion of the city (thus the need for evacuations) to an unpopulated location where it could be destroyed.[49]

Land mines have been especially problematic. An estimated hundred million land mines have been left over from recent conflicts. In Angola, roughly 40 percent of the population has experienced amputations due to land-mine accidents.[50] In Cambodia, where a decade-long civil war following the overthrow of the genocidal Khmer Rouge regime was concluded in 1991, land mines continue to kill and maim people regularly. A World Bank report noted that, in 2001, 173 people were killed and 640 people were wounded by mines or other forms of unexploded ordnance in spite of the fact that 313,586 antipersonnel land mines had been removed from the country between 1992 and 2001. As the report notes, "Mine and UXO contamination restricts access to homes, agricultural land, pastures, water sources, forests, schools, dams, canals, markets, business activities, health centers, pagodas, bridges, and neighboring villages. Thus the threat of UXO and mines impedes mobility, security, economic activity, and development."[51]

As noted above, land mines were the subject of a 1997 treaty, the Ottawa Convention, that bans their use and mandates their removal where they have been deployed. The treaty was the product of a remarkable coalition of states and NGOs determined to arouse global public interest in the problems posed by explosive remnants of war. In fact, American activist Jody Williams and the International Campaign to Ban Landmines (ICBL) shared the 1997 Nobel Peace Prize for their efforts to promote the land mine ban. While over 160 states have ratified the Ottawa Convention and have made significant progress in demining conflict zones, the United States has thus far refused to ratify the agreement, primarily due to its interest in continuing to use land mines for the defense of South Korea.

Many of the same states and NGOs that pushed for the international agreement to ban land mines have also promoted multilateral efforts to address problems associated with other explosive remnants of war, including antivehicle mines, grenades, artillery shells, mortars, and rockets. Cluster bombs, once described by William Arkin as "a greater hazard to civilians than virtually any other weapon that is legal,"[52] have recently been made the subject of a new multilateral agreement similar in form and content to the Ottawa Convention. In 2008, the Convention on Cluster Munitions (CCM) was concluded in Dublin. As of March 2015, 116 states had signed and 91 states had ratified the agreement, which entered into force on August 1, 2010. The United States, China, Russia, India, and Israel are among the many states that have yet to sign the CCM, which bans the production, stockpiling, transfer, and use of cluster bombs.[53]

Cluster bombs disperse "bomblets," or "submunitions," over a broad area when dropped from a plane or fired by rockets on the ground. The bomblets (202 per device in the cluster bomb used most commonly by the United States at the outset of the Afghan campaign) are designed to explode on impact, spraying the area with deadly shrapnel and, in some cases, incendiary material. For a variety of reasons, including submunitions units malfunctioning or landing on soft surfaces, anywhere from 5 percent to 20 percent of the bomblets fail to explode as intended. Bomb canisters can then remain on the ground for years before being accidentally detonated, with tragic consequences.

The war in Afghanistan was not the first time that cluster bombs had been used extensively by the United States, creating a significant postconflict problem with unexploded ordnance. In fact, cluster munitions have been in use for over fifty years. NATO reported in 2000 that 1,392 cluster bombs had been dropped during the Kosovo campaign, with a failure rate of 8 to 12 percent. Within a year of the end of the conflict, forty-seven people (over half of them children) had been killed, and 101 people had been injured by unexploded canisters. It is estimated that in the aftermath of the Persian Gulf War (1991), as many as two million unexploded cluster bomblets remained in Iraq and Kuwait.[54] These weapons are believed to have killed over 2,500 Iraqi civilians following the end of that war, far more civilians than were reported to have been killed during the war itself.[55]

Child Soldiers

Children are often the victims of explosive remnants of war, but land mines and cluster bombs are not the only war-related problems affecting children. Indeed, the impact of modern warfare on children is staggering. During the 1990s, as a consequence of war, approximately two million children were killed, over four million were disabled, over ten million were psychologically traumatized, over one million were orphaned, approximately twenty million were displaced, and three hundred thousand children were forced to serve in armies as soldiers, spies, sex slaves, or in other roles.[56]

The use of child soldiers is not new. During the American Civil War, to take one example, underage soldiers on both sides likely numbered between 250,000 and 420,000, including many under twelve who followed fathers, older brothers, and even teachers into the Union and Confederate armies.[57] As both conceptions of childhood and the technology of war have changed, the international community has become increasingly sensitive to the issue of child soldiers. In 1996, Graça Machel, then Mozambique's minister of education, prepared a report at the request of UN secretary-general Boutros

Boutros-Ghali titled *Impact of Armed Conflict on Children*. Much of what we know about the problem comes from this study and from surveys conducted by NGOs since then.[58]

In its most recent international survey, the London-based Child Soldiers International reports that ten states employed soldiers under eighteen in conflicts between January 2010 and June 2012. In general, paramilitary organizations and rebel groups are more likely to employ child soldiers, but there are nonetheless a number of governments that recruit and deploy soldiers under eighteen years of age.[59]

Children serve a variety of functions in armies; not all are, strictly speaking, soldiers. Some carry weapons and engage in combat, but others serve as (aside from the capacities mentioned above) couriers, minelayers, cooks, and domestic servants. In the Democratic Republic of the Congo (DRC), almost all of the girls questioned by surveyors reported having been raped in the army. The Lord's Resistance Army, a rebel organization in northern Uganda that has abducted an estimated twenty thousand children, has forced girls both to fight and to serve commanders as sex slaves.[60]

Although some children are taken out of schools and orphanages by soldiers, not all of those who end up in armies are abducted. Many enlist voluntarily, often to escape poverty or because the lack of educational or employment opportunities leaves few alternatives. Some see entry into an army or rebel force as deliverance from the violence and fear inflicted on civilian populations by those same groups. In some instances, governments encourage enlistment by requiring military training programs in schools and camps.[61]

The proliferation of small arms and light weapons, in addition to fueling intrastate conflict, has made it easier for children to participate in combat. Weapons are so common and inexpensive that armed forces need not worry about whether putting a gun in the hands of a child will be a waste of resources. As Machel reported, in Uganda in 1996 an AK-47 could be purchased for about the cost of a chicken. More important, however, is the fact that small arms are so light and simple to operate that ten-year-olds have no difficulty using them. The illegal trade in small arms and light weapons, which the international community has thus far been unable to address effectively, must be regarded as a contributing factor in the tragedy of child soldiers.

On May 25, 2000, the General Assembly of the United Nations adopted the Optional Protocol to the Convention on the Rights of the Child on the Involvement of Children in Armed Conflict to outlaw military recruitment and the use in combat of those under eighteen. The Optional Protocol entered into force on February 12, 2002. By the end of May 2015, 159 states had ratified the agreement. Although not a party to the Convention on the Rights of the Child, the United States is a signatory to that treaty and thus is eligible to be a party to the Optional Protocol. The United States ratified the Optional Protocol on January 23, 2003.[62]

PRIVATIZED MILITARY FIRMS

We turn now to an issue that holds the possibility of transforming how wars are waged in the twenty-first century: the rise of privatized military firms (PMFs). Over the course of the past quarter-century, states—both rich and poor—have increasingly turned to private companies to provide services that were previously considered the responsibility of governments alone.

On March 30, 2004, four employees of Blackwater USA (since sold and renamed Academi), a private security firm hired to protect the employees of one of the Defense Department's many suppliers in Iraq, were ambushed as they drove through the city of Fallujah. They were shot, and their bodies were dragged from their vehicle, mutilated, and burned. Two were suspended grotesquely from a bridge. Photographs of the grisly scene were published or broadcast in less discreet media outlets around the world.

The incident in Fallujah drew attention to an issue that had, up to that point, attracted relatively little notice. From the very beginning of the war, privatized military firms were employed in Iraq to perform services traditionally considered the responsibility of uniformed military forces. In Iraq at the time of the Fallujah killings, at least twenty thousand private military contractors were employed to protect diplomats (including the head of the Coalition Provisional Authority, Paul Bremer), American and Iraqi businessmen, aid workers, and many others.[63]

While the large number of private security contractors in Iraq may be surprising, the role of privatized military firms has been even more important in a number of other conflicts. During the 1990s, the government of Sierra Leone halted a bloody civil war and recaptured the country's diamond mines from rebel forces by hiring Executive Outcomes, a PMF based in South Africa. Executive Outcomes used airpower, armored vehicles, and a small but highly trained force to accomplish what the government had been unable to do in years of fighting.[64] More recently, private military contractors from South Africa were brought into northern Nigeria to assist in military operations against Boko Haram. Observers indicated that the contractors, using helicopter gunships, armored personnel carriers, and night-vision goggles, were routing Boko Haram fighters at night but giving way during the day to Nigerian armed forces who took credit for the military successes.[65]

Privatized military firms are employed by governments for a variety of reasons, some that appear legitimate and some that may not be. First, PMFs allow the military to contract out jobs that are temporary, that involve skills that are in short supply among the armed forces, or that can be performed more efficiently by contractors. Second, when private contractors sustain casualties, those casualties are not typically reported in the media and do not affect public opinion in democracies the way military casualties do. (The Pentagon did not include contractor casualties on its casualty lists in the Iraq war.) The use of PMFs, in other words, may serve to conceal the true human costs of military operations, but it may also permit defense establishments to keep fewer troops under arms, since shortfalls can be handled by calling in the private sector.

The rise of privatized military firms also means, however, that defense establishments may find themselves competing for the services of military professionals. In February 2005, the Department of Defense approved a plan to offer financial incentives (up to $150,000 for a six-year reenlistment) to stem the flow of experienced Special Operations Forces personnel to private security companies. The bonuses were devised to deal with a situation in which Army Green Berets or Navy SEALs with twenty years' experience and making $50,000 in base pay could leave the military and go to work for a private security firm at salaries close to $200,000 a year.[66]

Perhaps more troublesome for the international system is the fact that an industry has emerged that gives those who can pay, whether governments or corporations—or even rebel organizations and drug traffickers (PMFs are reported to have trained drug dealers in Mexico and UNITA rebels in Angola in military tactics and the use of advanced weapons)—access to military force. In spite of certain advantages associated with contracting out warfare, a tremendous potential for abuse exists as well.

In the realm of conventional weapons and war, security can be bought. Private contractors are available to supplement military forces and thereby reduce the need for large armies. High-tech weapons also play a role in reducing the number of troops needed for many missions; they have the added advantage of reducing casualties for the military that is able to attack from a distance while enjoying information dominance. But the security that is available for purchase is not absolute. Resourceful enemies are always able to find and exploit weaknesses. If those weaknesses are not to be found on the conventional battlefield, determined adversaries may decide to attack nonmilitary targets.

War, as we noted at the outset of this chapter, is a form of coercive violence. Militarily powerful states, such as the United States, have an incentive to contain the use of coercive violence with rules that protect noncombatants, exclude children from participation, and limit the kinds of weapons that can be used. All of these are laudable rules, but if, in combination with the distribution of power in the system, these rules preordain the outcome of most conflicts, we should not be surprised if some actors in the system decide to ignore the rules. This should not be construed as a justification for terrorism, the use of weapons of mass destruction, or any other form of unlawful warfare. It is, instead, a caution for those who would consider the possession of overwhelming military power a panacea for a pluralistic world.

ADDITIONAL RESOURCES

Books

Berkowitz, Bruce. *The New Face of War: How War Will Be Fought in the 21st Century*. New York: Free Press, 2003.

Caldwell, Dan. *Vortex of Conflict: U.S. Policy Toward Afghanistan, Pakistan, and Iraq*. Stanford, CA: Stanford University Press, 2011.

Eckert, Amy E. *Outsourcing War: The Just War Tradition in the Age of Military Privatization*. Ithaca, NY: Cornell University Press, 2016.

Keegan, John. *A History of Warfare*. New York: Alfred A. Knopf, 1993.

Knox, MacGregor, and Williamson Murray, eds. *The Dynamics of Military Revolution, 1300–2050*. Cambridge: Cambridge University Press, 2001.

McFate, Sean. *The Modern Mercenary: Private Armies and What They Mean for World Order*. New York: Oxford University Press, 2015.

Schelling, Thomas C. *Arms and Influence*. New Haven, CT: Yale University Press, 1966.

Singer, P. W. *Corporate Warriors: The Rise of the Privatized Military Industry*. Ithaca, NY: Cornell University Press, 2003.

Singer, P. W. *Wired for War: The Robotic Revolution and Conflict in the 21st Century*. New York: Penguin Books, 2009.

Websites

Campaign to Stop Killer Robots: www.stopkillerrobots.org/
Child Soldiers International: www.child-soldiers.org/index.php
International Action Network on Small Arms: www.iansa.org/
International Campaign to Ban Landmines: www.icbl.org
Small Arms Survey: www.smallarmssurvey.org
Stockholm International Peace Research Institute: www.sipri.org/
U.S. Army Chief of Staff's Professional Reading List: www.history.army.mil/html/books/105/105-1-1/index.html
U.S. Department of Defense: www.defense.gov/

Films

Beasts of No Nation (2015, Netflix): Set in an unnamed African country, this film details the experiences of a fictional child soldier. Directed by Cary Joji Fukunaga.

The Fog of War (2004, Sony): An extended interview with former secretary of defense Robert S. McNamara by noted documentary filmmaker Errol Morris.

War School (2009, Ctrl. Alt. Shift): A brief but jarring film about child soldiers. Directed by Ben Newman.

Chapter Three

Nuclear Weapons, Deterrence, and Arms Control

The unleashed power of the atom has changed everything save our modes
of thinking, and we thus drift toward unparalled catastrophe.

—Albert Einstein quoted in the *New York Times*, May 25, 1946

At 2:45 AM on August 6, 1945, a lone American B-29 bomber named the
Enola Gay, after the pilot's mother, took off from the Pacific island of Tinian,
flew 1,600 miles in five-and-a-half hours to Hiroshima, Japan, and dropped
the most destructive weapon ever used in warfare up to that time—a nuclear
bomb ten feet long, twenty-eight inches in diameter, and weighing nine
thousand pounds. Forty-three seconds after it left the *Enola Gay*, the bomb,
code-named "Little Boy," exploded 1,900 feet above ground with a destructive yield equivalent to fifteen thousand tons of TNT.[1] The explosion lasted
about one second; the temperature at ground zero, the point directly below
the detonation, rose to six thousand degrees centigrade, a temperature greater
than the surface temperature of the sun. The temperature was so hot and intense that birds ignited in midair. One witness said, "It was as if the sun had
crashed and exploded."[2]

The effects on the residents of Hiroshima were horrific; one eyewitness
later reported, "Men whose whole bodies were covered with blood, and
women whose skin hung from them like a kimono, plunged shrieking into
the river. All these become corpses and their bodies are carried by the current
toward the sea."[3] The number of people killed was estimated to be between
sixty and eighty thousand, and more recent calculations indicate that by the
end of 1945, 140,000 had died.

When he felt the shock wave of the bomb hit the plane and saw the mushroom cloud rising over the city, the copilot of the bomber, Captain Robert

Lewis, asked, "My God, what have we done? If I live a hundred years, I'll never quite get these few minutes out of my mind."[4]

Even after the bombing of Hiroshima, Japan did not surrender; the government was torn between the civilian leaders who wanted to sue for peace and the military leaders who preferred death to the disgrace of surrender. Three days after the bombing of Hiroshima, at 3:47 AM, a B-29 named *Bock's Car*, for the pilot, took off from Tinian with another nuclear weapon—code-named "Fat Man"—and flew to Nagasaki. The bomb exploded 1,650 feet above the city at 11:02 AM with a destructive force estimated to be equivalent to twenty-one thousand tons of TNT. Unlike Hiroshima, Nagasaki was surrounded by hills, and these provided some limited protection from the blast. Still, forty thousand people died in the bombing and its immediate aftermath; by the end of 1945, eighty thousand had died in Nagasaki.

The day after the bombing of Nagasaki, Emperor Hirohito, speaking on the radio for the first time, told the Japanese people that "the enemy has begun to employ a new and most cruel bomb, the power of which to do damage is indeed incalculable, taking the toll of many innocent lives. Should we continue to fight, it would not only result in an ultimate collapse and obliteration of the Japanese nation, but also it would lead to the total extinction of human civilization."[5] Despite the continuing opposition of its military leaders, Japan surrendered unconditionally, and the most costly war in human history ended. But if the development and first use of nuclear weapons ended the war, they raised profound questions, questions that have remained to this day like shadows of the mushroom clouds that rose ominously over Hiroshima and Nagasaki.

Nuclear weapons are the most destructive weapons devised, built, and used by human beings. Although it would have been possible to kill as many Japanese with nonnuclear bombs, guns, or even knives and clubs, nuclear weapons made it dramatically faster and easier—both technically and morally—to do so. More people were killed in the March 1945 firebombing raid on Tokyo than were killed in either Hiroshima or Nagasaki, but those earlier attacks had involved hundreds of planes dropping thousands of bombs.

The day after the bombing of Hiroshima, a brilliant, young political science professor at Yale named Bernard Brodie picked up a copy of the *New York Times* and read this headline: "First Atomic Bomb Dropped on Japan; Missile Is Equal to 20,000 Tons of TNT; Truman Warns Foe of a 'Rain of Ruin.'" Brodie had written extensively on naval and military strategy. After reading the lead article concerning the bombing of Hiroshima, Brodie told his wife, "Everything that I have written is obsolete."[6]

Soon after the war ended, Bernard Brodie assembled a small group of civilian strategists to think about the implications of nuclear weapons for international politics and security. The group published in 1946 a remarkably prescient collection of essays, in which one of the contributors asserted, "To speak of it [the nuclear weapon] as just another weapon was highly mislead- ing. It was a revolutionary development which altered the basic structure of war itself."[7] Brodie pointed to the revolutionary implications of nuclear weapons. Ever since the time of Carl von Clausewitz, military strategists had believed that an attacker should have a superiority of three to one in order to ensure success.[8] Brodie turned this equation on its head: "If 2,000 bombs in the hands of either party is enough to destroy entirely the economy of the other, the fact that one side has 6,000 and the other 2,000 will be of relatively small significance."[9] Nuclear weapons, according to Brodie, negated the teachings of the greatest military strategists.

Other policymakers and strategists thought of nuclear weapons as significantly more powerful than previous weapons but not radically different. Herman Kahn was the strategist who best represented this position.[10] In the decades following the development and use of nuclear weapons by the United States, these two positions, broadly speaking, have characterized the ways of thinking about nuclear weapons.[11] In specific terms, six different approaches to dealing with nuclear weapons have been developed since 1945: (1) nuclear pacifists have contended that the use of nuclear weapons is never justified; (2) some Americans argued soon after World War II that the only way to reassure the Soviets was to give nuclear weapons to them; (3) Soviet and American postwar leaders presented several plans for the international control of nuclear weapons; (4) when these proposals came to naught, strategists argued that nuclear weapons should be used to deter other states' use of nuclear weapons or conventional weapons; (5) some contended that nuclear weapons should be subject to quantitative and qualitative limitations; and (6) others suggested,

Table 3.1.   Nuclear Weapons Stockpiles, 1945–2010

Year	U.S.	Russia	U.K.	France	China	Israel	India	Pakistan	TOTAL
1945	2								2
1955	2,422	200	14						2,636
1965	31,139	6,129	436	32	5				37,741
1975	27,519	19,055	492	188	180	20			47,454
1985	23,368	39,197	422	360	243	42			63,632
1995	10,904	27,000	422	500	234	63			39,123
2005	8,360	17,000	281	350	235	80	44	38	26,388
2010	5,000	12,000	225	300	240	80	80	70	17,995

Source: Robert S. Norris and Hans M. Kristensen, "Global Nuclear Weapons Inventories, 1945–2010," *Bulletin of the Atomic Scientists* (July/August 2010): 77–83.

Table 3.2.   Global Nuclear Weapons Inventories, 2014

Country	Deployed Strategic[1]	Nonstrategic[2]	Nondeployed Warheads[3]	Total Inventory	Growth Trends
USA	1,922	200	5,384	7,506	Decrease
Russia	2,484	2,000[4]	4,000	8,484	Decrease
UK	160	—	65	225	Decrease[5]
France	290	—	10	300	Decrease (slight)
China	—	—	250	250	Decrease (slight)[6]
India	80–100	—	—	80–100	Growth
Pakistan	—	—	90–100	90–110	Growth
Israel	—	—	80–200	80–200	Growth (slight)
North Korea	—	—	<10[7]	<10	Growth
		Total nuclear weapons in the world: 17,105			

1. Deployed nuclear weapons are assigned to delivery systems and available for use.
2. Lower-yield warheads are intended for short-range applications or even battlefield use.
3. Nondeployed nuclear weapons are weapons held in reserve that are not assigned to a deployed delivery system or have been retired and are awaiting dismantlement.
4. According to the Russian government, these nonstrategic nuclear weapons are assigned to armed forces but held in central storage.
5. The United Kingdom has stated that it plans to reduce its inventory of nuclear weapons to less than 180 warheads within fifteen years.
6. The Chinese have kept a relatively small, steady arsenal at roughly its current size since the 1980s, although Chinese concerns that growing United States and Russian offensive and defensive capabilities could undermine its deterrent may lead the country to consider increases in the future. Indeed, according to 2010 data, China had approximately 240 total nuclear weapons at the time, while 2013 data puts that number at 250.
7. North Korea is not believed to be capable of fixing its warheads to delivery systems, although in the aftermath of its third nuclear test on February 12, 2013, many experts believe that it is making progress toward this goal.

Source: The Center for Arms Control and Non-Proliferation, Lesley McNiesh; updates by Justin Bresolin, Sam Kane, and Andrew Szarejko; available at http://armscontrolcenter.org/fact-sheet-global-nuclear-weapons-inventories-in-2014/.

following those who believe nuclear weapons are not fundamentally different from previous weapons, that they could be used to fight and win wars. In this chapter, these six views will be described.

Before turning to these six approaches, however, it is important to note the growth in the number of nuclear weapons from the two that existed in August 1945 to the tens of thousands that existed during the Cold War and their decline in more recent years. Table 3.1 presents a snapshot of the number of nuclear weapons in the world's arsenals from 1945 to 2010, and table 3.2 presents the states that possess nuclear weapons as of 2014.

NUCLEAR PACIFISM

Absolute pacifists contend that no weapons should ever be used. Others do not reject the use of all military force but argue that nuclear weapons are so destructive and indiscriminate that they should never be used. This "nuclear pacifist" position was that of the eminent diplomat and scholar George Kennan, who argued:

> We would have to begin by accepting the validity of two very fundamental appreciations. The first is that there is no issue at stake in our political relations with the Soviet Union—no hope, no fear, nothing to which we aspire, nothing we would like to avoid—which could conceivably be worth a nuclear war. And the second is that there is no way in which nuclear weapons could conceivably be employed in combat that would not involve the possibility—and indeed the prohibitively high probability—of escalation to a general nuclear disaster.[12]

Kennan subscribed to this position at least by 1950 and held to it throughout the Cold War.[13]

On September 24, 2009, at the United Nations Security Council Summit on Nuclear Non-Proliferation and Nuclear Disarmament, President Barack Obama quoted Ronald Reagan: "A nuclear war cannot be won and must never be fought."[14] This statement expresses a sentiment that nuclear pacifists would support without hesitation. It is worth noting, however, that the United States has never been willing to make a "no first use" of nuclear weapons pledge. The Obama administration's 2010 Nuclear Posture Review rules out American first use of nuclear weapons against countries that are in compliance with the Non-Proliferation Treaty, a policy that would exclude Iran and North Korea.[15]

NUCLEAR POWER SHARING

In August 1939, the Soviet Union and Nazi Germany signed a nonaggression pact that protected Germany's eastern flank. The following month Germany attacked and occupied Poland, the event that catalyzed World War II in Europe. Many people believed that the Nazi-Soviet Pact had enabled Hitler to begin his conquests and therefore blamed the Soviet Union for cooperating with Hitler. After Poland, Germany attacked and occupied most of Western Europe, and in June 1941, Germany attacked the Soviet Union. The United Kingdom was now faced with a dilemma: Should it cooperate with the dictatorial state that had enabled Germany to attack Western Europe, or should it go its own way? Winston Churchill provided a characteristically forceful, unambiguous answer: "I have only one purpose, the destruction of Hitler, and my life is much simplified thereby. If Hitler invaded Hell I would make at least a favourable reference to the Devil in the House of Commons."[16] The reference to Stalin as the devil was not lost on anyone, least of all Stalin

himself, and throughout the war the relationship among the "Big Three"—
Roosevelt, Churchill, and Stalin—was tense.

From 1942 on, Stalin repeatedly demanded that the United States and
Britain open a second front so that Germany would have to move some of its
two hundred divisions on the eastern front to the western front, where it had
twenty divisions. Roosevelt first promised Stalin to open a second front in
the western part of Europe in 1942, but this was not done until June 6, 1944.
This delay was caused by a number of factors, including a shortage of landing
craft, but, irrespective of the reasons, the delay caused deep resentment on the
part of the Soviets. By the end of the war, distrust and suspicion characterized
the relationship between the United States and Great Britain, on the one hand,
and the Soviet Union, on the other.

When the United States bombed Hiroshima and Nagasaki, the military
superiority of the United States was unquestioned, even though Stalin tried
to dismiss nuclear weapons as simply "long-range artillery." What could the
United States do to reassure the Soviets that nuclear weapons would not be
used against them?

On September 11, 1945, one month after the bombings of Hiroshima and
Nagasaki, in a memo to President Truman, Secretary of War Henry L. Stimson stated:

> In handing you today my memorandum about our relations with Russia in re-
> spect to the atomic bomb, I am not unmindful of the fact that when in Potsdam
> I talked with you about the question whether we could be safe in sharing the
> atomic bomb with Russia while she was still a police state. I still recognize the
> difficulty and am still convinced of the ultimate importance of a change in Rus-
> sian attitude toward individual liberty but I have come to the conclusion that it
> would not be possible to use our possession of the atomic bomb as a direct lever
> to produce the change. I have become more convinced that any demand by us
> for an internal change in Russia as a condition of sharing the atomic weapon
> would be so resented that it would make the objective we have in view less
> probable.[17]

Stimson went on to argue that "unless the Soviets are voluntarily invited into
the partnership on a basis of cooperation and trust, we are going to maintain
the Anglo-Saxon bloc over against the Soviet [and that would result in] a
secret armament race of a rather desperate character."[18]

McGeorge Bundy, who as a young man assisted Stimson in writing his
memoirs, contended that Stimson was in favor of a three-power agreement
with the United States, the Soviet Union, and the United Kingdom "to control
and limit the use of the atomic bomb as an instrument of war."[19] He dismissed
Stimson's idea of sharing nuclear weapons with the Soviet Union as some-

thing only casually and briefly mentioned to President Truman. Regardless of whether Stimson presented this idea seriously, it nevertheless stands as an alternative for dealing with nuclear weapons.

Curiously, the proposal to share nuclear weapons with the Soviet Union was revisited in modified form three decades later. In March 1983, President Ronald Reagan called for the development of a "Strategic Defense Initiative," which journalists, focusing on its space-based components, quickly dubbed "Star Wars." Reagan's idea was to develop a defensive system that would protect the United States and its population from a missile attack from the USSR or other countries. Such a system would require some of the most advanced technology that the United States possessed; one expert described the technical problems associated with missile defense as akin to "hitting a bullet with a bullet." Despite the level of technological sophistication, President Reagan proposed to give the technology to the Soviets:

> If a defensive system could be found and developed that would reduce the utility of these [offensive missiles] or maybe even make them obsolete, then whenever that time came, a President of the United States would be able to say, "Now we have both the deterrent, the missiles—as we have had in the past, but now this other thing that has altered this—." And he could follow any one of a number of courses. He could offer to give that same defensive weapon to them to prove to them that there was no longer any need for keeping these missiles. Or with that defense, he could then say to them, "I am willing to do away with all my missiles. You do away with all of yours."[20]

The United States did not deploy missile-defense technologies until the early twenty-first century, almost twenty years after they were first proposed by President Reagan. By that time, the Cold War had ended, the Soviet Union had disappeared, and there was no further talk of providing the technology to Russia.

INTERNATIONAL CONTROL: THE BARUCH AND GROMYKO PLANS

In December 1945, a committee chaired by Under Secretary of State Dean Acheson was appointed to study policies related to nuclear energy, and the following month a group of consultants headed by David Lilienthal, then head of the Tennessee Valley Authority, was formed. After three months of work, the Acheson-Lilienthal Report was released; it called for the creation of an international authority to exercise control over all nuclear research and development. The proposed International Atomic Development Authority would also be granted the power to manage, license, and inspect all nuclear facilities. The proposal furthermore called for an agreement banning nuclear weapons and for the suspension of U.S. nuclear weapons production and development until the international authority was established.

In June 1946, the U.S. representative to the newly established United Nations Atomic Energy Commission (UNAEC), Bernard Baruch, presented a plan that incorporated the provisions of the Acheson-Lilienthal Report and called for the cessation of the manufacture of atomic weapons and the establishment of an international authority that would have a monopoly on nuclear research and development. If violations were charged against a member of the UN Security Council, the alleged violator would not be allowed to exercise its veto power in the Council. In addition, the Security Council would be allowed to impose, by majority vote, sanctions on violators.

The Soviet Union opposed the Baruch Plan, for several reasons. First, if accepted, the plan would have prohibited the USSR from ever developing nuclear weapons; in essence, the Soviet Union would have been frozen in a position of strategic inferiority vis-à-vis the United States. Second, perhaps recalling their treatment by their American and British allies in World War II, Soviet leaders believed that the international authority would be dominated by Western leaders who would be hostile toward the USSR. Last, the Soviets believed that the Baruch Plan would open Soviet borders to Western inspectors, some of whom would be spies. The Soviet Union had lost twenty-five million citizens in World War II and viewed outsiders with suspicion. As the Soviet representative to the UNAEC, Andrei Gromyko, noted years later, "The Baruch Plan, so energetically trumpeted by the American side, was stillborn, and it could not have been otherwise, given its content and aims."[21]

Gromyko presented a Soviet counterproposal that called for the destruction of all stocks of nuclear weapons within three months of the signing of the agreement. Only after the destruction of all nuclear weapons would sanctions for violations of the agreement be established. Such sanctions would be administered by the UN Security Council and would be subject to the veto of any permanent member. This proposal was as unacceptable to the United States as the Baruch Plan had been to the Soviet Union.

The Baruch and Gromyko plans, the first attempts to achieve nuclear disarmament, failed for two principal reasons. First, the Soviet Union was unwilling to accept permanent inferiority relative to the United States and, second, the two sides had very different approaches concerning the verification of any potential agreement. When these negotiations failed, policymakers focused on finding means to manage the new, revolutionary weapons of mass destruction rather than turning them over to international control.

NUCLEAR DETERRENCE

If nuclear weapons could not be eliminated, they would have to be controlled. One of the oldest means of controlling weapons, as old as humanity, is to deter their use; the old Roman maxim, "If you want peace, prepare for war," is the quintessential statement of deterrence. The new weapons made deterrence all the more important.[22]

Nuclear strategists defined deterrence as the possession of sufficient power to inflict unacceptable damage on a potential aggressor. They considered the concept to be based on several fundamental assumptions. First, states were postulated to be the only important actors in international relations. Second, decision makers were presumed to be rational—that is, they would make decisions on a cost-benefit basis seeking to maximize benefits and minimize costs. In this sense, all decision makers, whatever their nationality, ideology, or ethnicity, would reach the same decisions when confronted with the same data. Third—and this is the fundamental assumption of deterrence—if a threat is sufficiently large and believable (or "credible," in the lexicon of deterrence theory), resort to war will be rejected. Fourth, deterrence views the severity of threats as a function of destructive capability—the greater the destructive capability, the greater the threat. According to this assumption, the number of nuclear weapons possessed by a state matters.

Over time, strategists (mostly civilian and American) developed theoretical notions related to deterrence. The mission of deterrence was important; it concerned the types of conflict that states sought to deter. When the Eisenhower administration announced its policy of "massive retaliation," by which the United States would "retaliate, instantly, by means and at places of our own choosing," many felt that this threat was not believable. Criticism came from a number of sources, including the strategic studies community (including B. H. Liddell Hart, Henry Kissinger, and William Kaufman), the military (Gen. Maxwell Taylor), and the political realm (Senator John F. Kennedy).[23] During the 1960 presidential campaign, Senator Kennedy said:

> Under every military budget submitted by this [Eisenhower] Administration, we have been preparing primarily to fight the one kind of war we least want to fight and are least likely to fight. We have been driving ourselves into a corner where the only choice is all or nothing at all, world devastation or submission—a choice that necessarily causes us to hesitate on the brink and leaves the initiative in the hands of our enemies.[24]

After Kennedy became president in January 1961, his administration announced a new nuclear deterrence strategy: "flexible response."

Another important aspect of nuclear deterrence concerned the object of threat. In the Kennedy administration, there were debates among those who thought that people and cities were the most efficacious objects of threat, a targeting policy referred to as "countervalue," and others who thought that military bases and defense plants were the best targets, referred to as "counterforce" doctrine.

The last notion that was debated concerned the number of nuclear weapons needed to ensure effective deterrence. Early in his administration, President Kennedy ordered his secretary of defense, Robert McNamara, to determine how many nuclear weapons were enough to deter a Soviet attack. McNamara had recruited a group of bright, young quantitative analysts, his "whiz kids," and they had concluded that the ability to kill 25 percent of the Soviet population while destroying 40 to 50 percent of Soviet industrial capacity would provide effective deterrence. McNamara told the president that this level of destruction could be accomplished with two hundred intercontinental ballistic missiles (ICBMs) and that to be sure that all two hundred targets would be destroyed, two missiles would be assigned to each. The president then asked McNamara whether he intended to request four hundred missiles from the Congress. McNamara responded that he recommended the president request the smallest four-digit number possible: one thousand ICBMs. McNamara warned the president that if he requested a smaller number, the administration would be "politically murdered."[25]

Throughout the Cold War, the United States and the Soviet Union had their nuclear weapons pointed at one another; they were, to use Robert Oppenheimer's analogy, like two scorpions trapped in a bottle. Despite the horrific potential for destruction in the Cold War era, deterrence was relatively straightforward. If the United States or the Soviet Union were attacked with nuclear weapons, the source of the attack could be identified and a retaliatory attack would be ordered.

With the growing importance of nonstate actors in international relations, deterrence is no longer as simple and straightforward, a fact noted by President George W. Bush in the 2002 *National Security Strategy of the United States*: "New deadly challenges have emerged from rogue states and terrorists. None of these contemporary threats rival the sheer destructive power that was arrayed against us by the Soviet Union. Traditional concepts of deterrence will not work against a terrorist enemy whose avowed tactics are wanton destruction and the targeting of innocents."[26]

The president pointed to the challenges to deterrence theory raised by the emergence of terrorism. First, terrorists do not have territory that can be attacked. Second, they do not have an identifiable population that can be attacked. Third, terrorist leaders may not conform to the rational decision-making model on which deterrence theory is based.

NUCLEAR ARMS CONTROL

Ballistic missiles dramatically reduced the time required to cause death and destruction. Prior to the advent of missiles, it took hours for bombers to go from the United States to the USSR or vice versa. In August 1957, the Soviet Union tested the first ICBM. Thereafter, it would take thirty minutes for a missile to travel from the Soviet Union to the United States. Suddenly, the United States, which had been physically isolated from the destructiveness of Europe's wars, was vulnerable to attack, a fact that was underscored by an influential strategist, Albert Wohlstetter, in a noteworthy article arguing that American bombers were vulnerable to a preemptive attack.[27] Wohlstetter's warning struck a raw nerve with Americans, who remembered the surprise attack on Pearl Harbor. In the new world of intercontinental ballistic missiles, there were a number of ways in which nuclear war could start, including a surprise attack, accident, or escalation from a conventional conflict.

In 1961, several books were published that called for the limitation of nuclear weapons.[28] These books constituted the foundation of a theory of arms control, whose essential feature, according to Thomas Schelling and Morton Halperin, was "the recognition of the common interest, of the possibility of reciprocation and cooperation even between potential enemies with respect to their military establishments."[29]

Until the Cuban missile crisis, nuclear war seemed to be a hypothetical possibility, the nightmare of nuclear strategists; however, in October 1962 the United States discovered a clandestine attempt by the Soviet Union to install nuclear missiles in Cuba, ninety miles from the shores of the United States. In response, President Kennedy demanded that Moscow remove the missiles. For a tension-filled thirteen days, the United States and the USSR were on the brink of war. The crisis was resolved only when the United States made a public pledge not to sponsor an invasion of Cuba and a private pledge to remove its intermediate-range ballistic missiles from Italy and Turkey. It was as if Kennedy and the Soviet premier, Nikita Khrushchev, had gone to a precipice, looked into the abyss of possible nuclear war, and backed away.

In the aftermath of the Cuban missile crisis, the United States and USSR signed an agreement calling for the installation of a "hotline" between Washington, D.C., and Moscow. This gave the superpowers' leaders the ability to

communicate quickly, reliably, and secretly, a capability that had been miss-
ing throughout the Cold War until that point. A second arms control agreement was negotiated in a three-month period by the three existing nuclear
powers: the United States, the Soviet Union, and the United Kingdom. That
instrument, the Limited Test Ban Treaty, prohibited its signatories from conducting nuclear tests in the atmosphere. At a minimum, this was a significant
"clean air act,"[30] although many thought that it was more important as one of
the first significant arms control agreements in the Cold War.

Other countries became concerned about the threats posed by various types
of weapons and moved to place limits on them. For example, in the 1960s a
number of states were concerned about the possible spread of nuclear weapons and negotiated the Non-Proliferation Treaty. In 1969 the United States
and Soviet Union opened negotiations to limit long-range nuclear weapons:
the Strategic Arms Limitation Talks (SALT). The first SALT agreements—
the Anti-Ballistic Missile (ABM) Treaty and an interim agreement on offensive arms—were signed in 1972, to be followed by a new round of negotiations called SALT II that resulted in an agreement in 1979. This agreement
was signed, but not ratified, by the United States.[31]

The Strategic Arms Reduction Treaties, known by the acronym START,
were two agreements designed to reduce the numbers of long-range nuclear
weapons in the arsenals of the United States and the Soviet Union. In July
1991, President George H. W. Bush and his Soviet counterpart, Mikhail Gorbachev, concluded START I, which called for a one-third reduction in the
number of nuclear warheads and bombs held by the United States and USSR.

When the Soviet Union disintegrated in December 1991, the status of the
START I Treaty was called into question, because former Soviet long-range
nuclear weapons were stationed in what had become four independent states:
Russia, Ukraine, Belarus, and Kazakhstan. The three non-Russian states
agreed to ratify the START I Treaty and to destroy or turn over their nuclear
weapons to Russia.

In January 1993, President George H. W. Bush and President Boris Yeltsin
of Russia signed the second Strategic Arms Reduction Treaty (START II),
which called for reductions of 50 percent in the levels of weapons allowed
by START I. The George W. Bush administration adopted an approach to
Russian-American strategic nuclear arms control that was radically different
from those of previous administrations. Whereas the START I treaty was
more than seven hundred pages long, the Strategic Offensive Reductions
Treaty (SORT) signed in Moscow in May 2002 was only three pages long and
contained no provisions for verification. It declared that the total number of
strategic nuclear weapons would not exceed 2,200 as of December 31, 2012.
In the absence of verification provisions, the United States and Russia agreed

that the verification regime created by the 1991 START I treaty would be used to verify SORT.

The SORT agreement was unusual, as, for the most part, nuclear arms control efforts ground to a halt under George W. Bush. During his Senate confirmation hearings, secretary of state nominee Colin Powell announced that the administration would not seek ratification of the Comprehensive Test Ban Treaty, which had been rejected by the Senate in 1999. Toward the end of his first year in office, President Bush made good on a campaign pledge by announcing that the United States would withdraw from the ABM Treaty of 1972. The declaration marked the first time since World War II that any state had withdrawn from an arms control treaty. (North Korea gave notice of its intent to withdraw from the Nuclear Non-Proliferation Treaty in 1993, but it suspended that notice as a consequence of negotiations with the United States over the future of its nuclear weapons program. In 2003, North Korea did actually withdraw from the NPT.)

President Obama entered office in 2009 intent on reviving efforts to reduce the world's stockpiles of nuclear weapons. On April 5, 2009, in a speech in Prague, he stated his desire to move toward a world without nuclear weapons. Spurred into action by the planned expiration of START I on December 5, 2009, and by the desire to show progress toward nuclear disarmament prior to the NPT Review Conference scheduled for May 2010, the Obama administration negotiated an agreement with Russia called New START. Signed in April 2010, and designed to supersede the 2002 Strategic Offensive Reductions Treaty, the New START Treaty required that Russia and the United States reduce their strategic nuclear arsenals to 1,550 warheads each within seven years of the agreement's entry into force. Both sides were limited to a combined total of no more than seven hundred deployed ICBMs, SLBMs, and nuclear-capable heavy bombers. The treaty included provisions for on-site inspections, data exchanges, and the use of so-called national technical means of verification. The U.S. Senate gave its consent to the ratification of the treaty on December 22, 2010, and the treaty entered into force.[32]

During the Cold War, arms control had three principal objectives: (1) to reduce the probability of war occurring; (2) if war occurred, to reduce the damage caused by war; and (3) to reduce the economic cost of preparing for war.[33] These objectives informed arms control efforts from the late 1950s to the end of the Cold War. To what extent are these objectives relevant in the post-9/11 environment?

Arms control remains vitally important, particularly concerning efforts to limit the spread of weapons of mass destruction, the subject of chapter 6. Russian-American efforts to limit their weapons, while not as important as they were during the Cold War, remain vital if only because the United States and Russia possess 93 percent of the nuclear weapons in the world. During the Cold War, nuclear weapons threatened to cause a global cataclysm. That threat is no longer as great, although the capability remains. However, the possibility that weapons of mass destruction could be used is greater today than during the Cold War.

NUCLEAR WAR FIGHTING

Since the beginning of the nuclear age, some strategists and political leaders have argued that nuclear weapons are capable of accomplishing a number of different missions and that they should be used in support of U.S. national priorities. In the extreme, some have argued that the United States should have the capability to fight a nuclear war and prevail. This is referred to as a "nuclear war-fighting" strategy. The Reagan administration proposed this strategy and sought the capabilities to support it. Advocates of this approach argue that nuclear weapons can be used to compel as well as to deter other states; they point to the Soviet withdrawal from Iran in 1946 and the Korean armistice of 1953 as cases in which the threat of nuclear weapons played a role.

The option to use nuclear weapons for political or military purposes requires a large number and variety of weapons so that a number of different contingencies can be addressed. Advocates of this approach argue that even though nuclear weapons are the most powerful weapons ever invented, they do not increase a state's influence unless they are, in some sense, used. Paradoxically, preparing to use nuclear weapons best ensures their nonuse. If, however, their use becomes necessary, the most militarily effective weapons should be used.

Opponents of this approach contend that the very act of envisioning the use of nuclear weapons, the most destructive weapons ever devised, makes their use more likely. In addition, if states deploy their weapons so that they are usable, they must make them usable within a short period of time. This "hair-trigger" situation is exceedingly dangerous.

The option of "fighting and winning" a nuclear war characteristic of the strategic policy of the Reagan administration was resurrected by the George W. Bush administration in its call for a new class of nuclear weapons, "bunker busters." In 2002, the administration called for funds to explore the possibility of developing a new earth-penetrating warhead that would be used to destroy underground command bunkers and nuclear weapons storage sites. The administration argued that the conventional "bunker buster" bombs would not penetrate deeply enough to destroy some targets and that new nuclear weapons were needed to accomplish this mission. In 2009, the Department of Defense announced plans to deploy a nuclear bunker buster called the Massive Ordnance Penetrator (MOP) on B-2 bombers. In its 2010 Nuclear Posture Review, the Obama administration renounced the development of these weapons.

LIVING WITH NUCLEAR WEAPONS

John Steinbruner has said, "Even with the potential for a major strategic engagement with nature looming in the background, the pattern of nuclear weapons deployment remains the largest and most imminent physical threat to any and all human societies."[34] Because of the awesome potential of these weapons, a number of options have been proposed for dealing with them, ranging from never using them to employing them in contemporary military operations.

The arms control approach for dealing with nuclear weapons was developed in the 1960s primarily to control Soviet and American nuclear weapons. The United States and Russia still possess the lion's share of nuclear weapons in the world; however, seven other countries now possess nuclear weapons. Therefore, in the future efforts must be made to include all nine states that possess nuclear weapons in order to implement more effective, comprehensive controls.

Arms control is an appropriate strategy only for those states whose relations are a mixture of cooperation and conflict; without cooperation arms control is impossible, but without conflict it is unnecessary. It was the genius of those responsible for the development of the arms control approach that within an extremely conflictual relationship they were able to build a useful theory on as narrow a basis for cooperation as the mutual desire to avoid nuclear war. The post–Cold War objectives of arms control differ somewhat from the objectives associated with the initial arms control approach, because the underlying assumptions about the mixture of cooperation and conflict in international relations have changed. Where the desire to cooperate extends no further than measures designed to avoid nuclear war, all that can reasonably be expected of arms control is assistance in preventing the parties from stumbling into a war that neither wants. But once a more cooperative relationship has been developed, the possibilities greatly increase.

Former U.S. ambassador to NATO Ivo Daalder has drawn upon this distinction in suggesting that the future of arms control may lie with "a cooperative approach, applicable to states with largely compatible political and security interests" rather than "a competitive approach, applicable to states with fundamentally different political and security interests." While "competitive arms control" has as its primary objective preventing war, "cooperative arms control" seeks to "transform political relations in a manner conducive to creating a pluralistic security community."[35]

Proponents of the arms control approach must also extend their focus beyond the nation-state to encompass nonstate actors in a world increasingly influenced by such actors. While the principal fear and focus of the Cold War concerned the Soviet-American nuclear balance, today the focus is on the possibility of nuclear or other weapons of mass destruction falling into the hands of terrorists or rogue states. Concepts like deterrence and coercive diplomacy (compellence) developed during the Cold War are only partially applicable to a world in which states are no longer the only, or even the major, political actors. In this new environment, it is vital to develop new ways of thinking about issues of security so that, as strategist Herman Kahn put it many years ago, the living will not envy the dead.

ADDITIONAL RESOURCES

Books

Brodie, Bernard, ed. *The Absolute Weapon: Atomic Power and World Order*. New York: Harcourt, Brace, 1946.

Bundy, McGeorge. *Danger and Survival: Choices about the Bomb in the First Fifty Years*. New York: Random House, 1988.

Caldwell, Dan. *The Dynamics of Domestic Politics and Arms Control: The SALT II Treaty Ratification Debate*. Columbia: University of South Carolina Press, 1991.

Cirincione, Joseph. *Nuclear Nightmares: Securing the World Before It Is Too Late*. New York: Columbia University Press, 2013.

Freedman, Lawrence. *The Evolution of Nuclear Strategy*, 3rd ed. New York: Palgrave Macmillan, 2003.

Krepon, Michael. *Better Safe Than Sorry: The Ironies of Living with the Bomb*. Stanford, CA: Stanford University Press, 2009.

Larsen, Jeffrey A., and James J. Wirtz, eds. *Arms Control and Cooperative Security*. Boulder, CO: Lynne Rienner, 2009.

Mandelbaum, Michael. *The Nuclear Revolution: International Politics before and after Hiroshima*. Cambridge: Cambridge University Press, 1981.

Morgan, Patrick. *Deterrence Now*. Cambridge: Cambridge University Press, 2003.

Rhodes, Richard. *The Making of the Atomic Bomb*. New York: Simon and Schuster, 1986.

———. *Dark Sun: The Making of the Hydrogen Bomb*. New York: Simon and Schuster, 1996.

———. *Arsenals of Folly: The Making of the Nuclear Arms Race*. New York: Vintage, 2008.

Williams, Robert E., Jr., and Paul R. Viotti, eds. *Arms Control: History, Theory, and Policy.* 2 vols. New York: Praeger Security International for ABC-CLIO, 2012.

Websites

Arms Control Association: http://www.armscontrol.org/
Center for Nonproliferation Studies: http://www.nonproliferation.org/
Defense Threat Reduction Agency: www.dtra.mil
National Nuclear Security Administration, Department of Energy: nnsa.energy.gov
Natural Resources Defense Council: www.nrdc.org/nuclear/default.asp
Ploughshares Fund: http://ploughshares.org/
Stimson Center: www.stimson.org
Stockholm International Peace Research Institute (SIPRI): www.sipri.org
Union of Concerned Scientists: www.ucsusa.org

Films

The Cold War. A twenty-four-part series on the development and playing out of the Cold War produced by CNN in 1998. Particularly noteworthy are interviews with many of the principal participants.

The Day After. A 1983 movie starring Jason Robards, JoBeth Williams, and John Lithgow that focuses on a Soviet nuclear attack on the United States. Directed by Nicholas Meyer, ABC Circle Films.

Dr. Strangelove or: How I Learned to Stop Worrying and Love the Bomb. The classic film directed by Stanley Kubrick and starring Peter Sellers, Columbia Pictures, 1964.

Fail Safe. A 1964 movie starring Henry Fonda and Walter Matthau that focuses on a military computer error that deploys American bombers to destroy Moscow and the attempt by the president (Fonda) to call them back. Directed by Sidney Lumet, Columbia Pictures.

On the Beach. This 1959 movie depicts the situation in Australia following a Soviet-American nuclear war and the radiation cloud that results from it. Directed by Stanley Kramer, Stanley Kramer Productions.

War and Peace in the Nuclear Age. A thirteen-part PBS series on the development and deployment of nuclear weapons. Boston: WGBH, 1989.

Chapter Four

Chemical and Biological Weapons

> The proliferation of chemical weapons, as well as their means of delivery, constitutes a threat to international peace and security.
>
> —United Nations Security Council Resolution 2118 (2013)

Two weeks after the 9/11 attacks, a letter containing a suspicious white powder arrived at NBC News in New York. After the powder was determined to be anthrax, over 1,300 NBC employees were tested for exposure and infection. One week later, in Boca Raton, Florida, a photo editor at American Media entered the hospital with a high fever. Three days later he was dead of inhalation anthrax, America's first anthrax victim in a quarter of a century. Tests indicated that the strains of anthrax used in the two incidents were identical.[1]

On October 14, 2001, a letter containing anthrax was opened in Senator Tom Daschle's office at the Capitol. After testing determined that approximately thirty congressional staffers had been exposed to anthrax, the House and Senate recessed while congressional office buildings were decontaminated. Mail addressed to Congress was held up for months as the U.S. Postal Service put in place a system to irradiate all letters and packages sent to Capitol Hill, the Pentagon, the CIA, and other government offices. Meanwhile, numerous postal workers in New Jersey and in the Washington, D.C., area were testing positive for anthrax exposure. Two who worked in the Washington postal facility handling congressional mail died in late October.

Initially, most Americans assumed the anthrax-laced letters, which contained radical Islamist statements, were a new phase in the terrorist attack on the United States. In mid-October 2001, Vice President Dick Cheney even suggested that the anthrax might be linked to Osama bin Laden. Laboratory analysis, however, revealed that the anthrax sent to Senator Daschle's office had come from a strain developed in the United States and that the fineness of the particles were such that the sample could have been produced only in a highly sophisticated lab.

As evidence gathered by the FBI increasingly pointed in the direction of some disgruntled military lab worker at either the U.S. Army's Dugway Proving Ground in Utah or Fort Detrick in Maryland, the trail seemed to grow cold. For months after the Postal Service was virtually shut down along the East Coast due to bioterrorism, no prime suspects were publicly identified. Barbara Rosenberg, director of the Federation of American Scientists' biological weapons monitoring program, suggested that the problem was not that the FBI knew too little but that it knew too much.[2] She speculated that the investigative trail led in a direction that, if pursued, would reveal that the United States had been violating both its international commitments under the Biological Weapons Convention and domestic law by secretly pursuing biological weapons research. Finally, in February 2010, the FBI closed its investigation of the case having concluded that the perpetrator was Dr. Bruce Ivins, a biochemist at the U.S. Army Medical Research Institute of Infectious Diseases at Fort Dietrick, Maryland. Dr. Ivins had committed suicide in 2008.[3] While some skeptics were unconvinced by the FBI's evidence, others suggested that the case had merely demonstrated the extraordinary difficulty of tracing the origins of a well-conceived biological weapons attack.

The post-9/11 anthrax cases revealed an extremely potent new source of insecurity in a world that, for Americans at least, already seemed more threatening than ever before. Many Americans stocked up on Cipro and other antibiotics recommended for the treatment of anthrax. Others rushed to doctors to check up on cold and flu symptoms that in previous years would have been stoically endured at home. Some stopped opening the mail. Ultimately, five people died as a direct result of the anthrax attacks. But the randomness of the fatalities (which included an elderly woman in Connecticut), the apparent lack of any effective preventative measures, and the long delay in finding the perpetrator raised the frightening specter of a future in which the most powerful country on earth might be unable to protect its citizens from biological warfare.

Chemical and biological weapons (CBW) have a long and disturbing history. Around 590 BC, the Athenians used a noxious plant to contaminate the water supply of Cirrha, a city under siege. When the defenders became afflicted with diarrhea, the Athenians, facing little resistance, entered Cirrha and slaughtered its residents. According to Thucydides, the Peloponnesians used sulfur fumes in an effort to take the town of Plataea. "Insect bombs" were used on a number of occasions in the ancient world to defend walled cities from attackers. Those who attempted to tunnel under walls sometimes found themselves confronted with swarms of bees released in the tunnels by defenders. In medieval Europe, catapults were sometimes used to launch active beehives over the walls of besieged cities or into the ranks of opposing armies.[4]

While ancient peoples often displayed remarkable ingenuity in the development of what today might be called CBW, the full potential of chemical and biological warfare would not be unleashed until the Industrial Age. The world was, in many ways, a very different place when chemical weapons first made an impact on modern warfare during World War I. Soon after the war began, there were chemical attacks. In August 1914, it was tear gas used by the French against the Germans. Two months later, the Germans employed a crude chemical compound that caused violent sneezing against the French. These early experiments in chemical warfare were, however, mere child's play compared with what was to follow. In April 1915, in the Second Battle of Ypres, Germany used chlorine gas with devastating effect. Among the ten thousand casualties caused by the attack, five thousand died. In September 1915, at Loos, the British attempted to retaliate with chlorine gas of their own, but a shift in the wind caused the British to suffer as much from the attack as the Germans did.[5]

Undeterred by similar setbacks on all sides, the combatants escalated the use of chemical weapons. Chlorine gas was followed by phosgene, a gas with ten times the lethality of chlorine. Then came the most awful chemical agent used in the Great War: mustard gas, which caused vomiting and serious blisters, both internally and externally. Those exposed to mustard gas often died agonizing deaths. Most survivors were seriously incapacitated—often blinded—or physically disfigured for life.

In all, chemical weapons caused almost 1.3 million casualties, including close to one hundred thousand deaths, during World War I. It was a horrific experience that helped to create a strong taboo among states against the use of chemical weapons. But as devastating as man-made gases were during the Great War, disease quickly reasserted itself as the more efficient killer. More people died of typhus and Spanish influenza in the four years following the war than had died of war-related causes during the four years of the war. And in the case of the Spanish influenza pandemic, the geographical spread of mortality was far greater than that associated with the war.

What does the use of poison gas in World War I have in common with the spread of the Spanish influenza following the war—other than, of course, extreme lethality? In a better world, one in which technological advances were not linked so often to security threats, perhaps there would be no link. Unfortunately, the same motives that led the Germans, French, and British to use, collectively, over one hundred thousand tons of gas in World War I would lead others to begin using microbes as weapons. After all, there is no need to manufacture gas (not to mention conventional bombs and bullets) if one can spread among the enemy population a disease that will be just as effective at sowing death and destruction. Some in the world today continue to operate on the basis of this proposition—and they know much more about disease than anyone knew in 1918.

THINKING ABOUT WMD

The ominous phrase *weapons of mass destruction* (or simply WMD) refers not only to the nuclear weapons discussed in the previous chapter but also to biological and chemical weapons. While it should be emphasized that not all weapons in these three categories are intended to produce mass destruction—there are, for example, low-yield nuclear weapons with tactical uses and chemical weapons designed to incapacitate rather than kill—nuclear, biological, and chemical weapons can threaten security in ways that appear genuinely apocalyptic. There are significant differences between nukes on the one hand and bugs and gas on the other. Unfortunately, the differences are ones that complicate rather than simplify the job of seeking security against WMD.

What nuclear, biological, and chemical weapons have in common is, first, the potential to kill millions of people quickly and with disturbing ease. Second, each type of weapon in the WMD category is especially difficult (some might say virtually impossible, at least when civilian populations are the target) to defend against. Third, each of these types of weapons has only limited value to those governments and armies that respect the laws of war and their prohibitions against indiscriminate killing. In fact, as we saw in the last chapter, governments have regarded nuclear weapons as being useful primarily, if not exclusively, for deterrence. However, the indiscriminate and seemingly unlimited lethality of nuclear, biological, and chemical weapons make them particularly attractive to those who neither bear the responsibility of protecting a state and its citizens nor respect the rules that sometimes keep states from committing mass murder. In other words, the very qualities that make weapons of mass destruction troublesome for states make them attractive to terrorists desiring to kill large numbers of innocents.

Western thinking about WMD and the threat such weapons pose has changed dramatically since the end of the Cold War. During the Cold War, politicians, soldiers, strategists, and many ordinary citizens worried constantly about the threat posed by WMD, particularly the large numbers of strategic nuclear weapons that the Soviet Union and the United States kept aimed at each other. With the collapse of the Soviet Union, what had seemed to be a permanent nuclear confrontation was brought to a peaceful end; for a time, defense budgets decreased and worries about WMD subsided. Peace, it seemed, had arrived.

The post–Cold War sense of security was short lived; new WMD threats quickly emerged. North Korea, one of just a handful of states clinging to communism, was in pursuit of nuclear weapons and in possession of ballistic missiles. The apparent hostility and irrationality of North Korea's leadership made its possession of nuclear weapons a troublesome prospect, to say the least. Even more troubling, however, was Iraq. Where North Korea's capability and intent with respect to the use of WMD was a matter of speculation, Iraq's was a matter of fact. During the 1980s, Iraq used chemical weapons in its war against Iran and against Kurdish rebels in its own territory.[6] Iraq's defeat in the Persian Gulf War in 1991 and the subsequent imposition of UN weapons inspectors brought to light the extent of Saddam Hussein's WMD programs.

Thanks in large part to North Korea and Iraq, WMD concerns in the West during the 1990s focused on the problem of "rogue states." Fears of an apocalyptic nuclear exchange signaling the failure of deterrence between the superpowers were replaced with fears of limited nuclear, chemical, or biological attacks launched by a state led by an undeterrable dictator. As Columbia University professor Richard K. Betts put it in a 1998 *Foreign Affairs* article, "There is less danger of complete annihilation, but more danger of mass destruction."[7]

In the aftermath of 9/11, WMD fears shifted again. Concern since then has been focused on the possibility that either a rogue state or terrorists might acquire and use WMD. Indeed, the Al Qaeda attacks on the World Trade Center and the Pentagon were intended to, and actually did, achieve a measure of mass destruction unprecedented in the history of terrorist attacks. The weapons of mass destruction used, of course, were commercial airliners with two hundred thousand pounds of fuel on board. In thinking about WMD, the significance of 9/11 was to remove any doubt there might have been that a terrorist organization such as Al Qaeda would use nuclear, chemical, or biological weapons if it had them. In fact, Osama bin Laden told his followers that the acquisition of WMD was a "religious duty."

At this point, it is worth recalling the discussion in chapter 1 of threats as products of capabilities and intentions. In spite of dramatic cuts in their arsenals, the United States and Russia continue to dwarf all other international actors in their WMD capabilities. But because their intentions toward each other are not now so obviously hostile as they were during the Cold War, their WMD capabilities appear not to pose an imminent threat to each other. Rogue states—or, as they have been labeled more recently by the U.S. government, "states of concern"—have vastly smaller WMD capabilities than the United States and Russia, but in the absence of benign intentions, they constitute a more significant threat to our security. Finally, terrorist and insurgent organizations such as Al Qaeda and the Islamic State are almost certainly further from being able to use nuclear, chemical, or biological weapons than most rogue states, and yet since 9/11 we have had little doubt about the malevolence of their intentions. As a result, the least significant WMD capability at present may be the threat we must worry about most. After all, when seeking security, we must always ask, "What if?"

CHEMICAL WEAPONS

Among those who worry about chemical and biological weapons (CBW), biological weapons are generally thought to be the more serious threat. Consequently, let us begin with chemical weapons in an effort to ease into a topic that even the experts—or, perhaps, especially the experts—find sobering.

Poison-tipped arrows, incendiary bombs, smoke (to hide troop movements), and hot oil or sewage dumped onto attackers from castle walls were the precursors of modern chemical warfare. Chemical weapons in the modern sense, however, had to await the Industrial Age and the development of modern chemical production processes. The use of tear gas and various poison gases during World War I marked the beginning of modern chemical warfare, but it almost marked the end as well, because revulsion at the use of the new weapons was so widespread. Unfortunately, in spite of remarkable restraint by all parties during World War II (although we must not forget the Nazis' use of poison gas in concentration camps and the use of chemical agents by the Italian and Japanese armies in their imperial wars), chemical weapons have not disappeared as a security threat.

Chemical weapons can be broadly defined as toxic manufactured gases, liquids, or powders that are designed to incapacitate or kill humans. There are four basic categories of chemical weapons: (1) lung, or choking, agents, such as chlorine and phosgene, which damage lung tissue and make breathing impossible; (2) blood agents, such as hydrogen cyanide, which prevent the flow of oxygen in the bloodstream; (3) blister agents, such as mustard gas, which cause chemical burns on skin and all other contacted body tissue, both internal and external; and (4) nerve agents, such as sarin and VX, which disrupt the central nervous system. In addition to these categories of potentially lethal chemical agents, there are nonlethal compounds known as incapacitating agents, such as tear gas, which causes temporary discomfort, and BZ, which causes cognitive disorientation. Finally, antiplant agents, such as the Agent Orange used by the U.S. military as a defoliant in the jungles of Vietnam, are also classified as chemical weapons and often have negative, if unintended, effects on human health (including cancer in the case of Agent Orange). Chemical weapons of all types are generally spread as liquids (especially in aerosol form) or gases (sometimes as vapors produced by a liquid compound).

Because they can cause death in painful and grotesque ways, often without warning, chemical weapons may inspire terror among civilians or unprotected combat forces. Defense analysts, however, generally point to certain limitations of chemical weapons. The effective delivery of chemical weapons depends in large part on environmental conditions. Chemical compounds that are delivered as aerosols or gases are easily dispersed by wind. In some cases, chemical weapons are rendered less effective, if not completely inert, by hot or cold temperatures. Furthermore (and in part because of these environmental factors), large quantities of chemical agents are often necessary to inflict even modest death tolls. A study in 1993 by the Office of Technology Assessment found that a ton of sarin might cause three to eight thousand deaths if used in *ideal* conditions in a highly populated area.[8] The Aum Shinrikyo sarin attack in the Tokyo subway system in 1995 injured or psychologically traumatized roughly five thousand people, but only twelve were killed. Admittedly, both the technology and the tactics employed in that attack were very crude, but it is worth noting that the use of chemical weapons in World War I resulted in slightly less than one death per ton of gas.

Therefore, and although many governments have invested heavily in chemical weapons over the years, a terrorist organization seeking the maximum lethal impact would very likely look to other weapons. On the other hand, chemical weapons are cheap and easy to produce. Large-scale manufacturing can be hidden amid legitimate commercial processes in dual-use factories. Raw materials are plentiful and easily obtained. Except when accidents occur, chemical weapons can be easily transported without detection. Furthermore, clouds of gas or unseen vapors that produce painful choking deaths, hideous blisters on exposed skin, or muscle twitching followed by rapid death are likely to be highly effective if the purpose of an attack is to induce terror in a civilian population.

Broadly speaking, there are two basic scenarios in which chemical weapons might be used. The first involves state action, most likely in connection with combat operations. The second is a terrorist attack. Actual cases of the military use of chemical weapons occurred in World War I, in various colonial wars (by the British in Afghanistan and by the Spanish and French in Africa), in Ethiopia (by the Italians during the 1930s), in China (by the Japanese during the 1930s), in the Iran-Iraq War (by both sides), and in Syria's civil war (by the government).

Between 1980 and 1988, Iran and Iraq fought a grim war noteworthy primarily for the number of casualties and the senselessness of the human slaughter that occurred. Altogether, the war caused over a million casualties. Perhaps not surprisingly, chemical weapons were used more extensively in the Iran-Iraq War than at any time since World War I. Iraq was the chief culprit, but Iran almost certainly used chemical weapons as well. Allegations concerning Iraqi use of chemical weapons surfaced early in the war, but international observers were unable to provide confirmation until 1984, when UN personnel determined that the Iraqi military had employed mustard gas and a nerve agent called tabun. Many other incidents were reported, but independent sources were unable to confirm most of them. Charges of chemical weapons use were part of both sides' propaganda during the war. Nevertheless, chemical attacks by Iraq were confirmed on various occasions in 1985, February 1986, and April 1987. In 1987, investigators found evidence of exposure to mustard gas among Iraqi troops, but it was unclear whether the exposure had been the result of an Iranian or an Iraqi attack.[9]

Beginning in April 1987 and continuing to October 1988, at the same time that Saddam Hussein's Revolutionary Guard was fighting Iran, Baghdad conducted a campaign of extermination against ethnic Kurds in northern Iraq. Four thousand Kurdish villages were razed, and somewhere between 50,000 and 180,000 Kurds were killed. Chemical weapons were used as part of the genocidal campaign.[10]

In March 1988, after Kurdish rebels moved into the predominantly Kurdish city of Halabja in northern Iraq, Iraqi planes dropped large numbers of chemical bombs over the course of several days. In what was likely an attack intended by Saddam Hussein both to push forward the genocidal campaign against the Kurds and to test Iraq's chemical warfare capabilities, a variety of chemical weapons, including mustard gas, sarin, tabun, and VX, were dropped on the city. An estimated three to five thousand civilians were killed in the attack; tens of thousands more were injured. Since the chemical attacks on Halabja and sixty other Kurdish towns, abnormally high rates of cancer, respiratory disease, birth defects, and infertility have been reported.[11]

In spite of the fact that Saddam Hussein was tried, convicted, and executed in 2006 for crimes against humanity and genocide, charges that were in part based on his government's use of chemical weapons against the Kurds, there are still dictators in the world willing to use chemical weapons. In Syria, where the regime of Bashar al-Assad found itself embroiled in a civil war after responding to Arab Spring protests in 2011 with violence, chemical weapons have been used on multiple occasions since the end of 2012. A UN inspection team reported "clear and convincing evidence" of the use of the nerve agent sarin in rocket attacks that the United States and its allies main tained could only have been carried out by Syrian government forces.[12] Even before the UN report was completed, Syria admitted for the first time that it possessed stockpiles of chemical weapons and, under pressure exerted by a unanimous UN Security Council, agreed to their destruction. With the Organisation for the Prohibition of Chemical Weapons (OPCW) supervising the process, well over a thousand metric tons of chemical weapons and precursor chemicals from Syrian stocks were destroyed by August 2014.

In March 2015, new reports of chemical weapons use in Syria surfaced, this time involving barrel bombs containing chlorine gas. Human Rights Watch and other groups maintained that the attacks, which occurred in rebel-held territory, could only have been been perpetrated by the government, given the targets and the use of helicopters to deliver the bombs.[13] Of course, the Syrian government's renewed use of chemical weapons in defiance of a UN Security Council resolution raised questions regarding the international community's willingness to enforce not only Security Council resolutions but also the terms of the Chemical Weapons Convention.

The primary example of the use of a chemical weapon in a terrorist attack up until now is the March 1995 Aum Shinrikyo attack on the Tokyo subway using the nerve agent sarin. Aum Shinrikyo (Supreme Truth), an apocalyptic cult founded in 1984 by Shoko Asahara, prophesied a global Armageddon during which the group would take over and govern a Japan devastated by a U.S. nuclear attack.[14] Around 1990, when cult members were defeated in Japanese parliamentary elections and the Japanese government began to investigate some of the cult's business deals for possible fraud, the group began to pursue weapons of mass destruction.

Through businesses owned by the cult, donations from cult members, and almost certainly fraud as well, Aum Shinrikyo amassed assets believed to have been in the neighborhood of a billion dollars in 1995. The organization used its wealth as well as the scientific expertise of many young, highly educated cult members to establish labs for the production of both chemical and biological weapons. Biological weapons came first. In the early 1990s the group is believed to have produced botulinum toxin, anthrax, and Q fever. The effort to produce chemical weapons began in 1993 and, after experiments with other nerve agents, focused on sarin.

In early 1994, according to Japanese prosecutors, Aum Shinrikyo began building a manufacturing plant designed to produce up to two tons of sarin a day. Although equipment failures and police investigations prevented the group from reaching its chemical weapons production goal, the demonstrated potential was alarming.

Between 1990 and 1995, Aum Shinrikyo members attempted on ten separate occasions to disseminate biological agents in Tokyo and the surrounding areas, including U.S. Navy bases. For a variety of reasons ranging from a failure of nerve on the part of operatives to poor bacterial strains, not a single casualty resulted from any of these attacks using biological agents. Consequently, the group began to focus on chemical weapons.

The use of sarin in an assassination attempt in 1993 failed, nearly killing the assailant. In June 1994, in the town of Matsumoto, the cult targeted three judges who were set to rule in a land fraud case involving Aum Shinrikyo. Late at night, for ten minutes, seven cult members sprayed vaporized sarin at the judges' living quarters. Seven people were killed and 144, including all three judges, were injured in the attack. The cult's deadliest and most notorious attack, however, came nine months later.

On March 20, 1995, five cult members carrying eleven doubled plastic bags containing a low-grade sarin solution and riding on separate subway trains converged on the Tokyo station closest to the Tokyo police headquarters. At the height of the Monday morning rush hour, the cultists punctured the bags on the floors of the subway cars in which they were riding and fled when their respective trains reached the station. As the sarin solution evaporated, passengers on the trains experienced vomiting, respiratory problems, seizures, and other signs of sarin poisoning. Trains containing the deadly vapors continued on their way from station to station—one for an hour and a half—before the system was closed down and cleanup began.

Twelve people died in the attack. Initial reports indicated that more than five thousand others were injured in the attack, but, according to Japanese officials, three-fourths of the approximately five thousand people examined in hospitals following the attack showed no signs of exposure to sarin. The actual number of people with physical injuries appears to have been closer to one thousand than to the figure of 3,938 cited by Japanese prosecutors, but the larger number of people reporting to hospitals suggests that psychological trauma may have affected far more people than were physically affected.

It is possible to view the Aum Shinrikyo attack on the Tokyo subway system as evidence that chemical weapons attacks are not as easy to mount as is often supposed. In fact, there *are* significant obstacles to terrorist organizations hoping to use chemical weapons as weapons of mass destruction. Most analysts, however, view the Aum Shinrikyo sarin attack with alarm, preferring to see it as a wake-up call. The cult, after all, had invested considerable resources in developing chemical and biological weapons and, over time, learned a number of lessons about what would and would not work. Just as those charged with defending society have learned a great deal from the March 1995 chemical attack, so too have those who are interested in using weapons of mass destruction against free societies. One of the lessons that terrorist organizations may have learned from Aum Shinrikyo is that biological weapons can have certain advantages over chemical weapons.

BIOLOGICAL WEAPONS

Human beings, as a species, have waged an epic struggle against disease from the beginning. Long before modern science began to uncover the role that microbes—viruses and bacteria—play in disease, some unscrupulous warriors sought to make disease their ally. One of the most notorious cases of primitive biological warfare may have been partially responsible for the plague that devastated Europe in the fourteenth century.

By 1340, traders operating between China and Europe had begun to carry the rat-borne fleas by which the bubonic plague from China was transmitted. In 1343, some Genoese merchants were attacked by Tartars at the Crimean trading post of Kaffa. The merchants saved themselves from the conventional Tartar attack by retreating behind the walls of Kaffa, but before the Tartars withdrew they catapulted plague-infested corpses over the walls. Some merchants subsequently died of the plague on their way home, but others survived to transmit the disease to Constantinople, Genoa, and Venice. From these commercial hubs the plague spread all over Europe, killing at least one-quarter of Europe's population by 1351.[15]

Some Native Americans were victims of a deliberate effort to spread disease during the French and Indian War. Sir Jeffrey Amherst, the commander of British forces in the war, ordered that smallpox-infested blankets be delivered to tribes loyal to the French in the Ohio River Valley. Whether the infected blankets were directly responsible is unknown, but smallpox did devastate several tribes soon thereafter.[16]

It was not until 1870 that biologists were able to prove that microorganisms cause disease. (Oddly enough, given its current significance as a biowarfare agent, the decisive experiment involved injecting anthrax into mice.) From that time on, it was possible to contemplate biological warfare in different terms, without the need to use corpses or infected materials as carriers of disease. Eventually, the disease-causing microbes—pathogens—themselves could be isolated and "weaponized."

Modern biological weapons employ living microorganisms, such as viruses and bacteria, or toxins produced by living organisms, to incapacitate or kill. Bacteria, viruses, and rickettsia are the three categories of microorganisms used as biological agents. Each type of microorganism produces a distinctive set of diseases. Bacterial diseases, which include anthrax, plague, and tularemia (rabbit fever), generally produce flu-like symptoms initially and are treatable with antibiotics. Anthrax and tularemia are not contagious; plague is. Among the rickettsia are Q fever, which is rarely fatal, and typhus. Both are treatable with antibiotics. Viruses, which do not respond to antibiotics, include smallpox and yellow fever. Following a global campaign of vaccination coordinated by the World Health Organization, smallpox was declared in 1980 to have been eradicated, but stocks of the smallpox virus were kept for research purposes by the United States and the Soviet Union. The existence of these stocks, combined with the fact that the smallpox vaccine is no longer routinely administered (or even widely available), makes many defense and public health officials worried about the potential reappearance of smallpox as a biological weapon.

Unlike microbes, toxins are nonliving substances, which means they do not reproduce or spread through contagion the way other biological agents do. As a result, toxins have more in common with chemical agents than with biological agents. In fact, some biological toxins can even be chemically synthesized. Nonetheless, toxins are considered to be biological weapons because they are derived from living organisms, such as molds and fungi.

In order to produce mass casualties, the microorganisms or toxins that make up biological weapons must be widely dispersed. Contagion—that is, the spread of disease from person to person—can play a role, at least in the case of a number of pathogens. Smallpox, for example, is highly contagious. In the case of bacteria that do not spread from person to person, or in the case of toxins, however, mass casualties can be produced only by using means of delivery that cause the biological agent to come in contact with large numbers of people. This generally means creating an aerosol spray with a liquid containing the biological agent. When prepared properly, such an aerosol is likely to be tasteless, odorless, and invisible. As a result, victims of a biological weapons attack may not know what has happened until well after symptoms have begun to develop.

The time frame for the appearance of symptoms following a biological weapons attack depends on the bacteria, rickettsia, or virus used. The incubation period for smallpox is from ten to fourteen days, and for plague from one to six days. Botulism has an incubation period of from twelve to seventy-two hours. Q fever, however, has an incubation period of from two to three weeks. Further complicating the ability of defense and public health officials to know that a biological weapons attack has occurred is the fact that disease symptoms, when they finally appear, are likely to be mistaken for symptoms that would accompany naturally occurring illnesses. Consequently, the first people to have evidence that a biological attack had occurred might be hospital lab technicians, public health epidemiologists, pharmacists, or even funeral directors. This is one reason that the U.S. government after 9/11 attempted to vaccinate all emergency-room workers with the smallpox vaccine.

Most microorganisms that might be used as biowarfare agents present special problems where "weaponization" is concerned. Some are killed by ultraviolet radiation and are therefore not suitable for use outdoors during the day. Most require extraordinarily careful handling to avoid the infection of lab workers or people living close to labs. In 1979, in Sverdlovsk (now Ekaterinburg), anthrax was accidentally released from a Soviet biological weapons lab. Sixty-four people died from what Soviet officials originally suggested was an anthrax outbreak caused by contaminated meat.

In spite of the tragedy at Sverdlovsk, anthrax is thought to be one of the biological agents best suited for use as a weapon. It is extraordinarily hardy, capable in nature of surviving in the soil fully exposed to the elements for decades. It can be freeze-dried, which means it can be milled into an extremely fine powder that, like the anthrax sent to Capitol Hill in September and October 2001, can be suspended in the air like particles of dust. In this form it can easily be inhaled. From the lungs, anthrax enters the bloodstream and is often lethal. The previously cited 1993 study by the Office of Technology Assessment concluded that an airplane spraying 220 pounds of anthrax spores over Washington, D.C., on a calm night would kill between one million and three million people.

The potential for biological warfare using only what nature provides in the way of pathogens is bad enough, but genetic engineering offers some truly horrifying possibilities. Dr. Ken Alibeck, who was first deputy director of the Soviet Union's biological weapons program from 1988 until his defection to the United States in 1992, has noted that Moscow's illegal biowarfare program had genetically modified anthrax to make it resistant to treatment using antibiotics.[17] Recombinant DNA technologies take the threat to another level. Imagine, for example, being able to make the deadly Ebola virus spread itself from person to person as easily as influenza. The creation of such diabolical diseases is no longer simply a sinister fantasy.

Biological weapons pose a particularly significant threat due to certain characteristics, some of which are unique and some of which are shared with other weapons of mass destruction. First, unlike nuclear weapons, for example, biological weapons can be produced without a large supporting industrial infrastructure. A typical college or even high school laboratory could be used to produce biological weapons. This leads to a second characteristic: low production cost. Third, biological weapons are accessible to rogue states and terrorist groups, a characteristic related to ease of manufacture, low production cost, and the relative ease with which clandestine manufacture and shipment can occur. While sophisticated systems like missiles or bombs can be used to deliver biological weapons, they are not required. Thus, ease of delivery is a fourth threat-enhancing characteristic of biological weapons. Fifth, the extraordinary lethality of many types of biological weapons makes them especially worrisome. Sixth, these weapons are very small; an anthrax spore may be just one to five microns in diameter, which is one-fiftieth the width of a human hair.

Ronald Noble, the secretary-general of the international law enforcement agency Interpol, has cited the following incident from 2006 to make the point that materials suitable for use in biological weapons may be obtained all too easily. Journalists with *The Guardian* were able to purchase, by mail, a sample of the smallpox genome. The company that provided the sample (for about $60) delivered the product without checking whether the order met a legitimate scientific need.[18]

Because biological weapons can be produced without a significant industrial infrastructure, their proliferation is likely to be both cheaper and more easily hidden than other kinds of weapons of mass destruction. Dual-use technology makes hiding a biological weapons program easier than hiding a nuclear weapons program or, in some instances, chemical weapons production. For example, fermenters are required to produce biological weapons in large quantities, and one might infer that the presence of a fermenter suggests an effort to produce biological weapons. The problem, however, is that fermenters are commonly used in biotech, pharmaceutical, and even beer-manufacturing processes.

The Arms Control Association, an advocacy group headquartered in Washington, D.C., has identified eight states, including some that have colluded with terrorists in the past, that are alleged either to have biological or chemical weapons programs or stockpiles or to be in violation of some aspect of the Biological Weapons Convention or the Chemical Weapons Convention. North Korea is suspected of having biological weapons capabilities and likely has a large stockpile of chemical weapons. Syria, believed to have an active biological weapons program, has actually used chemical weapons in its civil war. There have been past allegations regarding both types of weapons involving Egypt and Israel. Other states—China, Russia, Taiwan, Iran, and the United States among them—possess dual-use capabilities. On the other hand, a number of states, including Albania, Libya, and South Korea, have completed the destruction of chemical weapons stockpiles as required by the Chemical Weapons Convention.[19]

What possible motivation could there be for the use of chemical or biological weapons? The incentives—and disincentives—are different for countries and for nonstate actors.[20] A country contemplating a CBW attack against another country must expect, first, retaliation in kind if the victim of the initial attack has access to weapons of mass destruction. Second, it must expect the strong condemnation of the international community for violating well-established norms against the use of such weapons, as has happened recently with respect to Syria. For nonstate actors, such as terrorist organizations, rebel armies, or individual crackpots, the calculus is different. Retaliation in kind may not be possible, particularly if the person or organization using the weapon cannot be identified. As we have noted, an intentional release of deadly microbes would be followed by an incubation period of somewhere between a few days and a few weeks before the appearance of disease symptoms. Since even the onset of observable signs of disease might initially be assumed to have resulted from natural causes, individuals or groups employing biological weapons might well have time to go deep underground before their attack becomes obvious. The problem of deterrence (or, if deterrence fails, retaliation) is made even worse in the case of cults or terrorist organizations that have an apocalyptic worldview (as Aum Shinrikyo does) or readily accept the possibility of martyrdom (as in the case of Al Qaeda or the Islamic State). Because deterring the use of WMD by such groups seems unlikely, preventing them from acquiring (or maintaining) a WMD capability is imperative.

ADDRESSING THE THREAT

The 9/11 attacks prompted the U.S. government to reassess its preparedness for terrorist attacks of various types. One of the items that was emphasized on the homeland security agenda was defense against a possible weapons of mass destruction attack on the United States. The elements of a robust civil defense program include the stockpiling or distribution of protective masks or clothing (as has happened in Israel); equipment and training for decontamination; vaccinations for diseases used as biological weapons, such as smallpox; stockpiling of antibiotics for the treatment of certain disease outbreaks (e.g., stockpiling Cipro to treat anthrax); planning and training of emergency personnel for dealing with the use of WMD; and public education programs to increase understanding of the dangers and possible responses to weapons of mass destruction.

Preparation can literally make the difference between life and death. Israeli citizens are taught how to keep one room of their homes airtight in the event of a chemical or biological attack by taping plastic over the windows and doors. Poison gases and most toxic biological agents dissipate within hours; if individuals can avoid exposure during the immediate aftermath of an attack, they run a much smaller risk of death or injury.

The international community has addressed chemical and biological weapons in a variety of forums and will undoubtedly continue to do so in the future. The 1899 Hague Convention with Respect to the Laws and Customs of War on Land prohibited the use in war of projectiles containing poison gas. In response to the horrors of chemical warfare during World War I, the 1925 Geneva Protocol for the Prohibition of the Use of Asphyxiating, Poisonous or Other Gases, and Bacteriological Methods of Warfare was negotiated at the League of Nations. Although its ban on the use of chemical and biological weapons was designed to apply only to states that are parties to the Protocol, the agreement has become customary international law, which means that its provisions now bind all states regardless of whether they have accepted it.[21] The United States and Japan failed to ratify the treaty before World War II broke out, but during the war, President Roosevelt stated, "Use of such [chemical and biological] weapons has been outlawed by the general opinion of civilized mankind. This country has not used them, and I hope we never will be compelled to use them. I state categorically that we shall under no circumstances resort to the use of such weapons unless they are first used by our enemies."[22] Although the United States did not use chemical or biological weapons during World War II, it did not ratify the 1925 Geneva Protocol until 1975.

In 1969, amid negotiations toward a new agreement prohibiting them, the United States and France both renounced biological weapons. A treaty that went beyond the 1925 Geneva Protocol's ban on use to include a ban on the production and stockpiling of biological weapons was adopted in 1972. To date, this treaty—the Biological and Toxin Weapons Convention (BWC)—has been ratified by 173 countries, making it a significant statement by the international community opposing biological weapons. One of the underlying factors helping to bolster the BWC is a taboo against the use of diseases as weapons of war. This taboo has been expressed in many ways and in many different cultures over the centuries, suggesting that it may represent a universal moral norm.[23]

The most detailed multilateral treaty to date is the 1993 Chemical Weapons Convention (CWC), an agreement that prohibits the production and stockpiling of chemical weapons. Some 190 countries have ratified or acceded to the CWC (including Syria in September 2013), which entered into force in 1997. What makes the CWC superior to the BWC in one important respect is its verification system. The CWC created a body called the Organisation for the Prohibition of Chemical Weapons (OPCW), headquartered in The Hague, which includes 150 to 200 inspectors authorized by the treaty to conduct site inspections in countries that have ratified the agreement.

The United States, which developed a large chemical weapons stockpile during the Cold War, stopped manufacturing chemical weapons in

1968. Nonetheless, thirty thousand tons of chemical agents remained in the American stockpile at the end of the Cold War. Beginning in 1996, the U.S. Army began incinerating chemical weapons in a specially designed facility at Tooele, Utah. Two decades later, the process of destroying the chemical weapons stockpile continues at Tooele and other facilities.

While the Chemical Weapons Convention and the Biological and Toxin Weapons Convention may help to reduce the number of countries running chemical and biological weapons programs (and thus the number of weapons of mass destruction that could fall into the hands of terrorist organizations), neither agreement can guarantee our security against the threats posed by nonstate actors. To ensure our security, therefore, we must continue to think creatively about not only limiting the capabilities of those who might wish to do us harm but about changing their intentions as well. In the end, peace and security require more than defensive responses to the threats we perceive.

ADDITIONAL RESOURCES

Books and Articles

Garrett, Laurie. "The Nightmare of Bioterrorism." *Foreign Affairs* 80 (January/February 2001): 76–89.
Koblentz, Gregory D. *Living Weapons: Biological Warfare and International Security*. Ithaca, NY: Cornell University Press, 2009.
Lavoy, Peter, Scott D. Sagan, and James J. Wirtz, eds. *Planning the Unthinkable: How New Powers Will Use Nuclear, Biological, and Chemical Weapons*. Ithaca, NY: Cornell University Press, 2000.
Miller, Judith, Stephen Engelberg, and William Broad. *Germs: Biological Weapons and America's Secret War*. New York: Simon and Schuster, 2001.
Spiers, Edward M. *A History of Chemical and Biological Weapons*. London: Reaktion Books, 2010.
Tucker, Jonathan. *War of Nerves: Chemical Warfare from World War I to Al-Qaeda*. New York: Anchor, 2007.
Tucker, Jonathan B., ed. *Innovation, Dual Use, and Security: Managing the Risks of Emerging Biological and Chemical Technologies*. Cambridge, MA: MIT Press, 2012.
Vogel, Kathleen M. *Phantom Menace or Looming Danger? A New Framework for Assessing Bioweapons*. Baltimore, MD: Johns Hopkins University Press, 2013.

Websites

Arms Control Association: www.armscontrol.org
Biological and Toxin Weapons Convention Website: www.opbw.org

Centers for Disease Control and Prevention: www.cdc.gov
Federation of American Scientists: www.fas.org/programs/index.html
Organisation for the Prohibition of Chemical Weapons: www.opcw.org

Films

American Experience: *The Living Weapon*, NPT, 2007. Directed by John Rubin.
The Bloodless Massacre. Al Jazeera, September 9, 2013.
Council on Foreign Relations, James M. Lindsay, "Lessons Learned: Tokyo Sarin
    Gas Attack." March 20, 2012.
Council on Foreign Relations, Paul B. Stares, "Syria's Chemical Weapons Disarma-
    ment: Three Things to Know." September 18, 2013.

Chapter Five

The Terrorist Threat

Terrorism is a significant threat to peace and security, prosperity and people.

—UN Secretary-General Ban Ki-moon, May 2012

The terrorist attacks on U.S. soil on September 11, 2001, dramatically altered the global security environment. The North Atlantic Treaty Organization, a group that had been created to counter the Soviet military threat during the Cold War, invoked Article V, the collective security provision in the founding treaty, for the first time ever. Within eighteen months of the attacks, the United States and many of its NATO allies were at war in Afghanistan and Iraq; regime change was the objective in both wars. On the night of the 9/11 attacks, President George W. Bush noted in his diary, "The Pearl Harbor of the 21st century took place today."[1]

Terrorism was hardly a new phenomenon on 9/11. But what was new, and shocking, was the sophistication of the attacks and the enormity of the destruction they caused. The attacks killed more Americans than were killed at Pearl Harbor on December 7, 1941, but unlike that attack, most of those killed on September 11 were civilians. As many commentators noted at the time, it was the greatest loss of American life resulting from hostilities in a single day since the Civil War. British prime minister Tony Blair pointed out that more British citizens died in the attack on the World Trade Center than in any other terrorist act in British history, in spite of the fact that the Irish Republican Army carried out scores of attacks against British targets over the course of the twentieth century. What these observations highlight is that 9/11 demonstrated a new form of terrorism—one in which the objective was not merely to spread fear but also to kill as many people—particularly Americans—as possible. In the years since 9/11, an additional variant of terrorism has developed that, along with earlier "waves" of terrorism, will be described in this chapter.

DEFINING—AND FRAMING—TERRORISM

Although the term *terrorism* dates back only to the French Revolution, acts that we might today describe as terrorism have occurred throughout human history. What has changed—constantly—are the actors employing terrorism and the tactics they have used. Veteran terrorism scholar David Rapoport has described four distinct waves of terrorism in modern history: anarchist, nationalist, 1960s leftist, and the recent wave of religiously oriented terrorism.[2] Around the turn of the twentieth century, for example, there was a wave of assassinations by anarchists that were generally considered acts of terrorism: the president of France was assassinated in 1894; an Austrian empress and a Spanish prime minister fell in 1897; Italy's king, Umberto I, was killed in 1900; and an American president, William McKinley, was assassinated in 1901. The second wave was marked by the nationalist, anticolonial struggle in the developing world from the 1920s through the 1960s. The rise of leftist protests in the 1960s signaled a third wave, according to Rapoport. In the last several decades, a fourth wave of religiously inspired terrorists have exploited certain features of globalization, including enhanced access to information, finance, technology, and transportation, to engage in acts of unprecedented destructiveness. Other scholars have suggested the emergence of a fifth wave of terrorists whose "guiding dream is to create a new world—a utopian society to be realized *in this lifetime.*"[3] In this chapter, we will refer to the fourth and fifth waves as constituting the "new terrorism."

According to Walter Laqueur, terrorism is "the illegitimate use of force to achieve a political objective when innocent people are targeted."[4] Jessica Stern defines terrorism as "an act or threat of violence against noncombatants with the objective of exacting revenge, intimidating or otherwise influencing an audience."[5] These definitions lack a significant element contained in the statutory definition used in the United States where terrorism is defined as "premeditated, politically motivated violence perpetrated against noncombatant targets by sub-national groups or clandestine agents, usually intended to influence an audience."[6] Significantly, in both international and domestic law, only acts committed by nonstate actors ("subnational groups") or the "clandestine agents" of governments are considered acts of terrorism. This reflects the interest of states in maintaining their monopoly on the legitimate use of force and in excluding their own military activities from the definition of terrorism. However, both in law and in the definitions of most students of terrorism, large-scale attacks carried out by guerrilla groups or other military forces with belligerent status are not generally considered acts of terrorism.

The label *terrorist* is often applied as indiscriminately as terrorist attacks themselves. States typically seek to delegitimize the methods of those whose objectives they oppose while granting more latitude to those whom they wish to succeed. Likewise, most terrorists would prefer to wear the mantle of guerrillas or "freedom fighters." In 1982, the United States placed Cuba on its list of state sponsors of terrorism because of Cuba's support for leftist revolutionaries in Latin America and Africa. At the same time, the United States was assisting groups trying to overthrow the government of Nicaragua. And although the legal definition of terrorism in the United States refers to "politically motivated violence perpetrated against *noncombatant* targets," the media and government officials have routinely referred to the use of improvised explosive devices (IEDs) against military targets in Iraq and Afghanistan as acts of terrorism.

As many critics of the idea of a "war on terrorism" have pointed out, terrorism is a tactic and not an ideology. Consequently, it has been employed by a wide array of groups with very different objectives. Terrorism is, generally, a strategy of the weak against the strong or, in other words, a form of asymmetric warfare. Its users, targets, and methods change over time as different political issues emerge and are resolved or as new tactics and technologies are developed and countered.

According to data compiled by the U.S. National Consortium for the Study of Terrorism and Responses to Terrorism, there were 9,707 terrorist attacks worldwide in 2013.[7] In these attacks, sixty countries from around the world recorded 17,800 deaths and 32,500 injuries. In addition, 2,990 people were taken hostage. Most of these deaths—14,695—occurred in five countries (Iraq, Syria, Afghanistan, Pakistan, and Nigeria), and four groups were primarily responsible (Al Qaeda, the Taliban, Boko Haram, and the Islamic State).

Until 9/11, the attacks that caused the greatest loss of life generally involved the bombing of an airliner as in the January 1985 bombing of an Air India flight over the Irish Sea, which killed all 329 people onboard. The 9/11 attacks killed more than nine times that number, but to this point it remains an aberration. It is the primary goal of counterterrorism policies, which we examine at the end of this chapter, to prevent acts causing mass casualties such as the 9/11 attacks.

VARIETIES OF TERRORISM

Terrorism in the mid-twentieth century was often characterized as a form of political theater. This description suggested that most terrorist acts were designed primarily to attract an audience through media coverage of a compelling drama. For example, during the 1972 Munich Olympics, an event that was already the focus of international attention, a Palestinian group called Black September stormed the athletes' living quarters and took a group of Israeli athletes and coaches hostage. The drama was played out on live television over the course of almost twenty-four hours before German authorities attempted a rescue operation. In the end, seventeen people, including eleven of the Israeli hostages, were killed.

Although not all elements of the "new terrorism" appeared at the same time, analysts have noted that fourth-wave groups with new motivations and new tactics began appearing during the 1980s. Among the new terrorist organizations were a number of religiously motivated groups, some with an apocalyptic worldview, whose appearance seemed to usher in an "age of sacred terror."[8] Among the new tactics were suicide attacks, often designed to go beyond theatricality to the infliction of mass casualties. There were new targets as well. The United States, its citizens, and its embassies began to be targeted more frequently. To describe these changes, we examine the new terrorism under three headings: organizations, tactics, and targets.

Organizations

For much of the modern history of terrorism, states have been closely linked to terrorist organizations and their activities. Secretly supporting shadowy groups with compatible agendas—or actually creating such groups—has been regarded as a cost-effective way to harass an enemy that is too powerful to engage directly. During the 1980s, the government of Libya sponsored a series of terrorist attacks against Americans that culminated in 1988 in the bombing of a Pan Am airliner over Lockerbie, Scotland. After investigators traced the attack to two Libyan intelligence officers, the United States and the international community, acting through the UN Security Council, imposed sanctions on Libya. The Libyan government, having suffered under the sanctions for years, eventually turned over the suspects for trial and agreed to pay the victims' families $2.7 billion in compensation. There are many other examples, both past and present, of connections between states and terrorist organizations. For example, Hezbollah, a Lebanese organization regarded by a number of governments as a terrorist group, was supported financially by Iran and Syria for years. Lashkar-e-Taiba, the Pakistani organization behind the November 2008 terrorist attack in Mumbai, India, was formed with the active assistance of Pakistan's government during a time when Indo-Pakistani tensions over Kashmir were at a peak.

Organizations that are characteristic of fourth-wave terrorism generally function without state sponsorship. They can operate this way in part because they commonly have independent sources of revenue. While based in Sudan during the early 1990s, Al Qaeda was self-sufficient thanks to businesses owned and operated by Osama bin Laden, who was in fact a multimillionaire. When U.S. pressure on the Sudanese government resulted in Al Qaeda's departure for Afghanistan, the organization began relying more heavily on donations funneled through Muslim charities. There has been speculation as well that Al Qaeda may have profited from Afghanistan's lucrative opium trade.[9] Wherever the money came from, it was more than enough to pay for training camps, weapons, worldwide travel, and much more, including flight training for at least four people involved in the 9/11 plot. And it came with no restrictions imposed by state sponsors.

Significantly, one of the characteristics that distinguishes fourth-wave from fifth-wave terrorists is that the latter want to create a state and not simply rely on states. For example, the leaders of the Islamic State (also known as ISIS, ISIL, and Daesh) have announced the establishment of a worldwide caliphate. The caliphate has thus far amassed impressive wealth, but most has been acquired outside the normal operations of modern states. In 2014, the Islamic State's revenues included an estimated $600 million from extortion and taxes, $500 million stolen from state-owned banks in Iraq, $100 million from the sale of oil, and $20 million derived from kidnapping ransoms.[10] Thus, as of June 2014, the Islamic State's total assets equaled approximately $875 million. The group is able to minimize its expenses by capturing military equipment, appropriating land, and paying low salaries.

Terrorist groups operating with no attachments to a state pose a significant problem for policies based on deterrence. As we noted in chapter 3, deterrence is a policy designed to prevent the use of force by threatening the use of force as punishment.[11] The nuclear deterrent strategy employed by the Soviet Union and the United States has been credited with preserving the "long peace" of the Cold War.[12] It is important to note that deterrence has also been effective against rogue states, such as Iraq under Saddam Hussein or North Korea under Kim Jong-un. At the time of the Persian Gulf War (1990–1991), the United States was concerned that Iraq might use weapons of mass destruction against the American-led coalition forces. In his memoirs, James Baker, who served as secretary of state at the time, recalled:

> In hopes of persuading them [the Iraqis] to consider more soberly the folly of war, I purposefully left the impression that the use of chemical or biological agents by Iraq could invite tactical nuclear retaliation. (We do not really know whether this was the reason there appears to have been no confirmed use by

Iraq of chemical weapons during the war. My own view is that the calculated ambiguity regarding how we might respond has to be part of the reason.)[13]

While deterrence can inject a measure of caution into the policies of states that sponsor terrorism (with, it is hoped, corresponding effects on the terrorists being sponsored), it is difficult to formulate and implement an effective deterrence policy against most terrorist organizations. Terrorists with no state (and no state sponsor) to lose are unlikely to be deterred by the threat of retaliation. Whether the attempt to establish a new caliphate makes the Islamic State and allied organizations such as Boko Haram more responsive to deterrence strategies remains to be seen.

Soon after the 9/11 attacks, the George W. Bush administration noted the significance of nonstate actors to the concept of deterrence. In the 2002 edition of the *National Security Strategy of the United States*, the administration argued, "The nature of the Cold War threat required the United States—with our allies and friends—to emphasize deterrence of the enemy's use of force, producing a grim strategy of mutual assured destruction. With the collapse of the Soviet Union and the end of the Cold War, our security environment has undergone profound transformation." The report went on to say, "Traditional concepts of deterrence will not work against a terrorist enemy whose avowed tactics are wanton destruction and the targeting of innocents. The overlap between states that sponsor terror and those that pursue WMD compels us to action."[14]

The stability of deterrence rested, essentially, on a foundation of fear. Like deterrence, terrorism is also based on fear. In the case of terrorism, however, the objective is what Thomas C. Schelling labeled *compellence*—that is, using fear to *compel* the other side to take action.[15] Osama bin Laden and his followers sought in the 9/11 attacks to spread fear among the American public in an effort to compel the United States to remove its military bases from the Middle East and withdraw its support for the state of Israel. If fear played a central role in both the Cold War–era and the new post–9/11 international systems, it had very different results. In the Cold War deterrent system, fear promoted stability; it was essential for deterrence to operate successfully. During the Cold War, security was increased by a certain measure of insecurity. That is no longer the case.

Another characteristic of groups representing the new terrorism that affects both efforts to deter them and their choice of tactics is their religious motivation, coupled, in some cases, with an apocalyptic worldview. While the Islamic State, with its focus on purging apostate Muslim rulers and establishing a global caliphate, once again offers a perfect example, it would be a mistake to think that only Islam has produced terrorism motivated by some form of religious fundamentalism. Within the United States, a variety of extremist groups based on Christian identity (often infused with anti-Semitic and white supremacist views) have amassed weapons and preached war against the government for years. On April 19, 1995, the Murrah Federal Building in Oklahoma City was destroyed by Timothy McVeigh, a U.S. Army veteran, who employed a truck bomb in an attack inspired by the writings of Christian extremists.[16] In 1984, a plot by an extremist Jewish organization to destroy one of Islam's holiest sites, the Dome of the Rock in Jerusalem, was foiled by Israeli security.[17] Finally, Aum Shinrikyo, the cult responsible for the sarin gas attack on the Tokyo subway system in 1995 (described in chapter 4), provides another example of religiously motivated terrorism beyond the Muslim world.

Al Qaeda has described its campaign of terrorism as *jihad*, or holy war. In public statements, including the 1996 Declaration of War Against America, Osama bin Laden pronounced it a religious duty for Muslims everywhere to kill Americans. Bin Laden told one interviewer, "You say I am fighting against the American civilians. My enemy is every American man who is fighting against me even by paying taxes."[18] Al Qaeda recruits have been taught that they need not worry about killing noncombatants or trying to distinguish between those who are guilty and those who are innocent of crimes against Islam because God will reward the innocent in heaven and punish the guilty in hell.

Those who are attracted to fourth- and fifth-wave terrorist groups often differ from terrorists associated with more traditional terrorist organizations. Historically, most Islamic terrorists were young, single, and uneducated. The nineteen Al Qaeda perpetrators of the 9/11 attacks were, for the most part, older and more mature; several were married and had children; some were educated; and most had lived in the United States for several years prior to 9/11. Mohamed Atta, the suspected leader, was thirty-three years old and had studied urban planning in Germany for seven years. Khalid Sheikh Mohammed, who has been called "the principal architect of the 9/11 attacks," earned a degree in mechanical engineering from North Carolina Agricultural and Technical State University. Ramzi Yousef, the main plotter of the 1993 World Trade Center bombing, studied electrical engineering in Wales before moving to the United States. While these are isolated—and high-profile— examples, it has become increasingly likely that those who plot and carry out terrorist attacks will have been educated and will have traveled beyond their childhood homes.

Tactics

With money, educated supporters, extremist religious beliefs, and few of the restraints associated with state sponsorship, modern terrorist groups have abandoned the limits that terrorists once observed. Third-wave terrorists seeking to negotiate a political settlement with a state, like the Irish Republican Army or the Basque separatist organization Euskadi Ta Askatasuna (ETA), have generally understood that their use of violence must be carefully calibrated. An act of terrorism—or a campaign made up of many such acts—must be violent enough to command attention but not so violent that it becomes impossible for a government to even consider making concessions. Groups representing the fourth and fifth waves of terrorism seem not to be concerned about being too extreme, as illustrated by the beheadings of western hostages by the Islamic State and the kidnapping and rapes of school girls by Boko Haram. The willingness to commit atrocities, of course, makes fourth- and fifth-wave terrorists far more dangerous than previous ones.

Globalization—and in particular the spread of information and technology—makes it possible for terrorists unconstrained by a state sponsor or a traditional sense of limits to acquire or devise the means to conduct increasingly violent attacks. Trial testimony by former terrorists has indicated that Al Qaeda invested considerable time and money in reconnaissance missions all over the world in a search for gaps in security that it might be able to exploit. Terrorists have used the Internet both to gather information about potential targets and to share information about weapons and tactics. The overall effect of globalization on terrorism has been to increase the threat it poses while making terrorist organizations less hierarchical and more networked. As cyberexpert John Arquilla has noted, "In the long, often covert, 'cool war' against al-Qaeda and its affiliates . . . the driving force has been—and continues to be—an 'organizational race' to build networks."[19]

The central concern about groups that are characteristic of the new terrorism is their openly expressed desire, and their demonstrated ability, to conduct ever more destructive attacks. In August 1998, in the wake of the East African embassy bombings, the Clinton administration launched a cruise missile attack against sites affiliated with Al Qaeda. One of the sites was a chemical plant in Sudan owned by bin Laden. Soil samples from the site had indicated that it was likely being used to manufacture VX, a deadly chemical weapon. Documents captured from Al Qaeda camps in Afghanistan in 2001 described plans for the production of both biological and chemical weapons. And in 2004, British authorities found ricin, another chemical weapon, in a London apartment believed to have been rented by members of Al Qaeda. Combined with the "loose nukes" problem described in chapter 6, these and other evidences of terrorists' interest in acquiring and using weapons of mass destruction is deeply troubling.

Even in the absence of nuclear, chemical, and biological weapons terrorists have found ways to turn modern technologies to destructive ends. So-called improvised explosive devices (IEDs)—bombs detonated using a dazzling array of readily available technologies including cell phones, garage-door openers, and infrared devices—were used extensively in Iraq and Afghanistan against both military and civilian targets. Although the evidence thus far is mixed, many believe that it is only a matter of time until terrorists begin to mount attacks via drones and in cyberspace.

One of the characteristics of Al Qaeda (and Al Qaeda–inspired) operations is the use of closely coordinated attacks on multiple targets. While the bombings of the American embassies in Kenya and Tanzania (1998) and the 9/11 attacks represent the epitome of this ability, the same pattern can be observed in subsequent attacks in Madrid, London, and Mumbai. On March 11, 2004, ten bombs exploded on commuter trains in Madrid, all within minutes of 8:00 AM. Almost two hundred people died in the attacks; over 1,800 were injured. On July 7, 2005, London's transportation system was the target of a coordinated attack carried out by four British nationals with no known terrorist background. Four bombs were detonated during the morning rush hour, three in the Underground and one on a double-decker bus, killing 52 and injuring 950. In November 2008, the Pakistan-based terrorist organization Lashkar-e-Taiba launched a carefully planned attack on multiple locations in Mumbai, India. The attack spanned three days, as ten gunmen indiscriminately killed Indians and foreigners alike in highly populated areas, including a hospital, a Jewish center, a café, and two hotels. ISIS likewise staged an attack on multiple targets in Paris in November 2015, killing more than 130 innocent civilians.

Targets

Until the 1993 bombing of the World Trade Center, terrorism was a second- or even third-tier issue within the national security policy of the United States. What would, after 9/11, be called "the homeland" had rarely been attacked. In most years, more Americans died from lightning strikes or by drowning in their bathtubs than were killed in terrorist attacks.[20] Airline hijackings, which often involved American airlines, had been largely eliminated by the 1980s.

The 1993 attempt to bring down the World Trade Center, a disrupted plot to destroy American airliners over the Pacific Ocean, the bombing of two American embassies in East Africa, a disrupted plot to detonate bombs at Los Angeles International Airport on New Year's Eve in 1999, and the bombing on October 12, 2000, of the USS *Cole*, a destroyer berthed in a Yemeni port, all clearly indicated that the United States had become a prime target of Al Qaeda.

SUICIDE TERRORISM

It is important to note the increased incidence of suicide terrorism by groups associated with the new terrorism. Throughout history, terrorists have been known for their willingness to die for a cause. The Assassins, members of the Shia sect who regarded the murder of unrighteous leaders as a religious duty, carried out their attacks in the expectation that they would be captured and executed for their deeds. Modern suicide terrorism, however, goes a step beyond the probability of dying to the certainty that a successful attack will result in the death of the assailant.

According to researchers at the Terrorism and Low Intensity Conflict Program at the Institute for National Security Studies, from 1983 to 2013 there were 3,500 suicide attacks; in 2013 there were 291 suicide bombings in eighteen countries that killed 3,100 people.[21] Contrary to popular opinion, suicide terrorism is not motivated solely—or even primarily—by religious fundamentalism. For the 1980 to 2003 period, less than half the suicide terrorists whose affiliations are known were Islamic fundamentalists. Forty-five percent of the 524 suicide terrorists in the period, including 157 members of the antireligious Liberation Tigers of Tamil Eelam (LTTE) in Sri Lanka, were from secular groups. Even a large majority of Lebanese Hezbollah suicide attackers were communist or socialist (71 percent) or Christian (8 percent).[22]

Suicide terrorism is a tactic adopted by groups seeking to end an occupation of a territory the group considers to be its homeland. Suicide attacks occur as part of a campaign, meaning there are multiple attacks, often carried out over a period of years, directed against the same targets and with the same general aim. The targets are almost invariably democracies. Many examples could be cited. Hezbollah conducted a series of suicide attacks in 1983, including a bombing in which 241 U.S. Marines were killed, intended to drive the United States and France out of Lebanon. The Tamil Tigers, who often employed female suicide bombers, conducted multiple campaigns in an effort to force the Sri Lankan government to cede Tamil territories. Since 1996, Al Qaeda has been engaged in a suicide terrorism campaign intended to compel the United States to withdraw its military forces from Saudi Arabia where American bases were established prior to the 1991 Persian Gulf War. Hamas has undertaken several campaigns with the objective of forcing Israel to withdraw from the Occupied Territories.

The increase in the number of suicide attacks since 2003 was very closely tied to the American military occupation of Iraq and Afghanistan, along with the close cooperation between Pakistan and the United States in what was once called the "Global War on Terror" (GWOT). Pape and Feldman, in fact, note that 92 percent of all suicide attacks in the period from 2004 to 2009 can be explained by the pattern of deployment of U.S. military forces. Even what appears at first glance to be an exception to the rule, a brief suicide terrorism campaign in Uzbekistan in 2004, can be explained by the presence of an American air base in the country between 2001 and 2005. No suicide attacks have occurred in Uzbekistan since the base was closed in 2005.[23]

In the aftermath of the 9/11 attacks, the war in Afghanistan may have been a war of necessity. The Taliban regime had, after all, harbored those responsible for 9/11 and had refused to cooperate with the United States in bringing them to justice. The war in Iraq, however, was a war of choice.[24] Where suicide terrorism is concerned, the important point is that both wars likely increased the motivation of Al Qaeda, the Islamic State, and other terrorist groups to carry out suicide campaigns against the United States and its allies in the wars. Furthermore, there is considerable evidence that the long-term occupations of Afghanistan and Iraq, along with the use of drones against suspected terrorists in Pakistan, helped terrorist groups recruit more suicide bombers.

FIFTH-WAVE TERRORISTS

Although his analysis stretches the definition of terrorism used by most political analysts, religion scholar Jeffrey Kaplan has argued that the millenarian ideologies of groups such as the Lord's Resistance Army in Uganda and the *Janjaweed* in Sudan point to the emergence of a new wave of terrorism. Such a fifth wave, in fact, might include groups such as the Islamic State and Boko Haram that seek to move beyond Al Qaeda, from whom they originally drew their inspiration but with whom they are now in conflict. According Kaplan, fifth-wave terrorist groups are most noteworthy for a utopian ideology— sometimes religiously inspired—that seeks to establish an all-new society based on a model derived from a supposed "Golden Age" in the group's (partly imagined) past. It is an ideology that admits no compromise in the quest to promote the perfect man and society. Consequently, in its clash with the society or societies that must be replaced, fifth-wave groups tend to be extremely violent and even genocidal in keeping with their apocalyptic worldview. Such groups control their members in extreme ways, tending even to use rape as a method of subjugating women. Children are indoctrinated and often used as child soldiers. In short, fifth-wave groups present a toxic mix of beliefs and behaviors that are completely at odds with the values of the more liberal societies they seek to displace.[25]

Sadly, this grim description of fifth-wave organizations describes the Islamic State and Boko Haram all too accurately. In April 2014, Boko Haram kidnapped several hundred young girls from Chibok, Nigeria, and reports from some of those who escaped indicated that the girls had been raped and impregnated. The Islamic State's leaders have also approved the taking of child brides and rape of women in areas that have been captured. According to Kaplan, "Rape is the signature tactic of the fifth wave."[26]

COUNTERING TERRORISM

Addressing the challenge of terrorism, especially in its modern form where the aim is often the infliction of mass casualties, is a complex task for governments. It is a task complicated by the fact that terrorists constantly adapt their tactics in an effort to find and exploit the weaknesses of their targets. They also learn from each other, sometimes by way of training manuals, videos, and other instructional materials posted on the Internet. Under the circumstances, governments are also compelled to adapt their tactics and to learn from other governments. Where counterterrorism efforts are concerned, there are enormous benefits to be gained from cooperation among governments, as well as among agencies within governments.

Combating terrorism requires a range of activities that includes finding and either arresting or killing terrorists; disrupting terrorist operations before they can be carried out; and coping with the effects of those attacks that cannot be disrupted. And because terrorism occurs in a particular political and social context, combating it also requires addressing the underlying conditions that motivate it. Law enforcement agencies, intelligence organizations, and military forces have all been called upon to respond to the threat of terrorism. But so, too, have finance ministries, development agencies, and public health authorities.

Law Enforcement

Terrorism is a crime under both international and domestic law. Even in the absence of treaties and statutes that define and criminalize terrorism, most activities of terrorists would still be punishable under laws pertaining to murder and destruction of property. Furthermore, states have an interest in treating terrorists as criminals. To do otherwise is to risk conferring legitimacy on them and their causes. Terrorists seek acknowledgment of a grievance or recognition for a political cause. Their aim is to force states to negotiate, occasionally openly and directly, but more often tacitly and indirectly, using what Thomas Schelling called "the diplomacy of violence."[27] Not wanting to be blackmailed by groups that resort to indiscriminate violence, governments prosecute and punish individual terrorists whenever possible. In the course of prosecutorial investigations, they may gather useful information about terrorist organizations and their methods. They may also deny terrorists an important recruiting tool: the image of a criminal on trial or serving a long prison term is far less appealing than the image of a terrorist dying a martyr's death in battle.

On February 26, 1993, Al Qaeda made its first attempt to destroy the World Trade Center in New York. A large bomb in a rented truck exploded in the garage below the towers. Aided by one of the conspirators who tried to collect the deposit on the truck, investigators uncovered the terrorist cell responsible for the plot. Ramzi Yousef, who planned the attack, slipped out of the United States but was captured in Pakistan in 1995. In the course of the investigation, a laptop computer was found in the apartment where Yousef had lived in the Philippines. The computer's hard drive contained much of the evidence that was used to convict Yousef in 1997 of conspiracy in the 1993 bombing case.[28]

The capture of another Al Qaeda operative, Richard Reid, had much less to do with good police work than with good luck. Reid, the so-called shoe bomber, attempted to bring down an American Airlines flight from Paris to Miami on December 22, 2001. A British citizen with a string of convictions for petty crimes, Reid converted to Islam and was radicalized by the calls to *jihad* that he heard at the mosque in Brixton. In 1998, Reid traveled to Afghanistan to train at an Al Qaeda camp. He learned how to work with plastic explosives and was apparently given wide latitude to plan a suicide attack. After paying cash for a one-way ticket from Paris to Miami, Reid aroused the suspicion of French authorities and was denied the right to board his flight on December 21. After a brief investigation turned up nothing, Reid was allowed to fly the following day.

The explosive packed in the sole of one of Reid's athletic shoes likely would have blown a hole in the side of the plane as it crossed the Atlantic Ocean. Reid, however, was unable to light the fuse. An alert flight attendant confronted Reid, thinking he was trying to light a cigarette. When Reid attacked the attendant, other passengers subdued him. The plane was diverted to Boston, where Reid was arrested.[29]

Because Reid was arrested on American soil rather than on a battlefield in Afghanistan or Iraq, and because he was a British citizen, he was put on trial in a federal court rather than being sent to the military detention center at Guantánamo Bay on the island of Cuba. Like the trials of Ramzi Yousef and others, Reid's trial provided an open window onto the structure and operations of Al Qaeda. Valuable information about recruitment, training, operational planning, and the people involved at each stage came out in the trial and the pretrial investigation. While much of the information Reid revealed might have been gathered by other, more secretive methods, Reid's trial in an open court affirmed the values being defended in the conflict with Al Qaeda rather than compromising them.

War

A law-enforcement approach to terrorism serves the interest of democracies confronted by terrorist violence in affirming their values and denying terrorists recognition as lawful combatants. Terrorism is a crime, and terrorists deserve to be treated like criminals. However, an act of terrorism on the scale of the 9/11 attacks seems to demand a more forceful response. George W. Bush responded by declaring a "global war on terrorism."

Bush entered office emphasizing the need for the United States to act unilaterally in international affairs. Within six months of taking office, Bush had signaled his opposition to the Kyoto Protocol, the Anti-Ballistic Missile (ABM) Treaty, the Comprehensive Test Ban Treaty, and the International Criminal Court. He also refused to participate in a conference to provide verification measures for the 1972 Biological Weapons Convention and undermined a UN conference designed to control the spread of small arms and light weapons.[30]

Following the 9/11 attacks, however, the administration found that it was impossible to fight terrorism effectively without the cooperation of other states. The logic of counterterrorism was fundamentally multilateral. The administration actively cooperated with long-time allies such as Britain, France, and Germany, former competitors such as Russia, and even several hostile states, including Syria.

The American military response to the 9/11 attacks began in October, when a little more than four hundred Special Forces soldiers and CIA paramilitary forces working in tandem with American airpower and Northern Alliance forces overthrew the Taliban government and attacked Al Qaeda training camps in Afghanistan. The attack resulted in the destruction of the Al Qaeda terrorist training camps and the overthrow of the Taliban government, impressive accomplishments, to be sure; however, Osama bin Laden and Mullah Mohammed Omar, the leader of the Taliban, both avoided capture or death.

Following the invasion of Afghanistan, the Bush administration sought to develop a strategy for dealing with terrorism. In June 2002, President Bush stated in his commencement address at the U.S. Military Academy, "The gravest threat to freedom lies at the perilous crossroads of radicalism and technology." He argued that the policies of containment and deterrence were not applicable against nonstate actors, such as terrorist groups.[31] Several months later, the White House released *The National Security Strategy of the United States*, an annual report that typically received little public attention.[32] The eminent Yale historian John Lewis Gaddis contended that this one, however, was the most significant reconceptualization of American foreign policy since George Kennan laid out the doctrine of containment.[33] In the place of that foundation of U.S. post–World War II foreign policy, President Bush proposed that the United States be proactive, postulating that the traditional concept of state sovereignty need not be honored, given the threat posed by terrorists to the United States.

Preemption of threats, then, was proposed as a necessary element of American strategy. As a whole, the president's new approach came to be known as the Bush Doctrine. According to political scientist Robert Jervis, it had four elements:

> A strong belief in the importance of a state's domestic regime in determining its foreign policy and the related judgment that this is an opportune time to transform international politics; the perception of great threats that can be defeated only by new and vigorous policies, most notably preventive war; a willingness to act unilaterally when necessary; and, as both a cause and a summary of these beliefs, an overriding sense that peace and stability require the United States to assert its primacy in world politics.[34]

Although members of the Bush administration tried to present the central pillar of the Bush doctrine as "preemptive war," most international relations scholars believed that the policy could more accurately be described as one of "preventive" war, especially in its application to Iraq. The difference is significant. A preemptive war entails military action against an imminent threat, whereas a preventive war, according to political theorist Michael Walzer, "is designed to respond to a more distant threat."[35]

The Bush administration justified the invasion of Iraq in 2003 by arguing (1) that it possessed weapons of mass destruction, (2) that the Iraqi regime was directly linked to Al Qaeda and the 9/11 attacks, and (3) that the overthrow of Saddam Hussein would usher in a new democratic movement in Iraq and the rest of the Middle East. No weapons of mass destruction were found in Iraq, evidence linking Iraq and Al Qaeda has been discredited, and the long-term prospects for democracy in Iraq remain uncertain. Although the Bush administration continued long after the invasion of Iraq to portray it as part of the war on terrorism, considerable evidence suggests that one of its outcomes was to boost the recruiting efforts of Al Qaeda and other terrorist organizations.

Cooperative Security

Aside from the law enforcement approach, what alternative is there to combating terrorism through preventive war? Since the disintegration of the Soviet Union and the end of the Cold War, a number of security analysts, including the former and current secretaries of defense, William Perry and Ashton Carter, have focused on the need for and advantages of "cooperative security."[36]

A number of the central elements of cooperative security are relevant to the war on terrorism. First, proponents of cooperative security argue that strict controls and security measures for nuclear weapons, particularly those in the former Soviet Union, are urgently needed. We address the measures that have been taken to address the "loose nukes" problem in chapter 6. Second, the cooperative security approach argues for an internationally supported concept of effective and legitimate intervention—one that is multilateral in its orientation.

The unilateral approach favored by George W. Bush during his first eight months in office gave way to multilateralism when the World Trade Center fell, but the international cooperation that was forged in the days following 9/11 was fractured by the invasion of Iraq. Many of America's allies, in fact, questioned the legality of the invasion. Operating within the boundaries of international law (and the just war theory) is important in a struggle against terrorism. As just war theorist Michael Walzer has noted, "In a war for 'hearts and minds,' rather than for land and resources, justice turns out to be a key to victory. . . . There are now reasons of state for fighting justly. One might almost say that justice has become a military necessity."[37]

Cooperative security also calls for new initiatives promoting nonproliferation and security cooperation. Gone are the days when Ronald Reagan, as president of the United States, could say that the proliferation of nuclear weapons is "other states' business." In a world in which terrorists are actively seeking weapons of mass destruction, the United States, as the "world's last remaining superpower" and the biggest target of international terrorism, has a vital interest in nonproliferation.

Cooperative security was developed as a new way of thinking about threats in the post–Cold War era. It argues, fundamentally, for a multilateral approach to issues like those associated with the new terrorism. There are, however, some areas in which state sovereignty requires a certain degree of unilateralism in security policy. Homeland security is one such area.

HOMELAND SECURITY

Within days of the 9/11 attacks, President Bush announced the formation of an Office of Homeland Security within the Executive Office of the President. In

2002, Congress created the Department of Homeland Security, a cabinet-level agency intended to bring under one roof a wide array of existing programs related to security concerns within the borders of the United States. The Immigration and Naturalization Service was moved from the Department of Justice and combined with the U.S. Customs Service, formerly in the Treasury Department, to create Immigration and Customs Enforcement (ICE). The Transportation Security Administration was brought into Homeland Security from the Department of Transportation. Other agencies and programs—including the Federal Emergency Management Agency (FEMA), the Nuclear Incident Response Team, the Federal Computer Incident Response Center, and the Federal Protective Service—were included, all with the aim of improving the federal government's ability to coordinate planning for and responses to events like the 9/11 attacks.[38]

The creation of the Department of Homeland Security was a response to the obvious need for better coordination among agencies with responsibilities related to counterterrorism policy and other matters related to security within the borders of the United States. But it was also a response to the recognition that the domestic and international realms are increasingly difficult to separate. The ease of trade and travel associated with globalization have increased the possibilities that terrorists posing as tourists may be able to slip into targeted states or that a shipment of computers manufactured abroad may contain a radiological bomb. This means that questions concerning trade-offs between freedom and security will be a constant feature of a globalized world. It also means that we will constantly have to adjust our understandings of where the lines separating police, military, and intelligence functions should be drawn.

Since its establishment, the Department of Homeland Security has come under intense scrutiny for many different shortcomings. One of the most serious of these shortcomings may be its way of responding reactively rather than proactively to threats. Roger Cressey, who served on the National Security Council in the Clinton administration, puts it this way: "I think what Homeland Security has done well up to this point is to prepare defenses to respond to the last attack."[39] Responses to the 9/11 attacks and subsequent efforts to bomb airliners illustrate Cressey's point well. After 9/11, the Transportation Security Administration (TSA) was dramatically enlarged and airline passenger screening was enhanced. Regulations requiring the cockpit door of all airliners to be reinforced and locked during flight were implemented to try to prevent would-be hijackers from gaining access to the controls. After Richard Reid attempted to blow up an airplane by igniting explosives packed in his shoe, the TSA began requiring that passengers include their shoes among the personal items to be X-rayed at airport security checkpoints. The attempted

Christmas Day 2009 bombing of an airliner, which involved explosives packed in Omar Farouk Abdulmutallab's underwear, prompted the TSA to implement full-body scans of passengers. During the Cold War, the American and Soviet actions often could be characterized as an action-reaction cycle. Similarly, during the period following 9/11, terrorists' and counterterrorists' actions could also be characterized as an action-reaction cycle.

It is worth emphasizing, as we have noted before, that terrorism is a strategy of the weak. As such, it works by finding and exploiting the vulnerabilities of the target state. It is a difficult thing to find and remedy vulnerabilities before they can be exploited, but this is an important component of a good counterterrorism strategy. Ultimately, however, even greater efforts must be devoted to dealing with the root causes of terrorism.

The good news is that history is filled with terrorist organizations and particular modes of terrorism that were eliminated or simply disappeared. Assassinations, which were perpetrated by first-wave terrorists around the turn of the twentieth century, and airline hijackings, which were, on average, a weekly occurrence during the late 1960s and early 1970s, are uncommon today. Many terrorist groups have disappeared or ceased to constitute a threat, sometimes due to the success of counterterrorism policies, as with the defeat of the Liberation Tigers of Tamil Eelam in Sri Lanka and the elimination of the leadership of the Shining Path in Peru, or sometimes due to policy changes within the organization, as with the Provisional IRA in Northern Ireland. But just as some terrorist groups disappear, others, such as the Islamic State and Boko Haram, appear on the scene to signal a new wave.

ADDITIONAL RESOURCES

Books

Allison, Graham. *Nuclear Terrorism: The Ultimate Preventable Catastrophe*. New York: Times Books, 2004.

Benjamin, Daniel, and Steven Simon. *The Age of Sacred Terror*. New York: Random House, 2002.

Hoffman, Bruce. *Inside Terrorism*. Rev. and exp. ed. New York: Columbia University Press, 2006.

Kaplan, Jeffrey. *Terrorist Groups and the New Tribalism: Terrorism's Fifth Wave*. London: Routledge, 2010.

Levi, Michael. *On Nuclear Terrorism*. Cambridge, MA: Harvard University Press, 2007.

Riedel, Bruce. *The Search for Al Qaeda: Its Leadership, Ideology, and Future*. Washington, DC: Brookings Institution, 2008.

Sageman, Marc. *Leaderless Jihad: Terror Networks in the Twenty-First Century.* Philadelphia: University of Pennsylvania Press, 2008.

U.S. National Commission on Terrorist Attacks on the United States. *The 9/11 Commission Report.* New York: W. W. Norton, 2004.

U.S. Office of the Coordinator for Counterterrorism. *Country Reports on Terrorism 2013.* Washington, DC: U.S Department of State, April 2014. Available at http://www.state.gov/j/ct/rls/crt/2013/index.htm.

Websites

Federal Bureau of Investigation: www.fbi.gov/about-us/investigate/terrorism

Global Terrorism Database: www.start.umd.edu/gtd/

RAND Corporation, Terrorism and Homeland Security: www.rand.org/research_areas/terrorism/

UN Action to Counter Terrorism: www.un.org/terrorism/

U.S. Government Accountability Office, Topic Collection: Terrorism: www.gao.gov/docsearch/featured/terrorism.html

Films

The Battle of Algiers: A classic movie that focuses on Algerian terrorism and French counterterrorism in the Algerian struggle for independence. 1996, Igor Film. Directed by Gillo Pontecorvo.

Munich: A Stephen Spielberg film that focuses on Israel's effort to kill those responsible for the murder of Israeli athletes at the 1972 Munich Olympic Games. 2005, Universal.

Obama at War: A PBS/WGBH *Frontline* production originally aired in May 2015.

The Rise of ISIS: A PBS/WGBH *Frontline* production originally aired in October 2014.

Zero Dark Thirty: A feature film focusing on the hunt for Osama bin Laden. 2012, Columbia Pictures. Directed by Kathryn Bigelow.

Chapter Six

The Proliferation of Weapons of Mass Destruction

The deadly arms race, and the huge resources it absorbs, have too long overshadowed all else we must do. We must prevent the arms race from spreading to new nations, to new nuclear powers and to the reaches of outer space.

—John F. Kennedy, State of the Union Address, January 30, 1961

Following the Persian Gulf War of 1991, UN inspectors discovered that an Iraqi official had secretly hidden 650,000 pages of material concerning biological weapons on a chicken farm outside of Baghdad. After examining these materials, the inspectors realized that Iraq had developed both a defensive and an offensive biological weapons program, that it had weaponized biological agents, and had loaded them into 166 bombs and twenty-five missile warheads.[1]

In April 1999, Ayman al-Zawahiri, Osama bin Laden's deputy and a trained medical doctor, wrote a memo to Muhammad Atef, Al Qaeda's military commander, in which he proposed a secret program to develop biological and chemical weapons:

The enemy started thinking about these weapons before WWI [World War I]. Despite their extreme danger, we only became aware of them when the enemy drew our attention to them by repeatedly expressing concerns that they can be produced simply with easily available materials. The destructive power of these weapons is no less than that of nuclear weapons. A germ attack is often detected days after it occurs, which raises the number of victims. Defense against such weapons is very difficult, particularly if large quantities are used.[2]

In 2003, a Russian businessman offered $750,000 to any Russian weapons scientist who would provide him with weapons-grade plutonium for a foreign

105

client. The businessman was successful in contacting residents of Sarov, a city closed to outsiders by the Russian government because it had been the home of the Soviet Union's top nuclear weapons design laboratories. Fortunately, scam artists sold the businessman a canister of mercury rather than plutonium, but the episode raised the possibility of nuclear weapons materials being sold to the highest bidder.[3]

Two Armenian men—one a businessman and the other a physicist—pleaded guilty in a court in Tbilisi to charges of smuggling highly enriched uranium into the Republic of Georgia in 2010. The material, placed in a lead-lined cigarette box and brought into the country by train, is thought to have come from a Russian nuclear fuel plant in Novosibirsk. The two smugglers believed they were selling the material to an Islamist organization but were dealing instead with an undercover agent of the Georgian government.[4]

These events and others have caused scholars and policy analysts to call attention to the advent of a "second nuclear age." According to arms control expert Michael Krepon, "The [first] nuclear age was cobbled together through deterrence, containment, military strength, diplomatic engagement, and arms control. . . . The second nuclear age is about power imbalance and asymmetric warfare, not arms races."[5] The first nuclear age was dominated by Soviet-American competition, a concern about surprise attack, and nuclear deterrence. The second nuclear age is marked by a concern about the spread of nuclear weapons to new countries and nonstate actors such as terrorist groups, fear of nuclear terrorism, and a concern that deterrence will not be effective against nonstate actors.

The cases mentioned above are just a few of the many that could be cited to justify the concerns that experts have expressed regarding the spread of weapons of mass destruction—and the materials needed to make them—to rogue states and terrorist groups. In his comments on the 9/11 Commission's final report, Chairman Thomas Kean noted that every expert with whom the Commission met had predicted that Al Qaeda would attempt a second major attack. Although the human and economic losses caused by the attacks of September 11, 2001, were enormous, they could have been much worse had weapons of mass destruction been used. Imagine the impact of terrorist use of nuclear weapons. According to a Harvard University study, "A bomb with the explosive power of 10,000 metric tons of TNT (smaller than the Hiroshima bomb), if set off in midtown Manhattan on a typical workday, could kill half a million people and cause over $1 trillion in direct economic damage."[6] The destructiveness of weapons of mass destruction combined with the difficulty of defending against their use makes preventing their acquisition by global actors with strong incentives to use them one of the highest national security priorities of the twenty-first century.

There are two principal means of slowing or reversing the spread of weapons of mass destruction (WMD) to additional states and to nonstate actors: nonproliferation and counterproliferation. The Nuclear Non-Proliferation Treaty, the Chemical Weapons Convention, and the Biological Weapons Convention all seek to prevent the spread of weapons of mass destruction and thus are characteristic of the nonproliferation approach. The other major approach, counterproliferation, seeks to destroy or neutralize the threat of WMD programs or stockpiles that are already in place. While nonproliferation strategies generally involve multilateral cooperation, counterproliferation strategies are often pursued by states acting alone. In this chapter, we will review the historical attempts to limit the spread of WMD and the threats they pose, and suggest what can be done to slow proliferation.

THE NONPROLIFERATION APPROACH

In 1963, President John F. Kennedy predicted that there could be from fifteen to twenty-five states with nuclear weapons by the 1970s.[7] Kennedy was not alone; many others also recognized the danger to which he drew attention. In an effort to prevent the spread of these weapons, a number of states negotiated the Nuclear Non-Proliferation Treaty (commonly known by its acronym, NPT), which was opened for signature in 1968.[8] The NPT proposed a straightforward quid pro quo: if states that did not possess nuclear weapons agreed not to produce them, states that had nuclear weapons would help them develop peaceful uses of nuclear energy, such as nuclear power generation and civilian research. The nuclear-weapons states also agreed to work toward the elimination of all existing nuclear weapons. This bargain has been attractive to most states; at the time of the May 2015 NPT Review Conference, 189 states (including five of the nine nuclear weapons–possessing countries) were parties to the NPT.

That is the good news. The bad news is that the small minority of states that have not signed the NPT includes Israel, India, and Pakistan, countries that are in the most volatile areas of the world. India and Pakistan have a long history of bitter hostility, focused primarily on the disputed territory of Kashmir. In May 1999, the two states went to war in the Kargil region of Kashmir. It was the third armed conflict in Kashmir since 1947, but the first in which both sides possessed nuclear weapons. In fact, both India and Pakistan had tested nuclear weapons (Pakistan for the first time) in 1998.

Pakistan is a particular concern, for several reasons. Its population of 175 million includes many Islamic fundamentalists, including some who support Al Qaeda and the Taliban. The 9/11 Commission reported that there were 859 *madrassahs* (conservative Islamic schools) teaching more than two hundred thousand young people in Karachi alone.[9] According to former National Security Council staff members Daniel Benjamin and Steven Simon, before 9/11 Pakistan's military intelligence agency, the Inter-Services Intelligence directorate, was "a kind of terrorist conveyor belt" that transported "young radicals from their schools [in Pakistan] to Afghanistan for training in camps run by or affiliated with Al Qaeda. From there, they were taken to the border with Indian-controlled Kashmir, where they slipped across to launch their attacks."[10]

Despite the overthrow of the Taliban, the attacks on Al Qaeda, and the death of Osama bin Laden, there is still support in Pakistan for these groups. An obvious danger is that nuclear materials could be turned over to terrorists. Even under former president Pervez Musharraf, who supported U.S. operations against terrorists and the Taliban, one of Pakistan's nuclear weapons designers, Abdul Qadeer Khan, sold nuclear components to Libya, Iran, and North Korea and headed up what the 9/11 Commission termed "the most dangerous nuclear smuggling ring ever disclosed."[11] In addition, two of Pakistan's senior nuclear scientists, Sultan Bashiruddin Mahmood and Chaudari Abdul Majeed, are sympathetic to Islamic extremists and met with Osama bin Laden and his deputy, Ayman al-Zawahiri, discussing nuclear weapons with them.[12] Before his death, bin Laden stated that he was seeking weapons of mass destruction and that, for Muslims, it is a "religious duty" to develop them.[13] Al Qaeda repeatedly tried to buy or steal nuclear weapons, and documents captured from Al Qaeda bases in Afghanistan reveal "a significant effort to pursue nuclear weapons."[14] The possibility that the Pakistani government might at some point be taken over by elements sympathetic to such Islamic terrorist groups as Al Qaeda complicates the picture even further.

Two of the three states to which A. Q. Khan sold nuclear technology, North Korea and Iran, continue to present serious proliferation risks. On the other hand, Libya gave up its quest for nuclear weapons as part of an effort to get out from under economic sanctions that had been imposed soon after the bombing of an airliner over Lockerbie, Scotland, by agents of the Libyan government in 1988. North Korea tested nuclear weapons in 2006 and 2009 and is believed to have as many as ten weapons in its small stockpile. Iran has denied an intent to build nuclear weapons while insisting on its right to enrich uranium for research purposes. The effort to stop Iran's nuclear enrichment program included United Nations Security Council resolutions, economic sanctions, a sophisticated cyberattack ("Stuxnet"), and negotiations with the "P-5 plus one" (the five permanent members of the UN Security Council plus Germany).

The development of nuclear power programs was stimulated throughout the world by the NPT. Many people believed that nuclear power could help solve contemporary problems, whether in medicine, energy, or other civilian issue areas. It was believed that certain uses would be safe and separate from weapons use; however, only four kilograms (8.8 pounds) of plutonium or twelve kilograms (26.4 pounds) of highly enriched uranium (HEU) are needed to make a nuclear bomb. By the late 1990s, there were twenty metric tons of highly enriched uranium at 130 operational civilian research facilities in more than forty countries.[15] Today, there are ten states that each possess at least two tons of weapon-usable nuclear material (HEU or plutonium). Another seventeen states have enough HEU or plutonium for the fabrication of at least one nuclear weapon.[16] While most of the world's weapon-usable nuclear materials are in military stockpiles, some is to be found at civilian research facilities, often with inadequate security. In one particularly troubling episode, uranium just below the quality of HEU was stolen from a research reactor in Congo and wound up in the hands of the Italian mafia.[17] Although this nuclear material could not have been used to make a nuclear weapon without additional processing, it would have been suitable for a radiological weapon, or "dirty bomb." According to the IAEA, there have been eighteen documented cases of seizure of highly enriched uranium or plutonium. Other losses or thefts not reported to the IAEA are also known to have occurred.[18]

THE COUNTERPROLIFERATION APPROACH

The nonproliferation approach is only effective given international cooperation. If one state or group of states supplies chemical, biological, or nuclear materials to another state or terrorist group, proliferation occurs and this approach fails. The NPT was built on the assumption that multilateral cooperation would stop the spread of nuclear weapons, but the optimistic assumption of universal cooperation has not always proved to be correct. The question concerning proliferation today often appears to be not whether but when certain states or subnational actors will develop WMD.

Faced with the potential and actual spread of nuclear, biological, or chemical weapons, a second approach was developed—counterproliferation—to destroy or neutralize the threat of WMD. In contrast to the multilateral nature of nonproliferation, counterproliferation is generally a unilateral approach. Israel has used military strikes to destroy incipient nuclear programs in the Middle East on at least two occasions. In 1981, Israeli planes destroyed an Iraqi nuclear reactor in Osirak. The reactor was designed to produce the fissile material needed to build nuclear weapons. In 2007, Israeli planes struck another nuclear facility, this time in Syria. The Syrians had little to say about the attack on what, according to evidence offered by the CIA, was a nuclear facility being built with the assistance of North Korea.

The United States, which historically led global nonproliferation efforts, moved in the direction of counterproliferation during the George W. Bush administration. In the early 1990s, when it appeared that North Korea was developing nuclear weapons, the U.S. government seriously considered a preemptive attack on suspected North Korean nuclear weapons sites.[19] At the same time it was making military contingency plans for attacking North Korea, the United States pursued negotiations with Pyongyang to reduce the danger of proliferation diplomatically. In 1994, the United States, Japan, and South Korea signed with North Korea an Agreed Framework that called for the three states to provide oil and build two new nuclear reactors to replace two existing reactors that produced plutonium suitable for use in nuclear weapons.[20] The North Korean threat was neutralized—at least for several years—as a result of a multilateral, nonproliferation approach.

In August 1990, Iraq attacked and occupied its Arab neighbor to the south, Kuwait. In response to Iraq's aggression and to the threat that Iraq might disrupt the world energy markets and develop weapons of mass destruction, the United States, joined by more than thirty other countries, forced Iraq to withdraw from Kuwait and to accept inspections by UN teams. Inspections were conducted from 1991 to 1998. More Iraqi weapons were destroyed during this period than were destroyed during the war. In 1998, Iraq expelled the UN inspectors, and the United States became increasingly concerned that Iraq might be developing weapons of mass destruction.

The Clinton administration preferred the nonproliferation approach for dealing with the issue of nuclear proliferation, although it considered a counterproliferation strategy against North Korea. With regard to Iraq, the Clinton administration adopted a nonproliferation approach. In contrast, when George W. Bush entered office, U.S. policy shifted toward counterproliferation, a shift solidified by the 9/11 attacks, which significantly increased American security concerns. The Bush administration increasingly moved toward a military-oriented policy of preemption, a position that was made explicit in several important policy statements.[21] President Bush came to believe that Saddam Hussein could not be trusted, that Iraq was developing weapons of mass destruction, and that the United States had to take forceful action—alone if necessary—to remove this threat. On March 20, 2003, the United States, principally with the support of the United Kingdom, attacked Iraq, with four main objectives: (1) to find and destroy Iraqi WMD; (2) to overthrow Saddam Hussein; (3) to end Iraq's suspected cooperation with Al Qaeda and other terrorist groups; and (4) to establish a democratic government in Iraq, in hopes that democracy would spread throughout the Middle East.[22] In spite of an extensive search during and after the fall of the Iraqi regime, no weapons of mass destruction were ever found. A much-maligned nonproliferation approach with inspections by the International Atomic Energy Agency as the centerpiece was, in most respects, vindicated by the absence of Iraqi WMD.

CONTROLLING ACCESS TO WMD

For more than four decades, the international community has sought to halt, or at least slow, the spread of weapons of mass destruction. In 2001, the United States moved from a nonproliferation to a unilateral counterproliferation approach, but the invasion of Iraq for counterproliferation reasons may, ironically, have convinced other states of the need to acquire WMD as a hedge against U.S. intervention. As an Indian general noted after the 1991 Persian Gulf War, in which a technologically advanced force led by the United States routed Iraq's large, battle-tested Republican Guard, the principal lesson of the war was "never fight the Americans without nuclear weapons."[23]

Despite the fact that it is unquestionably the single most powerful country in the world, the United States cannot effectively prevent the proliferation of weapons of mass destruction by itself; it must have the cooperation and support of other countries, including those that could supply the dangerous ingredients of WMD, and of those (such as Afghanistan under the Taliban) that could harbor terrorists intent on developing WMD. Democrats and Republicans, conservatives and liberals, all agree that there is no greater danger facing the United States than the specter of terrorists armed with chemical, biological, or nuclear weapons. In his 2003 State of the Union address, President George W. Bush declared, "The gravest danger facing America and the world, is outlaw regimes that seek and possess nuclear, chemical, and biological weapons. These regimes could give or sell those weapons to terrorist allies, who would use them without the least hesitation."[24] Seven years later, President Obama, speaking to the Nuclear Security Summit in Washington, said, "It is increasingly clear that the danger of nuclear terrorism is one of the greatest threats to global security—to our collective security."[25]

Although international agreements—most notably the Nuclear Non-Proliferation Treaty, the Biological Weapons Convention, and the Chemical Weapons Convention—have not completely prevented the spread of weapons of mass destruction, they have created an international norm opposing WMD proliferation. In a world of two hundred states with competing interests, priorities, and policies, such a consensus has value; it sends the message that most of the world's states are opposed to the development, production, stockpiling, and deployment of weapons of mass destruction. Efforts to strengthen the agreements that undergird this consensus, such as the attempts to negotiate a verification protocol for the Biological Weapons Convention and conclude a fissile material cutoff treaty, are therefore vitally important.

Russia remains the largest potential supplier of weapons of mass destruction to rogue states and terrorist groups. In 1993, the former Soviet Union possessed an estimated thirty-two thousand nuclear weapons and thousands of scientists with knowledge of how to build weapons of mass destruction.[26] As of mid-2015, there were still some 8,500 assembled nuclear warheads in Russia. The potential for unsecured nuclear weapons to fall into the hands of rogue states or terrorists is colloquially referred to as the "loose nukes" problem.

In 1991, Senator Sam Nunn and Senator Richard Lugar introduced legislation to provide funds to increase the safety of Russian weapons of mass destruction and to provide for their destruction. The Nunn-Lugar initiative, subsequently called the Cooperative Threat Reduction Program, provided funds to provide work for unemployed Russian scientists and engineers who had worked on weapons programs prior to the disintegration of the Soviet Union.[27] This program accomplished a great deal. By mid-2012, the program resulted in the deactivation of 7,619 strategic nuclear warheads and the destruction of 902 ballistic missiles and thirty-three strategic missile submarines. In addition, the program resulted in the destruction of 2,936 metric tons of Russian and Albanian chemical weapons, the securing of twenty-four nuclear weapons storage sites, the building of thirty-nine biological threat monitoring stations, and assistance with the employment of fifty-eight thousand former Soviet weapons scientists.[28] In spite of the significant accomplishments of this program, with the xenophobic policies of Russian president Vladimir Putin, the program was ended. Michael Krepon noted:

> The most important post-Cold War initiative to reduce nuclear dangers undertaken by the United States has come to a quiet, unceremonious end. . . . A quarter of a century after the Cold War ended, bilateral relations have reverted to hard times. These programs are now deemed unnecessary and inappropriate by Russian President Valdimir Putin and by majorities in both houses of the U.S. Congress. Russia is no longer a supplicant, and the U.S. Congress is no longer feeling generous.[29]

Despite the success of the Cooperative Threat Reduction Program, with its cessation much remains to be done. Russia still possesses large quantities of fissile material and large numbers of nuclear weapons. Not all of its weapons and fissile material have been adequately secured. This is especially problematic because Russia has a serious terrorist threat within its borders, represented by non-Russian extremists, such as those from Chechnya, Dagestan, and Ingushetia, some of the leaders of which have expressed interest in using nuclear materials in their campaign against the Russian government.

Reportedly, Chechen terrorists placed a canister of radiological material in a Moscow park in 1995, conducted reconnaissance on Russian nuclear warhead storage sites and transportation trains on several occasions in 2001 and 2002, and considered attacking and taking over a Moscow nuclear facility with significant supplies of highly enriched uranium. In October 2002, forty-one heavily armed Chechen terrorists took over a Moscow theater, demonstrating their motivation and capability to use force and die for their cause. Reportedly, the terrorists had considered taking over the Kurchatov Institute, which had enough HEU to make dozens of nuclear weapons.[30] Importantly, there are links between Al Qaeda and Chechen terrorists; if the Chechens obtained weapons of mass destruction, it is possible that Al Qaeda could gain access to WMD through them.

Obviously, actual weapons of mass destruction pose the greatest danger to American security; however, the components of these weapons and the processes to produce them also pose a significant threat. Therefore, the United States has actively sought international cooperation in tracking the manufacture, import, and export of the components of WMD. One aspect of the effort to control access to weapon-usable materials has been the Convention on the Physical Protection of Nuclear Material. Adopted in Vienna, the headquarters of the International Atomic Energy Agency, in 1979, the treaty entered into force in 1987 and as of September 2015 has 153 parties. The agreement requires states to criminalize theft or diversion of nuclear material in their own territories while cooperating with other states when diversions occur. Unfortunately, the treaty applies only to nuclear material used for peaceful purposes.[31]

A report by the Carnegie Endowment concludes, "Because the most difficult part of making a nuclear bomb is acquiring the nuclear material, *all weapon-usable nuclear materials should be treated as if they were nuclear weapons, and the highest standards applied to weapons should become the global norm for all such materials regardless of use or location.*"[32] There are four principal ways to prevent additional countries and nonstate actors, such as terrorists and transnational criminal organizations, from obtaining nuclear weapons. First, all stocks of nuclear weapons and weapon-usable nuclear materials should be secured throughout the world, including the United States. Physical protection of nuclear materials involves guards, gates, and guns—that is, nuclear materials and weapons should be protected by both human and physical means. In cases where it is not possible to ensure the security of nuclear materials, they should be relocated to countries that are able to secure them or destroy them. In fact, the United States has assisted with such measures on several occasions. In 1994, Kazakhstan shipped six hundred kilograms of highly enriched uranium to Oak Ridge, Tennessee, for secure storage, eliminating what had been the largest existing stock of fissile materials outside of Russia. In 1998, the United States removed highly enriched uranium from a vulnerable site in Tbilisi, Georgia. In addition, the United States has airlifted stockpiles of highly enriched uranium from three "dangerously vulnerable" sites in Romania, Bulgaria, and Libya.[33]

A second measure to prevent terrorists and criminal groups from obtaining nuclear weapons is to convert civilian, research, power, and naval reactors that use weapon-usable fuels to alternate fuels. The United States has sponsored a number of programs to convert highly enriched uranium into fuel for civilian nuclear-power reactors. In fact, as of 2003, 20 percent of the electricity produced in the United States came from nuclear power plants, and half of this was produced from highly enriched uranium from dismantled Russian nuclear weapons. This means that 10 percent of the electricity produced in the United States came from Russian fissile material. This program was a quintessential "swords into plowshares" program, which some have called "megatons into megawatts."[34]

A third measure is to eliminate large stockpiles of weapon-usable materials. By the end of 2003, two hundred tons of highly enriched uranium from dismantled Russian nuclear weapons had been blended into low-enriched uranium in accordance with Russian-American agreements. If Russian warheads contain on average twenty-five kilograms of highly enriched uranium, the two hundred tons were the equivalent of eight thousand warheads.[35] As of the end of 2012, Russia's fissile material stock included 128 tons of weapons-grade plutonium, 695 tons of highly enriched uranium, and 49.8 tons of reactor-grade plutonium.[36]

A fourth step to reduce the risk of terrorists' gaining access to nuclear materials and weapons is to halt production of all weapon-usable material. As of 2004, there was enough weapon-usable material in the world to produce more than a hundred thousand nuclear weapons. In spite of that fact, a number of states continued to produce it. Of the nine states that are known to have or are suspected of having nuclear weapons, the United States, Russia, the United Kingdom, France, and China have halted the production of HEU and plutonium; it is believed that Israel, India, Pakistan, and North Korea continue to produce nuclear materials for weapons, and many countries suspect that Iran embarked on a program to enrich uranium in order to build nuclear weapons.[37]

More than fifty years ago, President Eisenhower first proposed halting production of fissile material that could be used to make weapons. President Clinton, in a speech before the United Nations General Assembly in 1993, called for an international agreement to ban the production of fissile material. After the General Assembly endorsed President Clinton's recommendation, the UN Conference on Disarmament established a committee to negotiate a Fissile Material Cutoff Treaty (FMCT). At the Nonproliferation Review Conference in 2000, the states party to the NPT called for halting the production of fissile material by 2005. As of 2015, negotiations toward an FMCT remained stalled. One of the initial causes of the delay in negotiations was the Bush administration's announcement in July 2004 that the United States would support a treaty only without verification provisions.[38] Critics of this position noted that the American action would cripple the attempt to stop the production of fissile material. Dr. Frank von Hippel, a former White House science advisor, has argued that a verifiable FMCT would be "a political challenge, but it is technically feasible to establish the means to effectively monitor and verify compliance with the treaty in order to detect and deter clandestine nuclear bomb production efforts."[39] Others have noted that this "trust but not verify" approach was characteristic of the George W. Bush administration's approach to the Strategic Offensive Reductions Treaty (SORT or Moscow Treaty), which entered into force in 2003 with no verification provisions, and of its refusal to participate in the negotiations to strengthen the verifiability of the Biological Weapons Convention.

COOPERATION OR CONFRONTATION?

For fifty years, beginning with President Eisenhower's "Atoms for Peace" proposal in 1953, the United States employed an approach to controlling the spread of weapons of mass destruction that placed a premium on international cooperation and diplomacy. That approach changed in 2003. The attacks on the United States on September 11, 2001, ushered in the "second nuclear age" and focused attention on the possibility of terrorist acts employing weapons of mass destruction and, consequently, increased fear that rogue states, including Iraq, might be developing and stockpiling WMD. Against this backdrop (and disregarding contrary evidence offered by UN weapons inspectors), the United States, the United Kingdom, and other allies attacked Iraq with the avowed purpose of finding and destroying Iraqi WMD. No such weapons were ever found.

Intelligence indicates that North Korea has around ten nuclear weapons. In fact, given the evidence concerning North Korea's nuclear weapons, it would have been more in keeping with the logic of the George W. Bush administration's policy of preemption, as described in the *National Security Strategy* of 2002, to attack North Korea before Iraq. That was not done, and now the United States must decide what to do about North Korea and other potential or actual proliferators, as well as what to do about the very real danger of terrorists' or criminals' obtaining nuclear materials or even nuclear weapons.

Iraq was the first application of the George W. Bush administration's military-based, preemptive policy of counterproliferation, and it raised a number of troubling questions. The rationale for the invasion was that Iraq possessed weapons of mass destruction that posed a clear and present danger to the United States. While evidence of old Iraqi WMD research programs was found, nothing to justify the prewar security concerns was uncovered. The invasion was undertaken on the basis of false intelligence assumptions, with enormous costs to both the United States and Iraq. Given the prohibitive costs of the policy of preemption, what other options exist?

An international, diplomatically based nonproliferation policy is frustrating and time consuming, but it was followed by the United States for three-and-a-half decades. Perhaps 9/11 changed everything and demanded a dramatic revolution in U.S. strategy; that was the position of the Bush administration.[40] Just as difficult cases make bad law, however, it may be that traumatic events such as 9/11 result in policies that are not sustainable or effective over the long term. A policy that patiently enlists the cooperation and support of the entire international community, less a few rogue states, is the best way to seek greater security in an insecure world.

Over a twenty-month period, the five permanent members of the UN Security Council (the United States, the United Kingdom, Russia, China, and France) plus Germany—the so-called P-5 plus one—negotiated restrictions on the development of Iran's nuclear weapons technology. In July 2015, the Joint Comprehensive Plan of Action (JCPOA) was announced and, as part of the agreement, Iran ageed to reduce its number of centrifuges used to make highly enriched uranium from 19,500 to 6,000. In addition, Iran agreed to dismantle its "heavy water" nuclear reactor at Arak that could be used to produce plutonium, which, like highly enriched uranium, is usable for weapons. In exchange for Iran's agreement to these restrictions and acceptance of inspections from representatives from the P-5 plus one countries and the International Atomic Energy Agency (IAEA), economic sanctions imposed on Iran would be lifted. Although Republicans in Congress and the government of Israel strongly criticized the agreement, the Obama administration and European governments strongly supported it, and it was implemented. Experts estimated that the provisions of the agreement would extend the amount of time that it would take Iran to develop nuclear weapons—"break-out time"—from two or three months to one year. In addition, if Iran violates the agreement, the P-5 plus one are committed to reimposing economic sanctions on Iran.

In his Prague speech, President Obama called for "a new international effort to secure all vulnerable nuclear material around the world in four years." The UN Security Council added its support for this objective in Resolution 1887, adopted on September 24, 2009. Then, in April 2010, President Obama hosted forty-seven world leaders at the Nuclear Security Summit in Washington to highlight the need for greater cooperation on securing nuclear stockpiles. States represented at the summit also committed themselves to securing all nuclear materials within four years. Follow-up summit meetings were held in Seoul in 2012 and The Hague in 2014.

The signatories to the Non-Proliferation Treaty held a review conference involving all of the signatories in May 2015, and at this conference they reaffirmed the objectives of the treaty and pledged to make renewed efforts to prevent the spread of nuclear weapons and to reduce the number of nuclear weapons held by those states possessing them.

There is a solid foundation on which to build multilateral efforts to restrain weapons proliferation. The three main treaties focusing on the control of weapons of mass destruction—the Nuclear Non-Proliferation Treaty, the Chemical Weapons Convention, and the Biological Weapons Convention—have been widely accepted by the international community; holdouts are generally regarded as rogues rather than models worthy of emulation. Furthermore, while the holdouts (and even some signatories) continue to present problems and require close monitoring, there have been a number of successes in the effort to curb WMD proliferation. Rather than uncovering ongoing WMD programs, the Iraq War revealed that the international inspection regime imposed after the 1991 Persian Gulf War had done more than many expected to disarm Saddam Hussein. In spite of assistance from Pakistan, Libya failed to acquire the nuclear weapons it had long sought and, under the pressure of international sanctions, eventually decided to give up its quest. South Africa, which had clandestinely developed nuclear weapons under its apartheid regime, reversed course and eliminated its nuclear weapons in the 1980s before its transition to democracy. Democratic transitions and improved relations between them encouraged Argentina and Brazil to give up WMD programs begun during periods of military rule. Ukraine and Kazakhstan, two states left with portions of the enormous Soviet nuclear arsenal following the breakup of the Soviet Union, opted to eliminate those weapons and sign the NPT as non-nuclear weapons states. In short, the news on the proliferation front is not all bad, even if there are many reasons to keep the issue near the top of the security agenda.

ADDITIONAL RESOURCES

Books

Bunn, Matthew. *Securing the Bomb 2010: Securing All Nuclear Materials in Four Years*. Cambridge, MA: Nuclear Threat Initiative and the Project on Managing the Atom, Harvard University, April 2010.

Chapter Six

Caldwell, Dan. "Security, Proliferation and Arms Control." In *Handbook of American Foreign Policy*, eds. Steven W. Hook and Christopher M. Jones. London: Routledge, 2011.
Cirincione, Joseph. *Nuclear Nightmares: Securing the World Before It Is Too Late.* New York: Columbia University Press, 2013.
Perkovich, George, and James M. Acton. *Abolishing Nuclear Weapons.* Adelphi Book 396. London: International Institute for Strategic Studies, 2014.
Sagan, Scott D., and Kenneth N. Waltz. *The Spread of Nuclear Weapons: A Debate Renewed.* New York: W. W. Norton, 2003.
Samore, Gary, ed. *The Iran Nuclear Deal: A Definitive Guide.* Cambridge, MA: Belfer Center for Science and International Affairs, Harvard University, August 2015.

Websites

Arms Control Association: http://www.armscontrol.org/
Carnegie Endowment for International Peace: www.ceip.org
Defense Threat Reduction Agency: www.dtra.mil
Federation of American Scientists: www.fas.org
International Atomic Energy Agency: www.iaea.org
Monterey Institute for International Studies, Center for Nonproliferation Studies: http://www.nonproliferation.org/
Nuclear Threat Initiative: www.nti.org
United Nations Office for Disarmament Affairs website for the 2015 NPT Review Conference: http://www.un.org/en/conf/npt/2015/

Films

Countdown to Zero (2010): This documentary argues that the likelihood of the use of nuclear weapons has increased since the end of the Cold War due to terrorism, nuclear proliferation, and theft of nuclear materials and weapons. The film features interviews with leading statesmen and experts, including Tony Blair, Jimmy Carter, Mikhail Gorbachev, and Robert McNamara. Lawrence Bender Productions. Directed by Lucy Walker.
Last Best Chance: An hour-long fictionalized, gripping portrayal of how nuclear weapons could be smuggled into the United States. Available from the Nuclear Threat Initiative at www.nti.org. Bread & Butter Productions, 2005. Directed by Ben Goddard.
The Peacemaker: A feature film starring Nicole Kidman and George Clooney focusing on antiproliferation efforts by the United States. DreamWorks, 1997. Directed by Mimi Leder.

Part Two

NEW SOURCES OF INSECURITY

Chapter Seven

Infectious Disease and Health Insecurity

Infectious disease which antedated the emergence of humankind will last as long as humanity itself, and will surely remain, as it has been hitherto, one of the fundamental parameters and determinants of human history.

—William McNeill, *Plagues and Peoples* (1976)

In 1976, a virus called Ebola hemorrhagic fever was identified in rural Zaire (now the Democratic Republic of the Congo). The disease was named after the Ebola River, and its effects on those infected by it were severe and often fatal. A Zairean doctor who was among the first to encounter the modern strain of Ebola reported his findings in these words:

The affliction is characterized by a high temperature around thirty-nine degrees Celsius; frequent vomiting of black, digested blood, but of red blood in a few cases; diarrheal emissions initially sprinkled with blood, with only red blood near death; epistaxis [nosebleeds] now and then; retrosternal and abdominal pain and a state of stupor; prostration with heaviness in the joints; rapid evolution toward death after a period of about three days, from a state of general health.[1]

In the decades that followed, there were sporadic outbreaks of Ebola in twenty-four other central African countries; the largest outbreak prior to 2014 occurred in 2000 in Uganda, where 425 were infected and 224 died.[2] When the last of seven Ebola-related deaths occurred in Sudan in 2004 and there were no other reported cases, the World Health Organization declared the outbreak over. From 1976 through 2004, there were approximately 1,850 reported cases and 1,200 deaths. But in December 2013, children playing close to some bats in the jungle in Guinea became very sick.[3] Initially,

121

their sickness was diagnosed as cholera or malaria; however, after several weeks, the disease was identified as Ebola. The government of Guinea had no experience in dealing with Ebola and had very limited medical resources, and the World Health Organization (WHO) had little experience in dealing with Ebola; to make things worse, its offices in West Africa and its regional office in Brazzaville, Republic of Congo, did not communicate well with WHO headquarters in Geneva.[4] A nongovernmental organization, Doctors without Borders (*Médecins sans Frontières*, or MSF), had substantial experience dealing with Ebola and intervened to address the growing spread of the disease.

The initial outbreak traveled four hundred miles to Guinea's capital, and the border between Guinea and Sierra Leone remained open, allowing the disease to spread to that country and from there to Liberia. The spread of Ebola was exacerbated by several factors, including the lack of adequate medical and quarantine facilities and personnel, the delayed response from the affected countries' governments and international community, and burial practices in West Africa, which called for the washing of the bodies of the deceased. Ebola was not an airborne disease; rather, it was spread through contact with bodily fluids including urine, semen, vomit, feces, and blood. Bodies remained highly contagious even after death.

As news of the spread of Ebola reached the rest of the world, panic ensued. In October 2014 alone, seventy-five airplane cabin cleaners at LaGuardia Airport walked off their jobs because they were afraid of being exposed to Ebola. A woman who vomited in the Pentagon parking lot but showed no other symptoms of Ebola caused the temporary closure of the entrance to the building. A health worker from Texas who was suspected of being exposed to Ebola but had no Ebola symptoms was quarantined on a cruise ship for nineteen days. In Mississippi parents pulled their children out of school because the principal of the school had visited Zambia, which is three thousand miles from West Africa.[5] Most significantly, the CDC, one of the most respected disease centers in the world, predicted an estimated 1.4 million cases of Ebola with 980,000 deaths by February 2015.[6]

As a result of these dire predictions and despite the slow response, within nine months of the Ebola outbreak the U.S. government pledged an initial $350 million to combat the disease and deployed military personnel to provide logistics and build hospitals and quarantine facilities. In addition, the United Kingdom pledged $200 million, the World Bank $400 million, and Cuba and Nigeria sent health care workers. Doctors without Borders was the first and most effective group on the scene and provided 5,300 workers; of these, twenty-eight were infected and fourteen died. Eventually, WHO deployed seven hundred people at seventy-seven field sites. The Centers for

Disease Control and Prevention (CDC) responded with the largest deployment in its seventy-five-year history by sending 165 staff members to West Africa and committing more than a thousand support personnel to the anti-Ebola campaign at CDC headquarters in Atlanta.

The 2014 Ebola crisis clearly demonstrated several realities of contemporary international security. First, it was clear Ebola was not an exception to what to expect for the future, but rather a precedent. Second, a rapid response by national, nongovernmental, and international actors was needed to stem disease outbreaks from becoming pandemics. And third, the Ebola crisis showed that public health issues were security issues. According to WHO director general Dr. Margaret Chan, "I have never seen a health event threaten the very survival of societies and governments in already very poor countries. I have never seen an infectious disease contribute so strongly to potential state failure."[7]

The traditional approach regards security purely in state-centric military terms; however, as the Ebola crisis demonstrates, the threat posed by infectious disease calls this view into question. Throughout recorded history (and long before there was an awareness of their existence), microbes have threatened the security of human communities, occasionally shaking the foundations of states and empires. In his *History of the Peloponnesian War*, Thucydides wrote not only about the military battles between the rival city-states of Athens and Sparta but also, in excruciating detail, about the epidemic that swept Athens in 430–429 BC, killing a quarter of its soldiers. A passage describing the breakdown of order due to what Thucydides calls simply "the plague" is worth noting:

> The bodies of the dying were heaped one on top of the other, and half-dead creatures could be seen staggering about in the streets or flocking around the fountains in their desire for water. For the catastrophe was so overwhelming that men, not knowing what would happen next to them, became indifferent to every rule of religion or law. Athens owed to the plague the beginnings of a state of unprecedented lawlessness. Seeing how quick and abrupt were the changes of fortune . . . people now began openly to venture on acts of self-indulgence which before then they used to keep in the dark. . . . No fear of god or law of man had a restraining influence. As for the gods, it seemed to be the same thing whether one worshipped them or not, when one saw the good and the bad dying indiscriminately. As for offences against human law, no one expected to live long enough to be brought to trial and punished.[8]

Based on Thucydides' description, as well as the description of Ebola by modern epidemiologists, some experts believe that the plague that devasted Athens was actually Ebola.[9] According to a modern historian of disease,

William McNeill, in a relatively short period of time the epidemic "inflicted a blow on Athenian society from which it never recovered."[10] Thucydides implied that the epidemic contributed to Sparta's victory over Athens. Many scholars consider Thucydides the father of the discipline of international relations; yet his progeny have focused narrowly on military aspects of security rather than on the broader view that Thucydides adopted.

Between 1347 and 1351, a catastrophic pandemic ravaged Eurasia and Africa north of the Sahara. Estimates of the number of deaths caused by the plague are necessarily rough, but scholars have suggested a mortality rate for Europe ranging from 25 to 45 percent of the population. In 1351, the Vatican put the number of plague deaths in Christian Europe at 23,840,000, which was about a third of Europe's population before bubonic plague struck in 1347. According to the medieval historian Froissart, "a third of the world died."[11] The significance of the plague may go well beyond the fact that no war in human history has killed a larger proportion of the world's population. Some have argued that the frequent recurrence of bubonic plague in Europe between the fourteenth and sixteenth centuries, always with large-scale suffering and death apparently unrelated to the piety (or impiety) of the victims, resulted in the breakdown of respect for the dominant religious institution, the Roman Catholic Church. Infectious disease thus created the social conditions in which the Protestant Reformation and the religious wars that followed could occur. By this account, the European experience with bubonic plague led to a fundamental transformation of the international system when the 1648 Peace of Westphalia, which ended the most destructive of Europe's religious wars, established the modern system of sovereign states.[12]

Historians often point to the technological superiority of the European conquistadors in explaining their impressive defeat of the native meso-American Indians in the sixteenth century. However, when Spanish explorer Cortés and his men reached the New World with their European weapons, even more destructive to native peoples was the smallpox virus that they also brought to the Americas. Although smallpox had caused many deaths in Europe, the conquistadors and other survivors of periodic European smallpox epidemics had built up some immunity to the virus. The indigenous peoples of Mexico and Central America had no such protection; the results were devastating to the immunologically unprepared populations. There were an estimated thirty million people in central Mexico when Cortés arrived in 1519; fifty years later, the indigenous population was three million, a tenth of what it had been. By 1618, the indigenous population had fallen to 1.6 million, and the primary culprit of this devastating population decline was disease.[13] The conquistadors' most effective weapon against the indigenous peoples of the Americas was smallpox, not gunpowder.

Disease is not always an ally of the invaders. Typhus, which is sometimes called "war fever" because of its common association with wartime conditions, was one of the principal causes of the destruction of Napoleon's Grand Army on its ill-fated march into Russia in 1812. Of the 422,000 French soldiers who began that campaign, only ten thousand returned to France. Roughly half of the fatalities are believed to have been caused by typhus and other diseases. During the Crimean War (1853–1856), the British lost ten times more soldiers to disease than to combat. Typhus affected both soldiers and civilians during and after World War I. In 1915, 150,000 people died of the disease in Serbia alone. From 1918 to 1922, it infected as many as thirty million people and claimed as many as three million victims in Eastern Europe and Russia.[14]

As World War I came to an end in 1918, pandemic influenza began circling the globe. Known as the Spanish influenza, not because of its place of origin (which was China) but because it affected 80 percent of the population of Spain, the pandemic quickly killed as many as one hundred million people around the world, six times as many as had been killed in all theaters of the war.[15] The influenza first hit the United States when two sailors reported ill in Boston. Spreading rapidly up and down the East Coast, it eventually affected almost a quarter of the U.S. population. Half a million Americans died, hospitals were filled to overflowing, and, in Baltimore and Washington, there were shortages of coffins.[16]

The pandemic was by no means confined to the United States or even to the Northern Hemisphere. Between September and November 1918, 5 percent of the population of Ghana died of influenza. Almost all of the thirty-eight thousand people living in Western Samoa got the flu in November and December 1918; 7,500 died of it.[17] Spanish influenza took four months to circle the globe in 1918 and 1919; in today's more globalized world, it could do so in four days.

These examples demonstrate the dramatic impact that disease has had on human history, an impact that many historians have failed to note adequately. Disease, in short, has posed significant threats to the security of peoples and political structures throughout history, and it continues to pose a substantial threat. Indeed, given the emergence of new diseases and the possibility of terrorists employing biological weapons, disease may very well be one of the greatest, if not *the* greatest, threats to security in the twenty-first century.

In this chapter, we will describe various infectious diseases and the threats that they pose, indicate what has been done to control these threats, and describe what else can be done to address the security implications of infectious diseases.[18]

INFECTIOUS DISEASES

Major advances in the scientific understanding of infectious diseases have occurred only within the past century. Before the twentieth century, with little understanding of the way infectious diseases attack their victims and spread to others, active defenses were impossible. Not even simple bacterial infections of the kind associated with dirt in an open wound could be treated effectively prior to the discovery of penicillin. The timely discovery and large-scale manufacture of penicillin, in fact, made World War II the first conflict in history in which those wounded in battle had a better than even chance of surviving without the loss of a limb. As the macabre scene of a Confederate hospital in Atlanta in the classic movie *Gone with the Wind* suggests, prior to the introduction of penicillin only amputation under relatively antiseptic conditions would save the life of a soldier with a spreading infection.

The remarkable advances of modern medicine have achieved only limited success in halting the carnage of infectious diseases, and even those limited successes are in danger of being reversed. Let us note first the successes and then the very real threats.

The most deadly infectious disease in history was smallpox. In the twentieth century alone, smallpox killed somewhere between three hundred and five hundred million people worldwide. In the 1930s, approximately fifty thousand people per year were infected in the United States alone; the mortality rate among victims was 30 percent. While the vaccination first developed by Edward Jenner in 1796 provided a proven means of limiting the spread of smallpox, the vaccine was not widely distributed enough to eliminate the threat. Not surprisingly, the United States and other wealthy countries were the first to eradicate smallpox within their territories, a feat accomplished in advanced industrial states by the 1950s. Progress was much slower in the developing world. In 1967, when the World Health Organization (WHO) created its Smallpox Eradication Unit, smallpox was still claiming 1.5 to 2 million lives annually. Through a concerted and well-funded effort to carry vaccines to the most remote parts of the world, WHO succeeded in eliminating smallpox. In 1980, WHO declared its eradication program a success.[19] However, both the United States and the Soviet Union kept samples of the virus in order to prepare defenses against a possible biological attack employing smallpox; the deadliest disease in history had not been completely eliminated. Following the attacks on 9/11, there was concern that terrorists might obtain samples of smallpox and deliberately infect the populations of target states.

Worldwide, infectious diseases kill more people than all other causes combined; in 1998, a total of fifty-four million people died of infectious diseases.[20]

By contrast, an estimated total of sixty million people died in World War II. During the past several decades, thirty previously unknown diseases have emerged, including HIV/AIDS, Ebola, Marburg fever, hepatitis C, SARS, avian flu, the Hanta virus, and a virulent form of flesh-eating streptococcus. Unfortunately, there is no end in sight to the emergence of new diseases due to three factors: the increased mobility of people, greater ubanization, and human encroachment into previously uninhabited areas. It appears that pestilence is not only the deadliest of the four horsemen of the apocalypse but also, perhaps, the most dangerous and the most adaptable.

In addition to newly emerging diseases, several of humanity's oldest and most deadly scourges are staging a comeback, including tuberculosis, cholera, and malaria. The world's deadliest diseases are lower respiratory infections such as pneumonia, which kill over four million people a year; diarrheal diseases (2 million); HIV/AIDS (2 million deaths per year); tuberculosis (1.8 million); malaria (1 million); measles (500,000); and pertussis, or whooping cough (200,000–300,000).[21]

Epidemiological studies indicate that approximately twenty well-known diseases are reemerging, and this is occurring in developed as well as developing countries. For example, tuberculosis was supposed to have been eradicated in the United States by 2000, but it is staging a robust return. In 1993, WHO identified tuberculosis as a global emergency, with particular areas of the world, including Russia, India, Southeast Asia, sub-Saharan Africa, and parts of Latin America, considered particularly vulnerable. The TB bacillus, which is spread through the air by coughing and sneezing, infects more than two billion people—almost one-third of the world's population—but only 5–10 percent of those with the infection ever develop symptoms and become contagious. Nonetheless, in 2008, there were 9.4 million infected with TB worldwide; an estimated 1.8 million deaths attributable to TB occurred that year. Those infected with HIV are especially vulnerable to tuberculosis, and vice versa, as the two diseases work together to attack the human body. TB infects approximately 30 percent of those who are HIV-positive and is the leading identifiable cause of death among those with HIV.[22]

Malaria is another well-known but often misunderstood disease with devastating effects. Caused by parasites injected into humans with the bites of certain mosquito species, malaria generally produces fever and chills in its victims. In more severe cases, the fever may be followed by anemia, seizures, or even heart and lung failure. Some who survive malaria return to full health (and may even develop resistance to the disease), but others are left with physical or mental handicaps. No vaccines exist at present, but a variety of treatments, including quinine and its synthetic relative, chloroquine, have been developed over the years. In the absence of a vaccine, prevention efforts have been focused on eradicating the mosquitoes that spread malaria, primarily by using insecticides and blocking their access to humans through the use of insecticide-treated mosquito nets.[23]

According to the most recent global report on malaria from the U.S. National Academies, malaria is endemic in more than one hundred countries, or half of the countries in the world. Roughly three hundred million people worldwide are infected with the disease, and up to a million die from it each year.[24] Some 90 percent of malaria-related deaths occur in sub-Saharan Africa, mostly among children. Malaria, like many other diseases, mostly afflicts the poor. Its resurgence is being driven by a number of factors, including "the rapid spread of drug resistance among malarial parasites, changing rainfall patterns, and water development projects such as dams, which create new mosquito breeding grounds."[25]

Even in the developed world, disease takes a ghastly toll. In the United States, infectious disease remains the third-leading cause of death. Many medical researchers are now worried that the overuse—and the misuse—of antibiotics may be stimulating the development of drug-resistant strains of bacteria, thus diminishing the world's capacity to overcome many common diseases. This concern raises an important and very disturbing aspect of humanity's battle with disease. Just as action-reaction processes sometimes characterize conflicts between or among countries, a pattern in which the defensive measures of one side prompt the development of countermeasures by the other side, so the human conflict with pathogenic microbes involves an unending quest for biological escalation dominance. Diseases mutate in ways that, at the risk of making them seem human, appear fiendishly clever. Thus, the influenza vaccine developed to protect the most vulnerable people in society (generally the elderly and the young) from the ill effects of one flu season are unlikely to have any effect against the influenza strains that spread through the population a year later.

As we have pointed out with respect to other security issues, actions taken to defend against threats often have the unintended effect of becoming threats themselves. In the case of antibiotics, drugs developed to defend against infection may actually assist pathogens in developing mutations that are not affected by the antibiotic. A pertinent example of problematic pathogen evolution is multidrug-resistant tuberculosis (MDR-TB) and even more lethal extensively drug resistant TB (XDR-TB) found in Central Asia and Africa. In a sense, the actions taken to defend against the tuberculosis threat have helped to produce a new threat.

What some of the world's emerging diseases lack (so far) in numbers of victims they more than make up for in the ghastliness of their effects on human beings. Whether spread deliberately or not, an outbreak of Ebola in the

United States would introduce an element of insecurity related as much to the disease's symptoms as to its contagiousness or lethality.

In 1967, a hemorrhagic fever closely related to Ebola, called Marburg fever (for the German city where it was first seen), briefly made the jump from Africa to Europe when three workers at a pharmaceutical plant fell ill with flu-like symptoms. They were hospitalized, but their condition rapidly worsened; nausea, enlarged spleens, and bloodshot eyes appeared first. Then came red rashes, raw throats, and acute diarrhea. In the second week, the entire body of those affected became red in color as blood flow was blocked throughout the capillaries. This was accompanied by severe pain. Next, the vomiting of blood, the peeling of skin, and uncontrollable bleeding appeared. Several patients died, and others were left with assorted disabilities. The disease was traced to a group of monkeys that had been shipped to European labs from Uganda.[26] Not only is there no vaccine or cure for the Ebola and Marburg hemorrhagic fevers, but both are considered by public health officials to be excellent candidates for use as biological weapons.

Unfortunately, Marburg fever and Ebola are not the only diseases to jump from an animal species to humans, so-called zoonotic diseases. In 1997, there was an outbreak in Hong Kong of avian influenza virus (H5N1) that killed six of eighteen people infected with it.[27] Before this outbreak, scientists had thought that it was not possible for birds to infect humans. Following the initial outbreaks, millions of chickens, ducks, and other birds in Asia were killed in an attempt to destroy the virus. Yet in 2004, forty-four confirmed human cases of avian flu were documented in Thailand and Vietnam. Of those people infected, thirty-two died. While avian influenza cases remain rare— only 826 cases have been recorded from 2003 to 2015 from sixteen coutries worldwide—the disease remains worrisome because of its high lethality, at 53 percent.[28]

In November 2002, a new disease—severe acute respiratory syndrome, or SARS—was first identified in southern China. During the next two years, nine thousand cases were identified, and nine hundred people died of this new disease. Although SARS was mainly present in five Asian countries (China, Taiwan, Singapore, Vietnam, and Thailand), it spread to nineteen additional countries and had global implications. The outbreak of SARS in Canada caused a downturn in U.S. tourist visits there, with significant economic repercussions for Canada. SARS had a major impact on China. When the government after a long delay acknowledged the existence of the disease, an estimated "250,000 students, migrant workers and SARS-fearing citizens fled Beijing."[29] In addition to public panic, SARS resulted in close to a 1 percent decline in China's GDP. Fortunately, within two years of the initial outbreak of SARS, a treatment regimen and a vaccine had been developed.

In spite of the brief incursions into the developed world that Marburg fever, Ebola, avian flu, SARS, and certain other emerging infectious diseases have made, it may be tempting to think of such diseases as someone else's problem. After all, most of these newly discovered diseases were native to Africa and Asia and, with some rare exceptions, were largely confined to these areas. Other debilitating diseases, such as cholera and malaria, are primarily found in developing countries, and the public health systems of developed countries like the United States have, with few exceptions, either beaten back these scourges or kept them at bay.

It is unwise, however, to assume that the world's bacteriological and viral problems have always been stopped at the borders or that they will be in the future. Globalization has always encouraged a robust exchange of microbes along with goods and services. Recall that it was merchants returning from Asia to Europe who carried bubonic plague in the fourteenth century. Remember, too, that two sailors disembarking in Boston in 1918 brought the Spanish influenza to American shores. The approach of both American and international public health officials in combating infectious disease has been, according to Laurie Garrett, based on two false assumptions: "that microbes were biologically stationary targets and that the diseases could be geographically sequestered."[30] The greater the level of exchange of persons and products in the world—that is, the greater the degree of globalization—the greater will be the possibility that deadly pathogens also will travel.

Time is no ally. In 1350 BC the first epidemic of smallpox was identified in Egypt. It had spread to China by 49 AD, to Europe after 700, the Western Hemisphere by 1520, and Australia by 1789.[31] Thus, it took smallpox a little over three thousand years to circumnavigate the globe. By contrast, it took HIV/AIDS only about thirty years to do so. Globalization collapses time needed for the spread of infectious diseases.

Potential for the global spread of infectious diseases is related to the different incubation periods of infectious diseases and has a profound impact on public health. Smallpox, for example, has an incubation period from ten to fourteen days. Thanks to the ease and efficiency of international air travel, an individual who carries the smallpox virus could visit half a dozen or more of the world's major cities in the time between contracting the disease and first noticing the symptoms. Add to this disturbing reality the fact that more people than ever before are traveling long distances. In 1951, there were seven million airline passengers. The number topped five hundred million (or 1.4 million per day) by 1993, and it totaled 3.3 billion in 2014. As the Nobel Prize–winning geneticist Joshua Lederberg puts it, "The world is just one village. Our tolerance of disease in any place is at our own peril."[32]

HIV/AIDS

Nowhere is this truth more evident than in the case of the human immuno-deficiency virus (HIV) and acquired immune deficiency syndrome (AIDS). HIV/AIDS is recognized as a clear and present danger. Today, thirty-five million people worldwide are living with HIV/AIDS; 2.1 million new cases of HIV/AIDS infection occurred worldwide in 2013, and an estimated 1.5 million died from the disease in that year.[33] Since the disease was first identified over thirty years ago, thirty-nine million people have died worldwide, and seventy-eight million people have been infected. Over 90 percent of those infected with HIV are in the developing world, 24.5 million in sub-Saharan Africa alone.[34] Clearly, Africa is the epicenter of the AIDS pandemic.

One significant effect of the HIV/AIDS pandemic has been the creation of large numbers of "AIDS orphans." The Joint United Nations Programme on HIV/AIDS (UNAIDS) estimates that in 2013 there were 17.7 million children under eighteen who had lost one or both parents to AIDS; roughly 86 percent of these children are in sub-Saharan Africa, including 2.2 million in Nigeria.[35] AIDS orphans are less likely to remain in school and are more vulnerable to exploitation by sex traffickers or warlords. Many fear that the "lost orphan generation" created by AIDS deaths will exacerbate the child-soldier problem. With no parents to provide for and supervise them, orphaned children have been recruited by unscrupulous warlords and guerrilla groups as soldiers. Sadly, child soldiers existed before the scourge of AIDS, but by creating millions of orphans the HIV/AIDS pandemic has made the child-soldier problem much worse. It is likely to continue to worsen far into the future.

AIDS is a crisis for both the developed and the developing worlds. To date, more than 660,000 people have died with an AIDS diagnosis in the United States. This figure is approximately 133 percent of the total number of Americans killed in World War II, the Korean War, and the Vietnam War combined. For this reason, and because of the threat that the HIV/AIDS pandemic represents to the political, social, and economic stability of the world, in April 2000 President Clinton declared that AIDS represented a "national security threat." The National Intelligence Council, a U.S. government advisory body, issued a national intelligence estimate in 2000 titled "The Global Infectious Disease Threat and Its Implications for the United States." Currently the Central Intelligence Agency actively recruits medical analysts specializing in internal medicine, epidemiology, infectious diseases, and public health.[36]

Concern over infectious diseases is not a partisan issue. In his confirmation hearings to become secretary of state, Colin Powell noted that he, like President Clinton, viewed HIV/AIDS as a "national security threat." Former president George W. Bush stated that "AIDS is the greatest health crisis of our time."[37] Commenting on the 2014 Ebola outbreak, President Obama said, "I consider this a top national security priority. This is not just a matter of charity—although obviously the humanitarian toll in countries that are affected in West Africa is extraordinarily significant. This is an issue about our safety. It is also an issue with respect to the political stability and the economic stability in this region."[38] Both Republican and Democratic leaders in the United States have consistently portrayed infectious diseases as a threat to security.

A number of other governments, international and nongovernmental organizations, and individual analysts have focused on AIDS as a security threat. P. W. Singer, for example, writing in *Survival*, the journal of the respected International Institute for Strategic Studies, has argued that AIDS poses a direct danger to national and international stability and is a threat to the militaries of countries.[39] In regard to the AIDS threat to military forces, Singer notes that studies consistently indicate that the infection rates in African military forces are around five times that of civilian populations and that during times of war infection rates can be as much as fifty times higher.[40] The average rate of infection for African militaries is 30 percent, but for some countries it is much higher. Estimates indicate that infection rates are as high as 50 percent for the Congo and Angola, 66 percent for Uganda, 75 percent in Malawi, and 80 percent in Zimbabwe. The United Nations draws many of its peacekeeping forces from the ranks of African militaries. If AIDS infection rates continue to grow, many African militaries will be unable to provide forces. Singer concludes, "AIDS is indeed a security threat and should be treated as such, with the high-level attention and resources necessary to defend against it. Fighting AIDS is not just a matter of altruism, but enlightened self interest."[41]

In an early analysis of the link between AIDS and security, the nongovernmental International Crisis Group argued that AIDS is significant in five different senses: as a personal issue, an economic issue, a communal security issue, a national security issue, and as an international security issue.[42] On the personal level, AIDS threatens the "lives, health, family structure, and well being of individuals and entire communities."[43] In an economic sense, "AIDS puts at risk human capital and natural resource development, and business investment, which form the foundation of national economies."[44] AIDS affects not only a country's economic performance but also its community and social cohesion. According to the British House of Commons, "Evidence suggests that in societies facing economic crisis and lack of clear political leadership the presence of AIDS with its associated stigma may cause instability. The citizens are aware of the increase in illness and death, the stigma associated with it; and the lack of leadership leads to blame."[45] AIDS has the potential to threaten both individual states' national security and broader international security.

Acknowledging the tragic effects of, and the threat posed by, the AIDS pandemic, in his 2003 State of the Union address George W. Bush announced the establishment of the President's Emergency Plan for AIDS Relief (PEP-FAR), describing it as "a work of mercy beyond all current international efforts to help the people of Africa."[46] Bush pledged that the United States would provide $15 billion over a five-year period. Initially, the Bush administration identified fourteen countries (twelve of them in sub-Saharan Africa) to which aid would be directed: Guyana, Haiti, Botswana, Côte d'Ivoire, Ethiopia, Kenya, Mozambique, Namibia, Nigeria, Rwanda, South Africa, Tanzania, Uganda, and Zambia. Congress later instructed the president to add a fifteenth country outside of the Caribbean or Africa, and Vietnam was accordingly added to the list in the summer of 2004. In 2008, PEPFAR was reauthorized for an additional five years at up to $48 billion.

Since its inception through 2014, the PEPFAR program has provided anti-retroviral treatment for 7.7 million people worldwide, HIV testing and counseling for 56.7 million people (including 14.2 million pregnant women), 6.5 million voluntary medical male circumcision procedures, care and support for more than 5 million orphans and at-risk children, and training for more than 140,000 new health care workers in PEPFAR-supported countries.[47] Commenting on PEPFAR in his memoirs, George W. Bush wrote, "I hoped it would serve as a medical version of the Marshall Plan." The program became the largest appropriation of funds by a country to combat a single disease in history, and many historians believe that it will be remembered as the most positive accomplishment of the forty-third president's two terms in office.

ADDRESSING THE THREAT OF DISEASE

Clearly much can be done to confront the threats posed by infectious diseases. The past can be a guide to the future. As we noted earlier, the World Health Organization, with the cooperation of member states, was able to eradicate endemic smallpox. The way this was accomplished suggests how threats in this area might be addressed. The most striking aspect of WHO's effective campaign to eliminate smallpox was the cooperation of states, international organizations, and nongovernmental organizations. Indeed, cooperation by various types of international actors is key to confronting the threat of infectious disease.

The Gavi Alliance (formerly the Global Alliance for Vaccines and Immunizations) provides an example of what can be accomplished through a

broad-based, cooperative approach among global actors including governments, international organizations, NGOs, and the private sector. Established
in 2000 with an initial grant of $750 million from the Bill and Melinda Gates
Foundation, the Gavi Alliance makes vaccines and immunizations available
to those in the world's poorest states. Through the end of 2014, the Alliance
estimated that its program of immunizations, along with its investments in
other vaccination efforts in seventy-three developing countries, had prevented the future deaths of 3.1 million people, most of them children. A total
of 257 million children worldwide received vaccinations as a consequence of
almost $5 billion in donations from states and nonprofit organizations fun-
neled through the Gavi Alliance during its first decade of existence.[48]

The Gates Foundation, which is the wealthiest foundation in the world,
has thus far distributed over $30 billion, much of it to improve global health.
New York Times columnist Thomas Friedman has called Bill Gates a "super-
empowered individual" because of his ability to act as a "game-changer"
on matters of global concern, including the infectious disease threat. In
2010, Gates and investor Warren Buffett challenged their fellow billionaires
to pledge to give away at least half of their fortunes to charity, and, as of
2015, more than 130 of the richest people in the world, including Facebook
founder Mark Zuckerberg, Oracle founder Larry Ellison, and CNN founder
Ted Turner, had taken this pledge. The actions of these individuals and the
philanthropic organizations that they have supported provide a reminder of
the increasing importance of nonstate actors in international relations.[49]

The response to date to the threat of HIV/AIDS offers both positive and
negative lessons. Resources are vital. The contrasts between health expenditures in developing and developed states are stark. The World Heath Organization has calculated (on the basis of 2004 data) that health spending in
the states of the Organisation for Economic Co-operation and Development
(OECD) averages $2,716 per person per year. In contrast, there are sixty-four
WHO member states in which health spending is under $50 per person per
year. OECD member states contain 18 percent of the world's population and
spend 80 percent of the world's health care dollars.[50]

When the first effective treatments for HIV/AIDS were developed in the
1990s, the cost of treating someone infected with the disease was between
$10,000 and $15,000 per year, putting treatment far beyond the reach of
almost everyone in the developing world. A combination of developments
helped to increase access to antiretroviral (ARV) drugs. First, the major
pharmaceutical companies holding patents on the drugs began to negotiate
lower prices in an effort to make treatment programs more affordable to those
governments, international organizations, and NGOs attempting to slow the
spread of HIV/AIDS in the developing world. Second, the Clinton adminis-

tration announced that it would not intervene on behalf of drug companies in cases in which African countries decided to violate international patents for ARV therapies. Third, in 2001, an Indian drug manufacturer began to produce a generic form of the most popular form of combination therapy. This made treatment far more affordable and touched off a round of price cutting by companies making patented drugs. Fourth, after leaving office, Bill Clinton created the William J. Clinton Foundation, which had as one of its global priorities improving access to health care in the developing world. The Clinton Foundation, together with Doctors without Borders and other NGOs, entered into negotiations with drug companies and governments to secure even lower prices for drugs used in the treatment of HIV/AIDS. Finally, PEPFAR began operating in 2004 with the primary objective of providing funding for HIV/ AIDS treatment in some of the world's poorest, and most seriously affected, countries.[51]

It is vital that wealthy countries make and maintain their commitment to confront the threats posed by infectious diseases. In this regard, the commitment by the United States in the President's Emergency Plan for AIDS Relief is noteworthy but must be fully funded. The effects of the 2008 economic crisis combined with lagging political will have resulted in a failure to fully honor financial commitments to improve access to health in the developing world.

Another important aspect of addressing the pandemic of HIV/AIDS and other infectious diseases concerns female literacy. Studies indicate that the number of women infected with HIV/AIDS constitutes more than half of people living with AIDS, and that HIV/AIDS is the leading cause of death for women in their reproductive years (fifteen to forty-nine years old). This is due to the ways in which HIV/AIDS is transmitted. In many cases in the developing world, older males who frequent prostitutes or use intravenous drugs marry younger women and infect them with HIV/AIDS. Because two-thirds of the world's illiterate people are women, many women are unaware of the dangers of and precautions against HIV/AIDS infection. Increasing women's literacy programs is one way of addressing the problem of AIDS and other health issues. For example, women who read are more likely to be able to provide for their families and to obtain medical care for their children. Increasing women's literacy is also a means of addressing population control and economic development in that, as studies have shown, "for every three years of education that you provide a woman, it tends to reduce their own individual birth rate by one child."[52] The World Bank has found that "women with a post-secondary education are three times more likely than uneducated women to know that HIV can be transmitted from mother to child."[53] Educating women can have salutary economic effects; for example, increasing the level of education and resources available to female farmers to the same level as male farmers increased crop yields as much as 22 percent.[54] In its study of the world of 2020, the National Intelligence Council stated, "A growing body of empirical literature suggests that gender equality in education promotes economic growth and reduces child mortality and malnutrition."[55]

In December 2004, the U.S. National Intelligence Council noted the very real and substantial threat of disease in the report on its 2020 Project. The Council concluded that while terrorism could slow globalization, a widespread pandemic could stop it altogether.[56] Such a development would have profound implications for the future of civilization as we know it. For this reason, the threat of infectious disease may be the most serious that exists.

ADDITIONAL RESOURCES

Books and Articles

Brower, Jennifer, and Peter Chalk. *The Global Threat of New and Reemerging Infectious Diseases: Reconciling U.S. National Security and Public Health Policy*. Santa Monica, CA: RAND Corporation, 2003.

Crawford, Dorothy. *Deadly Companions: How Microbes Shaped Our History*. New York: Oxford University Press, 2009.

Garrett, Laurie. *Betrayal of Trust: The Collapse of Global Public Health*. New York: Hyperion, 2000.

———. "The Lessons of HIV/AIDS." *Foreign Affairs* 84 (July/August 2005): 51–65.

———. *Ebola: Story of an Outbreak*. New York: Hachette, 2014.

McNeill, William. *Plagues and Peoples*. New York: Anchor Books, 1976.

Oldstone, Michael. *Viruses, Plagues, and History*. New York: Oxford University Press, 2000.

Price-Smith, Andrew T. *The Health of Nations: Infectious Disease, Environmental Change, and Their Effects on National Security and Development*. Cambridge, MA: MIT Press, 2002.

Singer, P. W. "AIDS and International Security." *Survival* 44 (Spring 2002): 145–58.

Tucker, Jonathan B. *Scourge: The Once and Future Threat of Smallpox*. Boston: Atlantic Monthly, 2001.

U.S. National Intelligence Council. *The Global Infectious Disease Threat and Its Implications for the United States*. NIE-99-17D. Washington, DC: January 2000.

Websites

Centers for Disease Control and Prevention: www.cdc.gov

Council on Foreign Relations. *Map: Vaccine-Preventable Outbreaks*: http://www.cfr .org/interactives/GH_Vaccine_Map/index.html#map

Doctors without Borders (*Médecins sans Frontières*): http://www.doctorswithout
  borders.org
Gavi: The Vaccine Alliance: www.gavi.org
National Institutes of Health: www.nih.gov
Roll Back Malaria Campaign, World Health Organization: www.rbm.who.int
United Nations Programme on HIV/AIDS (UNAIDS): www.unaids.org
World Health Organization: www.who.int

Films

The Andromeda Strain (1971): Based on the book by Michael Crichton, this science
  fiction movie deals with a new, almost completely fatal virus inadvertently brought
  to Earth from a satellite recovered from space. The virus threatens the world's entire population. Universal Pictures. Directed by Robert Wise.
Contagion (2011): A feature film starring Gwyneth Paltrow that follows the spread
  of an airborne virus that is fatal within days. Warner Bros. Directed by Steven
  Soderbergh.
Outbreak (1995): A feature film starring Dustin Hoffman and Morgan Freeman that
  focuses on Army medical researchers trying to stop a fast-spreading, deadly virus
  Warner Bros. Directed by Wolfgang Petersen.
Outbreak, Frontline (PBS/WGBH, 2015). An in-depth report on the orgins of the
  2014 outbreak of Ebola in West Africa.

Chapter Eight

Transnational Criminal Organizations and Trafficking

Organized crime constitutes nothing less than a guerrilla war against society.

—Lyndon B. Johnson

Willie Sutton, a career criminal with a special fondness for armed heists, is said to have told a reporter who asked why he robbed banks, "That's where the money is." Today the big money is found elsewhere—in drug trafficking, the sale of counterfeit goods, and even in that most tragic anachronism, human bondage. Organized crime groups, which were once generally localized like the Cosa Nostra in Sicily or the Green Gang in Shanghai, have evolved into transnational criminal organizations (TCOs) that are now able, like multinational corporations, to leverage the advantages of globalized markets to generate vast profits. And just as multinationals exploit the differences among states in areas such as finance, labor, and environmental protection, transnational criminal organizations exploit differences in criminal law and, more important, law enforcement. TCOs thrive where the state's capacity to make and enforce law is weak due to indifference, corruption, or conflict. Unfortunately, transnational crime is not just a beneficiary of political instability but also a major cause.

A study published in 2010 by the United Nations Office on Drugs and Crime (UNODC) estimated that transnational organized crime (TOC) generated $870 billion the previous year, or roughly 1.5 percent of the world's total economic output.[1] While revenues vary by region of the world and by activity from year to year—arms trafficking, for example, rises and falls in profitability as wars begin and end—trafficking income, on the whole, seems to be steadily rising. Given the illicit nature of the activities that TCOs are engaged in, accurate data is difficult to come by, but there are some clear indicators to be found in stories of law enforcement successes. For example, in the space of a decade counterfeit goods detected at Europe's borders increased tenfold.

The effects of transnational organized crime are not merely economic in character. There are significant impacts on human, national, and international security. As the May 2010 *National Security Strategy of the United States* noted, threats posed by TCOs "cross borders and undermine the stability of nations, subverting government institutions through corruption and harming citizens worldwide." Transnational organized crime compromises the stability of states, and thus constitutes a national security threat, in a number of ways. It provides funding for insurgents, often by trafficking resources such as oil, diamonds, or even wildlife found in areas controlled by the insurgents. At the same time, the wealth generated by trafficking may create a disincentive for warlords to make peace. Transnational organized crime may threaten or even undermine completely the rule of law by corrupting lawmakers and law enforcement officials with wealth generated by criminal activities or by intimidating them with threats or acts of violence. In its quest for profits, it may provide support for terrorists regardless of their targets or objectives. Finally, in the course of establishing networks for illicit trade in drugs, counterfeit goods, or human beings, transnational criminal organizations may open up new possibilities for trafficking in firearms, missiles, or even nuclear weapons.

The global reach of transnational criminal organizations has been facilitated by many of the features of what we commonly call "globalization." Globalization allows consumers in the advanced industrialized states to buy clothing manufactured in Bangladesh, computers assembled in Indonesia, and insurance policies sold by telemarketers in India, but it also allows consumers—sometimes the very same consumers—to buy heroin manufactured from poppies grown in Afghanistan, antiquities illegally exported from Egypt, and even young girls kidnapped and trafficked from Thailand. Not only are traffickers able to move commodities easily, but they can also move money with little trouble. Thanks to the rise of a globalized system of finance based on electronic transfers of funds and simple currency conversions, moving money around the world has never been easier, although those same systems combined with rules adopted after 9/11 have improved the ability of governments to track financial flows.

TRAFFICKING AND TRANSNATIONAL CRIMINAL ORGANIZATIONS

While globalization has created the environment, it is the trade—the illegal trade or *trafficking*—that raises security issues. The term *trafficking* refers to commerce involving legal goods (such as cigarettes or computers) traded illegally (by, for example, evading taxes or contravening export or import restrictions) and to commerce involving illegal goods (such as narcotics or human beings) when traded in any manner whatsoever.

Trafficking, although dramatically expanded by it, is not a product of globalization. In fact, both in the form of the illicit trade of legal goods and in the form of commerce in illegal goods, trafficking is an ancient activity that has involved, at various points in history, the bones of saints, Dutch tulips, and literature on birth control.

Although the list of legal and illegal items of trade has changed over time, even today a wide variety of commodities is trafficked. The list includes highly enriched uranium, endangered species of both plants and animals, stolen art, human organs, and illegally copied software, music, and movies (along with the commodities—and human lives—we will be focusing on in this chapter). Although it is impossible to know exactly how much wealth is generated by criminal enterprises, most experts believe that drug trafficking and arms trafficking are the two most lucrative forms of trafficking. In fact, drug trafficking is believed to rank behind only the global trade in petroleum as a source of wealth. Human trafficking is generally thought to rank third, with the illicit trade in cultural property, including art and antiquities, ranking fourth in total value.

Behind most of the trafficking that occurs are transnational criminal organizations (TCOs). Some of the biggest and most influential TCOs are well known—the Italian mafia, the Mexican drug cartels, the Japanese *yakuza*, and the Russian mobs, for example—but many more operate entirely in the shadows. What is perhaps most remarkable about TCOs is the extent to which their power has increased. All operate beyond the sovereignty of any state— that is, outside the law—but that has always been true of criminal enterprises. What is different now is that TCOs actually challenge the sovereignty of some states in areas well beyond the illegal activities that form the core of their identity. To put it differently, TCOs have come to control territory, extract rents (i.e., taxes) in areas under their control, provide services for local populations, and even wage war. All of these are functions that are normally associated with sovereign states.

In a few extreme cases, TCOs have gone beyond performing governmental functions and have actually taken over a state. The process may begin with bribery or attempts to intimidate public officials. Assassinations—of judges, legislators, police officials, and military officers—may follow. Eventually, as in Colombia in the 1990s, criminals and representatives of the state may decide some form of accommodation is preferable to continued violence. In 2001, a secret agreement called the Pact of Ralito was negotiated by a group

of Colombian paramilitary leaders, mayors, congressmen, and business leaders. It called for nothing less than the reform of the state—along lines favorable to the interests of the drug cartels. Some believe that Mexico's criminal
syndicates, engaged in a long-running struggle with the federal government
and with each other, are moving toward a strategy of coopting rather than
confronting the state.[2]

The wealth of some TCOs—especially certain drug cartels—has permitted
them to arm themselves with sophisticated weaponry and other technologies
capable in some instances of matching those wielded by states. For example,
Pablo Escobar reportedly tried to purchase surface-to-air missiles (SAMs) for
the Medellín cartel.[3] Mexican drug cartels have used the "narco submarines"
pioneered by Colombian cartels as well as drones (carrying, on average,
thirteen kilos per flight) to transport drugs into the United States,[4] especially
as U.S. Customs and Border Protection agents have become more adept at
finding tunnels under the border and tracking ultra-light aircraft flying over
the border. Although some improvements are occurring, states generally have
been ill adapted to addressing the problems that TCOs present. As Roy Godson and Phil Williams note, "Governments are equipped and experienced in
dealing with security threats from other governments. They are neither com-
fortable nor familiar with threats that are nonmilitary in character, that target
society and the economy rather than the state per se, and that cannot be dealt
with through traditional state-centric policy options."[5]

Different forms of trafficking raise different sorts of security issues. Human trafficking, for example, presents what is most commonly regarded as a
human rights issue rather than a security issue. In the United States, responsibility for combating human trafficking rests with the Department of State and
the Department of Justice, a clear indication that the issue has not been fully
"securitized." Of course, to those trapped in modern forms of slavery, human
trafficking is a security issue of the highest order. To security analysts, this
form of trafficking could be said to raise security issues only in the context
of human security, according to which most, if not all, of those matters that
affect the security of individual human beings (as opposed to those that affect
the state only) are securitized. It is fair to ask, though, whether enslavement
associated with war (as in Sudan) or with the economic activities of a sovereign state (as in North Korea) may move human trafficking toward inclusion
as a national security issue. There are some indications, including a special
report on human trafficking published by the director of central intelligence
in 1999, that such a move is occurring in the United States.[6]

Drug trafficking, like human trafficking, generates enormous wealth for
criminals but tragic consequences for many of the individuals who are caught
up in drug abuse or the violence commonly associated with it. It also seems

to lend itself to legal rather than military responses. Unlike human trafficking, however, drug trafficking has been not only criminalized (with responsibility for addressing drug problems in the United States vested in a variety of law enforcement agencies, including the Drug Enforcement Agency [DEA], and in the Office of National Drug Control Policy) but also securitized. Since the late 1980s, the U.S. military's Southern Command has been assigned the task of assisting Colombia's struggle against drug trafficking and, more broadly, seeking to interdict shipments of drugs destined for the United States. The intermixing of drug trafficking and revolutionary violence in Colombia, Afghanistan, and the Golden Triangle of Southeast Asia raises security concerns as well.

The nature and fundamental purpose of the commodity being traded makes arms trafficking a national security issue. The illicit trade in weapons has long been implicated as a key factor in promoting and sustaining wars and revolutionary violence. It is not necessary, in other words, to be an advocate of a broader security agenda in order to view arms trafficking as a bona fide security issue. At the same time, certain characteristics of the illegal trade in arms (such as its role in facilitating the growth in the number of child soldiers worldwide) have made the trade (both legal and illegal) a key concern among advocates of human security.

We focus on these three forms of trafficking—human trafficking, drug trafficking, and arms trafficking—both because they represent significant threats to the well-being of individual human beings across the globe and because they help to illustrate different stages in the securitization of political issues. Human trafficking represents the entering wedge: a crime and a human rights concern but not yet, at least outside the realm of human security, a fully securitized problem. Drug trafficking has made the transition, so armed forces actually stand behind at least a portion of the "war on drugs." Arms trafficking has been a security issue at least since Caribbean gunrunners supplied weapons to the Confederacy during the Civil War, but it nonetheless has much in common with other forms of trafficking.

HUMAN TRAFFICKING

The U.S. State Department estimates that six to eight hundred thousand people are trafficked internationally each year, although the number may be far higher.[7] Worldwide, there are an estimated 20.9 million people held in some form of forced labor, bonded labor (in which a person is required to work until a debt to a trafficker is paid off), or forced prostitution.[8] These are the basic forms of modern slavery. In some places, such as Sudan, slavery exists in a form not very different from that which existed in the United States up to the end of the Civil War. Elsewhere, as in South Asia, involuntary servitude is linked to industrialization, as people—often women and children—are forced to work in sweatshops making clothes, shoes, sporting goods, toys, or other consumer products sold worldwide. In Haiti, as many as three hundred thousand children, some as young as four years old, have been forced to work in exchange for food, shelter, and an opportunity to attend school. The *restaveks* (from the French *reste avec*, for "stay with") are given up by parents who are too poor to care for them.[9] Finally, according to human rights groups, one hundred thousand North Korean workers have been sent abroad to work long hours as loggers in Siberia, factory workers in China, construction workers in Kuwait, or other strenuous jobs with wages being confiscated by a North Korean government desperate for foreign currencies.[10] In this case, North Korea has assumed the role of a transnational criminal organization.[11]

One of the most disturbing forms of modern slavery is sex slavery. Eighty percent of those trafficked into the United States are women and young girls; most are victims of sex trafficking.[12] In Tel Aviv and Dubai, women lured by the prospect of legitimate work as waitresses or sales clerks are trafficked from Eastern Europe and Russia and forced into prostitution.[13] The phenomenon is global, and generally unidirectional, with sex slaves, like those engaged in forced labor, moving from poorer states to richer ones.

Human trafficking, like drug trafficking and arms trafficking, flourishes because it is lucrative. A study prepared for the International Labor Organization has estimated that forced labor generates a profit of $150 billion per year.[14] The same patterns of globalization that have fostered the dramatic growth of transnational trade in such legitimate commodities as automobiles and consumer electronics have benefited human trafficking. Human trafficking, in other words, represents the underside of globalization.

Traffickers not only treat human beings as commodities to be bought and sold but also prey on the worst forms of human tragedy. People in crushing poverty are the most vulnerable to the false promises that traffickers use to ensnare their victims. Likewise, when children are sold to owners of sweatshops or brothels, it is often a desperate attempt by parents to sustain themselves and their remaining children. Not surprisingly, child labor is most prevalent in the world's least developed countries. For this reason, economic security provides the best protection against most forms of human trafficking.

The exploitation of tragedy on the part of human traffickers reached disturbing new lows in the aftermath of the South Asian tsunami disaster in 2004. In Aceh (Indonesia), Sri Lanka, and elsewhere, human trafficking networks attempted soon after the tragedy to sell orphans to prospective adoptive parents and to sweatshops. Governments in the region responded by restricting travel by children, posting guards at some orphanages, and accelerating efforts to locate relatives of children orphaned by the disaster.[15] Following the earthquake that devastated Haiti in 2009, officials in both Haiti and the neighboring Dominican Republic made efforts to prevent orphaned children from being trafficked. A subsequent investigation, however, found that over 7,300 children were smuggled into the Dominican Republic from Haiti following the disaster.[16]

As noted earlier, globalization helps to explain certain elements of human trafficking. International travel has become (in historical terms) inexpensive and simple. The increasing wealth of many of the world's people has dramatically expanded markets for domestic laborers (especially maids and nannies, who, even if not trafficked, are sometimes vulnerable to exploitation or enslavement by unscrupulous employers), for consumer goods that are sometimes manufactured in sweatshops, and for sex tourism. And yet, at the same time, boundaries and other traditional barriers thrown up by sovereignty may provide certain protections to traffickers. Phil Williams explains the situation this way: "Where market opportunities are lucrative, criminal organizations, large and small, ignore borders and typically violate or transcend national sovereignty; where they need safe havens they hide behind borders and exploit sovereignty."[17]

There is no question that human trafficking is an egregious abuse of human rights and a serious issue in international relations, but is it, in any sense, a security issue? The answer, as with many of the issues we consider in this book, is twofold. First, as we have noted, to those who lose their freedom and, in many cases, their lives as a consequence of trafficking, there can be no more serious and immediate threat to their security. Only those of us who are completely unaffected by human trafficking would even think to ask the question in the first place.

But, as with the issues of environmental and economic security and in the case of disease, the determination by governments that an issue constitutes a security problem (that is, the securitization of an issue) is often driven more by realist, state-centered calculations than by humanitarianism. In these terms, human trafficking differs significantly from drug trafficking and arms trafficking, although perhaps not as much as is commonly believed.

Drug trafficking and arms trafficking are considered security concerns in part because of the connection of each to violence and even warfare. Perhaps even more significantly from the standpoint of the traditional understanding of security, drug trafficking and arms trafficking have a demonstrated capacity to undermine states and threaten the stability of governments. Drug profits have sustained revolutionary and paramilitary organizations, while arms sales have altered power balances in both interstate and intrastate conflicts. Human trafficking, however tragic its impact on its victims, appears not to destabilize governments or to promote large-scale violence. Consequently, traditionalists have seen no reason to securitize the issue.

DRUG TRAFFICKING

Worldwide there are two hundred million users of illicit drugs supporting an industry that, by some estimates, generates almost as much revenue each year as the petroleum industry. (As with all illegal commercial activities, an accurate accounting of drug trafficking revenues is difficult to obtain, but drugs are estimated to generate half of global revenues attributable to transnational organized crime, or roughly $450 billion per year.[18]) In the words of a recent report by the UN Office on Drugs and Crime (UNODC), "Drugs remain the backbone of transnational organized crime, commanding the largest share of revenues and fuelling violence, corruption, conflict, and addiction."[19]

Demand for illicit drugs is fed by a global network of production and distribution. It is this network, linked as it is to TCOs, corrupt or impotent governments, rebel groups, and sometimes terrorists, that makes drug trafficking a major transnational problem. But is it a security issue?

One way to answer this question is to note the way the United States has approached drug trafficking since 1982, when President Reagan brought together the heads of eighteen federal agencies in an effort to attach new weight to the federal government's drug-control efforts. National drug policy, which is directed by a "drug czar" who heads the Office of National Drug Control Policy that was created within the Executive Office of the President in 1989, has been both securitized and militarized.

In 1989, the Department of Defense was designated the "single lead agency" in America's war on drugs. With the Cold War winding down, defense dollars began to be shifted into an effort to stem the tide of illegal drugs entering the United States. From the beginning, however, drug interdiction efforts were focused on a single aspect of drug trafficking—namely, the flow of cocaine from South America into the country. Cocaine, at that time, was the most visible drug problem facing Americans. By 1989, there were at least eight million cocaine addicts in the United States, including a significant number of well-known entertainment and sports personalities, so it is not surprising that cocaine produced in the Andes should have been the focus of the early war on drugs.

Responsibility for the military component of the war on drugs was placed on the Miami-based Southern Command (SOUTHCOM), which provided military support, primarily in the form of ships and aircraft, to the Joint Interagency

Task Force (JIATF). This group, in turn, brought together not only the Defense Department but also the Coast Guard, the Customs Service, the Drug Enforcement Agency, and other federal agencies with responsibility for drug control efforts. Today, at the U.S. government's El Paso Intelligence Center, over twenty different U.S. government agencies and departments are represented.[20]

Aside from the fact that it largely ignored a wide range of drugs coming from other parts of the world (including heroin from South Asia), the war on drugs suffered from a number of problems. First, efforts to suppress drug production in one area inevitably create incentives for production in another area. Even the successes achieved in Colombia in the disruption of the Medellín and Cali cartels merely spurred the creation of scores of smaller cartels. Second, the focus on production rather than consumption is problematic in and of itself. It means that the United States is widely perceived as treating its drug problem by lashing out at poor countries around the world rather than by taking responsibility for ending drug use at home. Intervention to destroy drug crops or arrest drug traffickers in places such as Colombia or Afghanistan can arouse resentment at what appears to be another form of imperialism as powerful countries attempt to solve their drug problem "over there" on the supply side rather than at home on the demand side. Furthermore, to destroy coca plants or poppies is, generally, to destroy the livelihoods of poor farmers without affecting the obscene profits of middlemen.

Declaring war on drugs does not, of course, guarantee that the problem will be treated as a security issue or, more to the point, that it should be. Antidrug policies necessarily involve efforts to reduce both supply *and* demand. When the demand comes from one's own citizens, the idea of a war on drugs, even if only metaphorical, seems inapt.

Regardless of how one views the American war on drugs, there are plenty of reasons to treat drug trafficking as a security issue. First, drug traffickers regularly and persistently employ violence to intimidate government officials, battle with rival traffickers over access to markets and supplies, and use force to facilitate business in many other ways. The term *narcoterrorism* was, in fact, coined to describe the use of violence by drug syndicates against government officials, journalists, and others. In recent years, drug-related violence along the U.S.-Mexico border, involving both Mexican and American nationals, has reached epidemic proportions. A *Los Angeles Times* report on conditions in Reynosa, a border city with a population of seven hundred thousand where rival drug cartels are fighting for control, states, "This is a city under siege. It's a city where you avert your eyes when men clean their guns in the middle of the plazas. Where schoolchildren are put through the paces of *pecho a tierra* drills, literally, 'chest to the ground'—a duck-and-dive move for when the shooting starts."[21]

The language used by locals to speak of those who have fled the violence—calling them "refugees" and "displaced persons"—is the language of war. The mayor of Reynosa is among the refugees, having moved across the border into Texas in fear for his life. It is a well-founded fear; during the administration of President Felipe Calderón (2006–2012), the number of intentional homicides increased steadily due to the government's concerted effort to wage war on drug traffickers. Of approximately 120,000 intentional homicides during the six-year period, an estimated one-third to two-thirds (forty thousand to eighty thousand) were related to drug trafficking or organized crime based on the use of automatic weapons, the inclusions of messages, dismemberment, or evidence of torture.[22]

Concern in the United States about drug violence in Mexico has prompted enhanced security cooperation between the two countries. The U.S. Congress appropriated $1.6 billion in June 2008 to fund the Mérida Initiative, a plan to assist Mexico and the countries of Central America with equipment, training, and intelligence for the fight against drug trafficking. The Pentagon spent an additional $34 million in 2010 to train the Mexican military in counternarcotics operations using lessons learned battling the insurgencies in Iraq and Afghanistan.[23]

Beyond the actual use of violence by traffickers and military responses to it in places such as Colombia, Afghanistan, and Mexico, drug trafficking presents itself as a security issue for other reasons. Profits from drug trafficking are commonly used to purchase weapons. This means not only that arms trafficking and drug trafficking are frequently linked but also that drug cartels and other TCOs are sometimes better armed than the police (and even the military forces) of many states in which they operate. Drug profits support rebel groups and terrorist organizations as well. In Colombia, FARC (the Revolutionary Armed Forces of Colombia) funded its long-running effort to overthrow the government with drug money—as much as $300 million a year. The anti-Taliban Northern Alliance in Afghanistan funded its operations with heroin profits until the United States stepped in to provide support after 9/11. More recently, drug money has supported government officials, including Afghan president Hamid Karzai's brother. In Lebanon's Bekaa Valley, terrorist training camps have long operated side by side with fields cultivated with opium and cannabis. Finally, although considerable evidence suggests otherwise, there have long been suspicions that Al Qaeda profited from opium sales in the months leading up to 9/11.[24]

It takes very little in the way of drug profits to purchase a sizeable arsenal. The UNODC reports that on November 16, 2009, Nicaraguan authorities seized a shipment of weapons intended for Mexico's Sinaloa cartel. Included were fifty-nine assault rifles, twenty thousand rounds of ammunition, eight kilograms of TNT, two grenade launchers, and ten grenades. The estimated value of the shipment was less than $200,000. In contrast, when the Nicaraguan navy seized 2.4 tons of cocaine three days later, the estimated value of the shipment was $80 million.[25]

In addition to these direct security ramifications, drug trafficking is closely tied to many other global problems that raise security concerns. Beginning with their effects on consumers and working backward, we may note first that drugs have serious health consequences. Beyond the direct and readily observable health impact of illicit drugs like cocaine and heroin, the spread of HIV/AIDS has been linked to intravenous drug use. The societies in which drug abusers live and work must bear a variety of costs associated with the issue. Healthcare costs and productivity losses associated with illicit drug use in the United States each run into the billions of dollars each year. Crime is also closely correlated with the use of illicit drugs.

For Colombia, the problems associated with drug trafficking and the insurgency it sustained for almost three decades were staggering. Two million Colombians, out of a total population of thirty-six million, were displaced by guerrillas or drug traffickers. At the time, only Sudan and the Democratic Republic of the Congo had more internal refugees.[26]

In spite of the overthrow of the Taliban and the continuing presence of American troops in Afghanistan, opium production is booming there. Afghanistan accounted for 79 percent of global opium production in 2009, down from 84 percent the previous year. A report by the United Nations argued that the drug trade, which accounts for a staggering 60 percent of Afghanistan's gross domestic product, threatens to undermine democracy and strengthen terrorist organizations.[27]

As if the trade in illegal narcotics and wars between drug cartels were not bad enough, another form of drug trafficking exists that threatens to undermine global progress against infectious diseases. Because the pharmaceutical industry is globalized and highly profitable, a very large international trade in counterfeit drugs, assisted by the Internet, has arisen over the course of the past decade. The total value of counterfeit drug sales worldwide is thought to be $200 billion.[28] Given the lack of enforcement of regulations pertaining to prescription drugs, it seems likely that the value of counterfeit pharmaceutical sales could soon outpace trafficking in illegal drugs.

Not surprisingly, the world's poor are most seriously affected by the problems posed by counterfeit and mislabeled pharmaceuticals. Developing countries where regulation of prescription drugs is ineffective or even nonexistent and where people often cannot afford full-priced medications are particularly susceptible to unscrupulous manufacturers and sellers of fake drugs. In some cases, the fakes may be better than nothing, but often counterfeit drugs have serious consequences. Mass poisonings resulting in thousands of deaths have been traced to the use of diethylene glycol, an industrial solvent often used in antifreeze, in place of glycerin, a sweet syrup safe for human consumption, in cough and cold medicines. At least one hundred people in Panama died after taking liquid cold remedies laced with diethylene glycol.[29] Furthermore, when antibiotics and antimalarial drugs are manufactured with inadequate levels of the active ingredients, the development of drug-resistant strains of malaria and other infectious diseases can be hastened.

ARMS TRAFFICKING

Arms trafficking differs from human trafficking and drug trafficking in some ways that are important to note at the outset. First, the illegal trade in weapons is overshadowed by a vast legal—that is, government-sanctioned—trade in arms. (The legal global arms trade in 2011 was valued at $178 billion.[30]) Selling weapons, unlike selling human beings or nonmedicinal drugs, is not illegal in and of itself. Consequently, arms traffickers must either compete with states (or legal corporations operating with state sanction and, commonly, subsidies) or find niche markets in which legitimate arms merchants do not operate. In most instances, this means that traffickers sell to the only buyers with whom legal dealers will not do business: rebel armies, terrorist organizations, drug traffickers, and other actors that threaten states and international order.

Second, the impact of arms trafficking on security is neither indirect nor incidental. While it may be facile to suggest that weapons alone cause wars, the widespread availability of weapons is undoubtedly an important factor in both making the resort to war feasible and sustaining conflicts that are already under way. From 2008 to 2011, 79.2 percent of the world's legitimate arms sales (and, almost certainly, an even higher percentage of illicit sales) were directed toward developing states, a fact that reflects and also contributes to the war-proneness of the developing world.[31] Small arms, which are favorites of traffickers due to their widespread availability, their popularity with consumers, and their portability, were responsible for 44.1 percent of violent deaths (homicides, legal interventions, and direct conflict deaths) recorded from 2007 to 2012.[32]

Finally, arms traffickers have the perverse ability to turn conflict resolution and disarmament to their advantage as postwar demilitarization in one part of the world makes available a supply of weapons for sale elsewhere. The end of the Cold War, for example, resulted in the reduction of standing armies throughout NATO and the Warsaw Pact. While many weapons were destroyed or stockpiled in government arsenals, an unknown (but probably large) number of weapons entered into circulation via arms traffickers. As a result, arms traffickers may function as arbitrageurs of war and peace in the world.

One of the most notorious of these arbitrageurs is Viktor Bout, a Russian businessman who, in a report by the British government in 2000, was called "the Merchant of Death." (Bout was the inspiration for the Nicolas Cage character in the movie *Lord of War*.) Bout is alleged to have sold over seven hundred surface-to-air missiles, military helicopters and airplanes, and thousands of guns to FARC, the Colombian paramilitary organization. He has also sold weapons in Afghanistan and in various war zones in Africa. At a Bangkok hotel in March 2008, Bout offered undercover agents of the U.S. Drug Enforcement Agency posing as FARC representatives a wide range of weapons, including land mines, unmanned aerial vehicles (UAVs), and C-4 explosives. He was arrested at the conclusion of the meeting, which was taped, and, in August 2010, a Thai court ordered his extradition to stand trial in the United States. Following his conviction in a U.S. district court on charges of conspiring to kill U.S. citizens and providing aid to FARC, a designated terrorist organization, Bout was sentenced in April 2012 to twenty-five years in a federal prison.[33]

Arms traffickers are middlemen; they sell but do not manufacture weapons. Consequently, the arms that are available on the black market almost invariably were transferred first in legal transactions. Many such transactions have been designed to support the security policies of states. During the 1980s, billions of dollars worth of weapons were channeled into Afghanistan in order to aid Afghan rebels (the *mujahidin*) in their war against the Soviet Union. When the Soviet Union withdrew in 1989, vast quantities of weaponry disappeared. Much of it wound up on the black market. Among the most disturbing aspects of this situation was the disappearance of an unknown number of Stinger missiles onto the market. These shoulder-fired surface-to-air missiles, covertly supplied by the United States, had been used with devastating effect by the *mujahidin* against Soviet aircraft. Roughly 2,300 Stingers had been delivered to the Afghan rebels; six hundred were unaccounted for when Kabul fell to the Taliban. The CIA estimated that about one hundred had been purchased by the Iranians. The remainder were either in the hands of the Taliban and/or Afghan warlords or circulating, via the black market, all over the Middle East and Africa.[34]

Given the threat posed by surface-to-air missiles in the hands of terrorists, the CIA in 1996 authorized an effort to buy back the Stingers wherever they could be found. In early 1997, a CIA official approached the Taliban with an offer to buy the fifty-three Stingers believed to be in the Taliban government's possession. In spite of the generous terms being offered by the CIA, the Taliban refused to sell the missiles, insisting that they were being kept for use in a future conflict with Iran.[35] Soon after, Osama bin Laden began to court the Taliban.

Stingers, however, are not the only shoulder-fired antiaircraft missiles possibly being trafficked. In November 2004, a U.S. government official revealed that American intelligence agencies had tripled their formal estimate of shoulder-fired surface-to-air missile systems believed to be at large worldwide. The revision was based on a determination that at least four thousand of the weapons in Iraq's prewar arsenals could not be accounted for. The new government estimate indicated that six thousand of the weapons might be outside the control of any government, up from a previous estimate of two thousand. It is not known how many of the missiles are currently in the hands of terrorist organizations, but Al Qaeda, Hezbollah, the Liberation Tigers of Tamil Eelam, and the Provisional Irish Republican Army are among the dozen or so nonstate actors known to have possessed them. The low price of shoulder-fired missiles on the black market, said to be $5,000 in late 2004, suggests that the black market supply is plentiful and that these weapons are within the reach of almost any organization that might be interested in purchasing them.[36]

Many experts believe that the widespread availability of shoulder-fired missiles combined with the increasing difficulty of carrying bombs onboard commercial airliners means it is only a matter of time before terrorists attack civil aviation in the United States, perhaps even in a coordinated attack involving planes taking off or landing at many different airports. The U.S. State Department estimated in 2009 that there had been over forty shoulder-fired rocket attacks against civilian aviation worldwide, although none in North America. These attacks caused at least twenty-eight crashes and over eight hundred fatalities.[37] At Los Angeles International Airport, the threat has prompted the addition of more security fencing and additional patrols in the area surrounding the airport, but officials acknowledge that the enormous urban area surrounding the airport makes surveillance extremely difficult.[38] Considerable research has also been devoted to adapting counter-MANPADS (or "man-portable air defense system") technologies currently in use on U.S. military aircraft in zones of conflict to civilian airliners. While defense contractors have successfully tested systems for use in the airline industry, economic struggles have caused the industry to balk at the cost—estimated to be $1 to $3 million per plane—of equipping fleets with counter-MANPADS technologies.

In most of the world, trafficking in small arms presents a greater security concern than trafficking in relatively high-tech systems. Weapons like the

American-made M-16 rifle or the Russian-made (but widely copied) AK-47 have been the primary instruments of the many intrastate conflicts that have plagued the globe since the end of the Cold War. They are inexpensive and widely available, making it easy for aggrieved groups to take up arms against governments or other nonstate actors. These same characteristics facilitate illicit trade and make regulation more difficult to enforce. Their ease of use and light weight make small arms ideal for use by untrained combatants and even child soldiers. Making the problem even worse, the end of the Cold War was accompanied by both a loss of superpower control over the trade in small arms and the creation of a tremendous surplus of weapons. Furthermore, the existence of transnational criminal organizations trafficking in drugs and persons provided a ready-made network of dealers for the illicit weapons trade. In short, a broad convergence of factors brought the issue of small arms trafficking to the fore during the 1990s.[39]

As we noted in the discussion of drug trafficking above, arms trafficking is commonly fed by the profits generated by other forms of illegal commerce. Colombian drug cartels, major purchasers of weapons for many years, have been eclipsed since 2006 by Mexican cartels. In Sierra Leone during the 1990s, a rebel group called the RUF armed itself through the sale of diamonds mined and illegally exported from the country. Sierra Leone's bloody civil war, which was characterized by extraordinary levels of gratuitous violence that included hacking off the limbs of thousands of noncombatants, was sometimes described as a war about nothing, since the rebels often appeared unconcerned with political objectives. More important than any political objectives, however, was the fundamental economic objective of gaining and maintaining control of the country's diamond mines, since the wealth available from diamonds was the only means the rebels had of supporting their insurgency.

In Sierra Leone, Colombia, Mexico, Afghanistan, Burma, and many other places in the world, trafficking in one commodity tends to facilitate, and often finance, trafficking in other commodities. Rebel groups, transnational criminal organizations, and even terrorists understand that the distribution networks, methods of transportation, and money laundering systems that make drug trafficking possible often work just as well for arms trafficking (and vice versa). What this means is that addressing trafficking in all its forms requires dealing with networks. But it also requires an understanding of markets.

Trafficking, like legal trade, involves market transactions for which both interested buyers and sellers must exist. There is, in other words, a supply side and a demand side. As with most unregulated market transactions, the terms of trade are adjusted as supply and demand fluctuate. This means that a drop in demand brought about, for example, by vigorous enforcement of laws that make it illegal to travel abroad to engage in sex with a child or by a public education campaign that succeeds in reducing the number of cocaine users will, *ceteris paribus* (all other things being equal, as cautious economists like to say), cause the price of the commodity in question to decrease. Prices will also fall when supply increases faster than demand, as might happen when thousands of weapons become expendable at the end of a war or favorable growing conditions produce a bumper crop of the opium poppies from which heroin is derived.

The very existence of trafficking, which we defined at the outset as illegal trade, indicates that simply legislating against slavery, drug abuse, or selling weapons without an export license is inadequate. Enforcement is necessary as well, but not because enforcement, no matter how vigorous, is likely to eliminate trafficking. At best, enforcement simply imposes additional costs on traffickers. The seizure of a shipment of drugs or weapons reduces (usually by a very small amount) the total supply available. By the laws of supply and demand, prices increase and, in the end, the industry as a whole (if not the individual seller) profits just as much as it would have in the absence of the seizure. Looked at another way, the costs imposed by law enforcement are, for traffickers, just one of the costs of doing business, costs that ultimately will be paid by consumers.

Some argue, on the basis of the fundamental economics of trafficking, that decriminalization (perhaps in combination with taxation) is the solution. If every step taken to stamp out trafficking merely makes it more profitable for the traffickers who survive (or those who choose to get into the business when they see the enormous profits to be made), then antitrafficking efforts are like punching a pillow or squeezing a balloon: pressure in one spot creates expansion somewhere else. The problem is exacerbated by the fact that the world is divided into two hundred separate sovereign states; some have considerable capacity, along with the will, to develop and enforce laws against trafficking, and some do not. In the end, our ability to address trafficking may depend to a considerable degree on collective action. The international community, in this as in so many other respects, is only as strong as its weakest member.

ADDITIONAL RESOURCES

Books

Chivers, C. J. *The Gun.* New York: Simon and Schuster, 2010.
Farer, Tom. *Transnational Crime in the Americas.* New York: Routledge, 1999.
Glenny, Misha. *McMafia: A Journey Through the Global Criminal Underworld.* New York: Vintage Books, 2008.

Kan, Paul Rexton. *Cartels at War: Mexico's Drug-Fueled Violence and the Threat to U.S. National Security.* Washington, DC: Potomac Books, 2012.

Mandel, Robert. *Dark Logic: Transnational Criminal Tactics and Global Security.* Stanford, CA: Stanford University Press, 2010.

Miklaucic, Michael, and Jacqueline Brewer, eds. *Convergence: Illicit Networks and National Security in the Age of Globalization.* Washington, DC: National Defense University Press, 2013.

Naím, Moisés. *Illicit: How Smugglers, Traffickers, and Copycats Are Hijacking the Global Economy.* New York: Doubleday, 2005.

Trafficking in Persons Report 2015. Washington, DC: U.S. Department of State, July 2015.

Williams, Phil, ed. *Illegal Immigration and Commercial Sex: The New Slave Trade.* Portland, OR: Frank Cass, 1999.

Websites

Office of National Drug Control Policy: www.whitehousedrugpolicy.gov/
Polaris Project: www.polarisproject.org/index.php
The Protection Project: www.protectionproject.org/
United Nations Office on Drugs and Crime: www.unodc.org/unodc/index.html

Film

Lord of War (2005): A fictionalized account of the life of Russian arms dealer Viktor Bout, starring Nicolas Cage. Lionsgate Films. Directed by Andrew Niccol.

Chapter Nine

Insecurity in Cyberspace

Cyberspace is the nervous system—the control system of our country.

—President George W. Bush, *National Strategy to Secure Cyberspace* (2003)

In November 2014 Sony Studios was preparing the release of a low-budget comedy that contained as part of its plot the assassination of North Korea's leader. In response, North Korean hackers wiped Sony's servers clean and released sensitive data, including the private emails of Sony executives. President Obama responded to the attack and indicated that he did not consider it an act of war, but rather a costly act of cybervandalism;[1] however, National Security Agency director James Clapper called the attack "the most serious and costly cyber attack against the U.S. to date."[2] The North Korean cyberattack on Sony was only the latest of an increasingly large number of cyberattacks.

Military strategists throughout history have conceived of the domains of war as including land, sea, and air. With the launching of satellites and vehicles into space, a fourth domain of warfare was introduced. Cyberspace is the fifth domain. In contrast to kinetic weapons such as edged weapons, firearms, and explosives that rely on force, mass, and energy to inflict damage, cyberweapons are nonkinetic weapons, but they are still able to inflict damage, as the North Korean attack on Sony and a number of recent cyberattacks demonstrate.

On August 7, 2008, military units of the Republic of Georgia occupied South Ossetia, a region of the country then undergoing attacks from rebel groups. The following day, the Russian army also moved into South Ossetia to begin the kinetic phase of a brief but intense war between Russia and Georgia. Cyberattacks, however, were already under way by the time kinetic

weapons came into play. Hackers—or, more likely, Russian cyberwarriors—
shut down Georgian government websites using a distributed denial-of-service (DDOS) attack. Content on the Georgian president's website was altered
to include photos of Adolf Hitler. As the kinetic war intensified, Russian
cyberattacks targeted communications and financial systems in Georgia. All
Internet traffic into and out of the country was blocked, denying Georgians
access to email and to most sources of news. Banking operations and credit
card systems were paralyzed throughout the country, as was the mobile phone
system. Although the Georgian government responded to the cyberattacks by
moving some critical Internet sites to servers outside the country and shutting down others, the cyberwar, like the kinetic war, was a rout. The Russian
government denied responsibility for the cyberattacks, blaming instead Russian "hacktivists" (or hackers with a political agenda) who were upset with
the Georgian government's response to the aspiration of South Ossetians to
independence, but most experts believe the attacks were too extensive and
too well coordinated not to have been directed by the Russian government.[3]

The cyberattacks on Georgia in 2008 were preceded by similar attacks on
websites in Estonia, another former Soviet republic, the year before. The Russian government's responsibility for the cyberattacks on Estonia, however,
is even more difficult to establish. Some contend that those attacks were
more likely the work of hacktivists using botnets, or networks of remotely
controlled computers, rented from one or more transnational criminal organizations.

The conflict began when a decision by Estonian officials in April 2007 to
move a monument honoring the Soviet Union's struggle against Nazism in
World War II provoked a backlash from Russians, both in Estonia, where
rioting occurred, and in Russia, where access in and out of the Estonian
embassy was blocked. These visible manifestations of Russian anger were
accompanied by large-scale DDOS attacks on Estonian government websites.
Even with the assistance of computer experts from the United States and
NATO, the Estonian government had difficulty determining the origin of the
cyberattacks.[4]

Shutting down government websites, disabling servers, making public
private emails, and disrupting communications are modest—and nonlethal—
forms of cyberattacks, but they are only hints of what is possible in the realm
of cyberwar. More than fifty of the world's two hundred nation-states are
developing impressive capabilities to attack both military systems and civilian
infrastructure within the domain of cyberspace.[5] In addition, networked information systems have provided opportunities to transform the way traditional
(kinetic) warfare is waged and espionage is conducted. But security threats in
cyberspace are not confined to those generated by states and their security es-

tablishments. The difficulty of asserting jurisdiction, attributing responsibility, and enforcing rules in cyberspace makes it an ideal venue for the activities of terrorists, transnational criminal organizations, and individuals eager to make an impact on the world, whether for good or ill. In fact, Al Qaeda, the Islamic State, and other terrorist groups have used the Internet extensively to disseminate propaganda, recruit and train members, raise funds, conduct surveillance and select potential targets, and communicate. Many fear that terrorists will turn to cyberattacks as time goes on; indeed, there are several "e-jihad" or "cyber-jihad" websites that are devoted to and maintained by radical Muslim hackers. Lending support to this view, in November 2002, Omar Bakri Muhammed, one of Britain's most outspoken Islamic clerics, gave an exclusive interview to *Computerworld* in which he said that "in a matter of time you will see attacks on the stock market." He referred specifically to the markets in New York, London, and Tokyo.[6]

In some respects, cybercrime may constitute the most serious current security threat of all cyberspace issues, if for no other reason than that it is a very real and present danger. Much cybercrime goes unreported, sometimes because victims are unaware of it and sometimes because corporations that have had data stolen prefer to avoid letting their customers and shareholders know. In 2007, however, a theft of such large proportions occurred that it could not be covered up. Cybercriminals from Ukraine, Belarus, Estonia, China, and the United States stole forty-five million credit card records from American retailer T.J.Maxx. Direct losses alone totaled over $130 million.[7] In 2015, Russian hackers stole an estimated $1 billion from ATMs at banks in thirty countries. Furthermore, Home Depot, Target, and Chase were all targets of cyberthieves.

We generally assume that espionage, war, terrorism, and crime can be distinguished from each other according to whom the perpetrator is and what the motive for the attack is. But when the identity of those who commit cyberattacks is unknown and data that has both economic and strategic value is stolen, it may be difficult to discern the exact nature of an attack. So, for example, if hackers steal information from the computers of an American defense contractor (as, in fact, has happened), it may be impossible to know whether another state is spying or preparing the cyberbattlefield for war, or whether criminals are stealing information from which they hope to profit. Collusion among governments, transnational criminal organizations, and individual hackers complicates the picture even further.

In spite of the difficulties involved in distinguishing the various types of cyberthreats in the real world, in this chapter we will discuss cybercrime, cyberespionage, cyberwar, and cyberterrorism separately. First, however, it is important to look briefly at the connection between information and war in history. We will then look at some of the invisible vulnerabilities of cyberspace before examining cyberthreats and some of the means of addressing them.

INFORMATION AND WAR

Throughout history, there have been four fundamental sources of power: economic wealth, military force, ideas, and information. Almost four centuries ago, Francis Bacon wrote, "Knowledge itself is power."[8] Prominent leaders in the worlds of commerce, politics, and defense have suggested a shift in the contemporary world from the pursuit of military power to what former Citibank chairman Walter Wriston has called the "pursuit of information and the application of information to the means of production."[9] Former secretary of defense William Perry has written, "We live in an age that is driven by information. Technological breakthroughs . . . are changing the face of war and how we prepare for war."[10]

In reality, information has always been an important factor in diplomatic and military affairs. Sun Tzu wrote, "What enables the wise sovereign and good general to strike and conquer is foreknowledge."[11] But without an ability to transmit it quickly and accurately, information may be of little use. Consequently, some of history's greatest military commanders have stressed the importance of timely communications. In the Second Punic War, Hannibal used mirrors to communicate quickly and over long distances.[12] Genghis Khan relied on riders on horseback with spare horses. When one horse tired, it would be exchanged for another. As RAND Corporation analysts John Arquilla and David Ronfeldt note, "This gave the horsemen, in relative terms, something approximating an ability to provide real-time intelligence, almost as from a satellite, on the enemy's order of battle and intentions."[13]

When, during World War II, the Allies were able to break German and Japanese codes, they gained a measure of the foreknowledge of which Sun Tzu had written centuries earlier.[14] Franklin Roosevelt and Winston Churchill made extensive use of the Axis powers' decrypted messages—that is, the raw data that the Allies intercepted and processed. However, Churchill refused to rely on intelligence reports that had been "sifted and digested" and insisted on seeing the "authentic documents . . . in their original form."[15] Throughout the war, he was able to read through intercepted messages and to base momentous decisions in part on the information they provided.

Given the enormous volume of communications today, it would be impossible for a leader to review even a small percentage of the raw "unsifted and undigested" information received by a country or large corporation in a single day, as the following statistics dramatically demonstrate: in 2014 there were an estimated 2.5 billion email users worldwide sending almost three hundred billion messages per day and ninety trillion messages per year. Lockheed cyberanalysts monitor approximately two billion messages per day on the company's websites.

Of course, as any Internet user knows, most of these messages are spam, many containing viruses; nevertheless, the enormous difficulty of sorting out the wheat from the chaff and the significant from the meaningless or even malicious is obvious. Any organization confronted with this tidal wave of data could easily be overwhelmed, but the U.S. military has equipped itself to collect and process information as an integral part of its war-fighting capabilities.

In the fall of 2001, leaders in the White House were able for the first time to watch a live video feed of an ongoing battle as images of an attack on Taliban forces were transmitted by an unmanned aerial vehicle (UAV) from Afghanistan. The transmission was sent to Central Command headquarters in Florida and then on to Washington, D.C. When U.S. special forces raided Osama bin Laden's hideout in Abbottabad, Pakistan, they were directed there by information obtained by the NSA, which had implanted spyware on the mobile phones of Al Qaeda members, and the CIA helped to find the location of one of these phones, pinpointing bin Laden's compound.[16] Thus, cyberespionage enabled the United States to locate one of the most wanted criminals in history.

Modern electronics have transformed but not eliminated the information problem in security affairs. Greater quantities of information can be gathered, processed, stored, and transmitted than ever before in history. In fact, the cost of storing, processing, and transmitting a unit of information during the past fifty years has declined by a factor of up to a hundred million or more and is projected to continue to decline over the next decade. A 2004 National Intelligence Council report noted, "Today individual PC users have more capability at their fingertips than NASA had with the computers used in its first moon launches."[17]

But problems with finding the right pieces of information and using them effectively persist. Often there is so much data that national intelligence agencies—even in the most advanced countries—cannot process all of the information available in a timely fashion; this was made tragically evident on September 11, 2001. The flood of information sometimes compels leaders to turn to the most accessible sources of information: the print and electronic mass media.

In the 1991 Persian Gulf War, information was not only a management challenge but also a tool (actually, a weapon) that was used by the United States in some traditional ways. For example, in the early days of the war, to hinder Iraq's access to information and to limit its leaders' ability to communicate with one another and their military commanders, the United States took down Iraq's electrical power grid. The United States also used disinformation to confuse the Iraqis. For example, on the basis of information released by the U.S. military, CNN reported that the United States was preparing to invade Kuwait amphibiously. As a result, Saddam Hussein prepared his forces for an invasion from the sea. This may have been the first war in history in which the enemy leaders watched the same, nearly instantaneous, reports on the war.

Information has been employed as a central and very effective tool in the fight against terrorism. The information that four hundred special forces troops on the ground in Afghanistan provided to air-attack planners enabled the United States to decimate Al Qaeda and Taliban bases with minimal loss of U.S. forces. In addition, American special operations forces in Afghanistan printed thousands of leaflets advertising a reward that the United States offered for information related to Osama bin Laden and leaders of Al Qaeda. The United States has also reportedly lured some insurgents into traps after infiltrating Al Qaeda computers and leaving behind disinformation.[18]

The American military dropped over forty million leaflets over Iraq before Operation Iraqi Freedom began; another forty million were dropped during the campaign. Leaflets urged soldiers to surrender and ordinary citizens to ignore the directives of the regime. Not all psychological operations (or PSYOPS), however, used old-fashioned methods. Coalition forces sent cell phone text messages and emails to political and military leaders in Iraq in the days leading up to the invasion. These messages were intended to detail the costs of continued loyalty to Saddam Hussein.[19]

Around the world, regular military forces, insurgents and terrorists, and transnational criminal organizations have become heavily dependent on networked computers to manage and disseminate information (and disinformation). This alone would be sufficient to prompt the securitization of cyberspace, but there is more. Computers are used not just for information storage and communication but also to control automated systems. Advanced weaponry, GPS systems, air-defense radar systems, and many other features of the modern battlefield are "wired." But so are banks, stock exchanges, airlines, and most other private-sector institutions. Controlling the computers that control any of these things has been tempting political foes and criminals alike.

CYBERSPACE: INVISIBLE INSECURITY

What Is Cyberspace?

As we noted at the beginning of this chapter, war in cyberspace differs from war in each of the other domains in that it is waged digitally, without necessarily producing kinetic effects (although, as we will show later, digital attacks can be designed to blow up things). If, in the *Star Wars* films, the climactic battles had been waged using cyberweapons rather than kinetic weapons, droids would have merely stopped dead in their tracks and attacking fighter craft would have been diverted to a different planet. The movie studio could have trimmed its special effects budget dramatically—and the crowds would have stayed away. Because cyberspace is so different from the domains of conflict we ordinarily think about, it may be helpful to describe precisely what it is and how cyberwarriors, cyberspies, and cybercriminals operate in it.

Some naively equate cyberspace with the Internet, believing that all cyberwars would involve only the kinds of denial-of-service attacks that were waged against Estonia, Georgia, and Ukraine. According to this conception, being involved in a cyberwar might mean losing access to email—perhaps a blessing in disguise—or to Facebook—a real disaster—for a matter of days or weeks. But a denial-of-service attack is mere child's play in terms of cyberwar. What makes the potentialities of cyberwar so frightening is the degree to which we depend on the Internet—and many other computer networks—to control important physical processes. The Greek root of the term *cyberspace*, in fact, means *control*. Thus, the millions of computers linked to assembly lines, municipal power grids, air traffic control systems, stock markets, and the Predator drones being flown over Afghanistan, Pakistan, Yemen, and Somalia are all parts of cyberspace. Fighting in cyberspace therefore might be aimed at rendering kinetic weapons (or defenses against kinetic weapons) ineffective or shutting down essential services in major cities.

Former deputy secretary of defense Gordon England, in a May 2008 memorandum, defined cyberspace as "a global domain within the information environment consisting of the interdependent network of information technology infrastructures, including the Internet, telecommunications networks, computer systems, and embedded processors and controllers."[20] The Internet is a network of networks, but there are also computer networks that are not connected to the Internet. These, too, are a part of cyberspace. While it may be harder to hack into computers and control systems that are not connected to the Internet, it is not impossible, as the case of the Stuxnet worm, discussed below, proves.

What Makes Cyberspace Insecure?

Richard A. Clarke, who served as National Coordinator for Security, Infrastructure Protection, and Counterterrorism, explains why cyberspace is an attractive domain for conflict:

In the broadest terms, cyber warriors can get into these networks and control or crash them. If they take over a network, cyber warriors could steal all of its information or send out instructions that move money, spill oil, vent gas, blow up generators, derail trains, crash airplanes, send a platoon into an ambush, or cause a missile to detonate in the wrong place. If cyber warriors crash networks, wipe out data, and turn computers into doorstops, then a financial system could collapse, a supply chain could halt, a satellite could spin out of orbit into space, an airline could be grounded. These are not hypotheticals. Things like this have already happened, sometimes experimentally, sometimes by mistake, and sometimes as a result of cyber crime or cyber war.[21]

Both cybercriminals and cyberwarriors have a variety of weapons in their arsenals. To understand these weapons, however, it is necessary to wade into a field that is filled with terms that sound as if they were drawn straight from science fiction, such as *packet sniffers*, *SCADA* (supervisory control and data acquisition), *IP (Internet protocol) spoofing*, and others. The National Intelligence Council has noted, "Cyberweapons can take various forms including viruses (self-replicating programs that require human action to spread), worms (a sub-class of viruses that can spread without human action), Trojan horses (malicious software hidden within a legitimate program), denial-of-service attacks (bombarding servers with messages to make them crash), and phishing (rogue emails and websites that trick people into revealing password information)."[22]

Many types of attacks begin with a botnet, which is made up of a large number of computers that have been infected with malicious software (or *malware*) that allows them to be controlled remotely via the Internet. In most instances, owners of the individual computers in a botnet are not even aware that their machines are doing someone else's bidding. On receiving a command, computers in the botnet can be made to send simultaneous requests to a single website, overwhelming it and making it unavailable to other, legitimate users. This is how a distributed denial-of-service (DDOS) attack is conducted. Botnets can also be instructed to send spam containing viruses or other malware.[23]

The botmaster controls an asset that can be rented out to spammers for advertising purposes or to criminals for phishing, which is the use of malicious code to steal valuable information—such as bank account numbers and passwords—from another computer. Botnets can also be rented out to governments or to nonstate actors (including terrorist groups) for DDOS or other cyberattacks. Jean Ancheta, who was convicted in 2006 on various computer fraud charges, allegedly made over $100,000 by distributing adware through a botnet made up of four hundred thousand computers that he controlled.[24]

Most people encounter the work of botnets, whether they realize it or not, in the form of spam containing false alerts from heirs or lottery winners offering gifts of cash, banks or network security officers, ads for fly-by-night pharmaceutical companies, or offers of salacious photos of pop culture icons. One common phishing scheme that exploits human gullibility (and greed) involves an appeal from the son/daughter/lawyer/banker/business associate of a recently deceased African dictator/general/entrepreneur/human rights activist for help in moving millions of dollars out of Africa into a secure bank account abroad. While most know better than to reply with bank account numbers or other sensitive financial information, a few people who receive the appeals fall for them just as a few unwisely click on links in other forms of spam. If a million emails are sent out and a mere one one-hundredth of a percent (0.01 percent) result in a reply containing information that can be used to perpetrate identity theft or a click-through that downloads a virus, then another one hundred successes can be chalked up for criminal enterprises in their so-called social engineering schemes. Of course, sending a million emails—or even a hundred million—is virtually cost-free once addresses have been secured.

Unfortunately, avoiding email scams is no guarantee of safe computing. There are many other, and far more sophisticated, threats in cyberspace. To get a better sense of how some of these threats are generated, let us take a brief look at how information is transmitted and sometimes altered or intercepted.

Messages travel through the Internet in blocks of data called "packets." An email message or web page might be broken into several packets prior to entering the network. Once the packets are received, they can be reassembled. A "packet sniffer" makes it possible to intercept packets of information as they travel across the Internet. Hackers have used sniffers to intercept user names and passwords, which can then be used for entering otherwise protected networks. In July 1995, the FBI identified a hacker who was using the Harvard University computer system to break into various U.S. Department of Defense systems, including the Naval Research Laboratory, the Los Alamos National Laboratory, and the Naval Command, Control and Ocean Surveillance Center. To find the offender, the FBI used a packet sniffer to scan for messages that came from the hacker, who was using the alias "Gritón" (which means "screamer" in Spanish). The investigation led to an Argentine university student, Julio Cesar Ardita, who pleaded guilty to wiretapping and other charges related to computer crimes.[25] Of course, hackers are not the only ones who use packet sniffing; both the NSA (Room 641A) and the FBI ("Carnivore" program) used this technique to collect information as part of their counterterrorism programs.

Every packet of information traveling on the Internet has a source and a recipient, indicated by the Internet Protocol (IP) addresses assigned to all computers on the Internet. Another offensive use of computer technology is called "IP spoofing," which involves forging the source address of a message so that it appears to have originated somewhere else. In a typical IP spoofing attack, the false source is trusted by the recipient, thus allowing the sender entry into a network.

The most notorious computer attacks in recent years have consisted of "worms" and "viruses." Both types of attacks infect computers (hence the medical metaphor) and spread over entire networks. Computers operate strictly according to the instructions that they receive from human operators or from other computers. Such instructions can be changed ("infected"), causing the computer to operate in unexpected or even destructive ways. According to computer security expert Dorothy Denning, "The main difference [between worms and viruses] is that a worm is an autonomous agent that spreads entirely on its own, whereas a virus attaches itself to other software and spreads with that software."[26]

Homer tells us that Greek soldiers hid inside a large wooden horse that the Trojans brought inside the gates of their city. Once inside Troy, the Greeks emerged from the horse and routed the surprised Trojans. In computer terms, a *Trojan horse* is a form of malware that is downloaded onto a computer by a user who believes it to be something that it is not. Trojan horses may appear in the form of malware bundled with a popular media file or other application. When downloaded, the malware may copy or delete files on the computer, log and transmit keystrokes, or turn the computer into a botnet drone. Among the various types of Trojan horses are "logic bombs." Logic bombs are triggered by a specific event, such as typing a particular series of keystrokes, or by the arrival of a particular date or time on the computer's internal clock.

Those who study information operations define *hacking* as "activities conducted online and covertly that seek to reveal, manipulate, or otherwise exploit vulnerabilities in computer operating systems and other software."[27] Hackers generally do not have political agendas; they try to break into computer systems for the challenge, for the same reason that climbers scale mountain peaks—because they are there. In contrast, "hacktivists" combine hacking with political activism. Thus, a number of groups use the Internet in support of their causes. For example, terrorist groups such as Hamas, Hezbollah, Al Qaeda, the Islamic State, and the Zapatista National Liberation Army (EZLN) have used the Internet to garner support for their organizations.[28]

CYBERCRIME

On May 4, 2000, an email with the subject line "ILOVEYOU" began spreading all over the world. It contained an attachment, labeled "LOVE-LETTER-

FOR-YOU-TXT" that, when opened, replicated and sent itself to everyone on the victim's address list, indicating the victim as the sender. The "Love Bug" malware (a Trojan horse), designed to exploit people's curiosity, was created by Onel de Guzman, a former computer programming student in the Philippines who had written about the possibility of such a self-replicating virus as part of his undergraduate thesis. Although the malware quickly infected forty-five million computers worldwide and cost an estimated $10 billion in lost productivity and cleanup costs, Guzman was never charged with a crime. He did not profit from the prank and, at the time, the Philippines had no laws making it a crime to spread malware.[29]

The Love Bug transformed cybercrime by demonstrating that malware, combined with human gullibility, could make it a very simple matter for skilled hackers to gain access to sensitive information stored on millions of computers. An incident in 2009 and 2010 in which hackers exploited some of the same unsafe computing practices that helped spread the Love Bug so quickly illustrates how lucrative cybercrime can be.

In the fall of 2010, over one hundred people were arrested in the United States, the United Kingdom, and Ukraine in an operation targeting one of the largest cybercrime networks ever uncovered. Network bosses in Eastern Europe used a virus called Zeus to infect computers, making it possible for them to gather passwords for online bank accounts. Money was then transferred from the compromised bank accounts to other accounts held by "mules," or go-betweens, in the United States and the United Kingdom. The network stole approximately $70 million before the FBI solved the case and began making arrests. Given more time, the amount stolen could have been much greater.[30]

The available evidence indicates that cybercrime has been increasing dramatically in recent years and that it will continue to do so. The FBI's Internet Crime Complaint Center reported that it received more than 269,000 complaints with an adjusted dollar loss of more than $800 billion in 2014.[31] (This figure does not include corporate losses due to cybercrime, which are estimated to be in the billions of dollars annually.) As Steven R. Chabinsky, the deputy assistant director of the FBI's Cyber Division, noted in testimony before the Senate Subcommittee on Terrorism and Homeland Security in 2009, "The number of actors with the ability to utilize computers for illegal, harmful and possibly devastating purposes continues to rise."[32]

From the spread of Onel de Guzman's so-called Love Bug in 2000 to the bank fraud perpetrated with the Zeus virus in 2010, there is one thing that almost all major cybercrimes have in common: they are transnational in character. This creates a host of problems for law enforcement authorities. Those who commit cybercrimes may be protected from prosecution due to loopholes in the law of the state where they operate or the indifference or ineffectiveness of local police and prosecutors. Law enforcement authorities, aware that computer crimes are being committed on their territories, may be reluctant to devote scarce resources to investigating and prosecuting those crimes as long as most victims are located in other states. While states often seek the extradition of their own nationals to stand trial on criminal charges, most are not eager to bring criminal suspects of other nationalities to their shores. What the wealthiest states—those where most cybercrimes have their biggest effects—generally hope to see is vigorous enforcement of laws criminalizing computer crimes in the states where the cybercriminals operate. However, even wealthy states have difficulty policing what might be considered their portions of cyberspace.

CYBERESPIONAGE

Whether we like it or not, a vast amount of personal information about each of us in the developed world can be found somewhere on networked computers—that is, in cyberspace. Financial transactions including purchases (whether in online or brick-and-mortar stores), phone records, school transcripts, birth certificates, personal information posted on social networking sites, and much, much more is stored in cyberspace, ready to be recovered and exploited by those with the skills necessary to breach what are often woefully inadequate security protocols. The same is true for information stored by corporations and governments.

Because cyberspace is where most information is stored and most communication occurs today, cyberespionage has become a major threat to the security of states and nonstate actors. It has become a threat in part because the cost of entry into the cyberespionage game is so low. The principal investigator of a U.S. General Accounting Office report stated in 1996, "Countries today do not have to be military superpowers with large standing armies, fleets of battleships or squadrons of fighters to gain a competitive edge. Instead, all they really need to steal sensitive data or shut down military computers is a two-thousand-dollar computer and modem and a connection to the Internet."[33] Of course, the cost of the computer may be much lower today.

Cyberespionage is, in simple terms, spying in cyberspace. It involves gaining unauthorized access to computers, networks, and control systems to collect secret or proprietary information or to alter data. Of course, when the target of an electronic intrusion is a state's security apparatus (the defense ministry, intelligence agencies, and military forces), the line separating cyberespionage from cyberwar becomes difficult to discern.

According to reports, computer systems at NATO were attacked more than 3,600 times in 2013.[34] Government networks in the United States deal with thousands of probes each day.[35] Some of the probes of military systems in the United States have merited their own names (supplied by federal investigators), including "Solar Sunrise," a cyberattack on U.S. government computers in 1998; "Moonlight Maze," a cyberespionage effort attributed to Russia, which began in 1999; and "Titan Rain," an attack attributed to China, which exfiltrated ten terabytes of data beginning in 2003.[36] In addition, NATO discovered a five-year effort dubbed "Sandworm" by Russia to tap into Ukrainian computers.

The Moonlight Maze and Titan Rain incidents both involved the theft of information on computers connected to the Internet. Until recently, all hacking required either physical access to a computer on the network being hacked (as, for example, with the ability to type on its keyboard) or, more commonly, an Internet connection so that hackers could find networks containing sensitive information in the same way that email finds its intended recipients. This meant that the networks containing the most sensitive information or the most important control functions, such as those used to coordinate nuclear missile launches, could be secured from hackers by maintaining an air gap—that is, keeping them disconnected from the Internet. This is no longer considered a fool-proof strategy for keeping sensitive networks secure.

The U.S. military has over one hundred thousand computers connected to the Secret Internet Protocol Router Network (SIPRNET), an air-gapped network used to transmit classified information and orders among military units. In November 2008, SIPRNET was compromised by spyware that originated in Russia and jumped to air-gapped computers with a human assist. Using standard hacking procedures, the spyware was deposited on computers with dot-mil addresses (indicating Department of Defense sites) connected to the Internet. At that point, it searched for thumb drives used to transfer data from one computer to another. Individuals who plugged infected thumb drives into air-gapped but otherwise unprotected SIPRNET computers provided the human assistance needed for hackers to get into one of the government's most secure networks.[37]

Another serious breach of cybersecurity occurred in 2009 when hackers gained access to data on the F-35, the U.S. military's next-generation fighter plane then under development. Several terabytes of information related to the design and avionics of the F-35 was stolen. Pentagon officials believe the hack came from a computer in China, a view supported by the similarity of China's new J-20 fighter aircraft to the F-35.[38] The cost to the United States to develop the F-35 was $337 billion, the most complex and expensive weapons system ever devised.[39]

British and American intelligence agencies have publicly identified the People's Republic of China as the source of a number cyberespionage cases; in fact, in May 2014, U.S. government prosecutors announced indictments against five Chinese military officers associated with the 61398 Chinese hacker group.[40] This was the first time that the United States filed formal hacking charges against a nonstate actor. In September 2015, President Obama and Chinese president Xi Jinping announced that they had reached a "common understanding" that neither government would knowingly support the theft of business or corporate secrets. Despite this agreement, there was some concern that hackers would act independently of governments, and even if hackers are identified, the problem of how to respond arises. There was also concern that an agreement to refrain from spying in cyberspace would be unenforceable. As Shane Harris, the author of *@War*, has written, "There is . . . no obvious way to enforce a cyber arms agreement. Nuclear enrichment facilities can be inspected. Tanks, ships, and aircraft can be seen from a distance. A cyber weapon can be built on a computer. It is practically invisible until it's launched."[41]

Threats to punish China or Russia in some fashion might easily escalate with consequences that neither side desires. The only viable solution seems to be for government agencies and corporations that have been the targets of cyberespionage to do a better job of securing sensitive information. This, however, requires developing—and maintaining—the capabilities necessary to stay ahead of a determined adversary in the cat-and-mouse game of infiltration, detection, and exclusion.

CYBERTERRORISM

During his tenure as CIA director, George Tenet noted that terrorist groups including Hezbollah, Hamas, the Abu Nidal organization, and Al Qaeda were using computerized files, email, and encryption to support their operations.[42] The willingness of Al Qaeda, an organization with a decidedly retrogressive worldview, to use modern technology to attack symbols of modern wealth and power seems to suggest that it is only a matter of time before the organization turns to cyberterrorism. This, at least, was the conclusion of the National Intelligence Council in 2004, which stated, "We expect that terrorists will also try to acquire and develop the capabilities to conduct cyber attacks to cause physical damage to computer systems and to disrupt critical information networks."[43] And the National Academy of Sciences noted, "We are at risk. Increasingly, America depends on computers. . . . Tomorrow's terrorists may be able to do more damage with a keyboard than with a bomb."[44]

Terrorists have used the Internet extensively in recent years, but not to conduct cyberattacks—at least not thus far. Before we examine the possibility of cyberterrorism, let us consider what terrorists are doing in cyberspace.

Because terrorism is a form of psychological warfare that seeks to spread fear, terrorist organizations have used the Internet to disseminate images calculated to shock viewers. Grotesque videos of the beheadings of American and foreign workers captured by Al Qaeda, the Islamic State, and others in Syria, Iraq, Afghanistan, and Pakistan were posted on the Internet to make them available to audiences worldwide. More generally, terrorists have gone online to seek publicity and to disseminate propaganda. Virtually all of the world's major terrorist groups have active websites with information related to their organizations and causes. Typically, these websites attempt to justify their reliance on violent methods and to recruit supporters. One of the websites that Al Qaeda used at the time of the 9/11 attacks was alneda.com. It presented official statements from leaders of Al Qaeda and appears to have been used to transmit secret messages to Al Qaeda operatives around the world.[45] In July 2002, an American Internet entrepreneur acquired the alneda.com domain name when its registration was deleted in preparation for a move to a different server. The new owner left the existing content on the site but added tracking software so he could see where messages posted on the site were coming from. After five days, someone posted a message elsewhere on the Internet alerting Al Qaeda's supporters to the fact that alneda.com had been hijacked by an infidel.[46]

Terrorist organizations have also used the Internet to obtain information on potential targets. Dan Verton, author of *Black Ice: The Invisible Threat of Cyber-Terrorism*, notes, "Al-Qaeda cells now operate with the assistance of large databases containing details of potential targets in the United States. They use the Internet to collect intelligence on those targets, especially critical economic nodes, and modern software enables them to study structural weaknesses in facilities as well as predict the cascading failure effect of attacking certain systems."[47] When American investigators tracked Ramzi Ahmad Yousef, the mastermind behind the 1993 attempt to bring down the World Trade Center, to the Philippines two years after the attack, they found his laptop computer in the apartment where he had been living. The computer's hard drive contained much of the evidence that was used to convict Yousef in 1997 of conspiracy in the WTC bombing case. It also contained plans to blow up a dozen U.S. airliners over the Pacific. Included among the computer files were flight schedules, details of onboard detonations, and false identification documents including photos of some of the conspirators.[48]

Like many nonprofit and political organizations, terrorist groups use the Internet to raise money. Part of Al Qaeda's Internet presence has involved for-profit businesses and fake charities to provide the organization with revenue. According to testimony by Dennis Lormel, the head of the FBI's Terrorist Financial Review Group, "an Al Qaeda terrorist cell in Spain used stolen credit cards in fictitious sales scams and for numerous other purchases for the cell."[49]

Some terrorist groups have gone online to recruit and train new members. Websites focusing on matters of concern to Islamic fundamentalists are widely available; some contain downloadable videos of fighting in Chechnya, Afghanistan, and Iraq, as well as videos of prominent Al Qaeda leaders, such as Osama bin Laden and Ayman al-Zawahiri. Islamic *jihadi* groups have also used the Internet to distribute training materials related to bomb making, kidnapping, assassination, encryption, and poison. One of the most notorious of these training manuals is the *Encyclopedia of Jihad*, which is more than a thousand printed pages in length.

Finally, the Internet provides terrorists with the ability to plan and coordinate actions quickly, cheaply, and securely. Al Qaeda has used a sophisticated form of encryption called steganography, which involves hiding messages inside graphic files, such as photographs, for some communications between cells.

Why have terrorist organizations used the Internet to propagandize, recruit, raise money, plan, communicate, and coordinate but not to attack? Terrorism is a strategy that seeks to produce a profound psychological impact in the target society. It is, more to the point, about terrorizing large audiences. The theft of personally identifiable information from retailers, the spread of a crippling virus through cyberspace, or the infiltration of government computers—in other words, the more common types of cybersecurity breaches—rarely produce real fear in a society regardless of how costly or damaging to national security they may be. Terrorists hope to create panic, or at least dread, in an audience; cyberattacks are generally not suited for that. Thus, while there may be military reasons to prefer hacks over kinetic effects in some situations, terrorists invariably prefer explosions, in large part because they want to produce images suitable for television news broadcasts.[50]

There are certain types of cyberattack that might create the kind of dramatic effects that terrorists desire. For example, shutting off the supply of electricity to a major city or taking down the air traffic control system would likely generate fear, especially if such demonstrations of control over critical infrastructures were accompanied by credible threats to conduct additional cyberattacks. Fortunately, terrorist groups probably do not have the ability to conduct these kinds of attacks at present. Unlike many of the measures that states take in an effort to enhance national security, efforts to secure the critical infrastructures from state-based cyberattacks will provide protection against cyberattacks by terrorist organizations as well. This, of course, argues for taking measures to secure control systems that are vulnerable to cyberattacks before terrorists develop the capability to wage such attacks and before any state finds a reason to use what may be an existing capability.

CYBERWAR

Even though nonstate actors have not yet engaged in cyberwarfare, some states have. In July 2010, the industrial giant Siemens notified users of its supervisory control and data acquisition (SCADA) systems that a sophisticated worm was exploiting the company's default password in order to spread itself and steal industrial secrets. SCADA software, which is used to manage large-scale industrial processes, is supposed to be less vulnerable to malware because the computer systems running it are generally not connected to the Internet. However, the Stuxnet virus attacking Siemens' software was spread when flash drives used in computers connected to the Internet were inserted into control systems without an Internet connection, just as the malware of Russian origin that penetrated one of the Defense Department's air-gapped networks had done in 2008. Malware like the Stuxnet virus could be used to disrupt entire industries or even to shut down a regional power grid.[51]

Computer security experts concluded that the United States and Israel had created Stuxnet to sabotage Iran's nuclear program. The evidence supporting this theory was entirely circumstantial, but often circumstantial evidence is all that investigators have to go on when tracing cyberattacks. The first piece of evidence suggesting that Stuxnet had governmental origins was its complexity. Some suggested that it would have taken half a dozen or more skilled programmers working for six months to produce the malware's code. Also, while the virus was found on computers in a number of countries, including Indonesia and India, a large cluster of infected computers were in Iran. Iranian officials themselves suggested that Stuxnet was aimed at Iran's nuclear program but denied that delays in bringing the country's first nuclear power plant online were related to the worm.[52]

Cyberattacks such as Stuxnet would clearly be called "cyberwar" if they accompanied kinetic warfare, as the cyberattacks on Georgia in 2008 did. But if an attack is unattributed (and perhaps even unrecognized as having been an attack rather than an accident), then the label *cyberespionage* may be more appropriate. As we noted in the opening chapter, the determination that certain problems qualify as security issues is made by a social process that begins with a "speech act." The same is true in determining what merits the label *war*. In thinking about the relatively new problems associated with malicious activities in cyberspace, we should keep in mind that calling certain activities "cyberwar" rather than "cyberespionage" may be intended to heighten concern about threats to cybersecurity so that more resources will be devoted to remedies.

Regardless of whether all of the activities in cyberspace that are called "cyberwar" actually deserve that label, clearly the military forces of the United States and its NATO allies exhibit certain vulnerabilities to cyberattack. These vulnerabilities stem from the extraordinary degree of dependence on computers and networked information systems exhibited by these forces. Consider a recent description of this dependence by former U.S. deputy secretary of defense William J. Lynn III:

> Information technology enables almost everything the U.S. military does: logistical support and global command and control of forces, real-time provision of intelligence, and remote operations. Every one of these functions depends heavily on the military's global communications backbone, which consists of 15,000 networks and seven million computing devices across hundreds of installations in dozens of countries. More than 90,000 people work full time to maintain it. In less than a generation, information technology in the military has evolved from an administrative tool for enhancing office productivity into a national strategic asset in its own right.[53]

The U.S. military possesses capabilities that no other military force in the world can match, due in large part to its successful marriage of information systems to advanced technologies, including precision weapons. But, as retired Air Force officer and cyberexpert Gregory Rattray has pointed out, "Information systems now serve as both weapons and targets of warfare."[54] A military that depends for its effectiveness on access to information—including an ability to communicate instantaneously using electronic devices—and on the smooth functioning of advanced technologies could be crippled by an adversary that hacks into its computer networks. This is the concern that, above all others, has motivated the U.S. military to try to organize itself more efficiently for cyberwar.

In the aftermath of the 9/11 attacks, the Department of Homeland Security was established and had as part of its mission a focus on cyberthreats. The Federal Bureau of Investigation also stepped up its cybersecurity operations and analysis. In June 2009, the Department of Defense announced the creation of the U.S. Cyber Command within the U.S. Strategic Command. The new command, headquartered at Fort Meade, Maryland, alongside the National Security Agency, began operating in May 2010. Its missions are as follows: (1) to secure military networks and support traditional military activities with operations in cyberspace; (2) to integrate the cyber resources that currently exist in the different branches of the military; and (3) to work with allies, other government agencies, and industry to develop common responses to threats in cyberspace.[55]

In February 2015, the White House announced a new agency, the Cyber Threat Intelligence Integration Center, to help analyze and share digital threat information and data among the U.S. government, consumer groups, and private industry. The goal of this new organization is to issue warnings when a threat appears likely or a computer breach is spreading. In March 2015, observing "the digital world touches every aspect of our business," CIA director John Brennan announced a new, fifth division: the Directorate of Digital Information.[56] Soon after becoming secretary of defense, Ashton Carter announced a major initiative by the Department of Defense to work with Silicon Valley companies to counter cyberthreats, including investing in In-Q-Tel, a private company supported by the intelligence community. Carter also announced a new program to allow for cyberprofessionals to enter DOD for short periods of time as reserve officers.[57]

Organizational changes alone are inadequate to cope with cyberwar threats. Because a relatively small number of skilled programmers using inexpensive computer systems can generate a wide variety of cyberattacks, most experts believe that cyberspace is a domain in which offenses will have significant advantages over defenses, at least in the near term. This perspective was reflected by Admiral Michael S. Rogers, the director of U.S. Cyber Command, who stated, "We . . . need to think about how can we increase our capacity on the offensive side here, to get to that point of deterrence."[58]

In time, however, it may be possible to reconfigure the architecture of the Internet and other computer networks to create advantages for those seeking to prevent unauthorized access to sensitive information or control systems. The Internet, which was originally designed to provide for a redundant communications capability for military and U.S. government command and control centers and, later, to make it easier for a relatively small group of people—most of them scientists—to share information openly, is evolving rapidly. At least some in the world are pushing that evolution toward enhanced security. Meanwhile, it is worth considering what policy prescriptions can be devised to make cyberspace more secure.

COPING WITH CYBERTHREATS

Domestic Policy

The instances of hacking, cybercrime, cyberterrorism, cyberespionage, and cyberwar described in this chapter (along with many others that we have not mentioned) have grabbed the attention of governments, industry, and many individuals. In the United States, the administration of George W. Bush produced *The National Strategy to Secure Cyberspace* in February 2003 and, in 2008, President Bush announced the Comprehensive National Cybersecurity Initiative (CNCI) designed to establish security standards for government networks. Barack Obama established an office to coordinate federal efforts to secure cyberspace. The first director of the office, widely referred to as the "cyber czar," was appointed in December 2009.[59]

Within the government of the United States, the U.S. Cyber Command has been given the assignment of protecting military networks (including all dot-mil web addresses), and the Department of Homeland Security has been assigned the task of protecting other government networks (including all dot-gov addresses). Because the U.S. military has more resources and greater expertise in dealing with cyberattacks, the Obama administration in 2010 forged an agreement between Homeland Security and the Cyber Command under which Defense Department computing capacity could be used to deal with nonmilitary cyberattacks within the United States. While such an agreement has troubling implications for civil liberties, many experts regard it as an important step toward getting a handle on a threat that cannot be neatly divided between domestic law enforcement and international security.[60] In February 2013, President Obama issued Executive Order 13636, *Improving Critical Infrastructure Cybersecurity*, which focused primarily on two issues: information sharing and the protection of privately held critical infrastructure.

International Cooperation

As we noted in previous chapters, nuclear, chemical, and biological weapons have been the subjects of multilateral arms control agreements. Antipersonnel landmines and cluster munitions have been banned by treaties that have attracted broad support. While these precedents naturally suggest the possibility of developing arms control agreements applicable to cyberspace, several factors suggest that the tools of cyberwar may not be as easy to limit as weapons that operate in the other domains.

First, cyberwar capabilities are based on dual-use technologies. Nuclear warheads, canisters containing nerve agents, cluster bombs, and many other kinetic weapons do not have legitimate, nonmilitary purposes that complicate efforts to limit or even ban them; computers, fiber-optic cables, and Internet protocols that speed packets of data to their destinations do. As a consequence, almost any limits that might be imposed on either the hardware or the software used in cyberwar would risk limiting the many good and useful things that can be done with computer networks.

Second, from production to storage to actual use, malware is much easier to hide than kinetic weapons. Missiles must be launched from ground-based silos or pads, or from ships, submarines, or airplanes. Consequently, satellite reconnaissance, on-site inspections, and other forms of physical inspection can be used to find and count missiles. Chemical and biological weapons require labs for their manufacture and warehouses for storage. Again, physical inspection is possible. In contrast, cyberweapons, which are merely lines of software code designed to wreak havoc on an enemy's computer networks or computer-controlled technologies, may be created, stored, and launched from the same computers that are used to pay bills, download music, or check football scores. Inspectors looking to verify the absence of cyberweapons might have to scan trillions of lines of code scattered across millions of computers. Even then, there is no guarantee that cyberweapons, or malicious software codes, would be recognized for what they are. Virus-detecting software looks for existing forms of malware or for code that exploits known system vulnerabilities; innovative methods of attack or ones based on undetected vulnerabilities are much more difficult to find.

Third, an international agreement designed to limit cyberweapons would likely conflict with the privacy rights of individuals and the intellectual property rights of both individuals and corporations. Malware, whether it comes from a military unit, a transnational criminal organization, or an individual hacker, can be stored on or launched from computers belonging to innocent (and unaware) individuals or organizations. Few individuals, universities, nonprofit organizations, or businesses would be willing to make all the data stored on their computers available for periodic review by inspectors from a government or an international organization.

These are just a few of the problems associated with agreements intended to limit in some way the possession of cyberweapons. A different approach would be to prohibit the *use* of cyberweapons rather than their possession. But there is a problem with this strategy as well.

International law already prohibits states from launching cyberattacks, or any other forms of attack, except in self-defense. Gary Sharp, referring to the United Nations Charter's provision banning the threat or use of force by one state against other states, describes the principle in these terms: "*Any* computer network attack that intentionally causes *any* destructive effect within the sovereign territory of another state is an unlawful use of force within the meaning of Article 2(4) that may produce the effects of an armed attack prompting the right of self-defense."[61] The application of a ban on first use of cyberweapons, whether based on Charter limits on the use of force more generally or on a more specific treaty pertaining to cyberwar, would run up against the difficulties involved in attributing responsibility for sophisticated cyberattacks. On the other hand, some believe that an agreement defining the types of exploits that are to be considered cyberattacks under international law might help to dissuade state actors from pushing the limits where no shooting war has started while also providing a stronger legal basis for retaliation by the victim of proscribed cyberattacks.

In spite of the various barriers to arms control in cyberspace, there are a number of aspects of the cybersecurity problem that are ripe for international cooperation. For example, in 2001, the Council of Europe Convention on Cybercrime was concluded. The agreement, which entered into force in 2004, attempts to standardize the legal approaches to cybercrime being adopted by individual states and to promote cooperation in detecting and punishing such crimes. While the Convention is expanding its reach beyond Europe—the United States ratified it in 2006 and Canada, Japan, and South Africa have signed—one important member of the Council of Europe where cybercrime is common, Russia, has not yet joined.

While the United States began the new millennium with a go-it-alone approach to cybersecurity, that policy is beginning to change. Late in 2009, the Obama administration agreed to move forward with talks on cybersecurity in the framework of the United Nations Committee on Disarmament and International Security. The agreement on cyberespionage announced by presidents Obama and Xi in September 2015 is a modest step toward greater cybersecurity; however, it is not yet clear how effective such negotiations and agreements will be. Some states that have expressed interest in cyber arms control want to impose limits on information warfare, which they understand to include the spread of subversive ideas, while others, including the United States, are interested solely in addressing issues related to the spread of malicious code.

The Shape of Things to Come

There is much that is not yet clear about the future of cyberspace. Many have enthusiastically embraced the Internet as a tool that overcomes the barriers of time and distance in ways that promote trade and democracy while eroding traditional conceptions of state sovereignty.[62] This vision is based on the belief that the advantages of being connected in a wired world are so great that states can hardly choose to disconnect and that, once connected, they can scarcely control the flow of ideas across their borders. But states have always tried to stop at their borders those things they find threatening, whether armies, contagious diseases, contraband, or subversive ideas. Cyberthreats are no different. The United States, like many states around the world, is working to find ways to close its virtual borders to cyberattacks. China has taken extraordinary steps to close its virtual borders not only to malware but also to what its leaders view as subversive ideas. Thus the Chinese government employs an estimated forty thousand Internet police with the authority to take down websites, delete information, and make arrests. This, and similar situations in other states, has led Chris Demchak to suggest that state sovereignty—with the desire to maintain meaningful borders that sovereignty implies—will eventually be the norm in cyberspace, as it is in other domains.[63]

We may have to wait a few years to see whether cyberspace can be effectively partitioned and defended or whether cyber arms control is possible. What we know at this point is that the Internet, a remarkable technological innovation designed to connect people and facilitate the free flow of ideas, has become a domain in which terrorists and transnational criminal organizations operate freely, military and commercial secrets are stolen by unidentifiable hackers, and states are already waging cyberwar.

ADDITIONAL RESOURCES

Books

Arquilla, John, and David Ronfeldt, eds. *In Athena's Camp: Preparing for Conflict in the Information Age*. Santa Monica, CA: RAND Corporation, 1997.
———. *Networks and Netwars: The Future of Terror, Crime and Militancy*. Santa Monica, CA: RAND Corporation, 2001.
Clarke, Richard A., and Robert K. Knake. *Cyber War: The Next Threat to National Security and What to Do about It*. New York: Ecco, 2010.
Denning, Dorothy E. *Information Warfare and Security*. Reading, MA: Addison-Wesley, 1999.
Harris, Shane. *@War: The Rise of the Military-Internet Complex*. New York: Houghton Mifflin, 2014.
Kramer, Franklin D., Stuart H. Starr, and Larry K. Wentz, eds. *Cyberpower and National Security*. Washington, DC: National Defense University Press and Potomac Books, 2009.
Rattray, Gregory J. *Strategic Warfare in Cyberspace*. Cambridge, MA: MIT Press, 2001.
Singer, P. W., and Allan Friedman. *Cybersecurity and Cyberwar: What Everyone Needs to Know*. New York: Oxford University Press, 2014.

Websites

Computer Emergency Response Team Coordinating Center (CERT/CC): www.cert.org
Department of Homeland Security: www.dhs.gov

Institute for National Strategic Studies: www.ndu.edu

Institute for Security Technology Studies at Dartmouth College: www.ists.dartmouth
    .edu

Institute for the Advanced Study of Information Warfare: www.psycom.net/iwar.1
    .html

Films

Rise of the Hackers, *NOVA* (PBS, 2014). Directed by Kate Dart.

United States of Secrets, *Frontline* (WGBH/PBS, 2014). Directed by Michael Kirk.

WarGames: A classic 1983 movie starring Matthew Broderick and Ally Sheedy in
    which a young hacker is able to penetrate a Pentagon computer. MGM. Directed
    by John Badham.

Zero Day. 2003, Avatar Films. Directed by Ben Coccio.

Part Three

POLITICAL AND SOCIAL CONDITIONS OF INSECURITY

Chapter Ten

The State of the State: National Security and Human Security

In the decades to come, the most lethal threats to the United States' safety and security—a city poisoned or reduced to rubble by a terrorist attack—are likely to emanate from states that cannot adequately govern themselves or secure their own territory. Dealing with such fractured or failing states is, in many ways, the main security challenge of our time.

—Robert M. Gates, U.S. Secretary of Defense, 2006–2011

Immediately after the 9/11 attacks, Richard Perle, then chairman of the Defense Policy Board, said, "This could not have been done without help of one or more governments. . . . Someone taught these suicide bombers how to fly large airplanes. I don't think that can be done without the assistance of large governments. You don't walk in off the street and learn how to fly a Boeing 767."[1]

Perle was not alone in mistakenly assuming that there had to be a state behind the most destructive attacks on American soil in history. President Bush, Deputy Defense Secretary Paul Wolfowitz, and other high-level administration officials sought to link Al Qaeda specifically to Iraq after 9/11. Richard Clarke, the National Security Council official in charge of counterterrorism efforts, recounts a conversation with President Bush on the evening of September 12. The president, having previously been assured by the CIA and others that Al Qaeda was solely responsible for the attacks, said to Clarke and others in the Situation Room of the White House, "I want you, as soon as you can, to go back over everything, everything. See if Saddam did this. See if he's linked in any way."[2] The Bush administration's search for evidence of a direct link between Iraq and Al Qaeda continued right up to the beginning of the war with Iraq in March 2003. Evidence of contacts, including a Czech report (later discounted) of a meeting between hijacker Mohamed Atta and an Iraqi diplomat in Prague, was touted as "ties" or "links." In fact, on February

5, 2003, Secretary of State Colin Powell, addressing the UN Security Council in an effort to gain international support for the American war in Iraq, said, "Iraqi officials deny accusations of ties with Al Qaeda. These denials are simply not credible."[3]

While the Bush administration was clearly attempting to make a credible case for including military action against Iraq in the "global war on terrorism," key officials also seem to have been trapped in an outmoded worldview that made it difficult, if not impossible, to envision significant threats to the security of the United States emanating from nonstate actors. States have long been considered central to what security is all about, both as the primary objects of security and as the primary threats to the security of other states.

Until recently, most studies of international security focused on the state and on the problem of war. During the Cold War, in fact, the term *security studies* referred almost exclusively to the study of the military and the use of force in international politics. Harvard professor Stephen Walt, for example, wrote that "security studies may be defined as the study of the threat, use, and control of military force."[4] Much of security studies, in fact, was devoted even more specifically to problems related to nuclear deterrence and arms control. The centrality of the state can also be seen in the ubiquity of the term *national security*. (As students of international relations will know, the term *national* commonly substitutes for the term *state* or *nation-state*, as in *the national interest* and *national defense*.) When the United States reformed its defense and foreign policy apparatus after World War II, it did so through a legislative initiative called the National Security Act of 1947. One of the major creations of that act (as amended in 1949) was the National Security Council. In 1952, President Truman created the National Security Agency as the focus of activities related to electronic intelligence.

The same emphasis on the state can be seen in other countries as well. The chief intelligence agency of the Soviet Union for most of its history was the *Komitet Gosudarstvennoy Bezopasnosti* (KGB), or Committee for State Security. Today, the main security agency of the People's Republic of China is the Ministry of State Security. Indeed, this pattern is almost universal. It is state (or national) security that preoccupies virtually every government in the world.[5] This fact alone makes it important to examine the state and the closely related phenomenon of war as part of our survey of security.

STATES AND SECURITY: AN AMBIVALENT RELATIONSHIP

For roughly four centuries, states have been the fundamental constituents of global society. Peoples seeking to establish political communities in which to enshrine their most cherished values have aspired to the creation of states. The Wilsonian principle of self-determination, which holds out the promise that every nation should be able to incorporate itself in the form of a state, has become a part of international human rights law.[6] It has also become extraordinarily popular, at least if the growth in the number of states (and the tremendous human costs incurred to achieve that growth) is any indication.

States exist, and their number continues to increase, because they have proven themselves adept at protecting and promoting certain fundamental values. The values that we most commonly look to the state to provide are order, rights, security from external threats, and other collective goods.

To many theorists, the most important function of the state is to establish order or, in the words of the U.S. Constitution, to "insure domestic Tranquility." Thomas Hobbes was especially concerned with this point. In a world where the use of force or the threat of force is a constant, people must organize to protect themselves. Beginning in Western Europe at the end of the medieval period and gradually spreading across time and territory to encompass the entire globe, the effort to organize for mutual protection has produced a system of roughly two hundred autonomous states. Over time and in a variety of legal instruments, ranging from the Peace of Westphalia of 1648 to the United Nations Charter of 1945, the state has been legitimated in its role as society's primary manager of force.

It is important to emphasize that the state's role is to manage or control the use of force, not to eliminate it. Force, after all, may be necessary both to secure order within the state and to protect against external threats. States may legitimately use force to promote certain additional aims, such as the defense of norms, including respect for human rights and the prohibition against aggression, adopted by the society of states. Nor is the state's role merely to arbitrate among those who use force. It does not simply establish rules for duels and feuds and insurrections. It seeks to eliminate substate violence while preserving the possibility of state violence—if for no other reason than to quash substate violence in order to prevent the anarchy that prompted Hobbes to argue the need for a Leviathan. The problem, of course, is that the state's use of violence on behalf of security is subject to abuses of many kinds, including violations of the human rights of the state's own citizens and aggression against other states, abuses that are often rationalized by governments as necessary to deal with security threats. The power of the state can be—and often has been—a force for tremendous evil when it has not been subjected to adequate checks, when it has been wielded by unscrupulous rulers, and when it has been placed in the service of inhumane projects. One need think only of the forced collectivization of agriculture in Stalinist Russia, Hitler's "Final Solution," or Mao's Cultural Revolution (among many cases) to understand the pitfalls of a system in which states possess what approaches a monopoly on the legitimate use of force. The dimensions of the problem are illustrated by R. J. Rummel's findings that during the twentieth century more people died at the hands of their own governments than were killed in all of the century's wars combined.[7]

Controlling the state's use of force within its own borders is primarily a matter of constitutional arrangements and personal virtues. Beyond its borders, however, the state's use of force is limited by international law, international organizations, and, ultimately, the power of other states. In the more serious cases of the state's abuse of power internally, other states, acting under the authority of international norms and institutions, may be the only means of control available. This, in fact, was the reason NATO intervened in Kosovo in 1999.

To summarize, the state occupies a privileged position with respect to the use of force in the contemporary world. As Max Weber noted, "The state is the human community that (successfully) claims the *monopoly of the legitimate use of physical force* within a given territory."[8] Or, to put it more simply, the state may kill; other actors may not. Of course, the state is an institution—a legal abstraction even—so to say that the state may kill and others may not is to say that only those acting under the authority of the state (soldiers and police, for example) may legitimately use violence.

We may say, then, that the fundamental divide in the world, at least from the standpoint of security, is between those who have a right to use force (i.e., states and their agents) and those who do not. The way the world is organized, terrorists, criminal gangs, and disgruntled individuals have no right to employ violence. This is what Hobbes had in mind in presenting Leviathan as the necessary substitute for the "war of each against all."

Of course, to suggest that the dividing line between legitimate users of force and illegitimate ones is the line that separates the state from all others is a bit too simple. It denies the legitimacy of revolutionary violence, including the American Revolution, the French Revolution, and many more recent revolutions, at least some of which have been democratic in both intent and outcome. It leaves individuals and peoples everywhere without effective recourse against injustice when that injustice is cloaked with the authority of the state. It also grants the state too much authority. Even states, after all, cross the line when using force unjustly.

Nonetheless, the Hobbesian insight concerning the state and its relationship to the security of individual human beings is an important one for us to consider in thinking about states and war. It can help us to understand the centrality of the state (and national security) in the traditional paradigm, and it can alert us to a number of important ways that the new security agenda affects states

THE CHANGING STATE OF THE STATES SYSTEM

Our concern, however, is not only with the way that new conceptions of security affect states. States (and, perhaps more important, the international system that states constitute) are changing in ways that impact our under-standing of security.

Perhaps the most obvious change of the past century is the dramatic growth, mentioned earlier, in the number of members of the states system. The almost fourfold increase in the number of sovereign states from the twentieth century's beginning to its end was the result first and foremost of the fragmentation of multiethnic empires in Europe and Asia (including the breakup of the Austro-Hungarian and Ottoman empires after World War I and of the Soviet Union at the end of the Cold War) and of successive waves of decolonization in Africa, Asia, Oceania, and the Caribbean. At the begin-ning of the twentieth century, there were fifty-five independent states in the world; today the United Nations has 193 member states.[9] The dismember-ment of colonial empires proceeded so rapidly following World War II that the Trusteeship Council, one of the six main organs of the United Nations and a body dedicated to the oversight of dependent territories, was able to suspend its operations in 1994. The Trust Territory of the Pacific Islands, a strategic trust administered by the United States until 1990, was the last to appear on the agenda of the Trusteeship Council. Its dissolution yielded three new states (the Federated States of Micronesia, the Republic of the Marshall Islands, and the Republic of Palau), each a member of the United Nations in its own right, and the Commonwealth of the Northern Marianas, which remains a part of the United States.

As the number of states has increased, the willingness of states to join together in international organizations has also increased. The first inter-governmental organizations (to regulate navigation on the Elbe and Rhine rivers) were formed in the first half of the nineteenth century in response to the demands of the increased commercial interactions of Europe's states. International trade continues to motivate states to join international organi-zations ranging from those with broad mandates, such as the World Trade Organization, to those with narrower competencies, such as the International Coffee Organization. But scores of other concerns have prompted states to create international governmental organizations (IGOs). Many IGOs, such as the International Atomic Energy Agency (IAEA) and the Organisation for the Prohibition of Chemical Weapons (OPCW), focus on security issues.

The increase in the number of intergovernmental organizations has been accompanied by a greater willingness of states to join and of IGOs to invite them in regardless of their fitness for membership. The League of Nations, the first IGO to aspire to universal membership, never counted the United States among its members; it rejected Liechtenstein, San Marino, and Monaco as too small to be able to fulfill the obligations of membership; and it suffered the withdrawal of sixteen states (including Japan and Germany), as well as the expulsion of the Soviet Union in 1939. The United Nations, on the other hand, has achieved something very close to universal membership, including even international pariahs such as Burma, North Korea, and Sudan.[10]

The delegitimization of colonialism and the concomitant growth in size of the society of states have produced a system in which the gap between the strongest and weakest members of the states system, regardless of how strength is measured, has become enormous. In 2014, military expenditures by the United States comprised 34 percent of the world total and exceeded the military expenditures of China, Russia, Saudi Arabia, France, the United Kingdom, India, and Germany—the next seven highest-spending states—combined.[11] In economic terms, while annual gross domestic product per capita tops $52,000 in the twenty wealthiest states in the world, in over fifty of the world's states annual GDP per capita measures $5,000 or less.[12] The tiny South Pacific state of Tuvalu has a GDP of roughly $15 million, a portion of which is derived from a deal negotiated in 2000 to lease the country's Internet domain name (".tv") for approximately $2 million per year.[13] Whereas at one time such differentials would have invited the absorption of the weak into the empires of the strong, today the rules of international society expressly forbid such "solutions" to the weak state/strong state divide.

This leads to another important change in the states system: the persistence of "failed states." Because the security implications of failed states are so significant today, this issue will be considered separately below.

The increasing democratization of the world's states is another profound change that has significance for our assessment of states and war in the twenty-first century. In 1900, monarchs ruled thirty of the world's sovereign states; at the end of the twentieth century, Freedom House classified only ten states as monarchies, six of which were either on or adjacent to the Arabian Peninsula.[14] No country in the world met the criteria for democracy in 1900, according to Freedom House, but in 2014 there were 125 electoral democracies.[15] There are, of course, many complexities that are obscured rather than revealed by these statistics, and it is important to recognize, as Samuel Huntington noted, that history is not only "messy" but assuredly "not unidirectional."[16] Nevertheless, the changes that these numbers document are profound.

The democratization of states has gone hand in hand with the feminization of states. In 1900, only one country in the world (New Zealand) had extended the right to vote to all of its women. Today, only Saudi Arabia continues to deny women the right to vote. (Women are also barred from voting in the Holy See, which is the formal name for the Vatican city-state, but the only elections held there are those conducted by the all-male College of Cardinals for the selection of a new pope.) In 1900, not a single state in the world allowed women to stand for election to national offices. Today, women occupy roughly one in five seats in the world's national legislatures.[17] Although women occupied the top positions in only eight of the world's governments at the conclusion of the twentieth century, never before had so many women served as president or prime minister at one time.[18] The representation of women in governments around the world is appallingly low and progress has been incredibly slow, but the world is nonetheless very different from the way it was a century ago. Furthermore, it appears that the presence of women in democratic governments, even in small numbers, has had significant effects.

Noting the "pronounced gender gap with regard to foreign policy and national security issues," Francis Fukuyama has suggested that there is a connection between the widely observed democratic peace and the feminization of politics. According to what many scholars consider the closest thing to an irrefutable "law" of international politics, democracies do not wage war among themselves. This proposition, grounded in the theories of Immanuel Kant and Woodrow Wilson, has been the basis of policies adopted by Bill Clinton, George W. Bush, Tony Blair, and the European Union.[19] While we know that democracies do not fight each other, we do not know exactly why this is the case. It may be, Fukuyama suggests, that part of the answer lies in the fact that "developed democracies . . . tend to be more feminized than authoritarian states, in terms of expansion of franchise and participation in political decision making. It should therefore surprise no one," he continues, "that the historically unprecedented shift in the sexual basis of politics should lead to a change in international relations."[20]

The democratization and feminization of states are part of a larger trend toward the humanization of states and the international system. Individuals now matter in ways that they have not for most of history. This can be seen most clearly in the development of international humanitarian law in the nineteenth century and international human rights law in the twentieth century. It is manifested as well in the shift toward notions of human development and human security, away from more traditional understandings of state-led development and national security. As individuals have come to possess internationally recognized rights, states have been forced to cede a bit of their own sovereignty in deference to those rights.

There are also some subtle changes afoot that call into question many of our old ideas about security. Robert D. Kaplan, in an essay reflecting on the meaning of Fort Leavenworth in the nineteenth century and at present, suggests that the territorial nation-state, which, for centuries has been the focus of most thinking about security, is on the way out.[21] Richard Rosecrance, assessing changes in the nature of the state, also argues that land is becoming less significant in international relations. His thesis is that developed countries, at least, are rapidly becoming "virtual states" in which private-sector management and research functions are centralized in the territorial state while production is moved overseas to a group of "body nations" (such as China, Mexico, and India) that provide manufacturing for the world.[22] The economic success of a number of small states such as Singapore and Taiwan seems to demonstrate the declining significance of territory. It may be that this, too, is part of what prompted, over the course of the twentieth century, the delegitimization of wars of conquest and policies of imperialism.

Of course, noting these facts is not to suggest that the territorial state is already obsolete. Land, particularly in those situations in which oil deposits and other natural resources lie under it, may continue to be worth fighting over for some time to come, but its importance is on the decline for others. Territory and population remain the physical base of the state—for the present—so that security calculations must continue to take both into consideration.[23]

How have these changes in the states system affected our understanding of security? It may be better to ask how these changes *ought to* affect our understanding. As we noted at the beginning of this chapter, traditional modes of thought about national security are difficult to change.

First, the greatest threat to national security under the traditional paradigm—interstate war—has declined significantly as a consequence of some of the changes in the states system described above. In fact, one of the most striking developments in international politics since the end of World War II has been the decline in the incidence of large-scale interstate war. Militarized conflicts between states have not disappeared entirely by any means—the United States alone has fought large land wars in Korea, Vietnam, Iraq (twice), and Afghanistan—but across the globe there have developed large "zones of peace" in which interstate war has become extremely unlikely. Europe, where wars were a regular feature of continental politics for centuries, has become what Karl Deutsch labeled a "pluralistic security community."[24] North and South America and Southeast Asia have become stable regions that are generally free of interstate war, even though they have not achieved the level of economic and political integration that European states have experienced within the European

Union. The almost complete disappearance of war among the world's major powers may be the most noteworthy aspect of the larger story. John Mueller, in fact, has argued that great-power wars have become obsolete. He attributes this to an emerging consensus, solidified by the experience of two world wars, that war in the developed world is immoral and ineffective.[25]

Second, other changes in the states system noted above have resulted in the rise of "zones of turmoil," which are characterized by persistent and often seemingly intractable intrastate wars. According to the Uppsala Conflict Data Program, an average year over the course of the last two decades has seen forty armed conflicts scattered across the globe, the vast majority of which have been intrastate wars. Only one purely interstate armed conflict, between Djibouti and Eritrea, occurred in 2008. Virtually all contemporary wars occur in the developing world.[26]

Data compiled by the Correlates of War Project confirm that intrastate war has become the dominant form of armed conflict since World War II. Between 1945 and 1997, civil wars outnumbered interstate wars by a ratio of more than four to one (108 to 23). Battle deaths in civil wars (11.4 million) also dwarfed those in interstate wars (3.3 million).[27]

Intrastate conflict, which we discuss below, and economic insecurity, the subject of chapter 11, commonly appear in tandem. Both are also associated with the failure of states, an issue that, more than any other, has helped to advance the concept of human security.

WEAK STATES, FAILED STATES, AND COLLAPSED STATES

One of the problems with the traditional approach to the understanding of states and security is that the dramatic differences among states have often been underappreciated.[28] The false assumption that states are all fundamentally the same, at least with respect to their security interests, was especially prevalent during the Cold War, when the overwhelming majority of students of security studies focused on the United States, the Soviet Union, and their allies. Not surprisingly, given this focus, it appeared that states were principally concerned with external threats to their territorial and political integrity. To put it differently, national security required a capability to deter or defend against a military assault or espionage aimed at a coup d'état.

Because states vary widely in size, military might, political stability, and, perhaps most important, coherence (that is, literally, their ability to stick together), their security interests diverge in ways that the traditional understanding of national security fails to capture. The "ethnocentric obsession with external threats to state security" overlooks the fact that weak states are often concerned primarily with internal threats that commonly attend the creation and development of new states.[29] Sir Michael Howard wrote a quarter-century ago that "the problems of the twenty-first century will not be those of traditional power confrontations. They are more likely to arise out of the integration, or disintegration, of states themselves, and affect all actors on the world scene irrespective of ideology."[30] He could have said the same of the problems of the late twentieth century. Indeed, the historical record since 1945 suggests that security threats (understood narrowly as the threat of war and its effects) have been particularly significant in the developing world, where war has attended the creation and consolidation of new states (as in Pakistan, Vietnam, Algeria, and East Timor, to name but a few examples). As we noted above, far more fighting occurred in the world of weak states in the last half of the twentieth century than in the world of the strong states, and most of that fighting took the form of intrastate conflict rather than interstate conflict.

Weak states are problematic for a number of reasons. First, they fail to provide the basic security that states are supposed to offer their citizens. They fail, in other words, to offer a respite from the "state of nature," in which, according to Hobbes's famous description, "the life of man [is] solitary, poor, nasty, brutish and short."[31] As a consequence, there may be little protection against crime (including violent crime), little opportunity for education, little economic opportunity, and little access to health care.

Second, by failing to protect their citizens or to offer assistance with basic needs, weak states may burden their neighbors with refugees. According to the United Nations High Commissioner for Refugees, at the end of 2014 there were almost fifteen million refugees in the world. Stateless persons, internally displaced persons, and asylum seekers brought the total "population of concern" to almost fifty-five million, the highest figure ever recorded by the UNHCR. Syria, into the fourth year of its devastating civil war by that time, had produced 3.7 million refugees and 7.6 million internally displaced persons.[32]

Third, by failing to extend the rule of law over all of their territories, weak states may provide safe havens for terrorists, transnational criminal organizations, international fugitives, and other actors that are a menace to international society. This problem in particular has turned a key assumption of national security on its head.

For most of the history of the modern states system, national security has required assessing and responding to the threat—defined as a product of capabilities and intentions to do harm—posed by the strongest states in the system. The balance-of-power approach to security assumes that, for their own protection, states will arm themselves and form alliances in order to meet the threats posed by powerful potential enemies. Since the end of the Cold War, however, national security has required that strong states deal with passive threats posed by the weakest states in the system.

Since the end of the Cold War, the United States has stood as the world's only hyperpower, to use the term that French foreign minister Hubert Vedrine applied to the United States in 1999. The Persian Gulf War of 1991 demonstrated clearly the superiority of the American military over what was, at the time, thought to be a formidable Iraqi army. Events during the remainder of the 1990s, however, indicated that the U.S. military might not be capable of dealing as well with weak states as with strong states.

In country after country during the 1990s, the United States was confronted with humanitarian disasters that created pressure (in part as a consequence of media coverage and the public opinion it generated) for intervention. A more active post–Cold War UN Security Council both encouraged and assisted the interventionist impulse, with mixed results, in the former Yugoslavia, Somalia, Rwanda, Haiti, and elsewhere. During his eight years in office, President Bill Clinton was alternately criticized for doing too little—for failing to stop genocide in Rwanda, for example—and for doing too much—for conducting "foreign policy as social work."[33]

Each of the opportunities for intervention during the 1990s—those that were seized and those that were avoided—had at its core a state in which the most basic functions of government—establishing a minimal public order and providing basic services—had broken down. The problem for strong states in the post–Cold War world had become weak states, not the threat posed by other strong states. It was exemplified in one form or another by Afghanistan, Cambodia, Haiti, Côte d'Ivoire, Liberia, Rwanda, Sierra Leone, Somalia, Sudan, and Zaire. In fact, the problem arose so often that some felt a new taxonomy—dividing cases among the categories of "weak states," "failed states," and "collapsed states"—was required. It was the phenomenon of the failed state and its implications that more than any other transformed post–Cold War optimism about the triumph of democracy and the "end of history" into pessimism about "the coming anarchy."[34]

Robert Kaplan, one of the most influential pessimists, described the problem in a bleak account, originally published in 1994, of the situation in West Africa. "Even in the quiet zones [of Liberia, Guinea, Ivory Coast, and Sierra Leone] none of the governments except the Ivory Coast's maintains the schools, bridges, roads, and police forces in a manner necessary for fundamental sovereignty." It was not just West Africa, though, because Kaplan regarded the region as a microcosm of a much broader phenomenon:

West Africa is becoming a symbol of worldwide demographic, environmental, and societal stress, in which criminal anarchy emerges as the real "strategic" danger. Disease, overpopulation, unprovoked crime, scarcity of resources, refugee migrations, the increasing erosion of nation-states and international borders, and the empowerment of private armies, security firms, and international drug cartels are now most tellingly demonstrated through a West African prism.[35]

Fortunately, conditions in West Africa have improved since Kaplan wrote these words. Liberia's dictatorship has given way to a democratic government led by one of Africa's first female presidents, Ellen Johnson Sirleaf, and Sierra Leone is recovering from its decade-long civil war. But the stresses Kaplan observed there can still be observed in many other regions of the world as well as in West Africa's own troubled response to the Ebola crisis.

For those who live in (or near) failed states, "national security" must seem an ironic concept since the state is, whether directly or indirectly, the very cause of insecurity. Rather than providing protection against anarchy, failed states permit and sometimes even abet society's slide into the Hobbesian state of nature. Wars for control of territory or resources (such as the diamond mines of Sierra Leone or the oil fields of Angola) or for ethnic advantage or revenge are both common and extraordinarily devastating. Well over eight million people, primarily civilians, have been killed in failed-state conflicts since the end of the Cold War. Tens, or perhaps even hundreds, of millions more have been affected in other profound ways, especially by the denial of basic needs such as food, shelter, and health care.[36]

For the United States, the security issue related to failed states moved from the margins to the center as a consequence of 9/11. Two failed states, Sudan and Afghanistan, hosted Osama bin Laden and Al Qaeda training facilities in the years prior to 9/11. The American experience in another failed state, Somalia, in the October 1993 battle of Mogadishu (recounted in Mark Bowden's *Black Hawk Down* and in the movie based on it) was read by bin Laden as an example (along with Vietnam, Lebanon, and Afghanistan) of the ability of insurgents in a weak state to drive out a superpower.[37] In short, failed states, once a cause of debates in the United States over the nation's moral responsibilities and the proper configuration of the military, became a central concern, due to the platform they provided for the operation of Al Qaeda and other transnational terrorist organizations. The first major operation of the "global war on terrorism," consequently, was the war to overthrow the Taliban regime that had hosted bin Laden in Afghanistan. And lest there be any doubt about Afghanistan's status as a failed state in the fall of 2001, Barry Bearak indicated the true situation with this memorable line from a *New York Times* story on the possibility of war there: "If there are Americans clamoring to bomb Afghanistan back to the Stone Age, they ought to know that this nation does not have so far to go. This is a post-apocalyptic place of felled cities, parched land and downtrodden people."[38]

The Islamic State: A Consequence of Weak States

At the heart of the Peace of Westphalia was an agreement to eliminate religion as a reason for warfare by establishing a rule of mutual tolerance among (if not within) states. Both the Holy Roman Empire's bid to subdue Protestant principalities and the efforts of Protestant rulers to extend their control to Catholic territories were delegitimized by their joint acceptance of a principle encapsulated in the Latin phrase *cuius regio eius religio* (the ruler of the territory determines the religion practiced in it). While religious differences have factored into conflicts many times in the Westphalian era, now the basic principle is being threatened.

The Islamic State—also called the Islamic State in Iraq and ash-Sham (the term for Syria in classical Arabic) or the Islamic State in Iraq and Syria (ISIS)—has capitalized on state failure to inject into the modern world a distinctively premodern understanding of the way religion and the state are to interact. On June 29, 2014, the Islamic State publicly proclaimed a caliphate with Abu Bakr al-Baghdadi as the first caliph since the days of the Ottoman Empire. It is a theocratic state that considers itself unbound by the Westphalian principle of sovereignty with its corollaries of nonaggression and nonintervention. In fact, the formation of the caliphate signaled the Islamic State's intent to pursue a policy of expansion that would, according to prophecies in the Qur'an, lead to the Day of Judgment with its divinely forcordained apocalypse. For Muslims who subscribe to the most literal reading of the Qur'an, the establishment of the caliphate was a pivotal event; thousands began traveling from all over the world to the lands controlled by the Islamic State to lend their support to its efforts, military and political, to impose divine judgment on both Muslim and non-Muslim apostates.[39]

By the middle of 2015, and in spite of armed opposition on the ground supported by American and British airstrikes, the Islamic State controlled a swath of territory roughly equivalent to the size of the British Isles with a population estimated at six to eight million. Its territory, primarily in the most ineffectively governed regions of Iraq and most war-torn parts of Syria, demonstrates well the hazards posed by failed states and the tendency for conditions in them to threaten other states. To be clear, in the territories it controls the Islamic State exercises many of the functions associated with modern states. It enforces law, collects taxes, maintains both military and police forces, and even seeks to build alliances with like-minded organizations. (In March 2015, Boko Haram offered—and the Islamic State accepted—a pledge of allegiance that, in theory, extends the caliphate to West Africa.) In many respects, the Islamic State exercises more effective control over the territories it occupies than the states it has displaced did. However, the Islamic State does not have, and will likely never obtain, the recognition of other states.

It exists as a quasi-state (due to the absence of the critical element of recognition) only because the recognized states whose territory it occupies are themselves quasi-states (due to their inability to exercise effective control). Nation building, therefore, appears as an essential element of any strategy to defeat ISIS, a point recognized by President Obama in his pledge at the June 2015 G-7 meeting in Germany to accelerate efforts to train the Iraqi army to fight Islamic State units.[40]

INTRASTATE CONFLICT: THE MODERN FACE OF WAR

In the traditional paradigm, the greatest threat to the security of state—that is, to national security—is thought to be the hostile action of other states. The new security paradigm notes that groups within the state may pose a greater threat than other states as the explosions of interstate war are replaced by the implosions of intrastate war. But to acknowledge that intrastate conflict is the modern face of war is not to suggest that those in the politically stable states of the developed world can ignore what is happening elsewhere. As Syria's civil war and the rise of the Islamic State demonstrate, intrastate conflicts can have serious external ramifications.

Emboldened by the rapid success of the Arab Spring revolts in removing the corrupt leaders of Tunisia and Egypt in the first weeks of 2011, protesters took to the streets of Syria's major cities in March to demand the resignation of President Bashar al-Assad, whose security forces responded with violence. But rather than capitulate, the anti-Assad movement grew in numbers as well as in violence as protesters began to arm themselves against the government. Independent combat brigades formed all across Syria and battled the Syrian army for control of individual cities and town. In 2012, even the capital city of Damascus was experiencing urban warfare. As others have done before in the face of an insurgency, Assad responded brutally and indiscriminately. Both soldiers and civilians died by the thousands. By June 2013, the United Nations was estimating that ninety thousand people had been killed in the conflict. Two years later, credible estimates put the number killed in Syria at 220,000.

Meanwhile, the conflict in Syria grew more complicated as the chaos attracted Sunni militants eager to oust a repressive government dominated by Alawites, a small Shia sect. Two of the most effective Sunni rebel groups have been the al-Nusra Front, an affiliate of Al Qaeda, and the Islamic State. Their leading roles in the effort to overthrow the Assad regime coupled with their designation as terrorist organizations by the United States and other western governments has complicated external efforts to remove Assad from power by means of either diplomacy or force. But the Sunni challenge to Assad is hardly unified. In spite of common origins and aims (at least in broad terms), the al-Nusra Front and the Islamic State have not only rejected a merger but also clashed on the battlefield.

Syria has become a humanitarian nightmare. By the end of May 2015, there were approximately four million Syrian refugees scattered around the world with roughly three-quarters in neighboring Turkey and Lebanon. Another 6.5 million Syrians were displaced inside their own state.[41] As early as November 2011, the Independent Commission of Inquiry on Syria, a body appointed by the UN Human Rights Council, reported that Syrian military and security forces had committed gross violations of human rights with some potentially amounting to crimes against humanity.[42] The same group of investigators in February 2015 expressed frustration at the failure of the international community to respond to war crimes being committed in Syria.[43] On top of everything else, Syria's civil war has seen the use of chemical weapons by the Syrian government and beheadings by the Islamic State.

The civil war in Syria, although unique in many respects, is part of a disturbing pattern in international politics. Between 1946 and 2013, according to the Uppsala Conflict Data Program, there were 254 armed conflicts in the world. The vast majority of these conflicts (including all of the thirty-three armed conflicts ongoing in 2013) have been intrastate conflicts rather than interstate conflicts. While a number of the intrastate conflicts have been "internationalized" by the participation of outside states (as in Afghanistan, the Democratic Republic of the Congo, and Nigeria), the key point is that war is increasingly waged by rebel groups against states and not by states against other states.[44] While the number of internationalized intrastate conflicts (including the war in Ukraine, where Russia has supported Ukrainian separatists) raises questions about a possible reemergence of interstate war, former UN secretary-general Kofi Annan's statement remains valid: "In the world today intrastate conflict is the face of conflict."[45]

According to the International Institute for Strategic Studies in London, using a different data set from that employed by the researchers at Uppsala University, there were forty-two armed conflicts ongoing in the world in 2014, down from sixty-three in 2008. However, deaths due to armed conflict rose from 56,000 to 180,000 in that same period. Furthermore, 2013 saw the number of refugees and internally displaced persons (IDPs) go over fifty million for the first time since World War II as a consequence of intrastate conflicts in Syria, Iraq, Libya, Somalia, South Sudan, Nigeria, the Democratic Republic of the Congo, and elsewhere.[46]

Intrastate conflict, it should be noted, is also one of the faces of poverty. Oxford economist Paul Collier notes that of the roughly one billion people living in the world's poorest countries, 73 percent "have recently been through a civil war or are still in one."[47] In sub-Saharan Africa since 1990, there have been intrastate conflicts in Angola, Burundi, the Central African Republic, Chad, Côte d'Ivoire, the Democratic Republic of the Congo, Djibouti, Eritrea, Ethiopia, Guinea, Lesotho, Liberia, Mali, Mozambique, Niger, Nigeria, Rwanda, Senegal, Sierra Leone, Somalia, Sudan, Togo, and Uganda.[48] As chapter 11 notes, these conflicts have a direct and significant impact on economic development.

Unlike the large-scale wars of the first half of the twentieth century, which were based on state interests and involved the mobilization of all sectors of the state in support of a common cause, the intrastate wars that have dominated world politics in recent decades are often based on identity politics and involve the fragmentation of the state. The "identity" at the heart of these conflicts may be religious, ethnic, or racial, and while the groups involved may seek to seize control of a state or establish a new one, they do not fight out of loyalty to an existing state. On the contrary, groups like the Lord's Resistance Army in Uganda, the Chechen rebels in Russia, or Sunni militants in Syria seek to undermine the authority of the existing state.

The decline of state sovereignty has to be considered both a cause and a consequence of intrastate conflict. As Mary Kaldor notes, "The new identity politics arises out of the disintegration or erosion of modern state structures, especially centralized, authoritarian states. The collapse of communist states after 1989, the loss of legitimacy of post-colonial states in Africa or South Asia, or even the decline of welfare states in more advanced industrial countries provide the environment in which the new forms of identity politics are nurtured."[49] Governments have lost what was often almost exclusive control of weaponry, capital, and information as power has migrated from public to private actors. In some states, such as Colombia and Mexico, state sovereignty has been directly challenged by transnational criminal organizations. Beyond the erosion of sovereignty, however, what are the causes of intrastate conflict?

In an ambitious study titled *The International Dimensions of Internal Conflict*, Michael E. Brown draws a distinction between underlying and proximate causes of intrastate conflict. The former include such factors as weak states, elite politics, widespread economic problems, and problematic group histories. Proximate causes include factors such as "internal, mass-level factors (bad domestic problems); mass-level problems (bad neighborhoods); external, elite-level factors (bad neighbors); or internal, elite-level factors (bad leaders)."[50]

Some journalists and popular writers have ascribed intrastate and ethnic conflict to "ancient hatreds" between various groups. For example, in his book *Balkan Ghosts*, which reportedly influenced President Clinton's views on Bosnia, Robert Kaplan portrayed the root cause of the Balkan conflict as the mutual antipathies of the major ethnic groups in Bosnia.[51] Academic analysts, however, tend to discount this explanation of the cause of internal conflict, for several reasons.[52] First, scholars generally dismiss monocausal explanations of complex phenomena; even if "ancient hatreds" play a role in causing internal conflicts, other factors must be examined to explain why violence breaks out in some cases but not others, or why, when violence does occur, the level of intensity varies so widely.[53] Second, even if ethnic hostility exists, it may not result in groups killing one another. For example, the three major ethnic groups coexisted peacefully for decades in Yugoslavia before the Balkan wars of the 1990s began; something besides "ancient hatred" was clearly at work when the killing began. According to David Lake and Donald Rothchild, "By itself, ethnicity is not a cause of violent conflict. Most ethnic groups, most of the time, pursue their interests peacefully through established political channels. But when linked with acute uncertainty and, indeed, fear of what the future might bring, ethnicity emerges as one of the major fault lines along which societies fracture."[54]

Ethnic "fault lines" are very much in evidence. Members of ethnic groups identify with one another because of their shared national origin, tribal affiliation, social organization, or common language, religion, or race. Demographers estimate that there are somewhere from three to five thousand ethnic groups in the world today.[55] One study has identified 233 ethnic groups as targets of discrimination or as having organized for political assertiveness; this constitutes between 5 and 8 percent of the world's total number of ethnic groups.[56] Of the two hundred or so states that exist today, fewer than twenty—about 10 percent of the world's total—are ethnically homogeneous, "in the sense that ethnic minorities account for less than five percent of the population."[57] Some states have disintegrated along ethnic fault lines. Since the end of the Cold War, Czechoslovakia, Yugoslavia, the Soviet Union, and Ethiopia have fragmented, giving rise to almost two dozen new states. In a number of other states, a significant potential for ethnic fragmentation exists.

Ethnic groups often have ties to states outside of the countries in which they reside. In some cases states provide economic, and sometimes even military, aid to ethnic groups in other countries. For example, during the Soviet occupation of Afghanistan, the government of Saudi Arabia provided substantial aid to the Muslim *mujahidin* who were fighting the Soviets. Russian aid to separatists in the Crimea, a part of Ukraine since the breakup of the Soviet Union, resulted in its annexation by Russia. When ethnic groups receive aid from foreign governments, domestic disputes can turn into international conflicts.

Humanitarian Intervention, UN Peace Operations, and the Responsibility to Protect

The human toll of contemporary conflicts like the one in Syria, combined with their impact on other states, often prompts some consideration of intervention. When intrastate conflicts involve mass casualties among civilian populations or other "acts that shock the conscience of humankind," or in cases where there is "intent to destroy, in whole or in part, a national, ethnical, racial or religious group"—that is, genocide—the question of humanitarian intervention arises. Unilateral humanitarian intervention is often viewed with great skepticism owing to the belief that states are rarely willing to send military forces into harm's way for reasons unrelated to national interests. Even multilateral intervention may be considered suspect if it is not sanctioned and supervised by the UN Security Council. The problem, however, is that Security Council support for intervention of any kind can be difficult to muster, first, because of the divergent interests of the five permanent members (China, France, Russia, the United Kingdom, and the United States) and, second, because of the strong (and often self-serving) support for state sovereignty exhibited by China, Russia, and, at times, the United States. At a time when humanitarian intervention in Syria might have moderated or perhaps even ended the conflict without putting the Islamic State in an advantageous position, the Security Council was deadlocked by Chinese opposition to intervention on any grounds and Russian opposition to intervention against a client state.

At times a state with both the power and the will to intervene will do so without Security Council authorization. India's intervention in Bangladesh's war of independence in 1971, Vietnam's invasion of Cambodia in 1978 to oust the genocidal regime of Pol Pot, and the U.S.-led NATO intervention in Kosovo in 1999 provide good examples. At other times, however, political conditions in the Security Council are such that it is possible to secure a resolution authorizing UN-supervised peacekeeping.

Peacekeeping, which was originally conceived as an alternative to the more robust strategy of collective security, is intended to create the space in which brokered solutions to conflicts can occur while military forces operating under a UN Security Council mandate keep the opposing sides separated. The conflict resolution process may employ conciliation, mediation, or the offering of "good offices," sometimes involving the UN secretary-general or his personal envoy. Depending on the circumstances, UN peace operations may require the deployment of civilian police forces to assist in maintaining order or administrators whose function is to help a weak government build its capacity to provide essential services to the people of a war-torn state.

Peace enforcement is a more recent notion that the international community should act through the UN and other international organizations to end conflicts even when the opposing parties do not request assistance as is generally required for peacekeeping. These more assertive actions are sometimes referred to as "Chapter VII operations," because that section of the UN Charter refers to such actions, authorized by the Security Council, as blockade, enforcement of sanctions, forcible disarmament, and direct military action. From the founding of the UN in 1945 to the end of 2014, there have been seventy-one UN peace operations established; fifty-three have been established since the end of the Cold War. At the end of April 2015, there were sixteen active UN peace operations, including ones in South Sudan, the Democratic Republic of the Congo, Liberia, and (since 1964) Cyprus. The UN's first peacekeeping operation—the United Nations Truce Supervision Organization (UNTSO), established in the Middle East in 1948—is also its oldest; UNTSO continues to maintain observers in the region. For the fiscal year that ran from July 1, 2014, to June 30, 2015, UN peacekeeping operations cost approximately $8.47 billion, an amount apportioned among the members states of the UN based roughly on their ability to pay.[58]

Given the frequency of intrastate conflict, it is likely that the demand for peacekeeping and peace enforcement will continue into the foreseeable future. While there have been some notable failures in the UN's efforts to maintain international peace and security, some conflicts have been ended by UN intervention. Even the UN's worst failures have, arguably, helped to change the terms of debate, if not always the policies of states, regarding intervention. The UN's failures in the Balkans and in Rwanda provide important lessons.

In 1991, Croatia and Slovenia declared their independence from Yugoslavia, a multiethnic state created after World War I from the remnants of the Austro-Hungarian and Ottoman empires. These acts set in motion a chain of events that would soon lead to the worst war in Europe since World War II. In an effort to halt a spreading conflict, UN peacekeepers were sent to the former Yugoslavia in March 1992. By then, however, a new, horrific euphemism for genocide had been introduced into the lexicon of politics: *ethnic cleansing*. The size and mandate of the UN operation was inadequate to prevent the mass killing of innocent noncombatants. On the afternoon of July 10, 1995, Bosnian Serb paramilitaries attacked Srebrenica, a city the UN had declared a sanctuary for some forty thousand people seeking refuge from the war. UN peacekeepers in the city were hopelessly outnumbered and had to watch as some six thousand people were rounded up and killed. One account of the carnage reported:

> The Muslim men were herded by the thousands into trucks, delivered to killing sites near the Drina River, lined up four by four, and shot. One survivor, 17-year-old Nezad Avdic, recalled that as he lay wounded among the dead

Muslims, a Serbian soldier surveyed the stony, moonlit field piled with bodies and merrily declared: "That was a good hunt. There were a lot of rabbits here."[59]

Following the attack on Srebrenica, Serb forces threatened other "safe" areas. Only when the Serbs shelled the main marketplace in Sarajevo, killing more than fifty civilians, and three American diplomats died when their armored personnel carrier went off one of the treacherous roads leading into Sarajevo, was the international community moved to respond. Sixty thousand soldiers were sent to Bosnia to implement a peace agreement negotiated in Dayton, Ohio. In four years of war, an estimated two hundred thousand people were killed and two to three million were displaced from their homes.[60]

Even as ethnic cleansing was occurring in the Balkans, a second genocidal outburst was taking place under the helpless gaze of UN peacekeepers in Rwanda, where, for four centuries, two tribes—the Tutsi and the Hutu—had lived together. After Rwanda and Burundi gained their independence from Belgium in 1962, tensions between the Tutsi and Hutu flared into violence sporadically.

On April 6, 1994, the presidents of Rwanda and Burundi were killed when two missiles hit their plane as it approached the airfield at Kigali, the capital of Rwanda. The assassination unleashed a killing spree designed by Hutu extremists to wipe out Rwanda's Tutsi population. In just one hundred days, an estimated eight hundred thousand people were killed; almost five million were forced to flee for their lives.[61] The Carnegie Commission on Preventing Deadly Conflict called it "one of the most horrifying chapters in human history."[62]

A small UN peacekeeping force was present in Rwanda during the genocide. Its commander, Lieutenant General Romeo Dallaire, sought authority for an augmented force operating under Chapter VII ("peace enforcement") of the UN Charter rather than Chapter VI ("peacekeeping") in order to stop the genocide, assist in the return of refugees, and deliver humanitarian aid. Dallaire later estimated that with five thousand troops and a mandate under Chapter VII, he could have prevented most of the killing.[63] Why, then, were his requests not approved? Following the disastrous Somalia intervention, culminating in the *Black Hawk Down* incident in which eighteen American soldiers were killed in Mogadishu, both the UN and the U.S. government were hesitant to involve themselves in another African peace enforcement mission. In addition, the UN, the U.S. government, and NATO were trying to figure out what to do about the situation in the former Yugoslavia. As a result, there was little support for sending more troops to Rwanda.[64]

The abject failure of the United Nations to protect the security of targeted groups in Bosnia and Rwanda prompted a great deal of soul searching among those who might have acted differently. But it also led to a number of changes in the way the sovereignty of states was viewed. This became apparent, first, in the creation of international tribunals for the prosecution of individuals responsible for the atrocities, including genocide, that were committed in the territory of the former Yugoslavia and in Rwanda. The ad hoc tribunals created by the Security Council prompted the creation of the International Criminal Court in 1998. By seeking to hold individuals—including heads of state—responsible for war crimes, crimes against humanity, and acts of genocide, these courts signaled a repudiation of the traditional idea that acts of state stand above the law. (On the other hand, the support of major powers for traditional understandings of sovereignty helps to account for the fact that the United States, China, and Russia have not joined the International Criminal Court.) The general understanding of sovereignty was also challenged, if not fully changed, in the aftermath of Bosnia and Rwanda by efforts to redefine the responsibilities of states. UN Secretary-General Kofi Annan signaled the change in thinking in a 1998 speech on intervention in which he said, "The [UN] Charter protects the sovereignty of peoples. It was never meant as a license for governments to trample on human rights and dignity. Sovereignty implies responsibility, not just power."[65]

This new mind-set generated several efforts to think through the implications of a more humanitarian understanding of sovereignty. In 2000, the Canadian government—at the time a leader in the international movement to promote the concept of human security—established the International Commission on Intervention and State Sovereignty to study matters arising from the many opportunities for humanitarian intervention in the post–Cold War world. A year later, the Commission, which included former government officials, scholars, and politicians, released a report titled *The Responsibility to Protect*. The document argued that an international consensus was developing around the idea that there is a positive duty for the international community to act to protect civilians "suffering serious harm as a result of internal war, insurgency, repression, or state failure" if the government of the state in question is either responsible for the suffering or incapable of addressing it.

The responsibility to protect—commonly called "R2P"—is not part of international law. Instead, it is regarded by many as an emerging norm to guide the United Nations specifically and the international community more generally in considering when it may be permissible—or even necessary—to intervene. R2P was included in the 2005 World Summit Outcome Document. In 2009, Secretary-General Ban Ki-moon published a document titled *Implementing the Responsibility to Protect* as part of an effort to operationalize the concept. In 2011, faced with evidence of crimes against humanity in Libya, the UN Security Council adopted Resolution 1970, which noted the responsibility to protect and responded by imposing economic sanctions against the Gaddafi regime while also referring the situation to the International Criminal Court. A subsequent resolution, 1973, authorized UN member states to take "all necessary measures" to protect civilians in Libya. It was this resolution that NATO used as authorization for the bombing campaign that ultimately resulted in Gaddafi's overthrow.

NATIONAL SECURITY AND TRANSNATIONAL THREATS

Perceptions of national security are changing. At the beginning of September 2004, the *Washington Post* reported that Pentagon officials were considering a major shift in strategy, one that, if adopted, would require significant changes in American force structure. The shift then being contemplated was based on the view that traditional conceptions of national security had become outmoded as a consequence of the 9/11 attacks. As the *Post* story put it, "The plan's working assumption is that the United States faces almost no serious conventional threats from traditional, state-based militaries."[66] Worrying about states is out; worrying about substate actors is in. The final report of the 9/11 Commission explains the foundations of this shift in perspective and is worth quoting at some length:

> In the post-9/11 world, threats are defined more by the fault lines within societies than by the territorial boundaries between them. From terrorism to global disease or environmental degradation, the challenges have become transnational rather than international. That is the defining quality of world politics in the twenty-first century.
>
> National security used to be considered by studying foreign frontiers, weighing opposing groups of states, and measuring industrial might. To be dangerous, an enemy had to muster large armies. Threats emerged slowly, often visibly, as weapons were forged, armies conscripted, and units trained and moved into place. Because large states were more powerful, they also had more to lose. They could be deterred.
>
> Now threats can emerge quickly. An organization like Al Qaeda, headquartered in a country on the other side of the earth, in a region so poor that electricity or telephones were scarce, could nonetheless scheme to wield weapons of unprecedented destructive power in the largest cities of the United States.[67]

The dramatic rise of transnational threats associated with the increased capabilities of substate actors and their ability to operate out of failed states (or ungoverned territories in weak states) is transforming traditional assumptions underlying national security. States have long been viewed as the principal threats to the security of other states, but state-based challenges are increasingly perceived as emanating from the weakness rather than the strength of states. When states fail to carry out their fundamental purpose of establishing order in society, the security of their own citizens is, as it always has been, endangered. But transnational actors are now making state failures a threat to citizens in other states as well.

ADDITIONAL RESOURCES

Books

Beebe, Shannon D., and Mary Kaldor. *The Ultimate Weapon Is No Weapon: Human Security and the New Rules of War and Peace*. New York: PublicAffairs, 2010.

Brown, Michael E., ed. *The International Dimensions of Internal Conflict*. Cambridge, MA: MIT Press, 1996.

Carnegie Commission on Preventing Deadly Conflict. *Preventing Deadly Conflict: Final Report*. Washington, DC: The Carnegie Corporation of New York, 1997.

Dallaire, Romeo. *Shake Hands with the Devil: The Failure of Humanity in Rwanda*. New York: Random House, 2004.

Fukuyama, Francis. *State-Building: Governance and World Order in the 21st Century*. Ithaca, NY: Cornell University Press, 2004.

Kaldor, Mary. *New & Old Wars*. 2nd ed. Stanford, CA: Stanford University Press, 2007.

Kaplan, Seth D. *Fixing Fragile States: A New Paradigm for Development*. Westport, CT: Praeger Security International, 2008.

Lake, David, and Donald Rothchild, eds. *The International Spread of Ethnic Conflict: Fear Diffusion and Escalation*. Princeton, NJ: Princeton University Press, 1998.

Mandelbaum, Michael. *The Ideas That Conquered the World: Peace, Democracy, and Free Markets in the Twenty-First Century*. New York: PublicAffairs, 2004.

Ripsman, Norrin M., and T. V. Paul. *Globalization and the National Security State*. New York: Oxford University Press, 2010.

Rosecrance, Richard N. *The Rise of the Virtual State: Wealth and Power in the Coming Century*. New York: Basic Books, 1999.

Rummel, R. J. *Death by Government*. New Brunswick, NJ: Transaction, 1994.

Websites

Carnegie Commission for Preventing Deadly Conflict: http://www.wilsoncenter.org/subsites/ccpdc/index.htm

Freedom House: www.freedomhouse.org/

Fund for Peace, Fragile States Index: www.fundforpeace.org/web/index.php

International Peace Institute: http://www.ipinst.org/
UN Department of Peacekeeping Operations: http://www.un.org/en/peacekeeping/
    about/dpko/
U.S. Department of State: www.state.gov/
U.S. Institute of Peace: www.usip.org/

Films

Black Hawk Down (2001): This film, directed by Ridley Scott, is based on Mark
    Bowden's detailed account of the ill-fated U.S. Army operation in Mogadishu,
    Somalia, in 1993.
Ghosts of Rwanda (2004): A *Frontline* documentary, *Ghosts of Rwanda* looks back
    at the Rwandan genocide ten years after it happened in 1994.
Hotel Rwanda (2004): A feature film based on the efforts of Paul Rusesabagina, a
    hotel manager, to save the lives of Tutsi sheltered in his hotel during the Rwandan
    genocide. MGM. Directed by Terry George.
Shake Hands with the Devil (2007): A documentary recounting the efforts of Lieu-
    tenant General Romeo Dallaire and UN peacekeepers to respond to the Rwandan
    genocide without the support of the United Nations. Halifax Film Company. Di-
    rected by Robert Spottiswoode.

Chapter Eleven

Economics and Security

If commerce were permitted to act to the universal extent it is capable, it would extirpate the system of war.

—Thomas Paine, *The Rights of Man* (1791)

The connections between economics and security—for individuals, for states, and for the international system—are deep and strong. They are also complex and, in some instances, confusing. Certainly there must be a connection between wealth and security, but does wealth make its possessor more or less secure? Consider that in 2001, when Al Qaeda targeted the twin towers of the World Trade Center in New York City—an iconic symbol of American capitalism—the United States accounted for somewhere between a quarter and a third of global wealth. Far from offering protection, the enormous wealth of the United States made its most important financial center a target. But poverty provides no security from violence. Some of the poorest countries in the world—Sudan, Somalia, the Democratic Republic of the Congo, and Afghanistan—have been the scenes of continual conflict.

During and immediately after World War II, those who were responsible for creating a stable postwar order believed it was essential to attend to the economic foundations of security. Acutely aware that the heavy reparations imposed on Germany following World War I had crippled the Weimar Republic and provided an opening for the rise of fascism, Allied leaders not only resisted the impulse to demand that the Axis powers indemnify their victims but also determined (in the face of the Soviet threat) that they would assist in postwar reconstruction. Believing that protectionist trade policies such as the Smoot-Hawley Tariff Act of 1930 (which set U.S. tariffs at their highest level in over a century) had exacerbated the Great Depression and produced economic insecurity worldwide, economic planners made free trade the linchpin of the postwar order. And convinced, as Immanuel Kant and Adam Smith had been, that economic interdependence promoted peace, Europeans and Americans alike supported institutions that would bind the French and German economies together. From these and other reactions to the economic roots of World War II arose a wide range of regional and global economic institutions—the International Monetary Fund, the World Bank, the World Trade Organization (originally the General Agreement on Tariffs and Trade), and the European Union, among others—that had, and continue to have, as one of their primary aims promoting international security through free trade.

But the connection between economics and security is not just about international security—that is, the prevention of global war. For the millions of people at the end of World War II whose homes and workplaces had been destroyed by war, and for millions more living in soon-to-be-independent colonies who had never experienced the wealth associated with modernization, the economics-security nexus was important as a matter of human security. For the world's poor, then and now, poverty is not merely *related* to insecurity—it *is* a form of insecurity. Extreme poverty, in fact, entails the constant threat of death by starvation or preventable disease. It is what Norwegian scholar Johan Galtung has called "structural violence."[1] The point is well illustrated by this grim statistic: According to the World Food Programme, 3.1 million children under five die each year of causes related to poor nutrition.[2]

Economic concerns are part of both traditional and new security paradigms. The war-making capacity of states and nonstate actors alike is highly dependent on the availability of funding. Economic problems ranging from global depressions at one extreme to local labor disputes at the other can prompt violence. In many of the world's poorest states, political instability (and thus insecurity) is fed by a general awareness that those who rule live extravagantly while those who are ruled struggle merely to survive. In short, questions related to wealth and poverty run through almost every conceivable security issue. In this chapter, we seek to introduce some of the most salient respects in which economics impacts national security and human security. An important starting point for this discussion is the distinction between the wealthy and the impoverished parts of the world. Economic security means something quite different to the rich than it does to the poor.

WEALTH, POVERTY, AND SECURITY

Judged in terms of economic security, the fundamental divide in the world is between developed countries and developing countries. In the developed world, national security debates often entail questions related to defense spending. For example, a long-running debate in the United States over the cost of the F-22 fighter plane was settled in 2009 when former secretary of defense Robert M. Gates determined that the Air Force would acquire only 188 planes rather than the 648 originally planned. The cost per plane was ultimately $412 million,[3] an amount that exceeds the entire annual defense budget of some states. While states in the developing world also spend large sums on defense (at least relative to the size of their economies), their more pressing security concerns often involve matters such as basic law enforcement, disease prevention and control, and the mitigation of serious environmental hazards. Or, to take a different example, while citizens in the developed world may worry about fluctuations in the price of oil, many people in the developing world must worry about a decreasing supply of wood for cooking. These examples suggest something of the difference between thinking about the economics of national security versus the economics of human security.

The simple fact is that wealth is closely linked to power. As the historian Paul Kennedy noted, "Wealth is usually needed to underpin military power, and military power is usually needed to acquire and protect wealth."[1] Of course, wealth is tied not only to the maintenance of the military forces that are central to hard power but also to other means of exerting influence in international affairs, from maintaining embassies in distant places to providing foreign aid and paying dues to international organizations. The wealth-power nexus is so strong that some analysts regard a state's wealth, commonly measured in terms of gross domestic product (GDP) or gross national income (GNI), as the best means of estimating its power.

The steady increase in China's military capability since the beginning of its dramatic economic expansion illustrates the way wealth can generate hard power. To promote economic development, Deng Xiaoping instituted major reforms in the Chinese economy beginning in 1978. By opening up to foreign investment, allowing individuals to start businesses, and privatizing most state-owned enterprises, China achieved double-digit economic growth almost every year from 1978 to 2013. As the nation modernized and moved up the ranks of the world's largest economies (it is now second only to the United States[5]), military spending increased steadily. In fact, from 1988 to 2010, China's publicly acknowledged military spending increased nearly twenty-five-fold.[6] Even though Chinese economic growth began slowing somewhat in 2014, military spending increases have continued unabated. In March 2015, China announced that its official military budget would increase 10.1 percent for the year to approximately $145 billion.[7]

What has China's steadily rising military budget meant for the nation's hard-power capabilities? What previously was a large but unsophisticated military has become a force with significant capabilities in all five domains of warfare. China demonstrated an antisatellite capability in 2007. Its first aircraft carrier, built in the former Soviet Union and purchased from Ukraine, began sea trials in 2011. In the cyberdomain, the People's Liberation Army (PLA) has for years conducted a persistent program of cyberespionage that has drawn the ire of foreign governments and corporations. And while China's ability to project force remains limited in comparison with that of the United States, the PLA Navy now operates regularly in the Indian Ocean; in fact, since 2010 it has participated in antipiracy operations in the Gulf of Aden.[8]

Large economies create possibilities for large (and technologically advanced) militaries. Historically, this fact has prompted many governments to pursue policies associated with mercantilism or economic nationalism. Mercantilism, an economic belief that dominated the economic statecraft of the major European powers between the fifteenth and eighteenth centuries, held that the objective of states should be the accumulation of wealth, even at the expense of other states, since that wealth could be translated into power. Trade, rather than being regarded as a medium of exchange between equals, was considered an opportunity to enrich the state at the expense of its commercial partners when the terms of trade were favorable. This led to the use of tariffs and other trade barriers in an effort to generate favorable terms of trade. Of course, the most favorable terms of trade, and thus the greatest opportunities for accumulating monetary reserves, were to be gained by policies of imperialism; control over a colony allowed the imperialist state to engage in a form of trade in which virtually all of the benefits flowed in one direction. Colonialism thus appears as a key factor in accounting for the great economic divide separating the developed and the developing worlds.

In 1500, at the beginning of the age of European imperialism, the wealth gap between Europe and the rest of the world was small. In fact, Spanish explorers in the New World were on more than one occasion stunned by the wealth and sophistication of the societies they encountered. Tenochtitlán, the Aztec capital, had roughly ten times the population of Madrid when the forces of Hernán Cortés began their assault on it in 1519. And yet key technological and immunological advantages (Europeans carried diseases such as smallpox to which some of the peoples they encountered had no natural resistance) allowed Spain, Portugal, Britain, the Netherlands, and France to acquire empires that would enrich Europe at the expense of much of the rest of the world. Although most colonies in the Western Hemisphere had revolted and declared independence by the middle of the nineteenth century, a subsequent wave of empire building that would bring most of Africa under colonial rule was touched off by European rivalries in the second half of the century.

In the twentieth century, when peoples in Africa, Southeast Asia, and elsewhere began to dismantle colonial empires and establish states, most found themselves lagging far behind their former colonial masters in economic development. Where the colonizers had reaped the economic benefits of the Industrial Revolution, the colonized were generally kept from industrializing in order to avoid engaging in competition with industries located in the colonial power. It was, after all, the role of colonies to provide raw materials and markets, not manufactured goods.[9] This crucial economic factor, combined with the additional problems of bad governance and, in many instances, ethnic conflict (especially where borders drawn by colonial powers ignored important political and demographic divisions), ensured that one of the chief legacies of colonialism was a dramatic divide between developed and developing states.

What does it mean to be on the wrong side of the world's rich-poor divide? Particularly for those who live in the fifty or so least developed countries in the world—"the bottom billion," in Paul Collier's notable phrase[10]—security is an intensely personal concern with few assurances. In fact, the very reason we are compelled to speak of health security, water security, or food security is that such basics are anything but secure for most people in the developing world. To understand more precisely the nature of economic insecurity in the world's poorest states, it is worth considering some data from the United Nations Development Program's Human Development Index.

In 1990, under the leadership of Mahbub ul-Haq, the United Nations Development Program instituted an annual publication called the *Human Development Report*. The centerpiece of the report is the Human Development Index (HDI), a collection of data designed to provide a human-centered perspective on development in contrast to earlier state-centered measures (such as GDP alone) that often failed to account for how well human needs were being met.[11] There are 187 states included in the HDI. The bottom forty-three, including (at the very bottom of the list) Niger, Democratic Republic of the Congo, the Central African Republic, and Chad, are grouped in the Low Human Development category

For those living in states in the Low Human Development category, life expectancy at birth is 59.4 years, over twenty years lower than in Norway, Germany, Canada, or other high-HDI states.[12] Gross national income (GNI) per capita was $2,904 in 2013, compared with over $40,000 in the Very High Human Development states. Statistics on educational attainment also show great disparities. Those living in Low Human Development states have completed, on average, 4.2 years of education, compared with over twelve years in most countries at the top of the HDI. Finally, and perhaps most indicative of the human security dimensions of poverty, HDI data indicates that 34.3

percent of the population of Low Human Development states lives on less than $1.25 per day (adjusted for purchasing power parity), compared with 0.1 percent of the population in Very High Human Development states.

While the traditional security paradigm emphasizes wealth and its impact on power, the new security paradigm draws our attention to the interrelationship of poverty, weakness, and insecurity. The tendency of wealthy states to spread their influence across the globe has been witnessed for centuries. What we have recently come to understand more fully is that impoverished states tend to spread insecurity. In the first post-9/11 version of the *National Security Strategy of the United States*, the George W. Bush administration noted, "Poverty, weak institutions, and corruption can make weak states vulnerable to terrorist networks and drug cartels within their borders."[13] The 9/11 Commission echoed this observation, which in its final report noted, "Terrorism is not caused by poverty. Indeed, many terrorists come from relatively well-off families. Yet, when people lose hope, when societies break down, when countries fragment, the breeding grounds for terrorism are created."[14] Of course, terrorism is not the only security concern linked to poverty. Since World War II, the vast majority of the world's armed conflicts have occurred in the poorest parts of the world.

Development and Conflict

From Syria to Nigeria, from South Sudan to Afghanistan, from Iraq to the Democratic Republic of the Congo, intrastate conflict has become by far the most common form of conflict in the world. With very few exceptions, those states that are mired in civil war are underdeveloped. Michael W. Doyle and Nicholas Sambanis have noted that "low levels of per capita income . . . significantly exacerbate the risk of civil war." This, in fact, is "the most robust empirical finding in the literature" on the economic causes of conflict.[15] Syria, where civil war has raged since 2011, has a GDP per capita just over $1,000 according to World Bank data.[16] The same is true for Yemen and South Sudan. Other sites of ongoing civil wars are even poorer: the Central African Republic, Democratic Republic of the Congo, and Afghanistan are among the poorest states in the world, with per capita GDPs of $333, $484, and $665, respectively. Nigeria ($3,006) and Iraq ($6,863) rank higher thanks to oil income, but in neither case is the state's wealth distributed equitably.

Not all impoverished countries are at war, of course, but poverty is nonetheless an important risk factor for intrastate conflict. According to one estimate, the chance that a civil war will begin in a state with a GDP per capita of $250 within a five-year period is 15 percent. When GDP per capita rises to $500, the chance of war drops to 8 percent. Additional drops in the risk of war occur at a GDP per capita of about $1,200 (4 percent) and $5,000 (1 percent).[17] Paul Collier has noted that economic growth, and not just the existing level of development, is important in reducing the chance of civil war: "Societies that are growing faster per capita are significantly less at risk of violent conflict than societies that are stagnant or in decline."[18] While the traditional paradigm ties security to wealth (because of the links between wealth and power), the new paradigm requires that we attend to the mirror image where we see a connection between poverty and insecurity. Those in the developed world are often apt to overlook this part of the equation.

It is worth emphasizing that, in the new paradigm, poverty and insecurity are connected regardless of whether poverty causes war. At the level of the individual, poverty can wreak destruction without overt violence through disease, famine, or other challenges that confront those without adequate means. In recognition of this, the 1994 *Human Development Report* used the language of human security to frame that year's findings. It represented an attempt to shape the agenda for the 1995 World Summit on Social Development in Copenhagen and to capture the post–Cold War "peace dividend" for development. While it was not the first time the term *human security* had appeared in print, it was almost certainly the most prominent and most authoritative use of the term to that point. The report stated, "In the final analysis, human security is a child who did not die, a disease that did not spread, a job that was not cut, an ethnic tension that did not explode into violence, a dissident who was not silenced. Human security is not a concern with weapons—it is a concern with human life and dignity."[19]

THE ECONOMICS OF NATIONAL SECURITY

As we have noted, wealth and power are closely linked: wealth buys power, power protects wealth, and both are key components of national security. Wealth buys power in a number of ways, starting with its obvious link to defense spending. The United States, as we noted in chapter 3, spends more than any other country in the world on its military—over half a trillion dollars annually even without including international security assistance, contributions to UN peacekeeping operations, and the lingering costs of the wars in Afghanistan and Iraq. And yet this staggering sum has amounted to less than 5 percent of GDP. Defense spending of more than half a trillion dollars is possible only in a state with a very robust economy; the value of the U.S. economy is estimated to be approximately $18 trillion.[20]

A robust economy also facilitates a strong defense industrial base. The efficacy of defense spending—bang for the buck—depends to a considerable degree on the existence of innovative suppliers in a competitive market, something that is more likely in a strong economy. Of course, in a globalized economy, the economic health of one country is tied to the economic health of all others.

Economic concerns also link directly to national security via sanctions, which have been called "non-kinetic tools of warfare."[21] Because sanctions have been both important and controversial national security instruments, we devote special attention to them here.

Economic Sanctions

On March 6, 2014, after months of political instability in Ukraine provoked by poorly disguised Russian forces, President Obama signed Executive Order 13660 imposing sanctions against the individuals and institutions in Russia considered responsible for violating Ukrainian sovereignty. Two weeks later, after Russia announced the annexation of Crimea, the United States and the European Union imposed additional sanctions targeting Russian defense contractors, financial institutions, and energy companies, as well as individual members of Vladimir Putin's inner circle. The sanctions, according to the U.S. State Department, were intended to "send a strong message to the Russian government that there are consequences for their actions that threaten the sovereignty and territorial integrity of Ukraine."[22]

A year later, Russia's economy was reeling. The value of the Russian ruble had dropped, raising the cost of imported goods. The price of food increased, led by a doubling of the price of cabbage. Rosneft, a state-owned oil company, was forced to seek billions of dollars worth of loans from the government. And in a sign that the oligarchs, too, were worried about the state of the Russian economy, over $150 billion in capital exited the country in 2014.[23]

In spite of the many indications that sanctions, as intended, were imposing economic costs on Russia for its policy toward Ukraine, a number of questions remained regarding their efficacy. A sustained drop in the price of oil and gas, Russia's primary exports, may have had more impact on the economy than the sanctions did. In fact, some suggested that Putin actually benefited domestically from the sanctions because they allowed him to deflect blame onto the United States and the European Union for what would inevitably have been a serious economic downturn under any circumstances. A year after sanctions were imposed, there was little evidence that the Russian people were turning against Putin or his policy toward Ukraine. Perhaps reflecting that fact, the sanctions had not obviously altered Russian policy, although supporters of the sanctions could argue that, at a minimum, Russia's weakened economic position was likely inducing greater caution on Putin's part.

In spite of persistent questions about their effectiveness, economic sanctions have long been used to promote security by trying to influence the behavior of adversaries without the resort to war. According to former State Department official Richard Haass, sanctions may be defined as "mostly economic but also political and military penalties introduced to alter political and/or military behavior."[24] Actions have taken the form of "arms embargoes, foreign assistance reductions and cutoffs, export and import limitations, asset freezes, tariff increases, revocation of most favored nation (MFN) trade status, negative votes in international financial institutions, withdrawal of diplomatic relations, visa denials, cancellation of air links, and prohibitions on credit, financing, and investment."[25] Both states and international organizations have used sanctions to try to influence the actions and policies of states and corporations.

Sanctions are commonly regarded as an alternative to war, which Clausewitz defined as "an act of force to compel our enemy to do our will."[26] By substituting economic pressure for military force, those who advocate the use of sanctions hope to change an adversary's policies without the costs associated with war. Some, however, have argued that sanctions are often so costly that they are better understood as acts of war.[27] The sanctions imposed on Iraq between 1990 and 2003 offer an important, if extreme, example of "sanctions of mass destruction." A survey conducted in Iraq in 1999 on behalf of UNICEF found that mortality rates for infants and children in the heavily populated southern and central parts of the country had more than doubled since the imposition of sanctions at the time of Iraq's invasion of Kuwait in August 1990. The increased mortality rates suggested that half a million Iraqi children had died as a consequence of economic sanctions that were intended to punish Saddam Hussein's regime. Two UN officials responsible for administering the sanctions resigned in protest over what they regarded as a humanitarian catastrophe linked to sanctions.

In spite of their potential to cause great suffering, sanctions have been an important tool for the enforcement of international norms since the end of World War I. The Covenant of the League of Nations required members of the League to sever diplomatic and economic ties with states that waged war in violation of their obligations under the Covenant. During the 1930s, the League imposed sanctions twice: against Japan as punishment for its invasion of Manchuria and against Italy following its invasion of Ethiopia. In both cases, sanctions failed to alter the behavior of the target states, although they may have weakened both.

During the first four decades of its existence, the United Nations imposed economic sanctions only against Rhodesia in 1966 and South Africa in 1977. Although the dismantling of South Africa's apartheid regime did not come quickly, when it did happen there was a widespread perception that economic sanctions had played a significant role. Meanwhile, as it did with peacekeeping, the end of the Cold War opened the door to the much more frequent use of sanctions. Between 1990 and 2002 the United Nations imposed sanctions against Iraq (1990), the former Yugoslavia (1992), Libya (1992), Haiti (1994), Liberia (1992), Rwanda (1994), Somalia, UNITA forces in Angola (1994), Sudan, Sierra Leone, Afghanistan, Eritrea, and Ethiopia.[28] More recently, the UN Security Council imposed sanctions on Iran to punish it for its failure to accept international safeguards on its nuclear weapons program. At present, the United States has its own sanctions in place against Belarus, Burma, the Central African Republic, Cuba, Iran, Libya, North Korea, Somalia, Sudan, Syria, and Zimbabwe. In addition, there are prohibitions on trading with Balkan war criminals, Iraqis affiliated with Saddam Hussein's government, and individuals involved in trafficking drugs, conflict diamonds, or WMD components. Altogether, the United States has twenty-eight separate sanctions programs in place.[29] In a comprehensive description and analysis of economic sanctions, Meghan L. O'Sullivan identifies 122 cases in which sanctions were imposed by the United States or the United Nations on state or nonstate actors from 1990 through 2001.[30] It is not difficult to see why the 1990s have been called "the sanctions decade."[31]

There is substantial controversy over the effectiveness of economic sanctions. In work published in 1985 and updated in 1990, Gary Hufbauer, Jeffrey Schott, and Karen Ann Elliott studied 115 cases of economic sanctions imposed from 1914 to 1990 and concluded that sanctions were successful in forty (34 percent) of these instances. This study was criticized by a number of analysts as too optimistic concerning the effectiveness of sanctions.[32] Several observations concerning the literature on economic sanctions are important. First, virtually all of the studies on sanctions focus on interstate behavior. Second, almost all focus on the actions of wealthy states toward poorer states. In this sense, sanctions are actions of the powerful toward the weak. A reversal of this traditional pattern occurred in October 1973, when the Arab members of the Organization of Petroleum Exporting Countries (OPEC) imposed an embargo on oil shipments to the countries that supported Israel in the Arab-Israeli War. Within a matter of weeks, the price of oil went from $3 per barrel to $12, a 400 percent increase. The Arab oil embargo of 1973–1974 was an economic sanction imposed by the formerly weak against the strong. Thucydides wrote, "The strong do what they will, and the weak suffer what they must." The Arab oil embargo effectively turned Thucydides on his head.

TRADE AND MARITIME SECURITY

The economic well-being, and thus the security, of states is heavily dependent on international trade. As Michael Mandelbaum has noted, "Trade brings competition and competition is a force for economic efficiency. It raises productivity by forcing local firms to adopt the most efficient practices available, which is the key to productivity."[33] Trade also creates larger potential markets for goods and services, which in turn can ensure that large up-front costs for research and development will pay off. For example, the development of new aircraft, whether for civil or military aviation, requires large-scale investments that are likely to be profitable only if sales to foreign markets can be added to domestic sales. Furthermore, an open global market can ensure that manufacturers are able to source components for their products as cheaply as possible. Thus, an automobile manufacturer in the United States is available, via international trade and the global competition it facilitates, to source components ranging from tires to GPS systems efficiently.

While there are land borders, such as the U.S.-Canadian border, where trade occurs on a large scale—the two-way value of U.S.-Canadian trade in goods was $632 billion in 2013[34]—most of the world's trade moves by sea. The advantages of trade generally and maritime trade more particularly are so great that Paul Collier has identified the condition of being landlocked with bad neighbors, a situation that makes maritime trade difficult, if not impossible, as one of the four traps that prevent the world's most impoverished states from developing.[35] This, unfortunately, describes the geographical situation of a number of states in sub-Saharan Africa and Central Asia. Although not all of their neighbors are bad, Botswana, Zimbabwe, Zambia, Malawi, the Central African Republic, Rwanda, Burundi, Uganda, Kazakhstan, Kyrgyzstan, Uzbekistan, and many other struggling states lack the ocean ports that could improve chances of being able to participate fully in the global economy.

Global trade—and, with it, economic interdependence—has been facilitated by a number of factors. The willingness of the United States to finance the economic recovery of Europe following World War II was significant. The international effort to avoid a repetition of the economic nationalism that plagued the world in the interwar period, an effort represented by the Bretton Woods institutions, has also been important. The development of regional free-trade agreements—the ASEAN Free Trade Area, the North American Free Trade Area, and the Southern Common Market (MERCOSUR), for example—has facilitated trade beyond the bounds of the General Agreement on Tariffs and Trade and its successor, the World Trade Organization.

But efforts to eliminate barriers to trade are not the only factors contributing to a global trade that saw the value of world merchandise exports climb to $18.8 trillion in 2013.[36] Innovations in transportation have dramatically reduced the cost of moving goods around the world. Oil tankers, for example, have grown steadily: modern, ultra-large crude carriers have a capacity of five hundred thousand dead weight tons, roughly thirty times the capacity of the T-2 tankers that were built during World War II,[37] and greater capacity means lower unit shipping costs. For manufactured goods, the great transportation innovation of the twentieth century was the invention of shipping containers, followed by the development of intermodal transportation, so that a single container carrying, for example, laptop computers can cross the Pacific on a ship, be moved on arrival at the destination port to a rail car for the journey to an inland distribution center, and finally be put on the back of a truck to go to a retailer's warehouse. Today, eighteen million containers travel the world carrying mostly legal manufactured goods, but also occasionally illegal drugs, weapons, or other contraband.[38] Few containers are ever visually inspected on their journeys, a fact that has prompted security experts to worry about the possibility of container-borne WMD in a major port city such as Los Angeles, Singapore, or Hamburg. To address part of the WMD threat, after the 9/11 terrorist attacks U.S. Customs and Border Protection developed the Container Security Initiative (CSI), which seeks to screen cargo containers in foreign ports before they are loaded onto ships bound for the United States. While U.S. Customs and Border Protection agents are posted abroad in cooperation with officials from other countries, an important part of the program, given the enormous volume of trade involving containers, is nonintrusive inspection using X-ray and gamma ray scanners, as well as devices to detect radiation.[39]

Even as the elimination of trade barriers and the use of new, more efficient forms of shipping have lowered the costs of trade, the threats of terrorism and piracy are pushing costs in the opposite direction. In the South China Sea, the Straits of Malacca, and especially the western Indian Ocean, armed groups bent on robbery or hijacking for ransom regularly target oil tankers, container ships, and even cruise ships. In 2014, a total of 291 attacks against ships were recorded by the International Maritime Organization (IMO); of these, ninety-three occurred in the South China Sea, eighty-one in the Straits of Malacca and Singapore, and sixty-two in the Persian Gulf, Arabian Sea, off the coast of East Africa, and the wider Indian Ocean. Forty-five incidents were reported in the Gulf of Guinea off the coast of West Africa as well.[40]

For the better part of a decade, the world's most hazardous waters were those off the coast of Somalia. With onshore bases largely immune from Somali law enforcement and fast boats and substantial arsenals financed both by the proceeds of prior attacks and by international investors, Somali pirates engaged in increasingly audacious attacks until the international community was compelled to respond with a range of military, diplomatic, and legal actions. In 2008, the UN Security Council adopted Resolution 1851 calling for international cooperation against piracy and leading to the formation of the Contact Group on Piracy off the Coast of Somalia, which coordinated responses from various interested parties. In 2012, military forces from the European Union attacked pirate bases. The North Atlantic Treaty Organization (NATO) organized patrols by naval vessels from member states.[41] Additionally, other countries, including India and China, with a commercial interest in Indian Ocean trade contributed naval forces. For their part, shipping companies began employing armed guards from private military firms aboard ships in the region. In addition, the deployment of nonlethal weapons proved effective in defending against pirate attacks on occasion. For instance, in November 2005, the *Seabourn Spirit*, a luxury cruise liner with 151 passengers on board, used a long-range acoustic device (LRAD) emitting ear-piercing sounds to ward off a pirate attack about one hundred miles off the coast of Somalia.[42]

The combination of international military cooperation and the use by shipping companies of private security forces appears to have succeeded in pacifying the waters of the western Indian Ocean. The last time a tanker or freighter was hijacked by Somali pirates was 2012. According to IMO data, the number of incidents involving Somali pirates dropped to twelve in 2014, down from a high of seventy-eight in 2007.[43]

THE ECONOMICS OF HUMAN SECURITY

International trade is important, both for its impact on the economic well-being of states and for its potential to reduce the incidence of interstate conflict. Cooperation among major trading states to prevent terrorists from using shipping containers to deliver weapons of mass destruction or to reduce the threat of piracy is, consequently, something to be encouraged. But a focus on states and their commercial interests provides only half of what we need to know about the economics of security. Understanding why piracy off the coast of Somalia was such a problem in the first place requires that we consider economic security from the vantage point of those who have nothing to trade with the rest of the world. It requires that we consider the economics of human security.

Somalia has had a troubled history. After a decade-long war with Ethiopia punctuated by famines, Somalia experienced the overthrow of its Marxist government in 1991. When the major clans began to fight for control of the state, exacerbating the humanitarian crisis that had become almost a permanent feature of Somali life, the UN responded first with a humanitarian relief mission and then with a peace-enforcement mission. U.S. withdrawal from Somalia following the deaths of eighteen American soldiers in the October 1993 Battle of the Black Sea led to the collapse of the UN peace-enforcement effort.[44]

In spite of the creation of the Transition Federal Government (TFG) in 2003 and significant progress in unifying the country, Somalia has been for most of the past quarter-century a weak, if not failed, state. This, in part, has been due to a serious threat from al-Shabaab, a jihadist organization that, in 2012, declared its affiliation with Al Qaeda. As a consequence of war, terrorism, famine, and the inability of the government to provide even minimal physical security in much of the country, there has been little economic development in Somalia. There are no reliable figures for GDP. According to the Human Development Index, 81.77 percent of the population lives in multidimensional poverty (reflecting deprivations in education, health, and living standards), one of the highest figures in the world.[45] For most Somalis, drought, unemployment, violence, and extreme poverty are the norm. For a few Somalis, hijacking ships and demanding ransom offered a way to benefit from international trade. With the ransom for an oil tanker and its cargo exceeding $100 million, the proceeds from piracy were sufficient to make many Somalis—not just those attacking ships—incredibly wealthy.

Extreme poverty has had similar effects in other places. The number of those drawn into such activities is small, but poverty creates powerful incentives for people to work for drug cartels, arms traffickers, or cybercriminals. It prompts both internal and international migrations that, in turn, may put stress on the resources of another region or country. Where conditions are especially difficult, poverty may lead children to join an army that can promise regular meals, or it may lead them to answer ads for work that lead to sex slavery. Together with other conditions—the availability of cheap weapons or the existence of a repressive government, for example—poverty may lead to war. While mechanisms of causation are difficult to trace, there is certainly a strong correlation between poverty and intrastate conflict, as we noted earlier.

The links between extreme poverty and political instability are reason enough for security analysts to attend to the economics of development, but the problems of the poor are in fact more severe when considered from the standpoint of human security rather than national security. A few data points may help in describing the situation. In 2011 (the last year for which data is available), 17 percent of the population in the developing world had an income of less than $1.25 per day, the standard measure of extreme poverty according to development specialists. These are the "bottom billion," and there are in fact about a billion people living at or below this income level. About 2.2 billion people in 2011 lived on less than $2 per day.[46]

At these levels of poverty, undernourishment is common. Undernourishment, in turn, may result in high levels of child mortality, susceptibility to disease, and stunted development. It may also result in the failure of children to attend school, due either to the inability to pay even nominal school fees or to the necessity of working to survive. Extreme poverty is a significant risk factor for indentured servitude and other forms of slavery and human trafficking. It also makes children in war zones more susceptible to recruitment as child soldiers.

Whether the immediate causes of displacement are political repression or war, economic conditions, or environmental stresses, the poor are far more likely than the rich to become refugees. Their poverty, in many different ways, makes them insecure, but their insecurity also makes them poor.

For decades, the developed world has recognized the need to assist developing states for both altruistic and self-interested reasons. As Joseph Nye has argued, "Investments [in economic development] are a clear case of coincidence between self-interest and charity."[47] Developing states have also recognized the importance of development. In 1955, twenty-nine Asian and African countries met in Bandung, Indonesia, and declared that they were opposed to "colonialism in all of its manifestations" and thus not aligned with either the United States or the Soviet Union. By rejecting what they regarded as the neocolonial aims of both the capitalist and the communist worlds, these nonaligned states set out to create their own path to development. An important step in this process occurred in 1964 when seventy-seven states called for the creation of the UN Conference on Trade and Development (UNCTAD). (The nonaligned development caucus in the UN is still known as the "Group of 77" even though its membership has grown significantly since 1964.) Two so-called South Summits of the Group of 77 have occurred, the first in 2000 in Havana, Cuba, and the second in 2005 in Doha, Qatar. Among the principal objectives of the Group of 77 are trade, monetary, and institutional reforms, economic modernization, greater freedom for labor migration, the elimination of economic coercion, development aid, and debt relief. This effort to seize the initiative on development and reframe debates by articulating an agenda reflecting the interests of developing states was significant, but it was very nearly as state centered as the agenda it sought to replace. What some came to recognize in the 1990s, following the demise of the Soviet Union and the end of the Cold War, was that any state-centered development agenda was likely to leave most people in poverty even if, by some measures, their states could be said to be undergoing development. This recognition, in fact, prompted the creation of the Human Development Index that we discussed earlier.

On September 6, 2000, leaders from over 150 states (including one hundred heads of state) assembled at the United Nations in New York City for the Millennium Summit. Bill Clinton, in the final year of his presidency, and Vladimir Putin, in the first year of his, were present, as were Tony Blair of the United Kingdom and Jacques Chirac of France. Hugo Chavez, in office for a year and a half at that point, represented Venezuela, and Fidel Castro, then in power for over forty years, represented Cuba. Prime Minister Ionatana Ionatana represented the Pacific island state of Tuvalu, admitted to the United Nations as its 189th member state the day before the summit began. The official purpose of the meeting was to review the work of the United Nations as the organization entered a new century—and a new millennium.

In addition to a remarkable group photo befitting what was, up to that time, the largest gathering of world leaders in history, the primary product of the Millennium Summit was a document called the United Nations Millennium Declaration.[48] The Declaration provided a long and ambitious list of objectives related to the purposes of the United Nations divided into seven categories. Within the category labeled "development and poverty eradication," the Declaration articulated a number of specific objectives that would become the heart of what were to be called the Millennium Development Goals. Five of the objectives were defined with quantifiable targets—reducing by half the proportion of the global population subsisting on less than a dollar a day and living without safe drinking water, guaranteeing all children access to primary education, and reducing maternal mortality rates by three-quarters and child mortality rates by two-thirds—linked to a 2015 target date for the accomplishment of the objectives.

The Millennium Development Goals represented an unprecedented collective effort by the international community to address the problem of global poverty. It also reflected a sea change in the way states approached the problem. In what had been, up to the end of the Cold War, the traditional approach to development (at least as practiced by governments), there was an emphasis on aid to governments coupled with reform of government policies. The assumption was that aid and reform would eventually redound to the benefit of people living in poverty. Many foreign aid decisions, however, were made based not on a calculation of potential benefits to the world's poor but on the basis of national security assessments. Dictatorships with no track record of using aid money to benefit their populations were just as likely to receive foreign aid from the leading actors in the Cold War as more responsible regimes, especially if they were on the fence ideologically or occupied strategically significant territories. Freed from the political constraints imposed by the Cold War, the Millennium Development Goals looked beyond governments to human needs, replacing a top-down approach to development with a bottom-up approach to the elimination of poverty.

While there is considerable distance to go before it can be considered accomplished, much has been done toward meeting the goal of eradicating extreme poverty. Between 1990 and 2010, the number of people in the world living on less than $1.25 per day dropped by seven hundred million. Almost 50 percent of the population in developing regions lived in extreme poverty in 1990; the proportion was 22 percent in 2010. On the health front, an estimated 3.3 million lives were saved between 2000 and 2012 due to malaria interventions. Another twenty-two million lives were saved due to a global campaign between 1995 and 2012 to address tuberculosis. Additional health gains are indicated by a drop of almost 50 percent in mortality among children under five between 1990 and 2012. There have also been significant gains in education. The percentage of children in school increased from 83 percent to 90 percent between 2000 and 2012. In addition, gender inequalities in school attendance have largely been eliminated, as called for in the Millennium Declaration.[49] In September 2015, the United Nations adopted a new set of seventeen Sustainable Development goals with 169 specific targets geared toward improving the lives of people worldwide. The aim is to meet the new goals by 2030.

Progress in economic security, especially for those in extreme poverty, has been stymied by a variety of factors over the years: the politics of the Cold War, bad governance, ineffective development policies, violent conflict, exploitation, and more. The shift to human-centered development—and to a human security approach—has brought measurable improvements in the economic security of those in the developing world. Aid policies, while still reflecting political interests in many cases, have become smarter even as many developed states have increased their support to developing states. There is, however, a long way to go to ensure security for all. The evidence generated by the Arab Spring uprisings, the rise of the Islamic State, and political instability across large portions of sub-Saharan Africa suggests that investments in the economic security of the world's poorest people is actually an investment in our own security.

ADDITIONAL RESOURCES

Books

Baldwin, David. *Economic Statecraft*. Princeton, NJ: Princeton University Press, 1985.

Collier, Paul. *The Bottom Billion: Why the Poorest Countries Are Failing and What Can Be Done About It*. New York: Oxford University Press, 2007.

Copeland, Dale C. *Economic Interdependence and War*. Princeton, NJ: Princeton University Press, 2014.

Haass, Richard N., and Meghan L. O'Sullivan, eds. *Honey and Vinegar: Incentives, Sanctions, and Foreign Policy*. Washington, DC: Brookings Institution, 2000.

Hirschman, Albert O. *National Power and the Structure of International Trade*. Berkeley: University of California Press, 1980.

Knorr, Klaus. *Power and Wealth*. New York: Basic Books, 1973.

Knorr, Klaus, and Frank Trager, eds. *Economic Issues and National Security*. Lawrence: University Press of Kansas, 1977.

Sachs, Jeffrey D. *The End of Poverty: Economic Possibilities for Our Time*. New York: The Penguin Press, 2005.

United Nations Development Program. *Human Development Report*. New York: United Nations (annual).

Viotti, Paul R. *The Dollar and National Security: The Monetary Component of Hard Power*. Stanford, CA: Stanford University Press, 2014.

Websites

The Group of 77 at the United Nations: www.g77.org
Institute for International Economics: www.iie.com
International Monetary Fund: www.imf.org
U.S. Central Intelligence Agency *World Factbook*: www.odci.gov
World Bank: www.worldbank.org

Films

Actually, the World Isn't Flat, TED Talk by Pankaj Ghemawat.

Captain Phillips (2013): A film starring Tom Hanks and based on actual events that recounts the Somali pirate attack against the MV *Maersk Alabama,* a U.S.-flagged container ship. Scott Rudin Productions. Directed by Paul Greengrass.

Stolen Seas (2012): A documentary on Somali piracy directed by Thymaya Payne. Brainstorm Media.

Chapter Twelve

Resources, the Environment, and Security

> I am here today to say that climate change constitutes a serious threat to global security, an immediate risk to our national security, and, make no mistake, it will impact how our military defends our country.
>
> —President Barack Obama, Commencement Address to the U.S. Coast Guard Academy, May 20, 2015

As early as 1974, the Central Intelligence Agency published a research report titled "A Study of Climatological Research as It Pertains to Intelligence Problems." However, only in recent years have governmental leaders explicitly recognized the threat of climate disruption and sought to do something about it. In October 2014, the U.S. Department of Defense released a report that concluded, "The loss of glaciers will strain water supplies in several areas of our hemisphere. Destruction and devastation from hurricanes can sow the seeds for instability. Droughts and crop failures can leave millions of people without any lifeline, and trigger waves of mass migration."[1]

The world's environmental problems are widespread, and they are, in many instances, extreme. Consider this sampling:

- Although hurricanes and climate disruption cannot be linked directly, the increasing frequency and impact of hurricanes in recent decades is striking. In 1972, Hurricane Agnes killed 122 people; in 1992, Andrew caused $26.5 billion ($44 billion in 2012 dollars) in damage. Katrina struck New Orleans in 2005 and destroyed much of the city, causing $108 billion ($128 billion in 2012 dollars) in damage, killing more than 1,800 people, displacing more than 270,000, and causing significant damage to critical infrastructures, particularly related to oil production and refineries.[2] In

October 2012, Hurricane Sandy became the second most costly hurricane in American history, causing $50 billion in damage.[3]

- NASA's Global Climate Change projections indicate that the level of carbon dioxide in the atmosphere is the highest in 650,000 years at 400.06 parts per million; nine of the ten warmest years on earth have occurred between 2000 and 2015; global average temperature has increased 1.4 degrees (Fahrenheit) since 1880; Arctic sea ice is declining at a rate of 13.3 percent per decade.[4]
- Every year, approximately fifty thousand square miles of forest—an area roughly the size of Greece—disappears. Because the world's forests store 289 billion tons of carbon, deforestation is a significant contributor to global warming.[5]
- Species extinctions are occurring at somewhere between one hundred and one thousand times the nature average of fifteen per year. In fact, scientists have labeled the current period the Sixth Great Extinction Event. (The fifth occurred sixty-five million years ago when dinosaurs disappeared.)[6]
- On April 20, 2010, BP's Deepwater Horizon drilling rig exploded in the Gulf of Mexico. For three months, oil flowed into the sea at a rate of up to sixty thousand barrels per day. In the end, an estimated 4.4 million barrels of oil (not including over eight hundred thousand barrels collected from the bottom of the sea) entered the marine environment.[7] Although the Deepwater Horizon spill was the worst to have ever occurred in U.S. waters, a larger spill was deliberately caused by the Iraqi military in the Persian Gulf in 1991 during the Persian Gulf War.
- During the 1980s, an average of 5.5 *billion* tons of carbon dioxide was released into the Earth's atmosphere each year through the burning of fossil fuels. That amount increased to 7.7 billion tons annually from 2000 to 2008 and is projected to increase to 11.0 billion tons per year by 2030. The concentration of carbon dioxide in the atmosphere today is 38 percent higher than at the beginning of the Industrial Age.[8]

Clearly the world faces many environmental challenges, but is there any evidence to suggest that these challenges amount to a security threat? Over the past quarter-century, more and more analysts who concern themselves strictly with national security have begun to acknowledge important links between the environment and security. Those who think of security in terms of the lives and dignity of individual human beings see not just links between environmental problems and national security but also direct threats to human security. Today, within the new paradigm of security studies, it is essential to consider environmental security as it relates to individual humans, to corporations, to states, and to the international system.

Whenever human actions pose threats to the basic rights (and especially the right to life) of human beings, a security issue exists. Environmental problems have been "securitized" as a consequence of the recognition that human alterations of the natural environment do indeed threaten the lives and welfare of humans. In some instances, the threats posed by man-made environmental disasters are direct and obvious. The explosion at the Chernobyl nuclear power plant in 1986 resulted in thirty-one immediate deaths, an increase in the incidence of cancer in exposed populations, and enormous social disruption in the vicinity of the disaster. Experts estimate that six thousand people died as a consequence of the disaster in the years following the accident. As many as fifteen thousand people in Bhopal, India, died as a direct result of a deadly gas leak from a Union Carbide chemical plant in 1984; another two hundred thousand were injured.[9] London's "Great Smog" tripled the city's death rate over a four-day period in December 1952. The smog, produced by a combination of a natural temperature inversion and air fouled by the residues of coal smoke, was responsible for over four thousand deaths immediately and perhaps another eight thousand over the following months.[10]

The enormous complexity of ecosystems and the difficulty inherent in tracing anthropogenic (human-caused) effects on the environment make some analysts unwilling to treat environmental problems as security issues. Such skeptics argue, for example, that London's "Great Smog" was as much the product of the cold, damp air that enveloped the city as of the large quantity of sulfur dioxide and particulate matter in the air, or that the number of cancer deaths attributable to the Chernobyl disaster is simply unknowable. Similar claims are made regarding climate change. The objections of the skeptics can be met very simply and forcefully by noting, first, that the overwhelming weight of scientific opinion regarding human-induced environmental change sees far less uncertainty than the skeptics claim and, second, that in no other area involving human welfare would uncertainty be considered a legitimate reason for failure to act.

Originally, environmental issues were added to the security agenda by those who noted the environment's relationship to national security.[11] Here, with this relatively well-developed part of the new security paradigm, is a good place for us to begin our examination of environmental security.

Seen in terms of national security, environmental problems are "securitized" in two broad categories. There are, first, environmental threats that relate directly to warfare. This category includes environmental modification techniques used in fighting wars and damage to the environment that occurs as a consequence of warfare. The second category includes environmental threats not directly related to warfare. These may still be considered matters of national security in the case of environmental problems that threaten to cause a war. However, environmental problems that, because of their severity, threaten human lives and welfare even without the intermediate agency of war should also be included in this category and considered security issues, because of our concern for human security.

WAR-RELATED ENVIRONMENTAL THREATS

Around 2500 BC, what may have been the first use in history of environmental modification as a means of warfare occurred in the Middle East when King Urlama of Lagash ordered the construction of canals to divert water from neighboring Umma during a territorial dispute in the boundary region between the two kingdoms, which lay between the Tigris and the Euphrates. A better-known and far more dramatic instance of environmental warfare, according to Judaic and Christian tradition, occurred around 1200 BC during the great exodus of the people of Israel from Egypt. With the pharaoh's army in pursuit of the fleeing Israelites, Moses summoned divine assistance to part the waters of the Red Sea. After the Israelites had passed safely to the other side, Egyptian soldiers were drowned when the waters of the Red Sea closed over them.[12]

Herodotus describes how Cyrus, in 539 BC, invaded Babylon by diverting the waters of the Euphrates in order to allow his troops to march into the city on the dry riverbed.[13] Over two thousand years later, in 1503, Leonardo da Vinci and Niccolo Machiavelli devised a plan (never implemented) to divert the waters of the Arno River away from Pisa during a conflict between Florence and Pisa.[14] In the Netherlands, from the seventeenth century all the way up to 1940, a defensive network was based on plans to flood large portions of the country's low-lying land.[15]

The diversion of water is not the only environmental modification technique that has been used in warfare. Smoke (sometimes in combination with naturally occurring fog or dust) has been used to screen the movements of armies and ships for centuries. In the exodus from Egypt, smoke was used to hide the movement of the Israelites from the Egyptian army pursuing them. In 1632, the Swedish king Gustavus Adolphus used smoke generated by burning wet straw to cover a river crossing by his army. During the World War I battle of Loos in Belgium, British forces used smoke candles in the course of preparing for their first gas attack. So effective was the use of smoke to cover the British infantry assault at Loos that the British army continued to use smoke screens through the remainder of the war.[16] Modern navies routinely equip their ships with the capability to produce smoke screens.

The most dramatic modern-day instance of environmental warfare occurred in 1991, during the Persian Gulf War. Iraqi forces retreating from

Kuwait damaged 749 oil wells, setting 650 of them ablaze. Damaged wells burned or gushed an estimated six million barrels of oil per day. In all, six hundred million barrels of oil—equivalent to three months' worth of global petroleum consumption—were lost.[17]

Warfare (and preparations for war) can have devastating environmental impacts even when environmental resources are not being deliberately used as tools of war. The following examples merely illustrate the connection. A more comprehensive accounting of war-related environmental damage would require a volume of its own.

War sometimes has a devastating effect on other species, even to the point of threatening major species with extinction. As many as 100 of the 250 lowland gorillas and 300 of the 400 forest elephants populating the Congo's Kahuzi-Biega National Park are thought to have been killed between 1996 and 1999. Poachers using automatic weapons acquired from Rwandan soldiers following the 1994 genocide in Rwanda were responsible for many of the killings, but poaching was facilitated by the devastating impact of war on both conservation efforts and tourism. Rwandan and Congolese rebels using the national park as a base of operations also slaughtered animals for food and sold ivory to pay for weapons.[18]

War can also leave serious environmental hazards in its wake. Large areas of Iraq, Kosovo, and Afghanistan are today littered with low-level radioactive waste as a consequence of the U.S. military's use of depleted uranium weapons. Depleted uranium is a by-product of the uranium-enrichment process used to produce fissile uranium for nuclear weapons or reactors. Because depleted uranium, as a metal, is almost twice as dense as lead, it is used by the United States for tank armor and armor-piercing shells. Waste, including contaminated soil, produced by testing and training with depleted uranium weapons in the United States falls under Department of Energy guidelines for the disposal of radioactive waste. Concern over the health and environmental impacts of depleted uranium weapons led the U.S. Air Force in 1993 to stop using them in training exercises. (The decision was reversed in 2002.[19]) Of course, there are no environmental regulations that govern the use of such weapons in warfare. Consequently, in spite of the existence of hundreds of contamination sites in Iraq, Kosovo, and Afghanistan, as well as persistent questions among scientists concerning the long-term effects of depleted uranium on plant and animal life and groundwater, the United States has taken no steps even to assess the environmental impact of these weapons.

The ultimate, although unrealized, war-related environmental catastrophe is perhaps "nuclear winter." Jonathan Schell, in an apocalyptic bestseller that described the planet's possible condition following a general nuclear war, said that the United States could become "a republic of insects and grass" and that, indeed, the climatic catastrophe produced by a nuclear war might very well mean the extinction of human life.[20] Such a condition, or something approaching it, would be produced by the layer of dust and soot thrown into the atmosphere by multiple nuclear detonations.[21]

It is not combat alone that constitutes a security-related threat to the environment. A variety of environmental problems have also resulted from preparations for war.

In 1991, a Russian environmental group reported that the Soviet Union had regularly dumped radioactive waste into the Arctic Ocean during the Cold War. After initially denying the charges, the Russian government agreed in 1992 to appoint a commission to study the matter. When the report was completed the following year, it revealed that a large quantity of nuclear material had in fact been dumped. Six nuclear reactors with fuel, ten reactors without fuel, and portions of a nuclear icebreaker containing nuclear fuel had all been deposited in the Arctic Ocean. In addition, over seventeen thousand containers of radioactive waste had been dumped between 1959 and 1992. When barrels of nuclear materials floated on the surface after dumping, sailors had been ordered to shoot them with machine guns, ensuring not only that the barrels would sink but also that their contents would leak immediately into the ocean.[22]

In August 2000, the *Kursk*, a Russian submarine powered by two nuclear reactors, sank in the Barents Sea. Only a complex salvage operation conducted more than a year later prevented the *Kursk*'s reactors from joining those deliberately dumped into the Arctic Ocean as sources of long-term ecological damage.[23]

The U.S. Navy's use of midfrequency sonar to detect submarines at long distances has long been suspected of causing the deaths of marine mammals. In 2003, scientists studying the deaths of fourteen whales that beached themselves and died in the Canary Islands during nearby naval exercises reported evidence of depression sickness, likely caused by the whales' response to sonar.[24] In 2004, the Scientific Committee of the International Whaling Commission said that the evidence linking sonar to whale beachings "appears overwhelming."[25]

INDIRECT ENVIRONMENTAL THREATS

Environmental problems unrelated to warfare often constitute serious threats to human welfare and, consequently, raise issues of human security. Deforestation and desertification may deprive people of their livelihoods and even render subsistence farming impossible. Overfishing of the world's oceans to the point of causing the collapse of certain species of fish risks eliminating an important source of nutrition for humankind. Untreated sewage can affect supplies of drinking water, causing widespread illness and even death. Polluted air is a factor in respiratory diseases. Depletion of the ozone layer creates exposure to cancer-causing solar radiation. Climate change, which will be considered in greater detail later in this chapter, threatens many serious effects on humans, including, for some, the inundation of their homes. Even in the absence of war, environmental problems can bring death and destruction.

But there is some evidence that environmental damage may also lead to war. Thomas Homer-Dixon, a leading expert on the relationship between security and the environment, has stated that "scarcities of critical environmental resources—especially of cropland, freshwater, and forests—contribute to violence in many parts of the world."[26] While interstate violence is not a common consequence of environmental strains, violence within countries, especially developing states, can sometimes be attributed to environmental factors. The implications even for more advanced states are significant, since intrastate violence in the developing world can generate refugee flows, provoke humanitarian crises (with attendant pressures for intervention), and, in extreme cases, actually cause the collapse of states.

Water is the resource that most commonly causes tensions between states, although oil (which is discussed below) seems to generate more intense conflicts. Many of the world's most important rivers—the Nile, Euphrates, Indus, Ganges, Danube, and Paraná, to note just a few—are shared by two or more states. The construction of dams, such as the Ataturk Dam on the Euphrates River in Turkey and the Gabčíkovo-Nagymaros Project on the Danube in Hungary and Slovakia have created concerns downstream about environmental consequences of reduced water flows and about potential manipulation of supplies. In 1964, when Syria and Lebanon attempted to divert water from the Jordan River before it reached newly constructed irrigation canals in Israel, the Israelis used military force to prevent the construction of a dam. In parts of the world where fresh water is scarce, access to major rivers and lakes is clearly a matter of national security.[27]

Ultimately, it is human consumption—of water, food, air, and a host of other resources—that, together with the waste such consumption produces, is responsible for virtually all of the environmental problems we face today. That consumption increases with both population growth and development. Our prehistoric ancestors are thought to have consumed 2,500 calories of energy each per day, all in the form of food. Today the average human uses thirty-one thousand calories of energy per day (Americans consume on average six times that amount), with fossil fuels constituting the majority of that figure.[28] The significance of fossil fuels, and especially petroleum, as a cause of insecurity in the world today merits special attention.

OIL AND SECURITY

For much of the past century, oil has been "the prize," the one natural resource capable of empowering backward societies and bringing empires to their knees. It will have the same importance in international politics for years to come, although exactly how many more years is a contentious and crucial question. In the past half-century, some of the poorest states in the world have become some of the world's wealthiest states on the strength of oil revenues alone. Conversely, the world's most advanced states—the industrialized democracies of North America, Western Europe, and Japan—were temporarily crippled by an oil embargo in the 1970s. And Russia, reeling from the effects of its transition from communism to capitalism, rebounded economically on the strength of oil and natural gas exports, a factor that has significantly contributed to Vladimir Putin's longevity in office.

Have there been wars for oil? Some scoff at the idea, while others have taken to the streets with signs demanding, "No blood for oil." What is indisputable is this: Petroleum has been a vital resource for the world's industrialized states and has played a central role in the modern history of warfare. The most destructive war in history, World War II, was propelled in specific directions by the necessity of securing access to oil. As the Japanese military came to exert greater influence on Tokyo's foreign policy in the 1930s, a serious strategic problem presented itself: Japan possessed no petroleum. Although oil at the time met only about 7 percent of Japan's total energy needs, it supplied most of the Japanese military's energy demands. Furthermore, 80 percent of Japan's petroleum came from the United States, at a time when the two Pacific powers appeared to be on a collision course. The thirst for oil ultimately drove Japan across East Asia and into a war with the United States.[29] In the European theater, Germany's decision to push deep into the Soviet Union, however ill fated and unwise it may have appeared in retrospect, was considered necessary by the German military in order to gain control over oil supplies in the Caucasus.

Since the end of World War II, oil has become more, not less, important to the well-being of states. Economies have become more dependent on oil, as have military establishments. Indeed, it is difficult to overstate the importance of oil to modern societies. As important as the high-tech capabilities associated with command, control, communications, computers, and intelligence, surveillance, and reconnaissance (C^4ISR) have become to American military dominance, oil is still the lifeblood of the tanks, trucks, airplanes, and ships that constitute, in turn, the backbone—and the muscle—of modern armed forces. Petroleum is equally significant in the definition of economic power. It may be possible in the Information Age to order virtually any consumer good from virtually anywhere in the world over the Internet, but delivery still requires (despite the discussion of delivery of products from Amazon via drones) a FedEx cargo plane or a UPS truck, and neither moves without oil. The configuration of human habitation, with the relentless urbanization that has accompanied industrialization, is dependent on the means of transportation made possible by internal combustion engines burning petroleum-based fuels. Likewise, the agricultural revolution that has made it possible for fewer and fewer farmers to feed more and more city dwellers from the yield of ever smaller plots of land is based on petrochemical fertilizers and mechanized agricultural machinery.

The extent of American dependence on oil can best be captured in two key numbers. Petroleum accounts for 35 percent of the energy consumed in the United States; in the transportation sector, the figure is between 86 and 95 percent.[30] In recent years, a number of companies with incentives provided by governments have sought to develop commercially viable cars and trucks using alternative power sources such as electricity (Tesla Motors), gas-electric hybrid (Toyota's Prius), hydrogen, and nitrogen; however, despite these efforts, it will be decades before such technologies displace gasoline or diesel-powered vehicles.

Oil is a security concern not only because of its importance to the functioning of advanced industrialized states (and the military forces that protect their interests) but also because of where it is found throughout the world. The vast majority of the world's states have insufficient supplies of petroleum to meet their own needs and, consequently, must rely on imported oil. Net importers must therefore be concerned about the internal stability of petroleum-exporting countries and their continuing willingness to export oil. The security of oil pipelines and tankers is also a matter of considerable concern. On top of everything else, oil prices raise security concerns, since dramatic increases ("price shocks") have the potential for generating economic recessions in oil-dependent economies. Significant price decreases can also have significant effects on oil-exporting countries. In the one-year period from June 2014 to June 2015, the price of a barrel of oil dropped from more than $100 per barrel to $45 per barrel, a decrease that particularly affected countries such as Venezuela, whose oil revenues accounted for 96 percent of export earnings.[31]

Questions surrounding the dependability of oil-exporting countries (that is, the combination of their internal stability and their willingness to supply particular customers, including Ukraine, Japan, and the European Union) take on considerable urgency when one looks at who the leading oil exporters are. The top ten net petroleum exporters in 2013 were Saudi Arabia, Russia, the United Arab Emirates, Kuwait, Iraq, Nigeria, Venezuela, Qatar, Angola, and Canada.[32] Only Norway and Canada are considered "free," according to the annual assessment of political liberties and civil rights conducted by Freedom House. Saudi Arabia's monarchy, in contrast, is considered one of the world's most repressive regimes.[33] Several countries on the list are also among the world's most corrupt business environments.

The situation is scarcely any better when smaller suppliers and emerging producers, such as the former Soviet republics of the Caspian Sea basin, are considered. The oil-producing states of the region—Azerbaijan, Kazakhstan, Turkmenistan, and Uzbekistan—exported a little more than three million barrels of oil per day in 2013 and 2014.[34] All of these are dictatorships with corrupt leaders who are former Communist Party bosses from the period of Soviet rule. The political situation is even worse in certain other oil-producing states. Before the split of Sudan and the Republic of South Sudan, Sudan had estimated petroleum reserves of almost five billion barrels of oil. But civil war, mass killings in Darfur and South Sudan, and the presence of Al Qaeda in the 1990s made the Sudan inhospitable to Western oil companies. Eventually, the United States labeled Sudan's actions in Darfur "genocide." As this example demonstrates, petroleum exploration, production, and export often results in oil-importing states having to deal with governments that are repressive, corrupt, unstable, and even genocidal.

The addition of geographical realities to the mix generates additional problems. To begin with, boundary disputes tend to take on greater significance, increasing the risk of armed conflict, where oil is involved. Iraq's border dispute with Kuwait, which provided the pretext for Saddam Hussein's invasion in 1990, would have hardly merited more than an exchange of diplomatic notes had it not been for the vast quantities of petroleum lying beneath the desert. Although not currently militarized, one of the world's most contentious ongoing territorial disputes involves the conflicting claims of the Philippines, Malaysia, Brunei, Vietnam, Taiwan, and China to the Spratly Islands in the South China Sea. The expectation that large oil reserves are to be found beneath the waters surrounding the islands best explains the competing claims and China's increasingly aggressive activities in this area. As polar ice disappears, Russia has begun to assert itself militarily in the Arctic Ocean. Part of the reason seems to be the prospect of significant oil reserves in the Arctic region. But operations in the Arctic are not cheap. In September 2015 Royal Dutch Shell abandoned its efforts to drill for oil in the Chukchi Sea off Alaska.

Along with boundary disputes related to petroleum exploration and production, geography can raise concerns in relation to the movement of oil. In part due to the locations of the world's primary petroleum-exporting countries, much of the world's tanker traffic must pass through one or more maritime chokepoints en route to the oil-importing states. The most critical of these chokepoints is the Strait of Hormuz, separating the Persian Gulf from the Gulf of Oman and the Arabian Sea. Roughly seventeen million barrels of oil per day (approximately 30 percent of all sea-borne traded oil) pass through the Strait of Hormuz on the way to the United States, Japan, or (via the Suez Canal, another significant chokepoint) Western Europe.[35] Other significant chokepoints include the Strait of Malacca, Bab el-Mandab, the Danish Straits, the Turkish Straits, and the Panama Canal. The other principal means of transporting oil, via pipelines, also raises security questions. Pipelines often traverse the territories of war-torn or otherwise unstable states and present tempting, and generally undefended, targets for saboteurs.

The dilemmas associated with petroleum politics are becoming more, not less, difficult to address, because oil consumption continues to increase worldwide. The U.S. Department of Energy notes that global oil consumption grew from 86.1 million barrels per day in 2007 to 91.2 million barrels per day in 2013.[36] For its part, the United States used 19.05 million barrels of oil per day in 2014.

American consumption may not be the worst aspect of the demand problem in the future (although it appears unlikely that any state will catch the United States in per capita consumption). China and India, with respective populations of 1.3 and 1.2 billion, are experiencing dramatic economic growth. Automobile ownership in China, which was tightly restricted and beyond the reach of most Chinese until recently, is expanding rapidly. In 2014, there were 154 million private autos, compared with 240 million in the United States. The ratio of vehicles to people in the United States is 240 million vehicles to 315 million people.[37] If China were to have the same ratio of vehicles to people, it would have 990 million cars, a development that would have profound implications for the environment, not only in China but also around the world.

Energy production is highly dependent on technology; petroleum did not become the dominant source of energy until the discovery and development of cost-effective ways to drill for oil in the 1930s. Many analysts predicted that the world was running out of oil and that there were few places to look for undiscovered reserves. That perspective was shattered with the application of two new technologies to tap into oil and natural gas reserves: hydraulic fracturing ("fracking") and horizontal drilling. Since 2010, natural gas production has increased by 25 percent, and U.S. oil production has risen by 60 percent between 2008 and 2014.[38] An indicator of the change in the international oil market was the export of oil from the United States in October 2014 for the first time since 1975. The National Intelligence Council estimates, "By 2020, the US could emerge as a major energy exporter."[39]Against this background, it is worth noting the degree to which access to oil has already become a significant part of the U.S. definition of American national security.

In 1991 and again in 2003, the United States went to war against Iraq. On both occasions, most supporters and even some opponents of war were quick to argue that American forces were fighting in Iraq for reasons larger than oil—for Kuwaiti sovereignty or the principle of nonaggression (in 1991) or to topple Saddam Hussein, defeat global terrorism, or promote democracy or Iraqi human rights (in 2003). And yet the interest of the industrialized world in oil from the Persian Gulf States was, and is, undeniable. In November 1990, Secretary of State James A. Baker, in fact, was quite forthright about that interest when he explicitly linked the first American military confrontation with Iraq to jobs in the United States.[40]

Baker was not the first to connect Persian Gulf oil to U.S. national security. A decade earlier, a series of dramatic events had prompted President Carter to articulate a new approach to petroleum and national security. In January 1979, the shah of Iran, a faithful ally of the United States, was overthrown in an Islamic revolution. The hostility of the new regime to American interests was demonstrated in November when the American embassy in Tehran was overrun. Then, in December, the Soviet Union invaded neighboring Afghanistan.

Carter responded to these developments in his State of the Union Address on January 23, 1980, with what came to be called the Carter Doctrine. Noting that the Soviet invasion of Afghanistan threatened a region containing "more than two-thirds of the world's exportable oil," Carter said, "Let our position be absolutely clear: An attempt by any outside force to gain control of the Persian Gulf region will be regarded as an assault on the vital interests of the United States of America, and such an assault will be repelled by any means necessary, including military force."[41] To give force to the announcement, a new military command, the Rapid Deployment Joint Task Force, was formed in Tampa, Florida, with responsibility for the Persian Gulf region. Under President Reagan, this Rapid Deployment Force would become the Central Command.[42]

Reagan promoted the securitization of petroleum in other ways as well. In 1983, he signed National Security Decision Directive 114, which declared that "because of the real and psychological impact of a curtailment in the flow of oil from the Persian Gulf on the international economic system, we must assure our readiness to deal promptly with actions aimed at disrupting that traffic."[43] Military action was deemed necessary in 1986 when, as a response to threats to petroleum exports during the Iran-Iraq War, Reagan ordered the U.S. Navy to escort Kuwaiti oil tankers flying the American flag through the Persian Gulf and the Strait of Hormuz. The operation was not without significant costs. In 1987, the frigate USS *Stark* was struck by two Exocet missiles fired by an Iraqi fighter plane while operating in the Persian Gulf.

Thirty-seven Americans on board were killed. Just over a year later, another American warship patrolling the Gulf, the cruiser USS *Vincennes*, mistakenly fired on a civilian Iranian airliner, killing 290 people and fueling outrage in the region against the United States.

Fear that the Soviet Union might be advancing toward the vital oil resources of the Persian Gulf region when it invaded Afghanistan in 1979 was a factor in the U.S. government's decision to support Muslim militants—the *mujahidin*—who were to fight against the Soviets in Afghanistan throughout the 1980s. These militants, drawn from all over the Muslim world, included Osama bin Laden, who as a twenty-three-year-old traveled from his home in Saudi Arabia to Afghanistan to support the war in 1980. At the end of the war in 1988, bin Laden decided to transform the anti-Soviet effort into a foundation of future *jihad* by establishing a network called Al Qaeda.[44]

Those who bothered to read the annual White House summaries of national security strategy could not fail to be impressed by their acknowledgment of the continuing importance of Middle Eastern oil during the 1990s. The discussion of American security interests in the Middle East for many years contained the following line: "The United States has enduring interests in pursuing a just, lasting and comprehensive Middle East peace, ensuring the security and well-being of Israel, helping our Arab friends provide for their security, and maintaining the free flow of oil at reasonable prices." (The phrase *at reasonable prices* was dropped after the 1998 edition.[45])

Among the costs of petroleum production and consumption are those associated with military policies aimed at "maintaining the free flow of oil." Such "externalities" (that is, costs that are not fully allocated by the market) are significant. In addition to the costs of military deployments to protect friendly oil-producing regimes or oil transit routes, there are what may be broadly termed social costs. These include the costs associated with human rights abuses in authoritarian regimes that are propped up by oil revenues, as well as the costs of wars fought for control of oil reserves. On top of these, there are a variety of environmental costs, including those associated with the despoliation of wilderness areas (such as the Arctic National Wildlife Refuge) in the course of oil exploration and production, marine pollution when tankers such as the *Exxon Valdez* rupture or offshore oil platforms are damaged, air pollution from the burning of massive quantities of petroleum products, and climate change. The oil that spewed into the Gulf of Mexico following the explosion of BP's Deepwater Horizon rig provided a dramatic example of the environmental damage that can occur as a consequence of our dependence on oil, but most experts believe that the warming of the Earth's surface due to the accumulation of greenhouse gases, while much harder to discern and respond to, presents a far more serious threat to human security.

CLIMATE CHANGE

As we noted earlier, oil is not the only natural resource to raise security concerns. However, its significance for the economies of the industrialized world puts it in a category by itself. In addition, we have chosen to focus on petroleum because of the key role its use plays in what is perhaps the most important environmental issue of our time—climate disruption. As President Obama observed in April 2015, "Climate change can no longer be denied. It can't be edited out. It can't be omitted from the conversation. And action can no longer be delayed."[46]

It is becoming increasingly apparent that humans' dependence on oil (and other fossil fuels) bears primary responsibility for the profound and possibly irreversible climatic changes we are currently witnessing. NASA has noted that 97 percent of climate scientists believe that the Earth's warming trends during the last century are human induced.[47]

How is human consumption of petroleum related to climate change? Let us begin with a gallon of gasoline. When a gallon of gasoline is burned in an internal combustion engine powering a car, a truck, a lawnmower, a piece of construction equipment, or some other machine, five pounds of carbon dioxide (CO_2) are released into the atmosphere. Carbon dioxide is not a pollutant in the normal sense of that term. In fact, the release of carbon dioxide into the atmosphere is a necessary feature of our planet's vast carbon cycle; it occurs naturally in the respiration of animals and the decay of dead plants (among other ways). Its presence in the atmosphere makes life possible by trapping a portion of the sun's radiation and thereby helping to warm the surface of the Earth. The problem is that the use of fossil fuels, together with deforestation on a massive scale, has introduced carbon dioxide into the atmosphere on a scale unprecedented in human history.[48] When the Industrial Age began, the concentration of carbon dioxide in the atmosphere was approximately 280 parts per million; today it is more than 400 parts per million.[49] With that increase comes a more pronounced greenhouse effect, as more solar radiation is trapped near the surface of the Earth.

Over the course of the twentieth century, the average global temperature has increased; since 1880 average global temperatures have increased by 1.4 degrees Fahrenheit. The 2000–2009 decade was the warmest on record, and the World Meteorological Organization noted that 2014 was the warmest year on record. Sea levels have risen an average of 0.6 inches per decade since 1870, but recent years have seen an accelerated rise. In the last one hundred years, the sea level has risen seven inches. Arctic sea ice has been declining at a rate of 13.3 percent per decade. In 2009, the portion of the Arctic covered by ice was 24 percent smaller than the average coverage from 1979 to 2000.[50]

The impacts of changes are interrelated and compounded. The melting of the ice caps, along with icebergs and glaciers, causes sea levels to rise. This, in turn, produces beach erosion, flooding of coastal areas, and, eventually, the complete inundation of low-lying lands, including certain islands. Higher atmospheric temperatures cause evaporation of surface water to occur more rapidly. This means that storms, on average, will become more intense and that rainfall in some parts of the globe will increase. Overall, however, more rapid evaporation will result in a widespread drying of soils and a consequent expansion of deserts. Patterns of vegetation will also be changed across the world, with, in some cases, major impacts on agriculture. In parts of the world where subsistence agriculture is practiced, climate change is likely to produce, and in fact appears already to be producing, large numbers of environmental refugees.

Climate change, like virtually every other environmental threat, will affect the poor much more than it will the rich. The poor are, in many instances, dependent on the very resources and economic activities that are most likely to be affected by climate change. Subsistence agriculture, for example, may be affected in some regions by prolonged drought and in other regions by an increase in the number and severity of violent storms. Either drought or flooding can be devastating to communities living close to the margin of existence. Flooding, of course, is likely to be a particularly acute problem for people living in low-lying coastal areas, among them roughly seventy million Bangladeshis. However problematic and unpalatable many of the solutions will be, wealthy states (and wealthy individuals) will be able to purchase a measure of security against environmental threats, security that will simply be unavailable to many in the world. To put it bluntly but accurately, the rich will be able to buy their way out of many aspects of the problem.[51]

There are, of course, uncertainties inherent in efforts to predict global climate change and its effects, uncertainties that are often exploited by corporations and political leaders who have an interest in deferring remedial measures. The uncertainties are related to causal inferences and predictions, not to existing observations. There is no question concerning the increases in the Earth's average temperature and in the concentration of greenhouse gases in the atmosphere. The range of informed opinion concerning the likely effects of climate change—the area where uncertainty exists—runs from the view that those effects will be serious to the projection that they will be catastrophic.

Examining the areas of uncertainty is unlikely to provide any reassurance about future impacts, but it can make discussions of climate change more intelligible. To begin with, climate-change predictions must deal with uncertainties regarding potential changes in the carbon cycle. For example, it is possible that increases in atmospheric concentrations of carbon dioxide will stimulate the growth of the very vegetation that removes carbon dioxide from the atmosphere. Such an input in the carbon cycle might slow the rate at which greenhouse gases collect in the atmosphere.

There are a number of feedback processes that affect our ability to predict climate change. As snow and ice melt with the progression of global warming, highly reflective materials on the surface of the Earth disappear and reveal darker, more absorbent, materials, such as soil and water. The increased absorption of the sun's radiation has the potential to amplify global warming. Similarly, global warming increases the evaporation of water from the surface of the Earth, causing more clouds to form. The increased cloudiness might result in even more heat being trapped near the Earth's surface, or, because clouds also reflect solar energy away from the Earth, the net effect might be the opposite.

Another factor contributing to uncertainty is the potential for abrupt change. Climate changes that have been observed thus far have been incremental; projections typically assume continuing linear change. It is possible, however, that a tipping point might be reached, at which dramatic, and possibly even catastrophic, changes ensue. Among the possibilities are changes in ocean currents (and related impacts) of the type described in the Pentagon study noted below, or the sudden release—due to thawing—of the vast quantities of methane (another greenhouse gas) that are currently frozen in the Arctic tundra.

Finally, it is worth noting the uncertainties associated with computer modeling of climate change. While significant strides have been made in the construction of climate models, the models are both complex and dependent on enormous quantities of data. Minor uncertainties in data inputs can translate into more significant uncertainties when run through large and complex models. We should stress, however, that major climatic impacts are a certainty and, in fact, are already occurring.[52]

With this background in mind, it may be useful to consider what those who are responsible for the national security of the United States have to say about global warming. In 1972, Secretary of Defense James Schlesinger brought the Office of Net Assessment to the Pentagon to function as an in-house think tank charged with envisioning the future of warfare. OSD/NA (for Office of the Secretary of Defense/Net Assessment) had been born the previous year as a working group within the National Security Council in an effort to address President Nixon's complaints concerning the quality of the intelligence available to him. From the beginning, OSD/NA has been headed by Andrew Marshall, a man whose career as a professional strategist had begun at the dawn of the Cold War. In fact, as a young economist employed by the RAND

Corporation in the 1950s, Marshall was among the first to advocate a counterforce strategy for the use of American nuclear weapons as opposed to the existing countercity strategy.[53]

In 2003, at Marshall's direction, the Office of Net Assessment commissioned a report on the possible impact of global climate change on the security of the United States. The report, titled *An Abrupt Climate Change Scenario and Its Implications for United States National Security*, considers the implications for national security of a change in the major ocean currents that presently moderate the climate in many of the world's temperate zones.[54] Beginning with the standard assumption of gradual global warming, the report notes the possibility that the increase in fresh water in the oceans due to increased precipitation and the melting of ice in the polar regions might abruptly alter the operation of currents. Without the warmth generated in northern latitudes by ocean currents, average temperatures in parts of the world could drop five to ten degrees Fahrenheit. This, in turn, would change precipitation patterns, sharply reduce growing seasons, and increase the frequency of severe storms. The report's conclusions concerning the impact of the climate change described on national security are worth noting in detail:

> Violence and disruption stemming from the stresses created by abrupt changes in climate pose a different type of threat to national security than we are accustomed to today. Military confrontation may be triggered by a desperate need for natural resources such as energy, food and water rather than by conflicts over ideology, religion, or national honor. The shifting motivation for confrontation would alter which countries are most vulnerable and the existing warning signs for security threats.
>
> There is a long-standing academic debate over the extent to which resource constraints and environmental challenges lead to interstate conflict. While some believe they alone can lead nations to attack one another, others argue that their primary effect is to act as a trigger of conflict among countries that face preexisting social, economic, and political tension. Regardless, it seems undeniable that severe environmental problems are likely to escalate the degree of global conflict.[55]

The National Intelligence Council's 2020 Project acknowledges the scientific consensus that "the greenhouse effect is real." It takes a more circumspect view of the effects of global warming; nonetheless, the report concludes that the United States "is likely to face significant bilateral pressure to change its domestic environmental policies and to be a leader in global environmental efforts."[56]

In a 2007 report, a group of high-level, retired generals and admirals prepared a report for a defense contractor, the CNA Corporation, and concluded, "climate change can act as a 'threat multiplier' for instability in some of the most volatile regions of the world, and it presents significant national security challenges for the United States."[57] Seven years later, the same group revisited the subject of climate change and national security and concluded that the risks were accelerating.[58]

In 2014, the U.S. Department of Defense addressed the threat that climate change poses to national security and concluded, "Rising global temperatures, changing precipitation patterns, climbing sea levels, and more extreme weather events will intensify the challenges of global instability, hunger, poverty, and conflict. They will likely lead to food and water shortages, pandemic disease, and disputes over refugees and resources, and destruction by natural disasters in regions across the globe."[59]

INCREASING SECURITY
BY REDUCING CONSUMPTION

Environmental threats and resource issues are, as we have seen, connected in many different ways. Not surprisingly, many of the policies that can improve environmental security promise at the same time to ameliorate resource scarcities. Because petroleum consumption is central to much of the world's environmental security dilemmas, we begin our discussion of solutions there.

As previously noted, the development of the new technologies of hydraulic fracturing and the horizontal drilling of oil and gas wells have changed the energy picture in the United States, dramatically enabling the United States, for example, to surpass Russia as the world's largest gas producer and expanding its reserves from thirty to one hundred years.[60] That's the good news; the bad news is that there are a number of environmental problems associated with these new technologies, including increased air pollution, the contamination of drinking water, noise and dust from trucks serving drilling sites, and a dramatic increase in the number of earthquakes in some areas where fracking has been employed.[61] For example, during past decades, Oklahoma registered only about one-and-a-half earthquakes exceeding magnitude 3.0 on the Richter scale per year. Since the mid-2000s, the number of earthquakes of this magnitude have mushroomed to 585 in 2014 and more than 900 in 2015.[62] Both the U.S. Geological Survey and Republican governor Mary Fallin have recognized the possible connection between oil and gas drilling activity and seismicity.

Michael Klare has argued that the United States needs to separate oil imports from security commitments, reduce its "addiction" to imported oil, and move toward a "postpetroleum economy."[63] Undemocratic and even aggressive regimes have too often turned oil exports into American military hardware or even security guarantees from the U.S. government. This has been the pattern in the Middle East for over half a century; it is currently being duplicated in the Caspian Sea basin, a development that could have profound implications for future U.S. national security.

Reducing global oil consumption in general means conservation in the near term and a shift to new technologies in the longer term. A shift to alternative sources of energy holds some promise for reducing oil dependency and greenhouse gas emissions. Natural gas has the advantage of being a close substitute for oil in many applications while producing less CO_2 than oil. The problem with natural gas is that it is no less finite a resource than oil. It also happens to be most abundant in some of those same troubled parts of the world from which much of our oil comes.[64]

Some alternative sources of energy impose different costs. The construction of dams for hydroelectric power produces environmental impacts that we are only beginning to comprehend. It also carries the possibility of creating interstate tensions, as we noted earlier. Nuclear energy raises other security issues. Consider the prediction of the Defense Department's *Abrupt Climate Change* report: "As cooling drives up demand, existing hydrocarbon supplies are stretched thin. With a scarcity of energy supply—and a growing need for access—nuclear energy will become a critical source of power, and this will accelerate nuclear proliferation as countries develop enrichment and reprocessing capabilities to ensure their national security."[65]

It is, ultimately, conservation that is the key to addressing environmental threats, beyond merely the conservation of petroleum. The first step toward environmental security is simply to understand the true costs—in dollars and cents, certainly, but also in military commitments, climate change, polluted air and water, earthquakes, lost wilderness and biodiversity, and many other forms—of the choices we make as consumers. To ignore these costs is to put at risk both our quality of life and our security.

ADDITIONAL RESOURCES

Books

Campbell, Kurt, ed. *Climate Cataclysm: The Foreign Policy and National Security Implications of Climate Change.* Washington, DC: Brookings, 2008.
CNA Military Advisory Board. *National Security and the Accelerating Risks of Climate Change.* Arlington, VA: CNA Corporation, May 2014.
Diamond, Jared. *Collapse: How Societies Choose to Fail or Succeed.* New York: Viking, 2005.

Homer-Dixon, Thomas F. *Environment, Scarcity, and Violence.* Princeton, NJ: Princeton University Press, 1999.

Klare, Michael T. *Rising Powers, Shrinking Planet: The New Geopolitics of Energy.* New York: Metropolitan Books, 2008.

Maass, Peter. *Crude World: The Violent Twilight of Oil.* New York: Alfred A. Knopf, 2009.

Maslin, Mark. *Climate Change: A Very Short Introduction.* 3rd ed. Oxford: Oxford University Press, 2014.

Matthew, Richard A. "Is Climate Change a National Security Issue?" *Issues in Science and Technology* 27 (2011): 49–60.

Mazo, Jeffrey. *Climate Conflict: How Global Warming Threatens Security and What to Do About It.* London: International Institute for Strategic Studies, 2010.

U.S. National Academy of Science and Royal Society (UK). *Climate Change: Evidence and Causes.* Washington, DC: National Academies Press, 2014.

Yergin, Daniel. *The Prize: The Epic Quest for Oil, Money, and Power.* New York: Simon and Schuster, 1991.

———. *The Quest: Energy, Security, and the Remaking of the Modern World.* New York: Penguin, 2012.

Zedillo, Ernesto. *Global Warming: Looking Beyond Kyoto.* Washington, DC: Brookings Institution Press, 2008.

Websites

"Crisis Guide: Climate Change." *CFR Interactive.* New York: Council on Foreign Relations: www.cfr.org

The Earth Institute, Columbia University: www.earth.columbia.edu/

Energy Information Administration: www.eia.doe.gov

Greenpeace International: www.greenpeace.org/international/

Natural Resources Defense Council: www.nrdc.org/

"Slideshow: Ecological Disasters." *CFR Interactive.* New York: Council on Foreign Relations. www.cfr.org

United Nations Environment Programme: www.unep.org

Woodrow Wilson International Center for Scholars, Environmental Change and Security Program: https://www.wilsoncenter.org/

Films

Climate of Doubt, Frontline (WGBH/PBS, 2012). Directed by Catherine Upin.

Bhopal: A Prayer for Rain. London: Revolver Entertainment, 2014. A film starring Martin Sheen and Kal Penn focusing on the 1984 accident at a Union Carbide factory in Bhobal, India, which resulted in the deaths of up to fifteen thousand people. Directed by Ravi Kumar.

The Spill, Frontline (WGBH/PBS, 2010). Written by Marcela Gaviria and Martin Smith.

Chapter Thirteen

Seeking Security in an Insecure World

As Søren Kierkegaard once observed, life is understood backward but lived forward. Thinking about uncharted circumstances is risky, confusing, and contentious but must nonetheless be attempted

—John Steinbruner, *Principles of Global Security* (2000)

In the late 1980s, the United States and the Soviet Union were nearing the end of a long military and political struggle that had dominated international politics for four decades. Reflecting that struggle (and unaware that it was nearing an end), security studies focused heavily on deterrence and the threat of nuclear war. The respected journal *International Security* was publishing articles with titles like "The Consequences of 'Limited' Nuclear Attacks on the United States," "Controlling Nuclear War," and "Extending Deterrence with German Nuclear Weapons." Policy debates in the United States centered on the feasibility (and advisability) of the "Star Wars" space-based missile defense system and the prospects for bilateral nuclear arms control with the Soviet Union. Defense planners worried about the vulnerability of America's intercontinental ballistic missiles (ICBMs) to preemptive strikes by Soviet submarine-launched ballistic missiles (SLBMs). As had been the case since shortly after World War II, the world lived under the threat of nuclear annihilation.

On November 9, 1989, having forced the resignation of their communist leaders just two days earlier, crowds of East Germans began tearing down the Berlin Wall, the long-standing symbol of the rigid division of the world into two implacably hostile camps armed with the most destructive weapons ever devised. The dominoes began falling—in reverse—and in a remarkably short span of time the Soviet Union collapsed and the Cold War, the central political reality of the post–World War II period, was over.

245

It is instructive for several reasons to look back at the tensions of the mid-1980s and the euphoria of the early 1990s. First, it cannot help but produce humility among those of us who wish to make predictions about the prospects for security in the international system. Second, that period stands as an important signpost against which to measure the distance and, perhaps more important, the direction in which the world has traveled since September 11, 2001, which marked the end of the "post–Cold War" world and the beginning of a new era.

It is, of course, not enough to note that change has occurred. While there is much about the quest for security that does not change (so that Sun Tzu, Thucydides, and Clausewitz continue to reward those who read their observations on security), at another level, change is a constant. Indeed, it would be a betrayal of the reader's trust to have brought him or her to this point only to conclude that what was written during the Cold War remains sufficient for a clear understanding of international security. While the evidence presented to this point concerning the rise of new tactics and organizations of terrorism such as beheadings and the Islamic State, the wars in Afghanistan and Iraq, the threatening confluence of globalization and disease, or the advent of cyberwar may well be enough to make the point about the significance of changes in the security environment, part of our purpose here is to highlight the specific changes we believe to be most significant.

Surveying the problems of an insecure world, it is apparent that, first, nonstate actors—including ideologically driven individuals, terrorist networks, and transnational criminal organizations—have become significant threats to both states and individuals since the end of the Cold War and 9/11. Second, the threats we confront are increasingly transnational in character. Third, in large part due to the increasing significance of nonstate actors and transnational threats, security, now more than ever, is indivisible; we are all connected. Security is, fourth, increasingly subject to the law of unintended consequences—that is, actions taken to address specific threats often create insecurities in different areas. Fifth, when we return to the focus of the traditional approach to international security, we find that the geographical center of concern has shifted dramatically. And finally, we note that some old problems have risen from the ashes of the Cold War, like a modern-day phoenix.

THE RISE OF NONSTATE ACTORS

During the Cold War and (with various local and temporary exceptions) for centuries before that, seeking security meant taking actions to counter the threats posed by states. The Anglo-German naval arms race that preceded

World War I, the French development of the Maginot Line after World War I, the establishment after World War II of the North Atlantic Treaty Organization (NATO) in the West and the Warsaw Pact in the East, and the Soviet and American development and deployment of antiballistic missile systems were all manifestations of states' determination to protect themselves from other states.

Within the discipline of international relations, considerable attention has always been given to strategies for restraining the aggressive behavior of states. Balance-of-power theory and its Wilsonian rival, the theory of collective security, reflect this emphasis on restraining states. International law, international organizations, alliances, and many other features of modern international politics place the security of states front and center.

There are certainly good reasons to continue worrying about the security of states. When functioning properly, the state structures the political, economic, and social life of the community in such a way that freedom, commerce, and culture can flourish. But looking outward from within the state, other states may appear threatening. In fact, few social institutions can pose a greater threat to the state than other states.

Because states have, for a very long time, been central to the way we understand international security, it is difficult to shift the focus to threats posed by nonstate actors. As Ralph Waldo Emerson said, "People only see what they are prepared to see." There is, however, much to see beyond the state.

Attacks in New York and Washington on September 11, 2001; in Bali on October 12, 2002; in Madrid on March 11, 2004; in London on July 7, 2005; in Mumbai on November 26, 2008; in Boston on April 15, 2013; and in Paris on November 13, 2015, have made the threat to security posed by terrorist groups readily—and tragically—apparent. But terrorists are not the only nonstate actors to raise serious security concerns. The potential for individuals like A. Q. Khan, the Pakistani nuclear scientist who sold nuclear secrets and technology for personal gain, to threaten global security is evident. The negative impact that transnational criminal organizations have on security through the sale of weapons in conflict-prone regions, through the trafficking of human beings, through the financing of revolutionary violence and terrorism via drug trafficking, and through their own efforts to subvert states is also more apparent now than ever before. These and other examples of the problems caused by nonstate actors make it plain that states and the international system itself are no longer threatened solely, or even primarily, by other states.

Shifting the focus, even partially, from states to nonstate actors will have a significant effect on the way we view security. This is true first and foremost for this reason: In a system in which states are considered both the primary objects of and threats to security, interstate war must be the primary concern of those who think about security. And if war is the primary concern, the military will be the primary means of addressing that concern. The response to major threats involving nonstate actors bears this out. The threat posed by drug trafficking has, at least in the United States, elicited a "war on drugs," with a major role for the Department of Defense. The 9/11 attacks, perpetrated by a terrorist network, brought on a "war on terror." Regardless of whether war is the appropriate response, it appears to be what our state-centered mode of thinking leads us to whenever we identify a security threat.

The rise of homeland security, as a subject of both academic concern and government policy, is worth noting in this context. Homeland security is a concept that is clearly a product of a state-centered perspective, even though it arose as a response to threats posed by nonstate actors. To speak of homeland security is, on the positive side, to acknowledge that security concerns do not stop at the borders of the state. This point was brought home (quite literally) by the fact that the hijackers of the four airplanes that were brought down on 9/11 had lived and trained to pilot airplanes in the United States. On the other hand, the concept of homeland security is based on the idea that normal means of law enforcement are inadequate to deal with the new threats to security inside the state. It suggests that dealing with terrorism requires an internal security agency (the Department of Homeland Security) and an external security agency (the Department of Defense).

States continue to be the primary providers of security, but even in this realm nonstate actors are making inroads. Increasingly, we are being forced to think of security as a commodity that can be treated as either a public good or a private good. Like the nobles of the medieval period in Europe who built castles as private investments in security, more and more people worldwide who can afford to do so are retreating into gated communities or hiring private security firms for protection. But the privatization of security (and with it the legitimation of nonstate actors with security functions) is not limited to the individual level. States, too, appear to be privatizing more and more aspects of security, as was evident in the widespread use of private security firms by the United States in Iraq following the March 2003 invasion; indeed, at the high point of U.S. involvement in Iraq, the number of private military contractors about equaled the number of American military forces in Iraq.

THE RECOGNITION OF TRANSNATIONAL THREATS

One of the most obvious and, we believe, most significant changes in the post–Cold War security environment is the rise of transnational, as opposed to international, threats. Such threats are not new (as the post–World War I Spanish flu pandemic, to take but a single example, illustrates), but a number of factors have dramatically increased their significance. First, it must be acknowledged that one of the effects of the ending of the Cold War was to create a space in which it was possible for states in the developed world at least to begin giving serious attention to nontraditional threats. The demise of the Warsaw Pact created a "zone of peace,"[1] or a "unipolar moment,"[2] in which security against traditional threats in the vast majority of the developed world seemed assured. It seems reasonable to suggest that the dramatic reduction in the traditional state-centered threats that accompanied the end of the Cold War might explain the sudden interest of security analysts in nontraditional concerns.

Whether or not students of international security turned from nuclear deterrence to, say, epidemic disease as a self-interested means of preserving their policy relevance in the aftermath of the Cold War, one thing is certain: In the competition for scholarly attention and defense spending (two matters that are often connected), big threats trump small threats. To say that the end of the Cold War permitted academics and policymakers to pay more attention to small threats ("small" in relation to the threat of nuclear annihilation, that is) is by no means equivalent to saying that they invented these smaller, nontraditional threats. Most of those threats were always with us but had to be put on the back burner when Berlin was being blockaded, hydrogen bombs were being tested, the Soviet Union was sending nuclear missiles to Cuba ninety miles from the shores of the United States, and proxy wars were being fought in Asia, Africa, Latin America, and the Middle East.

Military threats to security have been and are likely to continue to be around for a long time to come; however, there are other problems that have not received adequate attention. Some should be (and in some cases now are) recognized as security threats. For example, smallpox, although no longer present in human populations, killed an estimated three to five hundred million people in the twentieth century alone. During the same period, an estimated hundred million people died as a consequence of war. Clearly, smallpox posed a greater threat to humans during the twentieth century than warfare; yet throughout the century students of international security focused on the threat of war rather than that of smallpox.

Transnational threats take a variety of forms, including those associated with nonstate actors, but what defines that category is the irrelevance of borders as devices for stopping the threats. Just as the humanitarian organization Doctors without Borders (*Médecins sans Frontières*) aspires to do good in the world without regard to the artificial barriers represented by the borders of sovereign states, so malevolence (in the form of disease, nihilistic ideologies, drugs, child prostitution, and many other problems) spreads widely across the globe with few obstacles. The problem, at one level, is globalization, which in its many guises creates a world increasingly vulnerable to computer- and communications-network disruptions, the spread of disease, financial instability, and many other problems. At another level, however, freedom is responsible. The freedom to travel to virtually any spot on the globe carries with it the possibility of transporting disease or terrorists in the process. The freedom to communicate via the Internet offers a medium through which scholars can plan a conference or terrorists can plan an attack. The freedom to purchase goods manufactured abroad presents the frightening prospect that, some day, a container ship bringing cars or computers or clothing from Asia may also carry a nuclear device. As Kenneth Waltz noted, "States, like people, are insecure in proportion to the extent of their freedom. If freedom is wanted, insecurity must be accepted."[3]

As we noted in chapter 10, the significance of transnational threats is now being acknowledged to some degree. The 9/11 Commission stated that "threats are defined more by the fault lines within societies than by the territorial boundaries between them. From terrorism to global disease or environmental degradation, the challenges have become transnational rather than international."[4] Similarly, President Bill Clinton noted in a May 2000 commencement address at the Coast Guard Academy that globalization and technological developments are "making us more vulnerable to problems that arise half a world away: to terror; to ethnic, racial and religious conflicts; to weapons of mass destruction, drug trafficking and other organized crime."[5] These, indeed, are among the very issues that we have examined in this book.

THE INDIVISIBILITY OF SECURITY

Security today is indivisible. As we noted earlier, a narrowly self-interested security policy cannot be narrowly self-interested. John Muir, the eminent environmentalist and founder of the Sierra Club, could have been talking about international security rather than nature when he wrote, "When we try to pick out anything by itself, we find it hitched to everything else in the Universe."[6] In its projection of likely security threats in 2030, the U.S. National Intelligence Council predicted, "The increasing nexus among food, water, and energy—in combination with climate change—will have far-reaching effects on global development over the next 15–20 years."[7] Consider the following examples that clearly demonstrate the effect of one issue on another.

First, the Wildlife Conservation Society estimates that annual trafficking of animals includes approximately four million birds, 640,000 reptiles, and forty thousand primates and that "at least a billion direct and indirect contacts among wildlife, humans and domestic animals result from the handling of wildlife and the wildlife trade annually."[8] With the increasing number of zoonotic diseases, trafficking in animals increasingly poses threats to public health. For example, in 2004 a man was apprehended at a Belgian airport illegally carrying eagles from Thailand, stuffed into tubes in his carry-on luggage. The birds were infected with avian flu virus (H5N1), and they, as well as several other birds in the airport quarantine area, had to be destroyed.[9] Had the smuggler not been caught, he could have unknowingly—and illegally—imported avian flu into Belgium.

Second, in 1999 the first case of West Nile virus was reported in North America in the Queens area of New York. Scientists who studied the virus found that it is transmitted via mosquitos, probably carried to North America by birds. Within several years, the virus was found in twenty-nine species of mosquitoes and more than a hundred species of birds and a number of mammals, including humans.[10] Its geographical range in North America encompassed Canada and the forty-eight states of the continental United States. Although the CDC estimated that fewer than 1 percent of those infected with the virus would develop a serious neurologic illness such as encephalitis or meningitis (inflammation of the brain or surrounding tissues), it nevertheless posed a new disease threat to those in North America. Scientists who studied the disease concluded that global warming caused by increasing levels of greenhouse gases may be contributing to the warmer winters and summer droughts that seem to promote the spread of the virus.

Third, scientists who have studied the 2014 reemergence of Ebola in Africa have concluded that human encroachment into previously uninhabited wilderness may have played a role in the transmission of the disease from bats to humans. Deforestation, therefore, appears to be linked to the reemergence of Ebola.[11]

Thus we see connections among various security issues. Economic insecurity may lead to slash-and-burn agriculture, with deforestation (and environmental insecurity) as a result. The devastation of an ecosystem may, in turn, create a refugee crisis that leads to ethnic conflict. An intrastate war may generate a market for arms traffickers. Trafficking in small arms and light weapons may then open up a network through which chemical, biological, or even nuclear materials are traded. The proliferation of weapons of mass destruction may make it possible for terrorists to acquire a nuclear device. And so on.

Consider the beginning of the chain above. Poverty, it should be clear, contributes to many other forms of insecurity. Former World Bank president James D. Wolfensohn put it this way:

> Poverty in itself does not immediately and directly lead to conflict, let alone to terrorism. Rather than responding to deprivation by lashing out at others, the vast majority of poor people worldwide devote their energy to the day-in, day-out struggle to secure income, food, and opportunities for their children. And yet we know that exclusion can breed violent conflict. Careful research tells us that civil wars have often resulted not so much from ethnic diversity—the usual scapegoat—as from a mix of factors, of which, it must be recognized, poverty is a central ingredient.[12]

Addressing the issue of global poverty requires more than anything else a simple recognition on the part of wealthy states that security is indivisible and that their willingness to take action is, in fact, an investment in their own security. To some extent, such a recognition is unavoidable. As Dominique Moïsi has noted, "In a transparent world the poor are no longer ignorant of the world of the rich, and the rich have lost the privilege of denial."[13] To act on this recognition, Wolfensohn recommended increasing foreign aid, reducing trade barriers, directing development assistance into proven programs, and acting multilaterally on global issues.

In September 2000, the United Nations General Assembly unanimously adopted the Millennium Development Goals (MDG), an ambitious set of plans that calls on the international community to eradicate extreme poverty and hunger; achieve universal primary education; promote gender equality and empower women; reduce child mortality; improve maternal health; combat HIV/AIDS, malaria, and other diseases; ensure environmental sustainability; and develop a global partnership for development. Progress toward the achievement of these goals was mixed, in part because of the rapid reversion to traditional modes of addressing national security in the wake of 9/11. A program for Sustainable Development Goals as a follow-up to the MDG upon its expiration at the end of 2015 was proposed and adopted in Rio de Janeiro in 2012.

We have examined many different threats to the well-being—the security—of individuals, states, and the international system. These have included traditional military threats posed by states, new threats (including the "new terrorism") presented by nonstate actors, and threats posed by infectious disease, poverty, the proliferation of weapons of mass destruction, cyberwar, transnational crime, ethnic conflict, and environmental degradation. Even the controversial White House document that outlined the George W. Bush administration's strategy of preventive war in September 2002 noted that "poverty, weak institutions, and corruption can make weak states vulnerable to terrorist networks and drug cartels within their borders."[14] The interconnectedness of these threats offers a compelling case, we believe, for the conclusion that security is, now more than ever, indivisible.

THE PROBLEM OF UNINTENDED CONSEQUENCES

We have noted that often the attempt to achieve greater security has the unintentional result of threatening security. For example, in chapter 9 we pointed out that the U.S. Department of Defense originally developed the precursor to the Internet to provide for assured, redundant communications among military bases and installations; if one communications node had been destroyed in an attack, the Internet would have provided an alternate means of communication. Over time, the Internet became a means by which the security of individuals, organizations, and states would be threatened. Or consider infectious diseases. The World Health Organization worked diligently to eradicate smallpox as a threat to the world's peoples. In order to develop defenses against an enemy employing smallpox as a weapon, the defense establishments of both Russia and the United States retained strains of smallpox. Now there is concern that these strains could become available to terrorists and be used to unleash the deadly disease on an unprotected world.

Unintended consequences—or "blowback," in the phrase used by the CIA[15]—may be most apparent in the military response to the 9/11 attacks. The Iraq War generated mistrust and animosity toward the United States and provided a training ground for Islamist militants. There is evidence that it duplicated the effects of the Soviet Union's war in Afghanistan during the 1980s in terms of providing a stimulus to global terrorism. In fact, the respected International Institute for Strategic Studies issued a report in October 2004 that indicated that the Iraq War had aided Al Qaeda's recruitment efforts.[16]

Even American "successes" against Al Qaeda may be making terrorism more difficult to address. In response to attacks on its leadership and its financing, Al Qaeda transformed itself into an ideology and a decentralized movement of jihadists. The loss of its base in Afghanistan resulted in the dispersal of militants all over the world and the spread of its ideology.[17]

The Syrian government of Bashar al-Assad engaged in horrific violations of its citizens' human rights, and the international community imposed sanctions on Syria hoping to force Assad out of office. After the United States formally withdrew its combat troops from Iraq in 2011, a new group affiliated with Al

Qaeda emerged: the Islamic State. Both Al Qaeda and the Islamic State were made up almost entirely of Sunni Arabs, and Assad turned to his Shia Iranian allies to oppose the Islamic State. The United States was now in the uncomfortable position of having to cooperate with Iran to oppose the Islamic State. So unintentionally, after expending American blood and treasure in Iraq, the United States was forced to work with its long-time opponent, Iran, in order to oppose a group that emerged from the remnants of Al Qaeda in Iraq.[18]

While it may be objected that more carefully constructed policies can avoid unintended consequences, history offers little encouragement. Providing Stinger missiles to the *mujahidin* in Afghanistan accomplished its primary purpose of inflicting serious losses on the Soviet Union, but "loose" Stingers now pose a significant threat to civil aviation. The military containment of Iraq during the 1990s was a policy success and, it seems, necessary, but the required stationing of U.S. forces in the Persian Gulf region thereafter was a factor in the decision of Muslim fundamentalists to attack American interests both in the region and in the United States itself. And the war in Iraq led to the formation and emergence of the Islamic State.

GEOGRAPHICAL SHIFTS

Even if we were not adopting an expanded view of security, we would be forced to note that the geographical focus of security studies has shifted dramatically in recent years. The broader view of security, however, provides even more reason for looking closely at different parts of the world, including Africa and Asia.

Many of the threats that we have described in this book come together in Africa. It is the area hardest hit by HIV/AIDS and malaria; it contains many of the world's poorest countries; it has both harbored terrorists and suffered from terrorist attacks; it is an important focus of trafficking of all types; it is the source of many of the refugees who seek to immigrate to European and other countries; and it has suffered more than any other continent from the effects of intrastate conflict. East Africa and the Horn, including Djibouti, Ethiopia, Eritrea, Kenya, Somalia, Tanzania, and Uganda, is an area of particular concern, given the conflicts in the region, the poverty, corruption, and high incidence of HIV/AIDS. Not surprisingly, Al Qaeda was active in Somalia and, according to reports, advised members of Mohammed Aideed's militia on how to use rocket-propelled grenades to shoot down U.S. Black Hawk helicopters. In addition, Al Qaeda operated out of Sudan and perpetrated the 1998 attacks on the American embassies in Nairobi, Kenya, and Dar es Salaam, Tanzania.

Other areas of Africa are also of concern and importance to American security. Africa's most populous country is Nigeria, with over 177 million people (more than half the population of the United States), about half of whom are Muslims.[19] Currently, Nigeria has the tenth largest reserves of oil and is the fourteenth largest exporter of natural gas in the world.[20] A number of African countries have majority populations of Muslims, and there is the possibility that Islamic radicalism will grow among them. Thus, addressing the threats of disease, poverty, intrastate conflict, and trafficking of drugs, humans, and diamonds is a matter of security. The United States and other wealthy, industrial states ignore these threats at their peril.

Other important developments with security implications are occurring in Asia as India and China continue to grow more powerful both politically and economically. China, in fact, has recently surpassed Japan to become the world's second-largest economy and will surpass the United States a few years before 2030.[21] In its report on global trends to the year 2020, the National Intelligence Council predicted that "the likely emergence of China and India, as well as others, as new major global players—similar to the advent of a united Germany in the nineteenth century and a powerful United States in the early twentieth century—will transform the geopolitical landscape, with impacts potentially as dramatic as those in the previous two centuries."[22] The population of China is currently 1.36 billion; India's population is 1.24 billion. Due to China's recently abandoned one-child policy, its population will age rapidly; by 2020 an estimated four hundred million Chinese will be over sixty-five. This will put increased demands on the younger members of Chinese society. From a more traditional security perspective, the greatest military threats to stability and peace in Asia in the near future will concern relations between China and Taiwan, on the one hand, and the two Koreas, on the other. Conflicts involving either of these pairings could rapidly escalate and draw in the United States.

China currently is embarked on an ambitious program to increase its influence in Africa and its control over the South China Sea. It is unusually active in Africa, sponsoring diplomatic initiatives, development projects, and commercial ventures. In 2012, President Obama announced that he had ordered a strategic "pivot" from the Middle East to Asia in order to counter rising Chinese power in the region. China, in turn, pursued an activist agenda: in January 2014, a Chinese naval group was dispatched to the James Shoal, an area claimed by both Taiwan and Malaysia; a month later three Chinese warships patrolled the Indian Ocean and traversed for the first time the Sunda Strait between the Indonesian islands of Java and Sumatra; in May 2014 close to eighty Chinese ships accompanied by seven naval vessels escorted a deep-sea oil exploration rig to a position 120 miles from the coast of Vietnam; and, in the spring of 2015, China embarked on an ambitious reclamation project in the Spratly Islands.[23] In addition to its geographical moves, China also embarked on an ambitious military buildup, purchasing and refurbishing an aircraft carrier from Ukraine and developing and testing a multiple, independently targetable warhead (MIRV) for its most powerful missile, the Dong Feng (DF-5) or East Wind, which is capable of reaching the United States from China.[24]

The combination of geographical shifts in the locus of insecurity and demographic changes with security implications points to what has been called the "urbanization of security."[25] A milestone in human history was passed in 2008 when, for the first time, over half of the world's population lived in urban areas.[26] Urbanization is especially noteworthy in the developing world, where cities like Dhaka, Kinshasa, and Lagos are rapidly moving into the ranks of the world's largest population centers. As of 2012, there were twenty-seven "megacities" with populations greater than ten million.

The implications of urbanization for security are mixed. One the one hand, no state has ever experienced significant economic development without a major shift in population from rural areas to cities. On the other hand, cities have often been breeding grounds for disease, crime, and various forms of social unrest. They are also where modern wars are often fought. During World War II, cities were targeted by all sides in strategic bombing campaigns intended to punish the target state and, eventually, compel its surrender. Today, the "new terrorism" focuses its attacks on major urban areas. Insurgents have learned that fighting from street to street in a city can neutralize some of the technological advantages of superior military forces. Civilians can be used as human shields, rubble-filled streets can block the movement of armored vehicles, and buildings can conceal the movement of insurgents from most forms of aerial surveillance. Consequently, from Mogadishu to Sarajevo, Grozny, and Fallujah, cities have become the primary battlegrounds of contemporary conflict.

NEW WINE IN AN OLD BOTTLE: THE REASSERTION OF RUSSIAN POWER

When the Soviet Union imploded and disintegrated in December 1991, many, particularly in the West, thought that a new era of peace and American hegemony had arrived; however, in Russia the feeling was quite different. To many in the west, Mikhail Gorbachev was a hero—the man who had ended the Cold War. But in Russia, Gorbachev was hated as the man who dismantled the power and influence of one of the two Cold War superpowers.

Boris Yeltsin succeeded Gorbachev, and then a young, hitherto little-known former KGB intelligence officer, Vladimir Putin, succeeded Yeltsin. Putin's rise to power coincided with an increase in global oil prices, and he was able to finance his administration primarily on Russian oil and natural gas sales. In addition, the previously state-owned enterprises were auctioned off, and many of the buyers became Putin's supporters. There developed a kind of "iron triangle" among the Russian government, organized crime, and businesses.[27]

The Russian constitution stipulated that no one could serve two *consecutive* terms as president, so Putin served two terms as president and then served one term as prime minister before running for the Russian presidency again.

In his third term as president, Putin embarked on an aggressive, xenophobic agenda. He first ordered an invasion and occupation of Crimea, a part of Ukraine. Western countries imposed economic sanctions against Russia and Putin's billionaire cronies. But Russia continued to support Russian dissidents in eastern Ukraine, calling for greater autonomy or even independence. Putin's actions toward Ukraine heightened fears in the Baltic states of Latvia, Lithuania, and Estonia, which had been ceded to the Soviet Union in 1939 as a result of the infamous Nazi-Soviet Pact. Of course, the difference between 1939 and the twenty-first century is that the Baltic states had become members of NATO, and were Russia to invade them, the other members of NATO would be obligated to come to their aid. To many, Putin's policies closely resembled those of the Cold War Soviet Union—new wine in an old bottle.

TWO VIEWS OF SECURITY FOR A NEW ERA

As we have noted throughout this book, the traditional view of security centers on the state. The perspective that puts *national security* front and center considers the central threats in the international system (and therefore the principal concerns of security studies) to be threats to the sovereignty, the territorial integrity, and the political and economic systems of *the state*. It is also state centered in that it views states as the primary sources of threats.

Seeking security in the twenty-first century requires attending to national security, because state-based threats to states still exist. We have noted the concerns raised by a reassertive Russia and the People's Republic of China. North Korea also poses a serious threat to the stability of East Asia due to its economic instability coupled with its ongoing nuclear program. Failed states, as we noted in chapter 10, pose a different kind of state-based problem, but one that is nonetheless very serious.

Because the traditional paradigm does not adequately address the various security threats that we have examined, it is important to go beyond national security. Our conclusions lead us to suggest that *human security* and *cooperative security* must be part of any comprehensive approach to security in the century ahead.

The concept of human security emerged in the early 1990s to bring together several distinct efforts to widen the traditional security agenda. Unlike national security, human security focuses on the individual human being rather than the state. It also includes a range of threats to human welfare that go well beyond the traditional focus on defense against aggression. Kofi Annan, the former UN secretary-general, described human security in these terms:

> Human security in its broadest sense, embraces far more than the absence of violent conflict. It encompasses human rights, good governance, access to education and health care and ensuring that each individual has opportunities and choices to fulfill his or her potential. Every step in this direction is also a step towards reducing poverty, achieving economic growth and preventing conflict. Freedom from want, freedom from fear, and the freedom of future generations to inherit a healthy natural environment—these are the interrelated building blocks of human—and therefore national security.[28]

Human security has its conceptual roots in international humanitarian law, international human rights, the concept of humanitarian intervention, and the dual concepts of economic development and human development. As with human rights, the adjective *human* signals a move not only toward thinking about the individual but also toward concern for humankind. Human security, in other words, is simultaneously individual security and universal security.

The structure of the international system complicates efforts to address many of the most serious problems we have discussed in this book. Sovereignty means that each of the two hundred states in the system is free to address (or ignore) global warming or human trafficking or terrorism, as it sees fit. This feature of the international system makes transnational threats particularly difficult to address. The failure of one state to reduce HIV/AIDS infection rates poses a threat to other states. The failure of one state to curb greenhouse gas emissions or to stop the destruction of rainforests has a negative impact on all states that are attempting to address global warming. Furthermore, nonstate actors—terrorists, arms traffickers, nuclear scientists willing to sell their services to the highest bidder—exploit differences among states and operate in the gaps of the international system.

These facts argue strongly for seeking security through the methods presented in the cooperative security paradigm, which, as we noted earlier, seeks to bring states together in ways that address the weaknesses of the international system as it is currently constituted. It approaches security as something to which all states are entitled and that can only be gained by mutual efforts. By treating security as a public good, it establishes the understanding that all states have a common interest in promoting a shared system of security and that "free riders" must be brought into a cooperative framework.

Cooperative security requires a degree of multilateralism that was absent from U.S. foreign policy during the administration of George W. Bush. President Obama has moved the United States toward more cooperative approaches in international affairs, but a variety of factors, including domestic political pressures and fiscal constraints, have limited the degree to which the United States can pursue an active multilateral agenda.

THE WAY FORWARD

Ken Booth's 1979 book *Strategy and Ethnocentrism* noted the failure of most security analysts to take adequate account of differences among cultures.[29] In the Cold War context in which Booth was writing, the Western emphasis on rationality as the foundation of nuclear deterrence theory was an especially striking example of this problem. Almost a decade later, however, scholars were still noting "the pitfalls of ethnocentrism due to American dominance of the field."[30] However much Western policymakers and scholars may have become sensitive to the problems posed by the difficulty of seeing beyond their own cultural constructs, we suspect that ethnocentrism may be an even greater problem today, in the middle of an ongoing struggle against mostly Muslim terrorist organizations, than it was during the Cold War. If our conclusions up to this point have been correct—that seeking security today requires countering threats from nonstate actors, recognizing threats that are transnational and, consequently, indivisible in character, dealing with the problems of unintended consequences, and operating in parts of the world that are especially unfamiliar to most of us in the West—then the ability to understand and even to empathize with those in other cultures is more important than ever before.

What policymakers, analysts, and even entire societies understand by "security" varies more than we ordinarily acknowledge, with the variations relating to political, social, technological, and other circumstances. The meaning of security differs across cultures, but within a culture it is also subject to change over time. This is so because political and social differences affect what societies desire to protect, because technological advances alter the types of threats that must be protected against, and, most important, because the very subjectivity of the concept of security ensures that individuals in different situations will value social goods and assess threats differently. The concept of security, to put it simply, is socially constructed.

To the extent that "security studies" has some common content that transcends political and cultural differences in the world, the influence of the privileged elites in the world must be credited. Certainly, the fears of male defense intellectuals discussing security at an arms control seminar in Cambridge, Massachusetts, in the early 1960s were quite different from the fears of Congolese women living through revolution and ethnic conflict in that same period. Not surprisingly, security studies in that era paid little attention to threats facing women in Africa.

Circumstances in large measure (but with some input from psychological factors) determine what we fear. Many feminists, noting the greater vulnerability of women to acts of sexual violence and physical abuse, have suggested that feminine conceptions of security differ from masculine conceptions as a consequence.[31] Because men are generally free from the fear of sexual violence and physical abuse, male-formulated notions of security manifest no concern for security as freedom from fear of sexual assault.[32] Similarly, security as defined by academics and strategists living and working in liberal democracies has tended to ignore the possibility that the state may generate fear among its own citizens.

As we noted in chapter 10, since World War II, developing states have been the scenes of most of the world's violent conflict. Much of that conflict has been intrastate and interethnic. This in itself should alert us to the divergence between our ethnocentric concern with insecurity defined in terms of external threats and the form of insecurity that most of the world actually experiences. As Mohammed Ayoob has observed, the primary security concerns of weak states are "internal in character" and are characteristic of "the early stages of state making."[33] A sophisticated understanding of security must take such considerations into account, particularly if concern for human welfare characteristic of human security or concern for complementary strategies characteristic of cooperative security is part of the mix.

Perhaps even more important than our ability to understand the impact of different circumstances on the way security is defined is the ability to assess our own circumstances accurately. The long litany of threats described in this book or in the threat assessments produced by many governments around the world may suggest not only that we live in an insecure world but also that the problems we face are insoluble. In fact, on many fronts there are reasons for optimism.

In many parts of the world, including Europe, where the two most destructive wars in history occurred within a span of thirty years, the possibility of war has become remote. Conflicts between democracies are routinely resolved without resort to force. While intrastate war continues to claim tens of thousands of lives each year in the developing world, elsewhere humankind seems to have achieved some success in understanding and addressing the causes of war.

There are, today, fewer nuclear weapons stockpiled in the world's arsenals than at any time in the last half-century. The United States and Russia have acknowledged a shared responsibility to reduce and, more important, secure their stockpiles of weapons and fissile material, although President Putin has canceled the Cooperative Threat Reduction Program. The vast majority of the world's states have pledged that they will never attempt to acquire nuclear, chemical, and biological weapons; many are active in efforts to deny the troublesome minority of states—and all nonstate actors—the ability to acquire weapons of mass destruction.

There has been significant progress in the fight against infectious diseases. The spread of HIV/AIDS has slowed; in fact, it hit its global peak of two million deaths in 2004.[34] The eradication of malaria appears to be a real possibility. The international response to the outbreak and spread of Ebola in West Africa in 2014 was delayed but ultimately effective. States, international governmental organizations, and nongovernmental organizations are working together to prevent and treat diseases among people who have never witnessed a vaccination program or visited a medical clinic.

There is cause for optimism, but not for complacency. Seeking security in an insecure world has always been an extraordinary challenge. Threats evolve, sometimes very rapidly; measures devised to enhance security will, in time, become ineffective. Think of the impact of the invention of gunpowder on castles and city walls, or of the appearance of drug-resistant diseases on vaccination programs. The nature—and number—of the threats we face is part of the challenge, but so is our interdependence. More than ever, the security of people all over the world is intertwined. This fact compels us to think creatively about security.

ADDITIONAL RESOURCES

Books

Battersby, Paul, and Joseph M. Siracusa. *Globalization and Human Security*. Lanham, MD: Rowman & Littlefield, 2009.
Carnegie Commission on Preventing Deadly Conflict. *Final Report*. Washington, DC: Carnegie Commission on Preventing Deadly Conflict, 1997.
Haass, Richard N. *The Opportunity: America's Moment to Alter History's Course*. New York: PublicAffairs, 2005.

Krepinevich, Andrew F. *7 Deadly Scenarios: A Military Futurist Explores War in the Twenty-First Century*. New York: Bantam Books, 2010.
Lipschutz, Ronnie D., ed. *On Security*. New York: Columbia University Press, 1995.
Shirk, Susan. *China: Fragile Superpower*. New York: Oxford University Press, 2008.
Steinbruner, John D. *Principles of Global Security*. Washington, DC: Brookings Institution, 2000.
U.S. National Intelligence Council. *Global Trends 2030: Alternative Worlds*. Washington, DC: National Intelligence Council, December 2012. http://www.dnl.gov/files/documents/GlobalTrends_2030.pdf.

Websites

Center for International Security and Cooperation: cisac.stanford.edu
Human Security Network: http://www.hpcrresearch.org/research/human-security -network
United Nations Foundation, Global Issues: www.unfoundation.org/global-issues/
U.S. Department of Homeland Security: www.dhs.gov/

Notes

PREFACE

1. Michael Krepon, *Better Safe Than Sorry: The Ironies of Living with the Bomb* (Stanford, CA: Stanford University Press, 2009); see also Paul Bracken, *The Second Nuclear Age: Strategy, Danger, and the New Power Politics* (New York: St. Martin's Griffin, 2013).

CHAPTER 1

1. *Levels & Trends in Child Mortality, Report 2014*, Estimates Developed by the UN Inter-Agency Group for Child Mortality Estimation (New York: UNICEF, 2014), 1.

2. World Health Organization, Global Health Observatory (GHO) Data, "HIV/AIDS," available at http://www.who.int/gho/hiv/en/.

3. International Labour Organization, "Forced Labour, Human Trafficking and Slavery," available at http://www.ilo.org/global/topics/forced-labour/lang--en/index.htm.

4. *Net Losses: Estimating the Global Cost of Cybercrime*, Economic Impact of Cybercrime II (Washington, DC: Center for Strategic and International Studies, 2014), 1, 3, available at http://www.mcafee.com/us/resources/reports/rp-economic-impact-cybercrime2.pdf.

5. All figures are from the *CIA World Factbook*, available at https://www.cia.gov/library/publications/resources/the-world-factbook/index.html.

6. Arnold Wolfers, "'National Security' as an Ambiguous Symbol," in *Discord and Collaboration: Essays on International Politics* (Baltimore: Johns Hopkins University Press, 1962), 147–65. This chapter originally appeared in *Political Science Quarterly* in 1952.

7. John Baylis, "International Security in the Post–Cold War Era," in *The Globalization of World Politics: An Introduction to International Relations*, eds. John

Baylis, Patricia Owens, and Steve Smith (Oxford: Oxford University Press, 1997), 194. K. J. Holsti has written, "Probably few concepts employed in statecraft and in the study of international politics have as vague referents as do *security* or *national security.*" *International Politics: A Framework for Analysis,* 7th ed. (Englewood Cliffs, NJ: Prentice Hall, 1995), 84 (original italics).

8. The billions of dollars spent to address potential problems that, it was feared, would result from the Y2K bug—a function of the transition to dates after December 31, 1999—could easily be regarded as expenditures designed to address national security concerns, at least according to most current definitions of security.

9. The shift in emphasis concerning the meaning of security was articulated early on in the following works (among others): Richard H. Ullman, "Redefining Security," *International Security* 8 (Summer 1983): 129–53; and Jessica Tuchman Mathews, "Redefining Security," *Foreign Affairs* 68 (Spring 1989): 162–77.

10. James N. Rosenau, "New Dimensions of Security: The Interaction of Globalizing and Localizing Dynamics," *Security Dialogue* 25 (September 1994): 255.

11. See Hedley Bull, *The Anarchical Society: A Study of Order in World Politics* (New York: Columbia University Press, 1977), 16–20. Bull defined international order as "a pattern or disposition of international activity that sustains those goals of the society of states that are elementary, primary, or universal." These goals, according to Bull, include preservation of the system itself, preservation of individual parts of the system (states), peace, and the limitation of violence.

12. See *People, States, and Fear: The National Security Problem in International Relations* (Chapel Hill: University of North Carolina Press, 1983).

13. See K. M. Fierke, *Critical Approaches to International Security* (Cambridge: Polity Press, 2007), 112–18. In addition to Buzan's *People, States, and Fear*, another of the leading works outlining the approach of the Copenhagen School is Barry Buzan, Ole Waever, and Jaap de Wilde, *Security: A New Framework for Analysis* (Boulder, CO: Lynne Rienner, 1998).

14. See Lars Schoultz, *National Security and United States Policy toward Latin America* (Princeton, NJ: Princeton University Press, 1987).

15. It may be objected that the transnational spread of disease, as with the Black Death that claimed roughly one-third of Europe's population in the 1300s, was an even greater threat to the security of states (or their medieval precursors) in the Middle Ages than it is today. However, the inability to understand pathogenesis in a prescientific era prevented any serious efforts—efforts beyond closing city gates to strangers—to securitize the problem of contagion. See Barbara W. Tuchman, *A Distant Mirror: The Calamitous 14th Century* (New York: Alfred A. Knopf, 1978).

16. Richard Rosecrance provides a particularly perceptive discussion of the declining significance of land for the modern state in *The Rise of the Virtual State: Wealth and Power in the Coming Century* (New York: Basic Books, 1999), 3–25.

17. Ullman, "Redefining Security," 129, 133.

18. See, for example, Buzan, Waever, and de Wilde, *Security: A New Framework for Analysis*; and Richard Wyn Jones, *Security, Strategy, and Critical Theory* (Boulder, CO: Lynne Rienner, 1999).

19. Wyn Jones, *Security, Strategy, and Critical Theory*, 103. Buzan, Waever, and de Wilde use the term *widening* in *Security: A New Framework for Analysis*.

20. See Buzan, Waever, and de Wilde, *Security: A New Framework for Analysis*, 2–5.

21. Gareth Evans, *Cooperating for Peace: The Global Agenda for the 1990s and Beyond* (St. Leonards, New South Wales: Allen & Unwin, 1993).

22. See *Human Development Report 1994* (New York: United Nations Development Program, 1994). The concept of human security has been promoted at the UN more recently by the joint action of Canada and Norway. See Astri Suhrke, "Human Security and the Interests of States," *Security Dialogue* 30 (September 1999): 265–76.

23. R. B. J. Walker, "The Subject of Security," in *Critical Security Studies: Concepts and Cases*, ed. Keith Krause and Michael C. Williams (Minneapolis: University of Minnesota Press, 1997), 63.

24. UN Department of Public Information, "Opening Session of Millennium Summit Hears Statements by 19 Heads of State, 10 Heads of Government, Two Vice-Presidents," UN Press Release GA/9750, September 6, 2000.

25. See, for one of the classic discussions of the security dilemma, Robert Jervis, *Perception and Misperception in International Politics* (Princeton, NJ: Princeton University Press, 1976).

26. The first statement of the idea of the security community was Karl Deutsch et al., *Political Community in the North Atlantic Area* (Princeton, NJ: Princeton University Press, 1957).

27. See Michael Krepon, *Better Safe Than Sorry: The Ironies of Living with the Bomb* (Stanford, CA: Stanford University Press, 2009).

28. For a British astronomer's discussion of this and many other dramatic threats to the survival of our planet, see Martin Rees, *Our Final Hour* (New York: Basic Books, 2003).

29. See Scott D. Sagan, *The Limits of Safety: Organizations, Accidents, and Nuclear Weapons* (Princeton, NJ: Princeton University Press, 1995); and Eric Schlosser, *Command and Control: Nuclear Weapons, the Damascus Accident, and the Illusion of Safety* (New York: Penguin Press, 2013).

30. *People, States and Fear: An Agenda for International Security Studies in the Post–Cold War Era*, 2nd ed. (Boulder, CO: Lynne Rienner, 1991), 146.

31. Wyn Jones, *Security, Strategy, and Critical Theory*, 99.

32. Robert Kaplan, *The Coming Anarchy: Shattering the Dreams of the Post–Cold War* (New York: Random House, 2000), 175–76.

33. For a noteworthy example of this, see Ken Booth, "Security and Self: Reflections of a Fallen Realist," in *Critical Security Studies*, eds. Krause and Williams, 83–119.

CHAPTER 2

1. See, for a compelling argument regarding the decline of violence in all aspects of life, Steven Pinker, *The Better Angels of Our Nature: Why Violence Has Declined* (New York: Viking, 2011).

2. Joshua S. Goldstein, *Winning the War on War: The Decline of Armed Conflict Worldwide* (New York: Plume, 2012), 13–22.

3. Spencer C. Tucker, "Casualties," *Encyclopedia of the Vietnam War: A Political, Social, and Military History*, 3 vols. (Santa Barbara, CA: ABC-CLIO, 1998), I:106.

4. Defense Casualty Analysis System, "U.S. Military Casualties—Vietnam Conflict Casualty Summary (As of May 22, 2015)," available at https://www.dmdc.osd .mil/dcas/pages/report_vietnam_sum.xhtml.

5. See Greg Campbell, *Blood Diamonds: Tracing the Deadly Path of the World's Most Precious Stones* (Boulder, CO: Westview Press, 2002); and Myriam S. Denov, *Child Soldiers: Sierra Leone's Revolutionary United Front* (New York: Cambridge University Press, 2010).

6. International Rescue Committee, *Mortality in the Democratic Republic of Congo: An Ongoing Crisis*, 16, available at www.theirc.org/special-reports/congo -forgotten-crisis. Mortality estimates in wartime are invariably controversial. The IRC's estimates of war-related excess deaths in the DRC have been disputed. See Human Security Report Project, "Shrinking Costs of War," Part II of *Human Security Report 2009* (Vancouver: Human Security Report Project, 2010), 36–48, available at http://www.hsrgroup.org/human-security-reports/20092010/overview.aspx.

7. Thomas C. Schelling, *Arms and Influence* (New Haven, CT: Yale University Press, 1966), 19.

8. Schelling, *Arms and Influence*, 1–2.

9. Schelling, *Arms and Influence*, 12–34.

10. The British decision to wage war in this fashion is extensively analyzed in Stephen A. Garrett, *Ethics and Airpower in World War II: The British Bombing of German Cities* (New York: St. Martin's, 1993).

11. Michael Walzer, *Just and Unjust Wars: A Moral Argument with Historical Illustrations*, 4th ed. (New York: Basic Books, 2006), 255.

12. Defense Casualty Analysis System, "U.S. Military Casualties—Persian Gulf War Casualty Summary Desert Shield/Desert Storm (as of June 1, 2015)," available at https://www.dmdc.osd.mil/dcas/pages/report_gulf_sum.xhtml.

13. Defense Casualty Analysis System, "U.S. Military Casualties—Operation Iraqi Freedom (OIF)—Military Deaths (Through April 30, 2003 as of May 22, 2015)," available at https://www.dmdc.osd.mil/dcas/pages/report_oif_ap2003.xhtml.

14. "NATO's Role in Kosovo," NATO, available at www.nato.int/kosovo/kosovo .htm.

15. Quoted in Andrew J. Bacevich, *Washington Rules: America's Path to Permanent War* (New York: Metropolitan Books, 2010), 173.

16. Quoted in George C. Herring, "America and Vietnam: The Unending War," *Foreign Affairs* 70 (Winter 1991–1992): 104.

17. Quoted in P. W. Singer, *Wired for War: The Robotics Revolution and Conflict in the 21st Century* (New York: Penguin Books, 2009), 221.

18. Singer, *Wired for War*, 19–32.

19. See *Losing Humanity: The Case against Killer Robots*, Human Rights Watch and International Human Rights Clinic, Human Rights Program at Harvard Law

School, November 2012, available at http://www.hrw.org/reports/2012/11/19/losing
-humanity.

20. Mark Prigg, "Who Goes There? Samsung Unveils Robot Sentry That Can Kill
from Two Miles Away," *Daily Mail*, September 15, 2014, available at http://www
.dailymail.co.uk/sciencetech/article-2756847/Who-goes-Samsung-reveals-robot
-sentry-set-eye-North-Korea.html.

21. Singer, *Wired for War*, 326–37.

22. Christopher Drew, "Drones Are Weapons of Choice in Fighting Qaeda,"
New York Times, March 17, 2009, available at www.nytimes.com/2009/03/17/
business/17uav.html.

23. Charlie Savage, "U.N. Report Highly Critical of U.S. Drone Attacks,"
New York Times, June 2, 2010, available at http://www.nytimes.com/2010/06/03/
world/03drones.html.

24. Peter Bergen and Jennifer Rowland, "Drone Wars," *The Washington Quarterly*
36 (Summer 2013): 8–9. For a broader perspective on the "drone war" in Pakistan, see
Sarah J. Watson and C. Christine Fair, "The Future of the American Drone Program
in Pakistan," in *Pakistan's Enduring Challenges*, eds. C. Christine Fair and Sarah J.
Watson (Philadelphia, PA: University of Pennsylvania Press, 2015), 72–97.

25. Bergen and Rowland, "Drone Wars," 8–9.

26. Bergen and Rowland, "Drone Wars," 12–13.

27. *Sun Tzu on the Art of War: The Oldest Military Treatise in the World*, trans.
Lionel Giles (Mountainview, CA: Wiretap, n.d.), 45 [e-book].

28. Defense Casualty Analysis System, "U.S. Military Casualties—Operation
Iraqi Freedom (OIF)—Military Deaths (Since May 1, 2003 as of May 22, 2015),"
available at https://www.dmdc.osd.mil/dcas/pages/report_oif_may2003.xhtml.

29. Defense Casualty Analysis System, "U.S. Military Casualties—Operation
Enduring Freedom (OEF) Casualty Summary by Casualty Category (as of June 1,
2015)," available at https://www.dmdc.osd.mil/dcas/pages/report_oef_type.xhtml.

30. Sam Perlo-Freeman, Aude Fleurant, Pieter D. Wezeman, and Siemon T.
Wezeman, "Trends in World Military Expenditures 2014," SIPRI Fact Sheet, April
2015, available at http://books.sipri.org/files/FS/SIPRIFS1504.pdf.

31. United Nations General Assembly, Approved Resources for Peacekeeping
Operations for the Period from 1 July 2014 to 30 June 2015, A/C.5/69/17, 14 January
2015.

32. See United Nations, "Regular Budget 2012–2013," available at http://www
.un.org/en/hq/dm/pdfs/oppba/Regular%20Budget.pdf.

33. According to researchers at the Dirksen Center, no record exists of Senator
Dirksen having actually uttered the famous remark attributed to him. See "A Billion
Here, a Billion There . . . ," The Dirksen Center, available at www.dirksencenter.org/
print_emd_billionhere.htm.

34. Dwight D. Eisenhower, *The White House Years: Mandate for Change, 1953–
1956* (Garden City, NY: Doubleday, 1963), 145.

35. W. J. Hennigan, "The F-22, the World's Priciest Fighter Jet, Finally Flies
in Combat," *Los Angeles Times*, September 24, 2014, available at http://www
.latimes.com/world/middleeast/la-fg-f-22-the-worlds-priciest-fighter-jet-finally-flies

-in-combat-20140923-story.html; "Montana Wheat Prices Slump to 5-Year Low," *Missoulian*, May 5, 2015, available at http://missoulian.com/news/state-and -regional/montana-wheat-prices-slump-to--year-low/article_ac6e8b12-e8d1-5659 -aac4-b2a982975d27.html.

36. Robert L. Paarlberg, "Knowledge as Power: Science, Military Dominance, and U.S. Security," *International Security* 29 (Summer 2004): 122–51.

37. Perlo-Freeman et al., "Trends in World Military Expenditures 2014."

38. Quoted in Charles W. Kegley Jr. and Eugene R. Wittkopf, *World Politics: Trend & Transformation*, 9th ed. (Belmont, CA: Wadsworth/Thomson Learning, 2004), 450.

39. *Global Burden of Armed Violence 2015: Every Body Counts* (Geneva: Geneva Declaration Secretariat, May 2015), 2.

40. "Speech by Lloyd Axworthy, Canadian Minister of Foreign Affairs, to U.N. Security Council Ministerial on Small Arms, September 24, 1999," International Action Network on Small Arms (IANSA), available at www.iansa.org/documents/un/ un_pub/statements/axworthy.htm.

41. See, among a wide variety of sources on the origins and distinctive characteristics of the SALW issue, Edward J. Laurance, *Light Weapons and Intrastate Conflict: Early Warning Factors and Preventive Action*, A Report to the Carnegie Commission on Preventing Deadly Conflict (New York: Carnegie Commission on Preventing Deadly Conflict, July 1998), 13–19; and Jeffrey Boutwell and Michael T. Klare, eds., *Light Weapons and Civil Conflict: Controlling the Tools of Violence* (Lanham, MD: Rowman & Littlefield for the Carnegie Commission on Preventing Deadly Conflict, 1999), 1–5.

42. Aaron Karp, "Laudable Failure," *SAIS Review* 22 (Winter–Spring 2002): 179.

43. "Notes for an Address by the Honourable Lloyd Axworthy, Minister of Foreign Affairs, to the 52nd Session of the United Nations General Assembly," September 25, 1997, International Action Network on Small Arms (IANSA), available at www.iansa.org/documents/un/un_pub/statements/axworthy.htm.

44. "Statement by John R. Bolton, U.S. Under-Secretary of State for Arms Control and International Security Affairs, UN Conference on the Illicit Trade in Small Arms and Light Weapons in All Its Aspects," July 9, 2001, available at disarmament.un.org/ cab/smallarms/statements/usE.html.

45. See "Towards an Arms Trade Treaty: Establishing Common International Standards for the Import, Export and Transfer of Conventional Arms," Report of the Group of Governmental Experts to examine the feasibility, scope, and draft parameters for a comprehensive, legally binding instrument establishing common international standards for the import, export, and transfer of conventional arms, United Nations General Assembly, A/63/334, August 26, 2008; Associated Press, "Treaty Regulating Global Arms Trade Takes Effect Wednesday," *New York Times*, December 23, 2014, available at http://www.nytimes.com/aponline/2014/12/23/world/ ap-un-united-nations-arms-trade-treaty.html.

46. Pieter D. Wezeman and Siemon Wezeman, "Trends in International Arms Transfers, 2014," SIPRI Fact Sheet, March 2015, available at http://books.sipri.org/ files/FS/SIPRIFS1503.pdf.

47. U.S. Department of State, "Introduction and Overview," *World Military Expenditures and Arms Transfers, 2014*, February 5, 2015.

48. Allan Hall, "Mustard Gas Blisters and a Daily Risk of Death: Bravery of Soldiers Still Clearing the 'Iron Harvest' of World War I Shells from Beneath Flanders' Fields," *Daily Mail*, November 10, 2013, available at http://www.dailymail.co.uk/news/article-2497732/The-iron-harvest-Meet-soldiers-tasked-clearing-hundreds-tonnes-deadly-World-War-I-shells-mines-beneath-fields-Flanders.html#ixzz2pUgxnQkI.

49. "A World War II Mine Forces Mass Evacuation," *International Herald Tribune*, February 9, 2004, available at www.iht.com/articles/128605.html.

50. Human Rights Watch, *Landmines: A Deadly Legacy* (Washington, DC: Human Rights Watch, 1993), 148–56.

51. *Breaking the Conflict Trap: Civil War and Development Policy* (Herndon, VA: World Bank, 2003), 31.

52. Paul Watson and Lisa Getter, "Silent Peril Lies in Wait for Afghanistan's People," *Los Angeles Times*, December 1, 2001, A1.

53. See "The Convention on Cluster Munitions," available at www.clusterconvention.org/.

54. Watson and Getter, "Silent Peril," A1.

55. John Donnelly, "Cluster Bombs Found to Spare Civilian Areas," *Boston Globe*, February 23, 2002, A1.

56. Carmen Sorger and Eric Hoskins, "Protecting the Most Vulnerable: War-Affected Children," in *Human Security and the New Diplomacy: Protecting People, Promoting Peace*, eds. Rob McRae and Don Hubert (Montreal: McGill-Queen's University Press, 2001), 134.

57. David M. Rosen, *Armies of the Young: Child Soldiers in War and Terrorism* (New Brunswick, NJ: Rutgers University Press, 2005), 5.

58. Graça Machel, *Impact of Armed Conflict on Children*, A/51/306 (New York: United Nations, August 26, 1996).

59. Child Soldiers International, *Louder Than Words: An Agenda for Action to End State Use of Child Soldiers* (London: Child Soldiers International, 2012), 11.

60. Coalition to Stop the Use of Child Soldiers, *Child Soldiers Global Report 2008*, Summary, 3, available at http://www.hrw.org/en/reports/2008/12/11/child-soldiers-global-report-2008.

61. See Machel, *Impact of Armed Conflict on Children*, 11–13.

62. For the text of the Optional Protocol and information on signatories, see the United Nations Treaty Collection, Optional Protocol to the Convention on the Rights of the Child on the Involvement of Children in Armed Conflict, May 25, 2000, available at https://treaties.un.org/pages/viewdetails.aspx?src=ind&mtdsg_no=iv-11-b&chapter=4&lang=en.

63. Dana Priest and Mary Pat Flaherty, "Under Fire, Security Firms Form an Alliance," *Washington Post*, April 8, 2004, 1.

64. P. W. Singer, *Corporate Warriors: The Rise of the Privatized Military Industry* (Ithaca, NY: Cornell University Press, 2003), 3–4.

65. Adam Nossiter, "Mercenaries Join Nigeria's Military Campaign Against Boko Haram," *New York Times*, March 12, 2015, available at http://www.nytimes

.com/2015/03/13/world/africa/nigerias-fight-against-boko-haram-gets-help-from
-south-african-mercenaries.html.

66. Thom Shanker, "Pentagon Sets Bonuses to Retain Members of Special Operations," *New York Times*, February 6, 2005, 4.

CHAPTER 3

1. Richard Rhodes, *The Making of the Atomic Bomb* (New York: Simon and Schuster, 1986), 711.

2. Quoted in Gwynne Dyer, *War* (New York: Crown Publishers, 1985), 96.

3. Quoted in Rhodes, *The Making of the Atomic Bomb*, 725.

4. Quoted in Rhodes, *The Making of the Atomic Bomb*, 711.

5. Quoted in Michael Mandelbaum, *The Nuclear Question: The United States and Nuclear Weapons, 1946–1976* (Cambridge: Cambridge University Press, 1979), 42.

6. Quoted by Fred Kaplan, *Wizards of Armageddon* (New York: Simon and Schuster, 1983), 9–10.

7. Frederick S. Dunn, "The Common Problem," in *The Absolute Weapon: Atomic Power and World Order*, ed. Bernard Brodie (New York: Harcourt, Brace, 1946), 4.

8. Carl von Clausewitz, *On War*, ed. and trans. Michael Howard and Peter Paret (Princeton, NJ: Princeton University Press, 1976).

9. Quoted in Kaplan, *Wizards of Armageddon*, 31.

10. Herman Kahn, *On Thermonuclear War* (Princeton, NJ: Princeton University Press), 1960.

11. Jeffrey Porro, "The Policy War: Brodie vs. Kahn," *Bulletin of the Atomic Scientists* (June 1982): 16–20.

12. George Kennan, "On Nuclear War," *New York Review of Books*, January 21, 1982, 8.

13. George Kennan, "The Atomic Bomb and the Choices for American Policy" (1950), in *The Nuclear Delusion: Soviet-American Relations in the Atomic Age* (New York: Pantheon Books, 1982), 3–6.

14. President Barack Obama, "Remarks by the President at the United Nations Security Council Summit on Nuclear Non Proliferation and Nuclear Disarmament," United Nations Headquarters, New York, New York, September 24, 2009, available at http://www.whitehouse.gov/the_press_office/Remarks-By-The-President-At-the-UN-Security-Council-Summit-On-Nuclear-Non-Proliferation-And-Nuclear-Disarmament/.

15. United States Department of Defense, *Nuclear Posture Review Report*, April 2010, ix, available at http://www.defense.gov/npr/.

16. Winston S. Churchill, *The Second World War: The Grand Alliance* (Boston: Houghton Mifflin, 1951), 370.

17. Henry L. Stimson and McGeorge Bundy, *On Active Service in Peace and War* (New York: Harper and Brothers, 1948), 642–46.

18. Stimson quoted in Godfrey Hodgson, *The Colonel: The Life and Wars of Henry Stimson 1867–1950* (New York: Alfred A. Knopf, 1990), 357.

19. Stimson quoted in McGeorge Bundy, *Danger and Survival: Choices about the Bomb in the First Fifty Years* (New York: Random House, 1988), 136.

20. "Transcript of Press Interview with President at White House," *New York Times*, March 30, 1983, 14.

21. Andrei Gromyko, *Memoirs*, trans. by Harold Shukman (New York: Doubleday, 1989), 140–41.

22. George Quester, *Deterrence before Hiroshima: The Airpower Background of Modern Strategy* (New Brunswick, NJ: Transaction, 1986).

23. See B. H. Liddell Hart, *Deterrence or Defense* (New York: Praeger, 1960); William W. Kaufman, *The McNamara Strategy* (New York: Harper and Row, 1964); Henry Kissinger, *Nuclear Weapons and Foreign Policy* (New York: Harper, 1957); Maxwell Taylor, *The Uncertain Trumpet* (New York: Harper and Brothers, 1960).

24. John F. Kennedy in Allan Nevins, ed., *The Strategy of Peace* (New York: Harper, 1960), 184.

25. Gregg Herken, *Counsels of War* (New York: Alfred A. Knopf, 1985), 155.

26. *National Security Strategy of the United States* (Washington, DC: White House, September 2002), available at georgewbush-whitehouse.archives.gov/nsc/nss/2002/.

27. Albert Wohlstetter, "The Delicate Balance of Power," *Foreign Affairs* 39 (January 1961): 211–34.

28. Donald Brennan, ed., *Arms Control, Disarmament and National Security* (New York: George Braziller, 1961); Hedley Bull, *The Control of the Arms Race* (London: Weidenfeld and Nicholson, 1961); and Thomas Schelling and Morton Halperin, *Strategy and Arms Control* (New York: Twentieth Century Fund, 1961).

29. Schelling and Halperin, *Strategy and Arms Control*, 2.

30. Elizabeth Young, *A Farewell to Arms Control* (Baltimore: Penguin Books, 1972), 86.

31. Dan Caldwell, *The Dynamics of Domestic Politics and Arms Control: The SALT II Treaty Ratification Debate* (Columbia: University of South Carolina Press, 1991).

32. Peter Baker, "Senate Passes Arms Control Treaty with Russia, 71–26," *New York Times*, December 22, 2010, available at http://www.nytimes.com/2010/12/23/world/europe/23treaty.html.

33. See Bull, *The Control of the Arms Race*, 3–29, and Bernard Brodie, "On the Objectives of Arms Control," *International Security* 1 (Summer 1976): 17–36.

34. John D. Steinbruner, *Principles of Global Security* (Washington, DC: Brookings Institution Press, 2000), 23.

35. Ivo Daalder, "The Future of Arms Control," *Survival* 34 (Spring 1992): 51–52.

CHAPTER 4

1. Andrew C. Revkin, "A Nation Challenged: Tracing the Spores—Testing Links Anthrax in Florida and at NBC," *New York Times*, October 18, 2001, 5.

2. Barbara Hatch Rosenberg, "Bioterrorism: Anthrax Attacks Pushed Open an Ominous Door," *Los Angeles Times*, September 22, 2002, M1.

3. Scott Shane, "F.B.I., Laying Out Evidence, Closes Anthrax Case," *New York Times*, February 19, 2010, available at www.nytimes.com/2010/02/20/us/20anthrax.html.

4. Edward M. Spiers, *A History of Chemical and Biological Weapons* (London: Reaktion Books, 2010), 28.

5. See Donald C. Richter, *Chemical Soldiers: British Gas Warfare in World War I* (Lawrence: University Press of Kansas, 1992).

6. See Timothy V. McCarthy and Jonathan B. Tucker, "Saddam's Toxic Arsenal: Chemical and Biological Weapons in the Gulf Wars," in *Planning the Unthinkable: How New Powers Will Use Nuclear, Biological, and Chemical Weapons*, eds. Peter R. Lavoy, Scott D. Sagan, and James J. Wirtz (Ithaca, NY: Cornell University Press, 2000), 47–78.

7. Richard K. Betts, "The New Threat of Mass Destruction," *Foreign Affairs* 77 (January/February 1998): 26.

8. U.S. Congress, Office of Technology Assessment, *Proliferation of Weapons of Mass Destruction: Assessing the Risks* (Washington, DC: Government Printing Office, 1993).

9. Thomas L. McNaugher, "Ballistic Missiles and Chemical Weapons: The Legacy of the Iran-Iraq War," *International Security* 15 (Fall 1990): 5–34.

10. See *Genocide in Iraq: The Anfal Campaign Against the Kurds*, A Middle East Watch Report (New York: Human Rights Watch, 1993), available at www.hrw.org/reports/1993/iraqanfal.

11. Richard A. Falkenrath, Robert D. Newman, and Bradley A. Thayer, *America's Achilles' Heel: Nuclear, Biological, and Chemical Terrorism and Covert Attack* (Cambridge, MA: MIT Press, 1998), 226–27.

12. Colum Lynch and Karen DeYoung, "In Syria, U.N. Inspectors Find 'Clear and Convincing Evidence' of Chemical Attack," *Washington Post*, September 16, 2013, available at http://www.washingtonpost.com/world/middle_east/kerry-un-will-enforce-deal-to-rid-syria-of-chemical-weapons/2013/09/16/0f1d9bf6-1eb6-11e3-94a2-6c66b668ea55_story.html.

13. "Syria: Chemicals Used in Idlib Attacks," Human Rights Watch, April 13, 2015, available at http://www.hrw.org/news/2015/04/13/syria-chemicals-used-idlib-attacks.

14. This account is based primarily on Jessica Stern, *The Ultimate Terrorists* (Cambridge, MA: Harvard University Press, 1999), 60–68.

15. Laurie Garrett, *The Coming Plague: Newly Emerging Diseases in a World Out of Balance* (New York: Penguin Books, 1994), 237–40.

16. Elizabeth A. Fenn, *Pox Americana: The Great Smallpox Epidemic of 1775–82* (New York: Hill and Wang, 2001), 88–91.

17. See Ken Alibeck, *Biohazard* (New York: Random House, 1999).

18. Ronald K. Noble, "Keeping Science in the Right Hands: Policing the New Biological Frontier," *Foreign Affairs* 92 (November/December 2013): 49.

19. "Chemical and Biological Weapons Status at a Glance," Arms Control Association, available at www.armscontrol.org/factsheets/cbwprolif.

20. See Falkenrath, Newman, and Thayer, *America's Achilles' Heel*, 167–215.

21. Julian Perry Robinson, "Chemical and Biological Weapons," in *Combating Weapons of Mass Destruction: The Future of International Nonproliferation Policy*, ed. Nathan E. Busch and Daniel H. Joyner (Athens: University of Georgia Press, 2009), 78.

22. Quoted in Thomas Graham Jr. and Damien J. LaVera, *Cornerstones of Security: Arms Control Treaties in the Nuclear Era* (Seattle, WA: University of Washington Press, 2003), 292.

23. On the taboo against the use of diseases as weapons, see Robinson, "Chemical and Biological Weapons," 77.

CHAPTER 5

1. Quoted in Bob Woodward, *Plan of Attack* (New York: Simon and Schuster, 2004), 24.

2. David C. Rapoport, "Modern Terror: The Four Waves," in *Attacking Terrorism: Elements of a Grand Strategy*, eds. Audrey Kurth Cronin and James M. Ludes (Washington, DC: Georgetown University Press, 2004), 46–73.

3. Jeffrey Kaplan, "The Fifth Wave: The New Tribalism?" *Terrorism and Political Violence* 19 (2007): 545.

4. Walter Laqueur, *The Age of Terrorism* (Boston: Little, Brown, 1987), 72.

5. Jessica Stern, *The Ultimate Terrorists* (Cambridge, MA: Harvard University Press, 2000), 11.

6. United States Code, Title 22, Section 2656f(d).

7. U.S. National Consortium for the Study of Terrorism and Responses to Terrorism, "Annex of Statistical Information," Bureau of Counterterrorism, Department of State, 2014, available at http://www.state.gov/j/ct/rls/crt/2013/224831.htm.

8. See Daniel Benjamin and Steven Simon, *The Age of Sacred Terror* (New York: Random House, 2002).

9. Benjamin and Simon, *The Age of Sacred Terror*, 143–45.

10. Sarah Almukhtar, "Despite Pressure, ISIS Finances Strong," *New York Times*, May 19, 2015, A10.

11. There are many analyses of deterrence; two of the best are Patrick M. Morgan, *Deterrence Now* (Cambridge: Cambridge University Press, 2003), and Alexander L. George and Richard Smoke, *Deterrence in American Foreign Policy: Theory and Practice* (New York: Columbia University Press, 1974).

12. John Lewis Gaddis, "The Long Peace: Elements of Stability in the Postwar International System," *International Security* 10 (Spring 1986): 99–142.

13. James A. Baker III, with Thomas M. DeFrank, *The Politics of Diplomacy: Revolution, War and Peace, 1989–1992* (New York: G. P. Putnam's Sons, 1995), 359.

14. *National Security Strategy of the United States* (Washington, DC: White House, September 2002), available at georgewbush-whitehouse.archives.gov/nsc/nss/2002/.

15. Thomas C. Schelling, *Arms and Influence* (New Haven, CT: Yale University Press, 1966), 70–72.

16. Benjamin and Simon, *The Age of Sacred Terror*, 439–45.

17. Paul Wilkinson, "Why Modern Terrorism? Differentiating Types and Distinguishing Ideological Motivations," in *The New Global Terrorism*, ed. Charles Kegley (New York: Pearson, 2002), 122.

18. Paul Watson, Tyler Marshall, and Bob Drogin, "On the Trail of the Real Osama bin Laden," *Los Angeles Times*, September 15, 2001, A16.

19. John Arquilla, "To Build a Network," *Prism* 5 (2014): 23.

20. Robert A. Pape and James K. Feldman, *Cutting the Fuse: The Explosion of Global Suicide Terrorism and How to Stop It* (Chicago: University of Chicago Press, 2010).

21. Yotam Rosner, Einav Yogev, and Yoram Schweitzer, "A Report on Suicide Bombings, 2013," *INSS Insight*, no. 507 (Tel Aviv: Institute for National Security Studies, January 14, 2014).

22. Pape and Feldman, *Cutting the Fuse*, 22.

23. Pape and Feldman, *Cutting the Fuse*, 26–42.

24. Richard N. Haass, *War of Necessity, War of Choice: A Memoir of Two Iraq Wars* (New York: Simon & Schuster, 2009).

25. Jeffrey Kaplan, *Terrorist Groups and the New Tribalism: Terrorism's Fifth Wave* (London: Routledge, 2010), 46–78.

26. Kaplan, "The Fifth Wave: The New Tribalism?" 548.

27. Schelling, *Arms and Influence*, 1–34.

28. Thomas L. Friedman, *The Lexus and the Olive Tree: Understanding Globalization*, rev. ed. (New York: Anchor Books, 2000), 403.

29. Philip Bobbitt, *Terror and Consent: The Wars for the Twenty-First Century* (New York: Anchor Books, 2009), 67–70.

30. Charles Kupchan, "The Rise of Europe, America's Changing Internationalism, and the End of U.S. Primacy," in *American Hegemony*, ed. Demetrios James Caraley (New York: American Academy of Political Science, 2004), 123.

31. George W. Bush, "West Point Commencement Speech," in *Foreign Affairs, America and the World: Debating the New Shape of International Politics*, ed. James F. Hoge Jr. (New York: W. W. Norton, 2002), 364–71.

32. *National Security Strategy of the United States*, http://nssarchive.us/.

33. John Lewis Gaddis, *Surprise, Security, and the American Experience* (Cambridge, MA: Harvard University Press, 2004).

34. Robert Jervis, "Understanding the Bush Doctrine," in *American Hegemony*, 3.

35. Michael Walzer, *Arguing about War* (New Haven, CT: Yale University Press, 2004), 146.

36. For the principal works that outline the major elements of the cooperative security approach, see Ashton B. Carter, William J. Perry, and John D. Steinbruner, *A New Concept of Cooperative Security*, Brookings Occasional Paper (Washington,

DC: Brookings Institution, 1992); Janne Nolan, ed., *Global Engagement: Cooperation and Security in the 21st Century* (Washington, DC: Brookings Institution, 1994); Ashton B. Carter and William J. Perry, *Preventive Defense: A New Security Strategy for America* (Washington, DC: Brookings Institution, 1999); and John D. Steinbruner, *Principles of Global Security* (Washington, DC: Brookings Institution, 2000).

37. Walzer, *Arguing about War*, 9.

38. On the creation of the Department of Homeland Security, see Donald F. Kettl, *System under Stress: Homeland Security and American Politics* (Washington, DC: CQ Press, 2007).

39. Quoted in Peter Katel, "Homeland Security," *CQ Researcher*, February 13, 2009, 133.

CHAPTER 6

1. Kenneth M. Pollack, *The Threatening Storm: The Case for Invading Iraq* (New York: Random House, 2002), 76–77.

2. Memo from Ayman al-Zawahiri to Muhammad Atef, April 15, 1999, quoted in Alan Cullison, "Inside Al-Qaeda's Hard Drive," *Atlantic Monthly* 294 (September 2004): 62.

3. "Plutonium Con Artists Sentenced in Russian Closed City of Sarov," *NIS Export Control Observer* no. 11 (Monterey, CA: Center for Nonproliferation Studies, Monterey Institute of International Studies, November 2003).

4. Julian Borger, "Nuclear Bomb Material Found for Sale on Georgia Black Market," *The Guardian* (London), November 7, 2010, available at www.guardian.co.uk/world/2010/nov/07/nuclear-material-black-market-georgia/print.

5. Michael Krepon, *Better Safe Than Sorry: The Ironies of Living with the Bomb* (Stanford, CA: Stanford University Press, 2009), 34, 169; see also Paul Bracken, *The Second Nuclear Age: Strategy, Danger, and the New Power Politics* (New York: St. Martin's Griffin, 2013).

6. Matthew Bunn, Anthony Wier, and John P. Holdren, *Controlling Nuclear Warheads and Materials: A Report Card and Action Plan* (Cambridge, MA: Nuclear Threat Initiative and the Project on Managing the Atom, Harvard University, March 2003).

7. John F. Kennedy, quoted by Glenn Seaborg, *Kennedy, Khrushchev, and the Test Ban* (Berkeley: University of California Press, 1981), 198–99.

8. For the text of the treaty and a listing of the current signatories, see http://www.un.org/disarmament/WMD/Nuclear/pdf/NPTEnglish_Text.pdf.

9. *Final Report of the National Commission on Terrorist Attacks upon the United States*, Authorized Edition [hereafter *9/11 Commission Report*] (New York: W. W. Norton, 2004), 367.

10. Daniel Benjamin and Steven Simon, *The Age of Sacred Terror* (New York: Random House, 2002), 146.

11. Dafna Linzer, "U.S. Shifts Stance on Nuclear Treaty," *Washington Post*, July 31, 2004, A1; *9/11 Commission Report*, 368.

12. David Albright and Holly Higgins, "A Bomb for the Ummah," *Bulletin of the Atomic Scientists* 59 (March/April 2003): 53–54.

13. "Interview with Bin Laden: 'World's Most Wanted Terrorist,'" ABCNews .com.

14. Matthew Bunn and Anthony Wier, *Securing the Bomb: An Agenda for Action* (Cambridge, MA: Nuclear Threat Initiative and the Project on Managing the Atom, Harvard University, May 2004), 5.

15. Bunn and Wier, *Securing the Bomb*, 36.

16. Matthew Bunn, *Securing the Bomb 2010: Securing All Nuclear Materials in Four Years* (Cambridge, MA: Nuclear Threat Initiative and the Project on Managing the Atom, Harvard University, April 2010), 26–27.

17. Jeffrey Fleishman, "Sting Unravels Stunning Mafia Plot," *Philadelphia Inquirer*, January 12, 1999.

18. Bunn and Wier, *Securing the Bomb 2010*, 5.

19. Leon V. Sigal, *Disarming Strangers: Nuclear Diplomacy with North Korea* (Princeton, NJ: Princeton University Press, 1998).

20. Joseph Cirincione, Jon B. Wolfsthal, and Miriam Rajkumar, *Deadly Arsenals: Nuclear, Biological, and Chemical Threats* (Washington, DC: Carnegie Endowment for International Peace, July 2005), 246–49.

21. See President George W. Bush's commencement address at West Point and the *National Security Strategy of the United States* (Washington, DC: White House, September 2002), available at georgewbush-whitehouse.archives.gov/nsc/nss/2002/.

22. Bob Woodward, *Plan of Attack* (New York: Simon and Schuster, 2004).

23. Quoted in Michael Ignatieff, *Virtual War: Kosovo and Beyond* (New York: Metropolitan Books, 2000), 211.

24. President George W. Bush, "State of the Union Address," *New York Times*, January 29, 2003.

25. "Remarks by the President at the Opening Plenary Session of the Nuclear Security Summit," Washington Convention Center, Washington, D.C., April 13, 2010, available at http://www.whitehouse.gov/the-press-office/remarks-president-opening-plenary-session-nuclear-security summit.

26. Robert S. Norris and William M. Arkin, "NRDC Nuclear Notebook: Global Nuclear Stockpiles, 1945–2000," *Bulletin of the Atomic Scientists* 56 (March/April 2000): 79.

27. Graham Allison, Ashton B. Carter, Steven E. Miller, and Philip Zelikow, *Cooperative Denuclearization: From Pledges to Deeds* (Cambridge, MA: Center for Science and International Affairs, John F. Kennedy School of Government, Harvard University, 1993).

28. American Security Project, Fact Sheet—The Nunn-Lugar Cooperative Threat Reduction Program: Securing and Safeguarding Weapons of Mass Destruction, July 25, 2012, available at http://www.americansecurityproject.org/fact-sheet-the-nunn-lugar-cooperative-threat-reduction-program-securing-and-safeguarding-weapons-of-mass-destruction/.

29. Michael Krepon, "Nunn-Lugar, R.I.P.," *South Asia Program* (Washington, DC: Stimson Center, January 28, 2015).

30. Matthew Bunn and Anthony Wier, "Preventing a Nuclear 9/11," *Washington Post*, September 17, 2004, B7.

31. International Atomic Energy Agency, "International Conventions & Legal Agreements: Convention on the Physical Protection of Nuclear Material," available at www.iaea.org/Publications/Documents/Conventions/cppnm.html.

32. George Perkovich, *Universal Compliance (A Strategy for Nuclear Security)* (Washington, DC: Carnegie Endowment for International Peace, 2005), 44 (original italics).

33. Bunn and Wier, *Securing the Bomb*, 3.

34. Bunn and Wier, *Securing the Bomb*, 3.

35. Bunn and Wier, *Securing the Bomb*, 79.

36. International Panel on Fissile Materials, "Countries: Russia," March 13, 2012, available at fissilematerials.org/countries/russia.html.

37. Perkovich et al., *Universal Compliance*, 90.

38. Linzer, "U.S. Shifts Stance on Nuclear Treaty," A1.

39. Quoted in "Arms Control Experts Say Ban on Production of Key Nuclear Materials for Weapons Should Be Universal and Verifiable," Media Advisory, Arms Control Association, July 30, 2004.

40. See *National Security Strategy of the United States, 2002*

CHAPTER 7

1. Laurie Garrett, *The Coming Plague: Newly Emerging Diseases in a World Out of Balance* (New York: Penguin Books, 1995), 104.

2. Danielle Renwick, "Backgrounder: Ebola Virus," Council on Foreign Relations, February 5, 2015, available at http://www.cfr.org/africa-sub-saharan/ebola-virus/p33661.

3. S. Briand, E. Betherat, P. Cox, et al., "The International Ebola Emergency," *New England Journal of Medicine* 371 (September 25, 2014): 1180–83.

4. Kevin Sack, Sheri Fink, Pam Belluck, and Adam Nossiter, "Ebola's Deadly Escape," *New York Times*, December 30, 2014.

5. Yanzhong Huang, "Are Americans Overreacting to the Ebola Virus?" Council on Foreign Relations, October 20, 2014, available at http://blogs.cfr.org/asia/2014/10/20/are-americans-overreacting-to-the-ebola-virus/.

6. Laurie Garrett, "How to Shut Down a Country and Kill a Disease," Foreign-Policy.com, October 22, 2014.

7. Quoted by Benjamin Syme Van Ameringen, "Ebola, Anarchy, and Failing States: The Crisis in West Africa," *Geopolitical Monitor*, November 24, 2014, available at http://www.geopoliticalmonitor.com/ebola-anarchy-failing-states-crisis-west-africa/.

8. Thucydides, *History of the Peloponnesian War*, trans. Rex Warner (New York: Penguin, 1980), 155.

9. P. E. Olson et al., "The Thucydides Syndrome: Ebola Deja Vu (or Ebola Resurgent?)," *Emerging Infectious Diseases* 2 (April–June 1996): 155–56.

10. William McNeill, *Plagues and Peoples* (New York: Anchor Books, 1976), 212–13.

11. Robert S. Gottfried, *The Black Death* (New York: Free Press, 1985), 77.

12. See Andrew T. Price-Smith, *The Health of Nations: Infectious Disease, Environmental Change, and Their Effects on National Security and Development* (Cambridge, MA: MIT Press, 2002), 11; see also Hans Zinsser, *Rats, Lice, and History* (Boston: Little, Brown, 1934), 132–75.

13. McNeill, *Plagues and Peoples*, 120–21; Jared Diamond, *Guns, Germs, and Steel: The Fates of Human Societies* (New York: W. W. Norton, 1997), 210.

14. See Zinsser, *Rats, Lice and History*.

15. Laurie Garrett, "The Next Pandemic?" *Foreign Affairs* 84 (July/August 2005): 6.

16. John M. Barry, *The Great Influenza: The Epic Story of the Deadliest Plague in History* (New York: Viking Press, 2004).

17. Garrett, *The Coming Plague*, 157.

18. In this chapter, we limit our focus to infectious diseases, but note that non-infectious diseases such as heart disease, diabetes, and cancer also pose significant threats to public health; see Mitchell E. Daniels Jr. and Thomas E. Donilon, Chairs, *The Emerging Global Health Crisis: Noncommunicable Diseases in Low- and Middle-Income Countries*, Task Force Report 72 (New York: Council on Foreign Relations, December 2014), available at http://www.cfr.org/diseases-noncommunicable/emerging-global-health-crisis/p33883.

19. Jeffrey D. Sachs, *The End of Poverty: Economic Possibilities for Our Time* (New York: The Penguin Press, 2005), 260. See also Donald R. Hopkins, *The Greatest Killer: Smallpox in History* (Chicago: University of Chicago Press, 2002).

20. Jordan S. Kassalow, *Why Health Is Important to U.S. Foreign Policy* (New York: Council on Foreign Relations and Milbank Memorial Fund, 2001), 6.

21. National Academies, "Global Killers" (Washington, DC: National Academies, 2014), available at http://needtoknow.nas.edu/id/threats/global-killers/.

22. "Tuberculosis," Fact Sheet No. 104, March 2010, World Health Organization, available at www.who.int/mediacentre/factsheets/fs104/en/print.html. See also Council on Foreign Relations and Milbank Memorial Fund, *Addressing the HIV/AIDS Pandemic: A U.S. Global AIDS Strategy for the Long Term* (New York: Milbank Memorial Fund, 2004), 13.

23. For an excellent primer on malaria and the methods being used in an effort to reduce its incidence, see Claire Panosian Dunavan, "Tackling Malaria," in *Infectious Disease: A Scientific American Reader* (Chicago: University of Chicago Press, 2008), 137–47.

24. Dunavan, "Tackling Malaria," 137–47.

25. Dunavan, "Tackling Malaria," 137–47.

26. Garrett, *The Coming Plague*, 53–55.

27. Garrett, "The Next Pandemic?" 12.

28. World Heath Organization, "Avian Influenza Weekly Update Number 481," May 1, 2015, available at http://www.wpro.who.int/emerging_diseases/Avian Influenza/en/.

29. Garrett, "How to Shut Down a Country and Kill a Disease."

30. Laurie Garrett, "The Return of Infectious Disease," *Foreign Affairs* 75 (January/February 1996): 66.

31. UNAIDS, "Global Facts and Figures 09," available at data.unaids.org/pub/FactSheet/2009/20091124_fs_global_en.pdf.

32. Joshua Lederberg, quoted by Michael S. Gottlieb, "The Future of an Epidemic," *New York Times*, June 5, 2001, 23.

33. Centers for Disease Control and Prevention, "HIV/AIDS: Basic Statistics," March 10, 2015, available at http://www.cdc.gov/hiv/basics/statistics.html.

34. Centers for Disease Control and Prevention, "HIV/AIDS: Basic Statistics."

35. UNICEF, "Monitoring the Situation of Children and Women," available at http://data.unicef.org/hiv-aids/trends.

36. See, for example, the recruitment announcement in the *Journal of the American Medical Association (JAMA)* 292 (December 15, 2004): 29–30.

37. President George W. Bush, "President Speaks to the United Nations General Assembly," September 21, 2004, available at georgewbush-whitehouse.archives.gov/news/-releases/2004/09/20040921-3.html.

38. President Barack Obama, "Remarks by the President After Meeting on Ebola" (Washington, DC: The White House, October 6, 2014), available at http://www.whitehouse.gov/the-press-office/2014/10/06/remarks-president-after-meeting-ebola.

39. P. W. Singer, "AIDS and International Security," *Survival* 44 (Spring 2002): 145–58.

40. UN Programme on HIV/AIDS, "AIDS and the Military," May 1998, available at www.unaids.org.

41. Singer, "AIDS and International Security," 154–55.

42. International Crisis Group, *HIV/AIDS as a Security Issue.*

43. International Crisis Group, *HIV/AIDS as a Security Issue*, 4.

44. International Crisis Group, *HIV/AIDS as a Security Issue*, 9.

45. British House of Commons, Select Committee on International Development, "HIV/AIDS: The Impact on Social and Economic Development," March 29, 2001; cited by International Crisis Group, *HIV/AIDS as a Security Issue*, 15.

46. George W. Bush, "President Delivers 'State of the Union,'" January 28, 2003, available at georgewbush-whitehouse.archives.gov/news/releases/2003/01/20030128-19.html.

47. U.S. Department of Health and Human Services, "PEPFAR's Program Results," available at https://www.aids.gov/federal-resources/around-the-world/pepfar/.

48. See GAVI Alliance, available at www.gavialliance.org/.

49. See Sam Howe Verhovek, "Philanthropy Inc.," *Los Angeles Times*, January 27, 2005, A18; "Foundation Fact Sheet," Bill and Melinda Gates Foundation, available at www.gatesfoundation.org/about/Pages/foundation-fact-sheet.aspx.

50. World Health Organization, "Spending on Health: A Global Overview," Fact Sheet No. 319, March 2007, available at www.who.int/mediacentre/factsheets/fs319/en/index.html.

51. See AVERT, "AIDS, Drug Prices and Generic Drugs," available at www.avert.org/generic.htm.

52. International Bank for Reconstruction and Development, *World Bank Atlas*, 35th ed. (Washington, DC: World Bank, 2003), 26.

53. *World Bank Atlas*, 18.

54. U.S. National Intelligence Council, *Mapping the Global Future*, Report of the 2020 Project (Washington, DC: Government Printing Office, December 2004), 39.

55. U.S. National Intelligence Council, *Mapping the Global Future*, 30.

56. U.S. National Intelligence Council, *Mapping the Global Future*.

CHAPTER 8

1. *Estimating Illicit Financial Flows Resulting from Drug Trafficking and Other Transnational Organized Crimes: Research Report* (Vienna: United Nations Office on Drugs and Crime, October 2011), 7, available at www.unodc.org/documents/data-and-analysis/Studies/Illicit_financial_flows_2011_web.pdf.

2. See Jorge Garay and Eduardo Salcedo-Albarán, "The Worst Is Yet to Come in Mexican Drug War," *Poder 360°*, October 21, 2010, available at http://esalbaran.com/eduardosalcedoalbaran/about_Me+by_Me/Entries/2010/10/21_The_Worst_is_Yet_to_Come_in_Mexican_Drug_WarAnalysts_talk_of_the_Colombianization_of_drug-trafficking_in_Mexico._If_thats_the_case,_what_weve_seen_so_far_is_only_the_beginning.html.

3. Terry Terriff, Stuart Croft, Lucy James, and Patrick M. Morgan, *Security Studies Today* (Cambridge: Polity, 1999), 150–51.

4. Paul Rexton Kan, "Mexican Drug Cartels as Vicious Firms," *Small Wars Journal*, March 15, 2015, available at http://smallwarsjournal.com/jrnl/art/mexican-cartels-as-vicious-firms.

5. Roy Godson and Phil Williams, "Strengthening Cooperation against Trans-sovereign Crime: A New Security Imperative," in *Beyond Sovereignty: Issues for a Global Agenda*, ed. Maryann K. Cusimano (New York: Bedford/St. Martin's, 2000), 111.

6. Amy O'Neill Richard, *International Trafficking in Women to the United States: A Contemporary Manifestation of Slavery and Organized Crime*, An Intelligence Monograph (Washington, DC: Center for the Study of Intelligence, Central Intelligence Agency, November 1999).

7. See Nicholas D. Kristof and Sheryl WuDunn, *Half the Sky: Turning Oppression into Opportunity for Women Worldwide* (New York: Vintage Books, 2010), 10. A decade ago the United Nations put the number at four million persons trafficked each year. See Amnesty International, *Broken Bodies, Shattered Minds: Torture and Ill-Treatment of Women* (London: Amnesty International Publications, 2001), 16.

8. International Labour Organization, "New ILO Global Estimate of Forced Labour: 20.9 Million Victims," June 1, 2012, available at http://www.ilo.org/global/about-the-ilo/newsroom/news/WCMS_182109/lang--en/index.htm.

9. Mike Thomson, "Haiti: After the Storm," *BBC Today*, December 3, 2009, available at http://news.bbc.co.uk/today/hi/today/newsid_8390000/8390444.stm.

10. Choe Sang-Hun, "North Korea Exports Forced Laborers for Profit, Rights Groups Say," *New York Times*, February 19, 2015, available at http://www.nytimes .com/2015/02/20/world/asia/north-koreans-toil-in-slavelike-conditions-abroad-rights -groups-say.html.

11. See Paul Rexton Kan, Bruce E. Bechtol Jr., and Robert M. Collins, "Criminal Sovereignty: Understanding North Korea's Illicit International Activities," *The Letort Papers*, U.S. Army War College, Strategic Studies Institute, April 2010, available at http://www.strategicstudiesinstitute.army.mil/pubs/display.cfm?pubID=975.

12. Kristof and WuDunn, *Half the Sky*, 10.

13. Misha Glenny, *McMafia: A Journey Through the Global Criminal Underworld* (New York: Vintage Books, 2009), 104–10, 157–59.

14. *Profits and Poverty: The Economics of Forced Labour* (Geneva: International Labour Office, 2014), 13.

15. See Jane Perlez and Evelyn Rusli, "Uncounted Costs: Legions of Orphans and Broken Hearts," *New York Times*, January 7, 2005, A3; John Carvel, "Agencies Warn on Adopting Orphans," *Guardian* (London), January 7, 2005, 6.

16. Gerardo Reyes and Jacqueline Charles, "Exclusive Investigation: Guards Cash in on Smuggling Haitian Children," *Miami Herald*, October 26, 2010, available at http://www.ijdh.org/2010/10/topics/education-topics/exclusive-investigation-guards -cash-in-on-smuggling-haitian-children/.

17. "Trafficking in Women and Children: A Market Perspective," in *Illegal Immigration and Commercial Sex: The New Slave Trade*, ed. Phil Williams (Portland, OR: Frank Cass, 1999), 146.

18. *Estimating Illicit Financial Flows Resulting from Drug Trafficking and Other Transnational Organized Crimes*, 7.

19. *The Globalization of Crime: A Transnational Organized Crime Threat Assessment* (Vienna: United Nations Office on Drugs and Crime, 2010), 276.

20. United States Drug Enforcement Administration, "Intelligence Topics at DEA: El Paso Intelligence Center," available at www.dea.gov/ops/intel.shtml.

21. Tracy Wilkinson, "Caught Behind Enemy Lines," *Los Angeles Times*, November 7, 2010, A1.

22. Kimberly Heinle, Octavio Rodríguez Ferreira, and David A. Shirk, *Drug Violence in Mexico: Data and Analysis Through 2013*, Special Report, Justice in Mexico Project, Department of Political Science & International Relations, University of San Diego, April 2014, vi–vii, available at https://justiceinmexico.files.wordpress .com/2014/07/dvm-2014-final.pdf.

23. Mary Beth Sheridan, "Military Is Broadening U.S. Effort to Help Mexico Battle Its Drug Cartels," *Washington Post*, November 10, 2010, available at http://www .washingtonpost.com/wp-dyn/content/article/2010/11/09/AR2010110907060.html.

24. See Steve Coll, *Ghost Wars: The Secret History of the CIA, Afghanistan, and Bin Laden, from the Soviet Invasion to September 10, 2001* (New York: Penguin, 2004), 485.

25. *The Globalization of Crime*, 129.

26. "Crisis Facing Colombians Is Called Worst in Hemisphere," *New York Times*, May 11, 2004, A8.

27. United Nations Office on Drugs and Crime, *Afghanistan Opium Survey, 2009*, 7, available at www.unodc.org/documents/afghanistan//Opium_Surveys/Annual_Surveys/2009_Annual_Opium_Survey_full.pdf.

28. Yian Q. Miu, "Crackdown Targets Counterfeit Drugs," *Washington Post*, November 20, 2009, A17.

29. Walt Bogdanich and Jake Hooker, "From China to Panama, a Trail of Poisoned Medicine," *New York Times*, May 6, 2007, 1.

30. U.S. Department of State, *World Military Expenditures and Arms Transfers, 2014*, "Introduction and Overview," February 5, 2015, available at http://www.state.gov/t/avc/rls/rpt/wmeat/2014/237233.htm.

31. Richard F. Grimmett and Paul K. Kerr, *Conventional Arms Transfers to Developing Nations, 2004–2011* (Washington, DC: Congressional Research Service, August 24, 2012), Summary.

32. *Global Burden of Armed Violence 2015: Every Body Counts* (Geneva: Geneva Declaration, May 2015), Executive Summary, available at http://www.genevadeclaration.org/en/measurability/global-burden-of-armed-violence/gbav-2015/executive-summary.html.

33. See Thomas Fuller, "Arms Suspect Vows to Win Case in U.S. After Extradition Order," *New York Times*, August 20, 2010, available at www.nytimes.com/2010/08/21/world/asia/21thai.html; and Pete Yost and Steve Braun, "U.S., Russia Face Off over Alleged Arms Trafficker," *Washington Post*, August 23, 2010, available at www.washingtonpost.com/wp-dyn/content/article/2010/08/22/AR2010082202841.html; "Profile: Viktor Bout," *BBC News*, April 5, 2012, available at http://www.bbc.com/news/world-europe-11036569.

34. Coll, *Ghost Wars*, 337.

35. Coll, *Ghost Wars*, 337–40.

36. Douglas Jehl and David E. Sanger, "U.S. Expands List of Lost Missiles," *New York Times*, November 6, 2004, 1.

37. *To Walk the Earth in Safety: The United States' Commitment to Humanitarian Mine Action and Conventional Weapons Destruction*, 8th ed. (Washington, DC: United States Department of State, Bureau of Political-Military Affairs, 2009), 7.

38. Greg Krikorian, "LAX Guards against Portable Missile Attacks," *Los Angeles Times*, December 14, 2004, B1.

39. See Edward J. Laurance, *Light Weapons and Intrastate Conflict: Early Warning Factors and Preventive Action*, A Report to the Carnegie Commission on Preventing Deadly Conflict, July 1998, 13–19; and Jeffrey Boutwell and Michael T. Klare, eds., *Light Weapons and Civil Conflict: Controlling the Tools of Violence* (Lanham, MD: Rowman & Littlefield for the Carnegie Commission on Preventing Deadly Conflict, 1999), 1–5.

CHAPTER 9

1. Amy Chozick, "Obama to See If North Korea Should Return to Terror List," *New York Times*, December 22, 2014.

2. Brian Bennett, "Cyberattack Peril Is Growing, Senators Are Told," *Los Angeles Times*, February 27, 2015, A12.

3. Richard A. Clarke and Robert K. Knake, *Cyber War: The Next Threat to National Security and What to Do About It* (New York: Ecco, 2010), 17–21.

4. Clay Wilson, "Cyber Crime," in *Cyberpower and National Security*, eds. Franklin D. Kramer, Stuart H. Starr, and Larry K. Wentz (Washington, DC: Potomac Books for National Defense University Press, 2009), 418–19.

5. Eric A. Fischer, Edward C. Liu, John W. Rollins, and Catherine A. Theohary, "The 2013 Cybersecurity Executive Order: Overview and Considerations for Congress," *CRS Report for Congress* R42984 (Washington, DC: Congressional Research Service, November 8, 2013), 1.

6. Dan Verton, "Exclusive: Bin Laden Associate Warns of Cyberattacks," *Computerworld*, November 18, 2002, available at http://www.computerworld.com.au/article/46027/exclusive_bin_laden_associate_warns_cyberattacks/.

7. Patrick Marshall, "Cybersecurity," *CQ Researcher*, February 26, 2010, 172.

8. Francis Bacon, *Religious Meditations*, quoted in *The Oxford Dictionary of Quotations*, 3rd ed. (New York: Oxford University Press, 1980), 28.

9. Walter B. Wriston, *The Twilight of Sovereignty: How the Information Revolution Is Transforming Our World* (New York: Charles Scribner's Sons, 1992), xii.

10. Quoted by Roger C. Molander, Andrew S. Riddile, and Peter A. Wilson, *Strategic Information Warfare: A New Face of War* (Santa Monica, CA: RAND, 1996), xi.

11. Sun Tzu, *The Art of War* (New York: Delacorte, 1983), 77.

12. John Arquilla, "The Strategic Implications of Information Dominance," *Strategic Review* 22 (Summer 1994): 25.

13. John Arquilla and David Ronfeldt, *In Athena's Camp: Preparing for Conflict in the Information Age* (Santa Monica, CA: RAND, 1997), 36.

14. F. W. Winterbotham, *The Ultra Secret* (New York: Dell, 1994); Ronald W. Clark, *The Man Who Broke Purple* (London: Weidenfeld and Nicholson, 1977).

15. Alvin Toffler, *Powershift: Knowledge, Wealth, and Violence at the Edge of the 21st Century* (New York: Bantam Books, 1990), 270.

16. Shane Harris, *@War: The Rise of the Military-Internet Complex* (New York: Houghton Mifflin, 2014).

17. U.S. National Intelligence Council, *Mapping the Global Future, Report on the 2020 Project* (Washington, DC: Government Printing Office, December 2004), 75.

18. David Sanger, John Markoff, and Thom Shanker, "U.S. Plans Attack and Defense in Web Warfare," *New York Times*, April 28, 2009, available at http://www.nytimes.com/2009/04/28/us/28cyber.html.

19. Lieutenant-Colonel Steven Collins, "Mind Games," *NATO Review*, Summer 2003, 13–16, available at http://www.nato.int/docu/review/pdf/i2_en_review2003.pdf.

20. Quoted in Daniel T. Kuehl, "From Cyberspace to Cyberpower: Defining the Problem," in *Cyberpower and National Security*, 27.

21. Clarke and Knake, *Cyber War*, 70.

22. U.S. National Intelligence Council, *Global Trends 2030: Alternative Worlds* (Washington, DC: National Intelligence Council, December 2012), 64.

23. Wilson, "Cyber Crime," 421.

24. Wilson, "Cyber Crime," 421.

25. See "The NCIS Argentine Computer Intrusion Investigation," *FBI Law Enforcement Bulletin*, October 1998, 9.

26. See Dorothy E. Denning, *Information Warfare and Security* (Reading, MA: Addison-Wesley, 1999), 269.

27. Gabriel Weimann, "Cyberterrorism: How Real Is the Threat?" *Special Report* 119 (Washington, DC: U.S. Institute of Peace, May 2004), 2.

28. David Ronfeldt, John Arquilla, Graham E. Fuller, and Melissa Fuller, *The Zapatista Social Netwar in Mexico* (Santa Monica, CA: RAND, 1998).

29. Mark Ward, "A Decade on from the ILOVEYOU Bug," *BBC News*, May 4, 2010, available at http://www.bbc.co.uk/news/10095957.

30. "More Than 100 Arrests, as FBI Uncovers Cyber Crime Ring," *BBC News*, October 1, 2010, available at http://www.bbc.co.uk/news/world-us-canada-11457611.

31. Federal Bureau of Investigation, Internet Crime Complaint Center, *2014 Internet Crime Report*, http://www.ic3.gov/media/annualreport/2014_IC3Report.pdf.

32. Marshall, "Cybersecurity," 172, 177.

33. U.S. General Accounting Office, *Information Security: Computer Attacks at Department of Defense Pose Increasing Risks*, GAO/AIMD-96-84 (Washington, DC: Government Printing Office, May 1996), 10.

34. Leo Cendrowicz, "NATO Frontline in Life-or-Death War on Cyber-Terrorists," *The Guardian*, October 30, 2014, http://www.theguardian.com/world/2014/oct/30/nato-frontline-cyber-terrorists-war.

35. Siobhan Gorman, "Cyber Attacks Test Pentagon, Allies and Foes," *Wall Street Journal*, September 25, 2010, available at online.wsj.com/article/SB1000142405274 8703793804575511961264943300.html.

36. Stuart H. Starr, "Toward a Preliminary Theory of Cyberpower," in *Cyberpower and National Security*, 85.

37. Clarke and Knake, *Cyber War*, 171–72.

38. Clarke and Knake, *Cyber War*, 233.

39. Harris, *@War*, xii–xvii.

40. Irving Lachow, "Cyber Terrorism: Menace or Myth?" in *Cyberpower and National Security*, 440.

41. Harris, *@War*, 114.

42. George J. Tenet, "Global Realities of Our National Security," Statement before the Senate Foreign Relations Committee on the Worldwide Threat in 2000, March 21, 2000.

43. U.S. National Intelligence Council, *Mapping the Global Future*, 95.

44. Quoted by Myriam Dunn Cavelty, "Cyber-Terror: Looming Threat or Phantom Menace? The Framing of the US Cyber-Threat Debate," *Journal of Information Technology and Politics* 4 (2007): 19.

45. "Testimony of Federal Bureau of Investigation Director Louis Freeh," Senate Select Committee on Intelligence, May 10, 2001, available at fbi.gov/congress/congress01/freeh051001.htm.

46. Patrick DiJusto, "How Al-Qaida Site Was Hijacked," *Wired*, August 10, 2002, available at http://archive.wired.com/culture/lifestyle/news/2002/08/54455?current Page=all.

47. Dan Verton, *Black Ice: The Invisible Threat of Cyber-Terrorism* (New York: McGraw-Hill Osborne Media, 2003), 109.

48. Thomas L. Friedman, *The Lexus and the Olive Tree: Understanding Globalization*, rev. ed. (New York: Anchor Books, 2000), 403.

49. Dennis Lormel, "Testimony before the Senate Judiciary Subcommittee on Technology, Terrorism and Government Information," July 9, 2002, available at www.fbi.gov/congress.congress02/idtheft.htm.

50. Lachow, "Cyber Terrorism," 450.

51. Robert McMillan, "After Worm, Siemens Says Don't Change Password," *Business Week*, July 19, 2010, available at www.businessweek.com/idg/2010-07-19/after-worm-siemens-says-don-t-change-passwords.html.

52. Ali Akbar Dareini, "Iran Loads Fuel Rods into 1st Nuclear Power Plant," *Washington Post*, October 26, 2010, available at http://www.washingtonpost.com/wp-dyn/content/article/2010/10/26/AR2010102600530.html.

53. William J. Lynn III, "Defending a New Domain: The Pentagon's Cyberstrategy," *Foreign Affairs* 89 (September/October 2010): 98

54. Gregory J. Rattray, *Strategic Warfare in Cyberspace* (Cambridge, MA: MIT Press, 2001), 8.

55. Lynn, "Defending a New Domain," 102.

56. Brian Bennett, "CIA Is Creating Digital Spying Division," *Los Angeles Times*, March 7, 2015, A1.

57. David E. Sanger, "Pentagon Announces New Strategy for Cyberwarfare," *New York Times*, April 24, 2015, A4.

58. Admiral Michael S. Rogers quoted in David E. Sanger, "U.S. Must Step Up Capacity for Cyberattacks, Chief Argues," *New York Times*, March 20, 2015, A4.

59. See Marshall, "Cybersecurity," 178–86.

60. Thom Shanker, "Pentagon Will Help Homeland Security Department Fight Domestic Cyberattacks," *New York Times*, October 20, 2010, available at www.nytimes.com/2010/10/21/us/21cyber.html.

61. Walter Gary Sharp Sr., *Cyberspace and the Use of Force* (Washington, DC: Aegis Research Corporation, 1999), 140.

62. For a prominent example, see Thomas L. Friedman, *The World Is Flat: A Brief History of the Twenty-First Century* (New York: Farrar, Straus and Giroux, 2005).

63. Chris C. Demchak, "Dilemmas of Arms Control and Cybersecurity," in *Arms Control: History, Theory, and Policy*, 2 vols., eds. Robert E. Williams Jr. and Paul R. Viotti (Santa Barbara, CA: Praeger Security International, 2012), 219–36.

CHAPTER 10

1. Steve Mufson, "U.S. Urged to Target Nations That Aid Terrorism; N.Y., Pentagon Attacks Are Called Acts of War," *Washington Post*, September 12, 2001, A12.

2. Richard A. Clarke, *Against All Enemies: Inside America's War on Terror* (New York: Free Press, 2004), 32. Later, according to Clarke (232), Wolfowitz argued that Osama bin Laden "could not do all these things like the 1993 attack on New York, not without a state sponsor." President Bush disputed the details but not the substance of Clarke's account of the conversation on September 12. See *Final Report of the National Commission on Terrorist Attacks upon the United States*, Authorized Edition [hereafter *9/11 Commission Report*] (New York: W. W. Norton, 2004), 334.

3. Secretary Colin L. Powell, "Remarks to the United Nations Security Council," New York City, February 5, 2003, available at http://2001-2009.state.gov/secretary/former/powell/remarks/2003/17300.htm.

4. Stephen M. Walt, "The Renaissance of Security Studies," *International Studies Quarterly* 35 (1991): 212.

5. A noteworthy exception to this rule is the Human Security Network, a loose affiliation of states organized by Canada and Norway in 1999 in order to focus attention on the security (defined as freedom from fear and freedom from want) of individuals. Of course, attention to human security supplements rather than displaces the normal focus on national security. See the website of the Human Security Network at http://www.hpcrresearch.org/research/human-security-network.

6. Common Article 1 of the International Covenant on Civil and Political Rights and the International Covenant on Economic, Social, and Cultural Rights states that "all peoples have the right of self-determination."

7. See R. J. Rummel, *Statistics of Democide: Genocide and Mass Murder since 1900* (New Brunswick, NJ: Transaction, 1997); and *Death by Government* (New Brunswick, NJ: Transaction, 1994).

8. Max Weber, "Politics as a Vocation," in *Max Weber: Sociological Writings*, eds. H. H. Gerth and C. Wright Mills (Abingdon: Routledge, 1991), 78.

9. In addition to the fifty-five autonomous states extant in 1900, there were seventy-five colonial dependencies and protectorates. See Freedom House, *Democracy's Century: A Survey of Global Political Change in the 20th Century*. There are more than 193 states in the world today, but exactly how many more depends on who does the counting. Recognizing (and therefore counting) states is a highly political matter that requires determining, for instance, whether the Republic of China (Taiwan) is autonomous, contrary to the claims of the People's Republic of China, or whether the Holy See is truly a state or a political/religious entity that is *sui generis*.

10. A. LeRoy Bennett and James K. Oliver, *International Organizations: Principles and Issues*, 7th ed. (Upper Saddle River, NJ: Prentice Hall, 2002), 81–82.

11. Center for Arms Control and Non-Proliferation, "U.S. Defense Spending vs. Global Defense Spending," available at http://armscontrolcenter.org/u-s-defense-spending-vs-global-defense-spending/.

12. *CIA World Factbook*, "Country Comparison: GDP–Per Capita (PPP)," available at https://www.cia.gov/library/publications/the-world-factbook/rankorder/2004rank.html. (The data used here are purchasing power parity GDP figures.)

13. *CIA World Factbook*, "Tuvalu," available at www.cia.gov/library/publications/the-world-factbook/geos/tv.html.

14. Freedom House, *Democracy's Century: A Survey of Global Political Change in the 20th Century.*

15. Arch Puddington, "Freedom in the World 2015: Discarding Democracy: A Return to the Iron Fist," Freedom House, available at https://freedomhouse.org/report/freedom-world-2015/discarding-democracy-return-iron-fist.

16. Samuel P. Huntington, *The Third Wave: Democratization in the Late Twentieth Century* (Norman: University of Oklahoma Press, 1991), 15.

17. Inter-Parliamentary Union, "Women in National Parliaments," Situation as of May 1, 2015, available at www.ipu.org/wmn-e/world.htm.

18. Robin Wright, "Mongolian Women Typify a New Global Activism," *Los Angeles Times*, February 22, 2000, A8.

19. There is an extensive literature on democratic peace theory. See, for example, Bruce Russett, *Grasping the Democratic Peace* (Princeton, NJ: Princeton University Press, 1993); James Lee Ray, *Democracy and International Conflict* (Columbia, SC: University of South Carolina Press, 1995); Spencer R. Weart, *Never at War* (New Haven, CT: Yale University Press, 1998); and Charles Lipson, *Reliable Partners: How Democracies Have Made a Separate Peace* (Princeton, NJ: Princeton University Press, 2003).

20. Francis Fukuyama, "Women and the Evolution of World Politics," *Foreign Affairs* 77 (September/October 1998): 33–36.

21. Robert D. Kaplan, *An Empire Wilderness: Travels into America's Future* (New York: Random House, 1998), 3–20. Part I of this book is titled "The Last Redoubt of the Nation-State."

22. Richard N. Rosecrance, *The Rise of the Virtual State: Wealth and Power in the Coming Century* (New York: Basic Books, 1999).

23. Barry Buzan, *People, States and Fear: An Agenda for International Security Studies in the Post–Cold War Era*, 2nd ed. (Boulder, CO: Lynne Rienner, 1991), 90–96.

24. Karl W. Deutsch et al., *Political Community and the North Atlantic Area: International Organization in the Light of Historical Experience* (Princeton, NJ: Princeton University Press, 1957). The phrases *zones of peace* and *zones of turmoil*, which appear below, are borrowed from Max Singer and Aaron Wildavsky, *The Real World Order: Zones of Peace, Zones of Turmoil* (Chatham, NJ: Chatham House Publishers, 1993).

25. John Mueller, *Retreat from Doomsday: The Obsolescence of Major War* (New York: Basic Books, 1989), 217. See also Steven Pinker, *The Better Angels of Our Nature: Why Violence Has Declined* (New York: Viking Books, 2011); and Joshua S. Goldstein, *Winning the War on War: The Decline of Armed Conflict Worldwide* (New York: Penguin Books, 2011).

26. See Lotta Harborn and Peter Wallensteen, "Armed Conflicts, 1946–2008," *Journal of Peace Research* 46 (2009): 577–87.

27. T. David Mason, *Sustaining the Peace after Civil War* (Carlisle, PA: Strategic Studies Institute, December 2007), 1.

28. See Inis L. Claude Jr., "Myths about the State," in *States and the Global System: Politics, Law and Organization* (New York: St. Martin's, 1988), 13–27.

29. Mohammed Ayoob, "Defining Security: A Subaltern Realist Perspective," in *Critical Security Studies: Concepts and Cases*, eds. Keith Krause and Michael C. Williams (Minneapolis: University of Minnesota Press, 1997), 121.

30. Michael Howard, *The Lessons of History* (New Haven, CT: Yale University Press, 1991), 4.

31. Thomas Hobbes, *Leviathan*, ed. C. B. Macpherson (New York: Penguin Books, 1968), chap. 13.

32. UN High Commissioner for Refugees, *UNHCR Global Report 2014*, available at http://www.unhcr.org/gr14/index.xml.

33. See Michael Mandelbaum, "Foreign Policy as Social Work," *Foreign Affairs* 75 (January/February 1996): 16–32.

34. Francis Fukuyama, *The End of History and the Last Man* (New York: Avon Books, 1993); Robert D. Kaplan, *The Coming Anarchy: Shattering the Dreams of the Post Cold War* (New York: Vintage Books, 2000).

35. Kaplan, *The Coming Anarchy*, 7–8.

36. Robert I. Rotberg, "Failed States in a World of Terror," *Foreign Affairs* 81 (July/August 2002): 127–40.

37. Clarke, *Against All Enemies*, 84–89.

38. Barry Bearak, "Taliban Plead for Mercy to the Miserable in a Land of Nothing," *New York Times*, September 13, 2001, A18.

39. Graeme Wood, "What ISIS Really Wants," *The Atlantic*, March 2015, available at http://www.theatlantic.com/features/archive/2015/02/what-isis-really-wants/384980/.

40. Julie Hirschfeld Davis and Michael D. Shear, "U.S. Will Step Up Training of Iraqi Forces Fighting ISIS, Obama Says," *New York Times*, June 8, 2015, available at http://www.nytimes.com/2015/06/09/world/europe/united-states-increase-training-iraqis-fighting-isis-obama.html.

41. Patrick Boehler and Sergio Pecanha, "The Global Refugee Crisis, Region by Region," *New York Times*, June 8, 2015, available at http://www.nytimes.com/interactive/2015/06/09/world/migrants-global-refugee-crisis-mediterranean-ukraine-syria-rohingya-malaysia-iraq.html.

42. See United Nations Office of the High Commissioner for Human Rights, Press Release, "The Findings of the Independent Commission of Inquiry on Syria," November 28, 2011, available at http://www.ohchr.org/EN/NewsEvents/Pages/DisplayNews.aspx?NewsID=11654&LangID=E.

43. Somini Sengupta, "U.N. Panel Threatens to Name Those It Accuses of War Crimes in Syria," *New York Times*, February 20, 2015, available at http://www.nytimes.com/2015/02/21/world/middleeast/un-panel-threatens-to-name-those-it-accuses-of-war-crimes-in-syria.html.

44. Lotta Themnér and Peter Wallensteen, "Armed Conflicts, 1946–2013," *Journal of Peace Research* 51 (2014): 541–54.

45. "Remarks by the Honorable Kofi Annan," Conference on Preventing Deadly Conflict among Nations in the 21st Century, University of California at Los Angeles, April 22, 1998.

46. Nigel Inkster, ed., *The IISS Armed Conflict Survey 2015* (London: International Institute for Strategic Studies, 2015).

47. Paul Collier, *The Bottom Billion: Why the Poorest Countries Are Failing and What Can Be Done About It* (New York: Oxford University Press, 2007), 17.

48. Norrin M. Ripsman and T. V. Paul, *Globalization and the National Security State* (New York: Oxford University Press, 2010), 141. Ripsman and Paul base their list on the work of the Peace Research Institute of Oslo.

49. Mary Kaldor, *New and Old Wars*, 2nd ed. (Stanford, CA: Stanford University Press, 2007), 81–82.

50. Michael E. Brown, ed., *The International Dimensions of Internal Conflict* (Cambridge, MA: MIT Press, 1996), 575.

51. Robert D. Kaplan, *Balkan Ghosts: A Journey Through History* (New York: Vintage Books, 1994).

52. Jack Snyder, "Nationalism and the Crisis of the Post-Soviet State," *Survival* 35, no. 1 (Spring 1993): 5.

53. Snyder, "Nationalism and the Crisis of the Post-Soviet State," 5.

54. David A. Lake and Donald Rothchild, *Ethnic Fears and Global Engagement: The International Spread and Management of Ethnic Conflict*, Policy Paper 20 (San Diego: Institute on Global Conflict and Cooperation, University of California, January 1996), 8.

55. Seyom Brown, *New Forces, Old Forces and the Future of World Politics*, Post–Cold War Edition (New York: HarperCollins, 1995), 162.

56. Ted Robert Gurr, *Minorities at Risk: A Global View of Ethnopolitical Conflict* (Washington, DC: U.S. Institute of Peace Press, 1993).

57. David Welsh, "Domestic Politics and Ethnic Conflict," *Survival* 35, no. 1 (Spring 1993): 65.

58. For data on peacekeeping operations, including details of past and present missions, personnel, and finances, see the website of the UN Department of Peacekeeping Operations, available at http://www.un.org/en/peacekeeping/. See especially "Peacekeeping Fact Sheet," Fact Sheet as of April 30, 2015, available at http://www.un.org/en/peacekeeping/resources/statistics/factsheet.shtml.

59. Stephen Engelberg and Tim Weiner, "Massacre in Bosnia: Srebrenica: The Days of Slaughter," *New York Times*, October 29, 1995, available at http://www.nytimes.com/1995/10/29/world/massacre-in-bosnia-srebrenica-the-days-of-slaughter.html.

60. For a detailed account of the early stages of the Balkan conflict, see Susan L. Woodward, *Balkan Tragedy: Chaos and Dissolution after the Cold War* (Washington, DC: Brookings Institution Press, 1995).

61. J. Matthew Vaccaro, "The Politics of Genocide: Peacekeeping and Disaster Relief in Rwanda," in *U.N. Peacekeeping, American Politics, and the Uncivil Wars of the 1990s*, ed. William J. Durch (New York: St. Martin's, 1996), 367.

62. Carnegie Commission on Preventing Deadly Conflict, *Preventing Deadly Conflict: Final Report* (Washington, DC: Carnegie Commission on Preventing Deadly Conflict, 1997), 3.

63. Romeo A. Dallaire, *Shake Hands with the Devil: The Failure of Humanity in Rwanda* (New York: Carroll and Graf, 2004).

64. Andrew Kohut and Robert C. Toth, "Arms and the People," *Foreign Affairs* 73 (November/December 1994): 47–61.

65. Quoted in James Traub, *The Best Intentions: Kofi Annan and the UN in the Era of American World Power* (New York: Farrar, Straus and Giroux, 2006), 93.

66. Thomas E. Ricks, "Shift from Traditional War Seen at Pentagon," *Washington Post*, September 3, 2004, A1.

67. *9/11 Commission Report*, 361–62.

CHAPTER 11

1. Johan Galtung, "Violence, Peace, and Peace Research," *Journal of Peace Research* 6 (1969): 167–91.

2. World Food Programme, "Hunger Statistics," available at http://www.wfp.org/hunger/stats.

3. W. J. Hennigan, "The F-22, the World's Priciest Fighter Jet, Finally Flies in Combat," *Los Angeles Times*, September 24, 2014, available at http://www.latimes.com/world/middleeast/la-fg-f-22-the-worlds-priciest-fighter-jet-finally-flies-in-combat-20140923-story.html.

4. Paul Kennedy, *The Rise and Fall of the Great Powers* (New York: Random House, 1987), xvi.

5. In 2014, the International Monetary Fund announced that China had overtaken the United States to become the world's largest economy measured in terms of purchasing power parity. This claim, however, has been contested. See Ben Carter, "Is China's Economy Really the Largest in the World?" *BBC News*, December 19, 2014, available at www.bbc.com/news/magazine-30483762.

6. June Teufel Dreyer, "Recent Developments in the Chinese Military," in *A Military History of China*, eds. David A. Graff and Robin Higham (Lexington: University Press of Kentucky, 2012), 296.

7. "China Boosts Military Budget by 10.1 Percent, Despite Slowing Economy," *South China Morning Post*, March 15, 2015, available at http://www.scmp.com/news/china/article/1729999/china-says-it-will-boost-military-budget-101-cent-year.

8. David Shambaugh, *China Goes Global: The Partial Power* (New York: Oxford University Press, 2013), 282–98.

9. With respect to sub-Saharan Africa in particular, the view that European colonial policies are chiefly responsible for underdevelopment was most forcefully articulated over forty years ago in Walter Rodney, *How Europe Underdeveloped Africa* (London: Bogle-L'Ouverture, 1972). Explanations for the continent's underdevelopment are vigorously contested in the historiography of Africa. For an important contribution to the debate, see Daron Acemoglu, Simon Johnson, and James A. Robinson, "The Colonial Origins of Comparative Development: An Empirical Investigation," *American Economic Review* 91 (December 2001): 1369–1401.

10. Paul Collier, *The Bottom Billion: Why the Poorest Countries Are Failing and What Can Be Done About It* (New York: Oxford University Press, 2008).

11. On the origins of the *Human Development Report*, see Gary King and Christopher J. L. Murray, "Rethinking Human Security," *Political Science Quarterly* 116 (2002): 587.

12. All data in this paragraph is drawn from United Nations Development Programme, Human Development Reports, Data, available at hdr.undp.org/en/data. GNI per capita figures are 2011 purchasing power parity (PPP) dollars.

13. *National Security Strategy of the United States* (Washington, DC: White House, September 2002), available at http://georgewbush-whitehouse.archives.gov/nsc/nss/2002.

14. *Final Report of the National Commission on Terrorist Attacks upon the United States*, Authorized Edition (New York: W. W. Norton, 2004), 378.

15. Michael W. Doyle and Nicholas Sambanis, *Making War and Building Peace: United Nations Peace Operations* (Princeton, NJ: Princeton University Press, 2006), 34.

16. GDP per capita data in this paragraph comes from World Bank, Data, "GDP per capita (current US$)," available at http://data.worldbank.org/indicator/NY.GDP.PCAP.CD/countries?display=default.

17. Joshua S. Goldstein, *Winning the War on War: The Decline of Armed Conflict Worldwide* (London: Plume, 2012), 292.

18. Paul Collier, *Wars, Guns, and Votes: Democracy in Dangerous Places* (New York: Harper Perennial, 2009), 125–26.

19. United Nations Development Program, *Human Development Report*, 1994 (New York: Oxford University Press, 1994), 22.

20. See International Monetary Fund, World Economic Output Database, April 2014, Report for Selected Countries and Subjects, available at http://www.imf.org/external/pubs/ft/weo/2015/01/weodata/weorept.aspx?pr.x=33&pr.y=7&sy=2014&ey=2015&scsm=1&ssd=1&sort=country&ds=.&br=1&c=111&s=NGDPD%2CNGDPDPC%2CPPPGDP%2CPPPPC&grp=0&a=.

21. Dick K. Nanto, "Economics and National Security: Issues and Implications for U.S. Policy," Congressional Research Service, January 4, 2011, available at https://www.fas.org/sgp/crs/natsec/R41589.pdf.

22. U.S. Department of State, "Ukraine and Russia Sanctions," available at www.state.gov/e/eb/tfs/spi/ukrainerussia/.

23. Michael Birnbaum, "A Year into a Conflict with Russia, Are Sanctions Working?" *Washington Post*, March 27, 2015, available at http://www.washingtonpost.com/world/europe/a-year-into-a-conflict-with-russia-are-sanctions-working/2015/03/26/45ec04b2-c73c-11e4-bea5-b893e7ac3fb3_story.html.

24. Richard N. Haass, *Economic Sanctions: Too Much of a Bad Thing*, Policy Brief 34 (Washington, DC: Brookings Institution, June 1998), available at http://www.brookings.edu/research/papers/1998/06/sanctions-haass.

25. Haass, *Economic Sanctions*.

26. Carl von Clausewitz, *On War*, ed. and trans. Michael Howard and Peter Paret (New York: Alfred A. Knopf, 1993), 83.

27. See John Mueller and Karl Mueller, "Sanctions of Mass Destruction," *Foreign Affairs* 78 (1999): 43–53; and Laura Sjoberg, "Sanctions as War," in *Rethinking the 21st Century: "New" Problems, "Old" Solutions*, eds. Amy Eckert and Laura Sjoberg (New York: Zed Books, 2009), 173–92.

28. James C. Ngobi, "The United Nations Experience with Sanctions," in *Economic Sanctions: Panacea or Peacebuilding in a Post–Cold War World?* eds. David Cortright and George A. Lopez (Boulder, CO: Westview, 1995), 17–18.

29. U.S. Department of the Treasury, Office of Foreign Assets Control, OFAC Sanctions Programs, available at www.ustreas.gov/offices/enforcement/ofac/programs/.

30. Meghan L. O'Sullivan, *Shrewd Sanctions: Statecraft and State Sponsors of Terrorism* (Washington, DC: Brookings Institution, 2003), 35–44.

31. David Cortright and George A. Lopez, *The Sanctions Decade: Assessing UN Strategies in the 1990s* (Boulder, CO: Lynne Rienner, 2000).

32. Robert A. Pape, "Why Economic Sanctions Do Not Work," *International Security* 22 (Fall 1997): 90–136.

33. Michael Mandelbaum, *The Ideas That Conquered the World: Peace, Democracy, and Free Markets in the Twenty-First Century* (New York: PublicAffairs, 2002), 323.

34. Office of the United States Trade Representative, "U.S.-Canada Trade Facts," available at https://ustr.gov/countries-regions/americas/canada.

35. Collier, *The Bottom Billion*, chapter 4.

36. World Trade Organization, "Modest Trade Growth Anticipated for 2014 and 2015 Following Two Year Slump," Press Release, April 14, 2014, available at https://www.wto.org/english/news_e/pres14_e/pr721_e.htm.

37. Andrew G. Spyrou, *From T-2 to Supertanker: Development of the Oil Tanker, 1940–2000*, rev. ed. (Bloomington, IN: iUniverse, 2011), 1, 31.

38. Lance E. Hoovestal, *Globalization Contained: The Economic and Strategic Consequences of the Container* (New York: Palgrave Macmillan, 2013), 3–5.

39. Michael Richardson, "A Time Bomb for Global Trade: Maritime-Related Terrorism in an Age of Weapons of Mass Destruction," *Maritime Security*, January–February 2004, 1–8.

40. International Maritime Organization, "Reports on Acts of Piracy and Armed Robbery Against Ships," Annual Report—2014, April 28, 2015, available at http://www.imo.org/OurWork/Security/SecDocs/Documents/PiracyReports/219_Annual_2014.pdf.

41. Conor Seyle, "How to End Piracy," *Foreign Affairs*, February 11, 2015, available at https://www.foreignaffairs.com/articles/africa/2015-02-11/how-end-piracy.

42. John Pain, "Cruise Ship Attacked by Pirates Used Sonic Weapon," *USA Today*, November 7, 2005, available at http://usatoday30.usatoday.com/tech/news/techinnovations/2005-11-07-cruise-blast_x.htm.

43. IMO, "Reports on Acts of Piracy and Armed Robbery Against Ships."

44. The classic account of what is known as the Battle of the Black Sea on October 3–4, 1993, is found in Mark Bowden, *Black Hawk Down: A Story of Modern War* (New York: Atlantic Monthly Press, 1999).

45. UNDP, Human Development Reports, Data, available at hdr.undp.org/en/data.

46. The World Bank, "Poverty Overview," last updated April 6, 2015, available at http://www.worldbank.org/en/topic/poverty/overview.

47. Joseph S. Nye Jr., "Terrorism," in *Power in the Global Information Age* (New York: Routledge, 2004), 212.

48. Resolution adopted by the General Assembly 55/2, United Nations Millennium Declaration, available at http://www.un.org/millennium/declaration/ares552e .htm.

49. *The Millennium Development Goals Report 2014* (New York: United Nations, 2014), 4–5.

CHAPTER 12

1. Coral Davenport, "Pentagon Signals Security Risks of Climate Change," *New York Times*, October 14, 2014, A14.

2. Joshua W. Busby, "Climate Change and National Security: An Agenda for Action," *Council Special Report*, no. 32 (New York: Council on Foreign Relations, November 2007), 1.

3. Estimates of cost were made by the National Hurricane Center, cited by Davis Porter, "Hurricane Sandy Was Second-Costliest in U.S. History," *Huffington Post*, February 12, 2013, available at http://www.huffingtonpost.com/2013/02/12/ hurricane-sandy-second-costliest_n_2669686.html.

4. NASA, "Global Climate Change and Global Warming," available at http:// climate.nasa.gov/evidence/.

5. *Global Forest Resources Assessment, 2010: Key Findings*, Food and Agricultural Organization, 2010, 4, available at foris.fao.org/static/data/fra2010/KeyFindings -en.pdf.

6. Neil MacFarquhar, "Trying to Lace Together a Consensus on Biodiversity Across a Global Landscape," *New York Times*, September 29, 2010, available at www.nytimes.com/2010/09/30/world/30nations.html.

7. Timothy J. Crone and Maya Tolstoy, "Magnitude of the 2010 Gulf of Mexico Oil Spill," *Science*, October 29, 2010, 634.

8. "Climate Change Primer: Human Impacts," Woods Hole Research Center, available at www.whrc.org/resources/primer_human.html; and "Climate Change Primer: Climate Change Fundamentals," Woods Hole Research Center, available at www.whrc.org/resources/-primer_fundamentals.html.

9. Jacqueline Vaughn Switzer, with Gary Bryner, *Environmental Politics: Domestic and Global Dimensions*, 2nd ed. (New York: St. Martin's, 1998), 12.

10. Eric Nagourney, "A Turning Point in Smog History," *International Herald Tribune*, August 14, 2003, 9. See also Peter Brimblecombe, *The Big Smoke: A History of Air Pollution in London since Medieval Times* (London: Methuen, 1987).

11. Among the early arguments for the view that environmental issues raise significant national security concerns, see Lester R. Brown, *Redefining National Security*, Worldwatch Paper 14 (Washington, DC: Worldwatch Institute, 1977); Jessica Tuchman Mathews, "Redefining Security," *Foreign Affairs* 68 (Spring 1989): 162–77; and

Thomas F. Homer-Dixon, "On the Threshold: Environmental Changes as Causes of Acute Conflict," *International Security* 16 (Fall 1991): 76–116.

12. Peter H. Gleick, "Water, War and Peace in the Middle East," *Environment* 36 (April 1994): 11. The biblical account is found in Exodus 14.

13. Gleick, "Water, War and Peace in the Middle East," 11.

14. Roger D. Masters, *Fortune Is a River: Leonardo da Vinci and Niccolo Machiavelli's Magnificent Dream to Change the Course of Florentine History* (New York: Diane, 1998).

15. John Childs, "A Short History of the Military Use of Land in Peacetime," *War in History* 4 (1997): 87.

16. Robert M. Gum and Maurice H. Weeks, "Smoke and Obscurants," *Military Review* 76 (September/October 1996): 84–90.

17. Matthew L. Wald, "Amid Ceremony and Ingenuity, Kuwait's Oil Well Fires Are Declared Out," *New York Times*, November 7, 1991, A3; Frederick Warner, "The Environmental Consequences of the Gulf War," *Environment* 33 (June 1991): 6–9, 25–26.

18. Ian Fisher, "In Congo War's Wake, a Massacre of Wildlife," *New York Times*, July 28, 1999, A10.

19. "Air Force Resumes Use of Depleted Uranium," *Boston Globe*, April 6, 2002, A2.

20. Jonathan Schell, *The Fate of the Earth* (New York: Alfred A. Knopf, 1982).

21. See Carl Sagan, "Nuclear War and Climatic Catastrophe: Some Policy Implications," *Foreign Affairs* 62 (Winter 1983/1984): 257–92; Starley L. Thompson and Stephen H. Schneider, "Nuclear Winter Reappraised," *Foreign Affairs* 64 (Summer 1986): 981–1005.

22. Jennifer Nyman, "The Dirtiness of the Cold War: Russia's Nuclear Waste in the Arctic," *Environmental Policy and Law* 32 (2002): 47–52.

23. Sophia Kishkovsky, "In 15 Hours, Submarine *Kursk* Is Raised from Sea Floor," *New York Times*, October 9, 2001, A7.

24. Anahad O'Connor, "Adding Weight to Suspicion, Sonar Is Linked to Whale Deaths," *New York Times*, October 9, 2003, A23.

25. "Whaling Commission's Science Panel Says Marine Mammals Threatened by Man-Made Noise," Press Release, Natural Resources Defense Council, available at www.nrdc.org/media/pressreleases/040720.asp.

26. Thomas F. Homer-Dixon, *Environment, Scarcity, and Violence* (Princeton, NJ: Princeton University Press, 1999), 12.

27. Peter H. Gleick, "Water and Conflict: Fresh Water Resources and International Security," *International Security* 18 (Summer 1993): 79–112.

28. Bill McKibben, "A Special Moment in History," *Atlantic Monthly* 281 (May 2001): 56–57.

29. Daniel Yergin tells this story well, and in considerable detail, in *The Prize: The Epic Quest for Oil, Money and Power* (New York: Simon and Schuster, 1992), 305–27.

30. U.S. Energy Information Administration, available at http://www.eia.gov/tools/faqs/faq.cfm?id=33&t=6; Michael T. Klare, *Blood and Oil: The Dangers and*

Consequences of America's Growing Dependency on Imported Petroleum (New York: Metropolitan Books, 2004), 7.

31. U.S. Central Intelligence Agency, "Country Comparison to the World," *World Factbook*, available at https://www.cia.gov/library/publications/the-world-factbook/fields/2116.html.

32. "Total Petroleum and Other Liquids Production-2013," Energy Information Administration, Department of Energy [hereafter EIA], available at http://www.eia.gov/countries/index.cfm?topL=exp.

33. "Freedom in the World, 2015," Freedom House, available at https://freedom house.org/report/freedom-world/freedom-world-2015#.VhMIP-sqXG4.

34. U.S. Energy Information Administration, "Total Petroleum and Other Liquids Production," available at http://www.eia.gov/countries.

35. U.S. Energy Information Administration, available at http://www.eia.gov/countries/regions-topics.cfm?fips=WOTC#hormuz.

36. U.S. Energy Information Administration, "International Energy Statistics," available at http://www.eia.gov/cfapps/ipdbproject/IEDIndex3.cfm?tid=5&pid=5&aid=2.

37. "China Soon to Have Almost as Many Drivers as U.S. Has People," *Wall Street Journal*, November 28, 2014, available at http://blogs.wsj.com/chinarealtime/2014/11/28/china-soon-to-have-almost-as-many-drivers-as-u s hns-people/.

38. Edward L. Morse, "Welcome to the Revolution: Why Shale Is the Next Shale," *Foreign Affairs* 93 (May/June 2014): 3.

39. U.S. National Intelligence Council, *Global Trends 2030: Alternative Worlds* (Washington, DC: National Intelligence Council, December 2012), 35.

40. See James A. Baker III, with Thomas M. DeFrank, *The Politics of Diplomacy: Revolution, War and Peace, 1989–1992* (New York: G. P. Putnam's Sons, 1995), 336–37.

41. Jimmy Carter, "State of the Union Address 1980," January 23, 1980, Jimmy Carter Library and Museum, available at www.jimmycarterlibrary.org/documents/speeches/su80jec.phtml.

42. Klare, *Blood and Oil*, 46–47.

43. "U.S. Policy toward the Iran-Iraq War," National Security Decision Directive 114, November 26, 1983, available via the National Security Archive, George Washington University, www2.gwu.edu/~nsarchiv/NSAEBB/NSAEBB82/iraq26.pdf.

44. *Final Report of the National Commission on Terrorist Attacks upon the United States*, Authorized Edition [hereafter *9/11 Commission Report*] (New York: W. W. Norton, 2004), 55–56.

45. The White House, *A National Security Strategy for a New Century* (Washington, DC: December 1999), 42.

46. Michael D. Shear and Coral Davenport, "Obama Uses a Visit to the Everglades to Press His Climate Agenda," *New York Times*, April 23, 2015, A18.

47. NASA, "Global Climate Change and Global Warming," available at http://climate.nasa.gov/evidence/.

48. McKibben, "A Special Moment in History," 64.

49. NASA, "Global Climate Change and Global Warming."

50. U.S. Environmental Protection Agency, *Climate Change Indicators in the United States*, Key Findings, 4–7, available at http://www3.epa.gov/climatechange/science/indicators/.

51. Timothy E. Wirth, C. Boyden Gray, and John D. Podesta, "The Future of Energy Policy," *Foreign Affairs* 82 (July/August 2003): 138–39.

52. This discussion of uncertainty in climate prediction is drawn from David G. Victor, *Climate Change: Debating America's Policy Options* (New York: Council on Foreign Relations, 2004), 12–16.

53. Marshall's work at RAND on counterforce targeting is discussed in Gregg Herken, *Counsels of War* (New York: Alfred A. Knopf, 1985), 79–81. For the origins of OSD/NA and Marshall's role in it, see Khurram Husain, "Neocons: The Men behind the Curtain," *Bulletin of the Atomic Scientists* 59 (November/December 2003): 68–70.

54. Peter Schwartz and Doug Randall, *An Abrupt Climate Change Scenario and Its Implications for United States National Security* (Washington, DC: Department of Defense, Office of Net Assessment, October 2003).

55. Schwartz and Randall, *An Abrupt Climate Change Scenario*, 14.

56. U.S. National Intelligence Council, *Mapping the Global Future*, 76.

57. CNA Military Advisory Board, *National Security and the Threat of Climate Change* (Arlington, VA: CNA Corporation, 2007), available at http://www.npr.org/documents/2007/apr/security_climate.pdf.

58. CNA Military Advisory Board, *National Security and the Accelerating Risks of Climate Change* (Arlington, VA: CNA Corporation, May 2014).

59. U.S. Department of Defense, *2014 Climate Change Adaptation Roadmap* (Washington, DC: Office of the Under Secretary of Defense for Installations and Environment, June 2014), available at http://www.acq.osd.mil/ie/download/CCAR print_wForeword_c.pdf.

60. U.S. National Intelligence Council, *Global Trends 2030: Alternative Worlds* (Washington, DC: National Intelligence Council, December 2012), v.

61. Fred Krupp, "Don't Just Drill, Baby—Drill Carefully," *Foreign Affairs* 93 (May/June 2014): 15.

62. Michael Wines, "Oklahoma Recognizes Role of Drilling in Earthquakes," *New York Times*, April 21, 2015.

63. Klare, *Blood and Oil*, 180–202.

64. Jeremy Rifkin, *The Hydrogen Economy* (New York: Tarcher, 2003), 125.

65. Schwartz and Randall, *An Abrupt Climate Change Scenario*, 19.

CHAPTER 13

1. Max Singer and Aaron Wildavsky, *The Real World Order: Zones of Peace, Zones of Turmoil* (Chatham, NJ: Chatham House, 1993).

2. Charles Krauthammer, "The Unipolar Moment," *Foreign Affairs* 70 (America and the World 1990/1991): 23–33.

3. Kenneth N. Waltz, *Theory of International Politics* (Reading, MA: Addison-Wesley, 1979), 112.

4. *Final Report of the National Commission on Terrorist Attacks upon the United States*, Authorized Edition [hereafter *9/11 Commission Report*] (New York: W. W. Norton, 2004), 361.

5. President William J. Clinton, "Remarks by the President at the U.S. Coast Guard Academy's 119th Commencement," U.S. Coast Guard Academy, New London, Connecticut, May 17, 2000, available at www.clintonfoundation.org/legacy/051700-speech-by-president-at-us-coast-guard-academy.htm.

6. John Muir, *My First Summer in the Sierra* (Boston: Houghton Mifflin, 1911), 110.

7. U.S. National Intelligence Council, *Global Trends 2030: Alternative Worlds* (Washington, DC: National Intelligence Council, December 2012), available at http://www.dni.gov/files/documents/GlobalTrends_2030.pdf.

8. William B. Karesh and Robert A. Cook, "The Human-Animal Link," *Foreign Affairs* 84 (July/August 2005): 43–44.

9. Denise Grady, "Making a Ferret Sneeze for Hints to the Transmission of Bird Flu," *New York Times*, March 28, 2006, D3.

10. Denise Grady, "On an Altered Planet, New Diseases Emerge as Old Ones Re-emerge," *New York Times*, August 20, 2002, D2.

11. Danielle Renwick, "Ebola Virus," *Backgrounders* (New York: Council on Foreign Relations, October 24, 2014).

12. James D. Wolfensohn, "Fight Terrorism by Ending Poverty," *New Perspectives Quarterly* 19 (Spring 2002): 42.

13. Dominique Moïsi, *The Geopolitics of Emotion: How Cultures of Fear, Humiliation, and Hope Are Reshaping the World* (New York: Anchor Books, 2009), 13.

14. *National Security Strategy of the United States* (Washington, DC: White House, September 2002), v, available at georgewbush-whitehouse.archives.gov/nsc/nss/2002/.

15. For a provocative discussion of the problem that popularized the use of the term *blowback*, see Chalmers Johnson, *Blowback: The Costs and Consequences of American Empire* (New York: Metropolitan Books, 2000).

16. Richard Norton-Taylor, "Thinktank: Invasion Aided al-Qaida," *Guardian* (London), October 20, 2004, available at www.guardian.co.uk/Iraq/Story/0,2763,1331362,00.html.

17. Douglas Frantz et al., "The New Face of Al Qaeda," *Los Angeles Times*, September 26, 2004, A1.

18. Peter Baker and Eric Schmitt, "Many Missteps in Assessment of ISIS Threat," *New York Times*, September 30, 2014, A1.

19. Central Intelligence Agency, *The World Factbook*, "Africa: Nigeria," www.cia.gov/library/publications/the-world-factbook/geos/ni.html.

20. Central Intelligence Agency, *The World Factbook*, "Country Comparison: Oil—Exports," available at www.cia.gov/library/publications/the-world-factbook/rankorder/2176rank.html; and "Country Comparison: Oil—Proved Reserves," available at www.cia.gov/library/publications/the-world-factbook/rankorder/2178rank.html.

21. U.S. National Intelligence Council, *Global Trends 2030*, 15.

22. U.S. National Intelligence Council, *Mapping the Global Future*, Report of the 2020 Project (Washington, DC: Government Printing Office, December 2004), 9.

23. Howard W. French, "China's Dangerous Game," *The Atlantic* (November 2014), 99; Helene Cooper and Jane Perlez, "China Objects to U.S. Flights Near Artificial Islands," *New York Times*, May 23, 2015, A3.

24. "China Goes Down the MIRV Path," *New York Times*, May 20, 2015, A22.

25. See Martin Coward, "Network-Centric Violence, Critical Infrastructure and the Urbanization of Security," *Security Dialogue* 40 (2009): 399–400.

26. UNFPA, *State of World Population 2007: Unleashing the Potential of Urban Growth*, June 27, 2007, available at http://www.unfpa.org/swp/swpmain.htm.

27. Karen Dawisha, *Putin's Kleptocracy: Who Owns Russia?* (New York: Simon and Schuster, 2014).

28. UN Department of Public Information, "Secretary-General Salutes International Workshop on Human Security in Mongolia," Press Release SG/SM/7382, May 8, 2000, available at www.un.org/News/Press/docs/2000/20000508.sgsm7382.doc.html.

29. Ken Booth, *Strategy and Ethnocentrism* (New York: Holmes and Meier, 1979).

30. Joseph S. Nye Jr. and Sean M. Lynn-Jones, "International Security Studies: A Report of a Conference on the State of the Field," *International Security* 12 (Spring 1988): 10–11.

31. For a useful overview of feminist perspectives on security, see J. Ann Tickner, *Gendering World Politics: Issues and Approaches in the Post–Cold War Era* (New York: Columbia University Press, 2001), 36–64.

32. Although her concern relates more to the nature of the state and to issues of jurisprudence, this is essentially the point made by Catharine A. MacKinnon in *Toward a Feminist Theory of the State* (Cambridge, MA: Harvard University Press, 1989).

33. Mohammed Ayoob, "Defining Security: A Subaltern Realist Perspective," in *Critical Security Studies: Concepts and Cases*, ed. Keith Krause and Michael C. Williams (Minneapolis: University of Minnesota Press, 1997), 121.

34. U.S. National Intelligence Council, *Global Trends 2030*, 12.

Selected Bibliography

Acton, James M. *Deterrence during Disarmament: Deep Nuclear Reductions and International Security*. Adelphi Book 417. London: International Institute for Strategic Studies, 2014.

Allison, Graham. *Nuclear Terrorism: The Ultimate Preventable Catastrophe*. New York: Times Books, 2004.

Arquilla, John, and David Ronfeldt, eds. *In Athena's Camp: Preparing for Conflict in the Information Age*. Santa Monica, CA: RAND, 1997.

Art, Robert J., and Kenneth N. Waltz, eds. *The Use of Force: Military Power and International Politics*. 7th ed. Lanham, MD: Rowman & Littlefield, 2009.

Avant, Deborah. *The Market for Force: The Consequences of Privatizing Security*. Cambridge: Cambridge University Press, 2005.

Axworthy, Lloyd. "Human Security and Global Governance: Putting People First." *Global Governance* 7, no. 1 (2001): 19–23.

Bacevich, Andrew J. *The New American Militarism: How Americans Are Seduced by War*. New York: Oxford University Press, 2005.

Baldwin, David. "The Concept of Security." *Review of International Studies* 23 (January 1997): 5–26.

Barnett, Jon. *The Meaning of Environmental Security: Ecological Politics and Policy in the New Security Era*. London: Zed Books, 2001.

Battersby, Paul, and Joseph M. Siracusa. *Globalization and Human Security*. Lanham, MD: Rowman & Littlefield, 2009.

Beckman, Peter R., Paul W. Crumlish, Michael N. Dobkowski, and Steven P. Lee. *The Nuclear Predicament: Nuclear Weapons in the Twenty-First Century*. 3rd ed. Upper Saddle River, NJ: Prentice Hall, 2000.

Beebe, Shannon D., and Mary Kaldor. *The Ultimate Weapon Is No Weapon: Human Security and the New Rules of War and Peace*. New York: PublicAffairs, 2010.

Benjamin, Daniel, and Steven Simon. *The Age of Sacred Terror*. New York: Random House, 2002.

———. *The Next Attack: The Failure of the War on Terror and a Strategy for Getting It Right.* New York: Henry Holt, 2005.

Beswick, Danielle, and Paul Jackson. *Conflict, Security and Development: An Introduction.* London: Routledge, 2015.

Betts, Richard. "Should Strategic Studies Survive?" *World Politics* 50 (October 1997): 7–33.

———. "The New Threat of Mass Destruction." *Foreign Affairs* 77 (January/February 1998): 26–41.

Betz, D. J., and T. Stevens. *Cyberspace and the State: Toward a Strategy for Cyber-Power.* Adelphi Paper 424. London: International Institute for Strategic Studies, 2011.

Biddle, Stephen D. *Military Power: Explaining Victory and Defeat in Modern Battle.* Princeton, NJ: Princeton University Press, 2006.

Booth, Ken. "Security and Emancipation." *Review of International Studies* 17 (1991): 313–26.

———. "Human Wrongs and International Relations." *International Affairs* 71 (January 1995): 103–26.

———. "Security and Self: Reflections of a Fallen Realist." In *Critical Security Studies: Concepts and Cases,* edited by Keith Krause and Michael C. Williams, 83–119. Minneapolis: University of Minnesota Press, 1997.

———. *Theory of World Security.* Cambridge: Cambridge University Press, 2007.

Booth, Ken, and Moorhead Wright. *American Thinking about War and Peace.* New York: Barnes and Noble, 1978.

Bracken, Paul. *The Second Nuclear Age: Strategy, Danger, and the New Power Politics.* New York: St. Martin's Griffin, 2013.

Brodie, Bernard, ed. *The Absolute Weapon: Atomic Power and World Order.* New York: Harcourt, Brace, 1946.

———. *Strategy in the Missile Age.* Princeton, NJ: Princeton University Press, 1959.

———. *War and Politics.* New York: Macmillan, 1973.

Brown, Lester. *Redefining National Security.* Washington, DC: Worldwatch, 1977.

Brown, Michael E., ed. *Ethnic Conflict and International Security.* Princeton, NJ: Princeton University Press, 1993.

———. *Grave New World: Security Challenges in the 21st Century.* Washington, DC: Georgetown University Press, 2003.

Brown, Michael E., and Richard N. Rosecrance, eds. *The Costs of Conflict: Prevention and Cure in the Global Arena.* Lanham, MD: Rowman & Littlefield, 1999.

Brown, Seyom. *The Causes and Prevention of War.* 2nd ed. New York: St. Martin's, 1994.

Bull, Hedley. *The Control of the Arms Race.* 2nd ed. New York: Frederick A. Praeger, 1965.

———. *The Anarchical Society: A Study of Order in World Politics.* New York: Columbia University Press, 1977.

Burgess, J. Peter, ed. *The Routledge Handbook of New Security Studies.* London: Routledge, 2012.

Burns, Richard Dean, ed. *Encyclopedia of Arms Control and Disarmament*. 3 vols. New York: Scribner's, 1992.

————. *The Evolution of Arms Control: From Antiquity to the Nuclear Age*. Lanham, MD: Rowman & Littlefield, 2013.

Busch, Nathan E., and Daniel H. Joyner, eds. *Combating Weapons of Mass Destruction: The Future of International Nonproliferation Policy*. Athens: University of Georgia Press, 2009.

Buzan, Barry, and Eric Herring. *The Arms Dynamic in World Politics*. Boulder, CO: Lynne Rienner, 1998.

Buzan, Barry, and Ole Waever. *Regions and Powers: The Structure of International Security*. Cambridge: Cambridge University Press, 2003.

Buzan, Barry, Ole Waever, and Jaap de Wilde. *Security: A New Framework for Analysis*. Boulder, CO: Lynne Rienner, 1998.

Caldwell, Dan. *The Dynamics of Domestic Politics and Arms Control*. Columbia: University of South Carolina Press, 1991.

————. *Vortex of Conflict: U.S. Policy Toward Afghanistan, Pakistan, and Iraq*. Stanford, CA: Stanford University Press, 2011.

Cameron, Maxwell A., Robert J. Lawson, and Brian W. Tomlin, eds. *To Walk without Fear: The Global Movement to Ban Landmines*. New York: Oxford University Press, 1999.

Carnegie Commission on Preventing Deadly Conflict. *Preventing Deadly Conflict: Final Report*. Washington, DC: Carnegie Commission on Preventing Deadly Conflict, 1997.

Carter, Ashton B., and William J. Perry. *Preventive Defense: A New Security Strategy for America*. Washington, DC: Brookings Institution, 1999.

Cerny, Philip G. "The New Security Dilemma: Divisibility, Defection and Disorder in the Global Era." *Review of International Studies* 26 (2000): 623–46.

Cha, Victor D. "Globalization and the Study of International Security." *Journal of Peace Research* 37 (2000): 391–403.

Chalecki, E. L. *Environmental Security: A Guide to the Issues*. Santa Barbara, CA: Praeger, 2012.

Chipman, John. "The Future of Strategic Studies: Beyond Grand Strategy." *Survival* 34 (Spring 1992): 109–31.

Chivers, C. J. *The Gun*. New York: Simon and Schuster, 2010

Cirincione, Joseph. *Bomb Scare: The History and Future of Nuclear Weapons*. New York: Columbia University Press, 2007.

————. *Nuclear Nightmares: Securing the World Before It Is Too Late*. New York: Columbia University Press, 2013.

Clarke, Richard A., and Robert K. Knake. *Cyber War: The Next Threat to National Security and What to Do About It*. New York: Ecco, 2010.

Clausewitz, Carl von. *On War*. Edited and translated by Michael Howard, Peter Paret, and Bernard Brodie. Princeton, NJ: Princeton University Press, 1976.

Cohen, Eliot. "A Revolution in Warfare." *Foreign Affairs* 75 (March/April 1996): 37–54.

Collier, Paul. *Wars, Guns, and Votes: Democracy in Dangerous Places*. New York: Harper, 2009.

Collier, Paul, and Ian Bannon. *Natural Resources and Violent Conflict: Options and Actions*. Washington, DC: World Bank, 2003.

Commission on Human Security. *Human Security Now: Protecting and Empowering People*. New York: Commission on Human Security, 2003.

Cote, Owen R., Jr., Sean Lynn-Jones, and Steven E. Miller, eds. *New Global Dangers: Changing Dimensions of International Security*. Cambridge, MA: MIT Press, 2004.

Crenshaw, Martha. *Explaining Terrorism: Causes, Processes and Consequences*. London: Routledge, 2010.

Croft, Stuart, and Terry Terriff, eds. *Critical Reflections on Security and Change*. Portland, OR: Frank Cass, 2000.

Cronin, Audrey K. "Behind the Curve: Globalization and International Terrorism." *International Security* 27 (2002): 30–58.

———. *How Terrorism Ends: Understanding the Decline and Demise of Terrorist Campaigns*. Princeton, NJ: Princeton University Press, 2011.

Dalby, Simon. *Environmental Security*. Minneapolis: University of Minnesota Press, 2002.

———. *Security and Environmental Change*. Cambridge: Polity, 2009.

Dallaire, Romeo. *Shake Hands with the Devil: The Failure of Humanity in Rwanda*. New York: Random House, 2003.

Dannreuther, Roland. *International Security: The Contemporary Agenda*. Malden, MA: Polity, 2013.

Del Rosso, Steven J., Jr. "The Insecure State: Reflections on 'The State' and 'Security' in a Changing World." *Daedalus* 124 (Spring 1995): 175–207.

Dessler, Andrew. *Introduction to Modern Climate Change*. Cambridge: Cambridge University Press, 2011.

Diamond, Jared. *Guns, Germs, and Steel: The Fates of Human Societies*. New York: W. W. Norton, 1997.

———. *Collapse: How Societies Choose to Fail or Succeed*. New York: Viking, 2005.

Diehl, Paul, and Nils Petter Gleditsch, eds. *Environmental Conflict: An Anthology*. Boulder, CO: Westview Press, 2000.

Drell, Sidney, and James E. Goodby. *The Gravest Danger: Nuclear Weapons*. Stanford, CA: Hoover Institution, 2003.

Duffield, Mark. *Development, Security and Unending War: Governing the World of Peoples*. Cambridge: Cambridge University Press, 2008.

Dyson, Freeman. *Weapons and Hope*. New York: Harper and Row, 1984.

Eberstadt, Nicholas. "Population Change and National Security." *Foreign Affairs* 70 (Summer 1991): 115–31.

Eckert, Amy, and Laura Sjoberg, eds. *Rethinking the 21st Century: "New" Problems, "Old" Solutions*. New York: Zed Books, 2009.

Elbe, Stefan. *The Strategic Implications of HIV/AIDS*. Adelphi Paper 357. London: International Institute for Strategic Studies, 2003.

Eriksson, Johan. *Threat Politics: New Perspectives on Security, Risk and Crisis Management*. Burlington, VT: Ashgate, 2001.

Evans, Gareth. *The Responsibility to Protect: Ending Mass Atrocity Crimes Once and for All.* Washington, DC: Brookings Institution Press, 2009.

Fierke, K. M. *Critical Approaches to International Security.* Cambridge: Polity Press, 2007.

Flynn, Stephen. *America the Vulnerable: How Our Government Is Failing to Protect Us from Terrorism.* New York: HarperCollins, 2004.

Freedman, Lawrence. "International Security: Changing Targets." *Foreign Policy* 110 (Spring 1998): 48–64.

———. *The Revolution in Strategic Affairs.* Adelphi Paper 318. London: Oxford University Press for the International Institute for Strategic Studies, April 1998.

———. *Evolution of Nuclear Strategy.* 3rd ed. New York: Palgrave Macmillan, 2003.

———. *Deterrence.* London: Polity, 2004.

Gaddis, John Lewis. *Surprise, Security and the American Experience.* Cambridge, MA: Harvard University Press, 2004.

Garrett, Laurie. "The Nightmare of Bioterrorism." *Foreign Affairs* 80 (2001): 76–89.

George, Alexander L., and William Simons. *The Limits of Coercive Diplomacy.* 2nd ed. Boulder, CO: Westview, 1994.

George, Alexander, and Richard Smoke. *Deterrence in American Foreign Policy: Theory and Practice.* New York: Columbia University Press, 1974.

Gerges, Fawaz A. *The Far Enemy: Why Jihad Went Global.* Cambridge: Cambridge University Press, 2005.

———. *The Rise and Fall of al-Qaeda.* Oxford: Oxford University Press, 2011.

Goldstein, Joshua S. *Winning the War on War: The Decline of Armed Conflict Worldwide.* New York: Plume, 2012.

Gray, Colin. "New Directions for Strategic Studies: How Can Theory Help Practice?" *Security Studies* 1 (Summer 1992): 610–35.

———. *Villains, Victims and Sheriffs: Strategic Studies and Security for an Inter-War Period.* Hull: University of Hull Press, 1994.

Guild, Elspeth. *The Second Nuclear Age.* Boulder, CO: Lynne Rienner, 1999.

———. *Security and Migration.* Cambridge: Polity, 2009.

Gurr, Ted Robert. "Peoples against States: Ethnopolitical Conflict and the Changing World System." *International Studies Quarterly* 38 (September 1994): 347–78.

Haftendorn, Helga. "The Security Puzzle: Theory-Building and Discipline Building in International Security." *International Studies Quarterly* 35 (March 1991): 2–17.

Hardin, Garrett. *Living within Limits: Ecology, Economics and Population.* Oxford: Oxford University Press, 1993.

Harff, Barbara, and Ted Robert Gurr. *Ethnic Conflict in World Politics.* 2nd ed. Boulder, CO: Westview, 2004.

Herz, John. "Idealist Internationalism and the Security Dilemma." *World Politics* 2 (1950): 157–80.

———. *International Politics in the Atomic Age.* New York: Columbia University Press, 1959.

Hillel, Daniel. *Rivers of Eden: The Struggle for Water and the Quest for Peace in the Middle East.* Oxford: Oxford University Press, 1994.

Hoffman, Bruce. *Inside Terrorism*. Rev. ed. New York: Columbia University Press, 2006.

Homer-Dixon, Thomas F. *Environment, Scarcity and Violence*. Princeton, NJ: Princeton University Press, 1999.

———, ed. *How the Twin Crises of Oil Depletion and Climate Change Will Define the Future*. New York: Random House, 2009.

Jervis, Robert. *Perception and Misperception in International Politics*. Princeton, NJ: Princeton University Press, 1976.

———. "Was the Cold War a Security Dilemma?" *Journal of Cold War History* 3 (Winter 2001): 36–60.

Job, Brian, ed. *The Insecurity Dilemma*. Boulder, CO: Lynne Rienner, 1992.

Jones, Clive, and Caroline Kennedy-Pipe, eds. *International Security in a Global Age: Securing the Twenty-First Century*. London: Frank Cass, 2000.

Kaldor, Mary. *New and Old Wars: Organized Violence in a Global Era*, 3rd ed. Cambridge: Polity, 2012.

Katzenstein, Peter J. *The Culture of National Security: Norms and Identity in World Politics*. New York: Columbia University Press, 1996.

Kay, Sean. *Global Security in the Twenty-First Century: The Quest for Power and the Search for Peace*. 2nd ed. Lanham, MD: Rowman & Littlefield, 2012.

Khalilzad, Zalmay M., and John P. White, eds. *The Changing Role of Information in Warfare*. Santa Monica, CA: RAND, 1999.

Kissinger, Henry. *Diplomacy*. New York: Simon & Schuster, 1994.

———. *World Order*. New York: Penguin Press, 2014.

Klare, Michael T. *Resource Wars: The New Landscape of Global Conflict*. New York: Henry Holt, 2001.

———. *Rising Powers, Shrinking Planet: The New Geopolitics of Energy*. New York: Metropolitan Books, 2008.

Knorr, Klaus. *The Power of Nations: The Political Economy of International Relations*. New York: Basic Books, 1975.

Knorr, Klaus, ed. *Historical Dimensions of National Security*. Lawrence: University Press of Kansas, 1976.

Knorr, Klaus, and Frank N. Trager, eds. *Economic Issues and National Security*. Lawrence: University Press of Kansas, 1977.

Koblentz, Gregory D. *Living Weapons: Biological Warfare and International Security*. Ithaca, NY: Cornell University Press, 2009.

Kolodziej, Edward A. "What Is Security and Security Studies? Lessons from the Cold War." *Arms Control* 13 (April 1992): 1–32.

———. "Renaissance in Security Studies? Caveat Lector!" *International Studies Quarterly* 36 (December 1992): 421–38.

———. *Security and International Relations*. New York: Cambridge University Press, 2005.

Kramer, Franklin D., Stuart H. Starr, and Larry K. Wentz, eds. *Cyberpower and National Security*. Washington, DC: National Defense University Press and Potomac Books, 2009.

Krause, Keith, and Michael Williams. "Broadening the Agenda of Security Studies." *Mershon International Studies Review* 40 (October 1996).

Krause, Keith, and Michael Williams, eds. *Critical Security Studies: Concepts and Cases*. Cambridge: Polity, 2002.

Krepinevich, Andrew F. *7 Deadly Scenarios: A Military Futurist Explores War in the Twenty-First Century*. New York: Bantam Books, 2010.

Krepon, Michael. *Better Safe Than Sorry: The Ironies of Living with the Bomb*. Stanford, CA: Stanford University Press, 2009.

Lake, Anthony. *6 Nightmares: Real Threats in a Dangerous World and How America Can Meet Them*. Boston: Little, Brown, 2000.

Lake, David A., and Donald Rothchild, eds. *The International Spread of Ethnic Conflict: Fear, Diffusion, and Escalation*. Princeton, NJ: Princeton University Press, 1998.

Laqueur, Walter. *A History of Terrorism*. New Brunswick, NJ: Transaction Books, 2001.

Larsen, Jeffrey A., and James J. Wirtz, eds. *Arms Control and Cooperative Security*. Boulder, CO: Lynne Rienner, 2009.

Lavoy, Peter, Scott D. Sagan, and James J. Wirtz, eds. *Planning the Unthinkable: How New Powers Will Use Nuclear, Biological, and Chemical Weapons*. Ithaca, NY: Cornell University Press, 2000.

Levi, Michael A. "Is the Environment a National Security Issue?" *International Security* 20 (1995): 35–62.

———. *On Nuclear Terrorism*. Cambridge, MA: Harvard University Press, 2007.

Levi, Michael A., and Michael E. O'Hanlon. *The Future of Arms Control*. Washington, DC: Brookings, 2005.

Lipschutz, Ronnie D., ed. *On Security*. New York: Columbia University Press, 1995.

Lott, Anthony D. *Creating Security: Realism, Constructivism, and U.S. Security Policy*. Burlington, VT: Ashgate, 2004.

Mandel, Robert. *Dark Logic: Transnational Criminal Tactics and Global Security*. Stanford, CA: Stanford University Press, 2010.

———. *Global Security Upheaval: Armed Nonstate Groups Usurping State Stability Functions*. Stanford, CA: Stanford Security Studies, 2013.

———. *Coercing Compliance: State-Initiated Brute Force in Today's World*. Stanford, CA: Stanford Security Studies, 2015.

Mandelbaum, Michael. *The Fate of Nations: The Search for National Security in the Nineteenth and Twentieth Centuries*. New York: Cambridge University Press, 1981.

———. *The Nuclear Revolution: International Politics before and after Hiroshima*. New York: Cambridge University Press, 1981.

Mathews, Jessica Tuchman. "Redefining Security." *Foreign Affairs* 68 (Spring 1989): 162–77.

Mazo, Jeffrey. *Climate Conflict: How Global Warming Threatens Security and What to Do About It*. London: International Institute for Strategic Studies, 2010.

Moran, Theodore H. "International Economics and Security." *Foreign Affairs* 69 (Winter 1990/1991): 74–90.

Morgan, Patrick M. *Deterrence Now*. Cambridge: Cambridge University Press, 2003.

Mueller, John. *Retreat from Doomsday: The Obsolescence of Major War*. New York: Basic Books, 1989.

Narang, Vipin. *Nuclear Strategy in the Modern Era: Regional Powers and International Conflict*. Princeton, NJ: Princeton University Press, 2014.

Neack, Laura. *Elusive Security: States First, People Last*. Lanham, MD: Rowman & Littlefield, 2007.

Newhouse, John. *War and Peace in the Nuclear Age*. New York: Alfred A. Knopf, 1989.

Nye, Joseph S. *Bound to Lead: The Changing Nature of American Power*. New York: Basic Books, 1991.

——. *The Paradox of American Power: Why the World's Superpower Can't Go It Alone*. New York: Oxford University Press, 2002.

——. *Soft Power: The Means to Success in World Politics*. New York: PublicAffairs, 2004.

——. *The Future of Power*. New York: PublicAffairs, 2011.

——. *Is the American Century Over?* Cambridge: Polity, 2015.

Nye, Joseph S., Jr., and Sean M. Lynn-Jones. "International Security Studies: A Report of a Conference on the State of the Field." *International Security* 12 (Spring 1988): 5–27.

Pape, Robert A., and James K. Feldman. *Cutting the Fuse: The Explosion of Global Suicide Terrorism and How to Stop It*. Chicago: University of Chicago Press, 2010.

Paris, Roland. "Human Security: Paradigm Shift or Hot Air?" *International Security* 26 (Fall 2001): 87–102.

Patrick, Stewart. *Weak Links: Fragile States, Global Threats, and International Security*. New York: Oxford University Press, 2011.

Paul, T. V. *Power versus Prudence: Why Nations Forego Nuclear Weapons*. Montreal: McGill University Press, 2000.

——. *The Tradition of Non-Use of Nuclear Weapons*. Stanford, CA: Stanford University Press, 2009.

Paul, T. V., Richard J. Harknett, and James J. Wirtz, eds. *The Absolute Weapon Revisited: Nuclear Arms and the Emerging International Order*. Ann Arbor: University of Michigan Press, 1998.

Payne, Keith B. *Deterrence in the Second Nuclear Age*. Lexington: University Press of Kentucky, 1996.

Perkovich, George, and James M. Acton. *Abolishing Nuclear Weapons*. Adelphi Book 396. London: International Institute for Strategic Studies, 2014.

Perry, William J. "Preparing for the Next Attack." *Foreign Affairs* 80 (2001): 31–47.

Plowman, J. Andrew. *Climate Change and Conflict Prevention*. Washington, DC: National Intelligence University, September 2014.

Powell, Robert. *Nuclear Deterrence Theory: The Search for Credibility*. Cambridge: Cambridge University Press, 1991.

Price-Smith, Andrew T. *The Health of Nations: Infectious Disease, Environmental Change, and Their Effects on National Security and Development*. Cambridge, MA: MIT Press, 2002.

Ralph, Jason G. *Beyond the Security Dilemma: Ending America's Cold War.* Burlington, VT: Ashgate, 2001.

Rhodes, Richard. *The Making of the Atomic Bomb.* New York: Simon and Schuster, 1986.

———. *Dark Sun: The Making of the Hydrogen Bomb.* New York: Simon and Schuster, 1996.

———. *Arsenals of Folly: The Making of the Nuclear Arms Race.* New York: Vintage, 2008.

Ripsman, Norrin M., and T. V. Paul. *Globalization and the National Security State.* New York: Oxford University Press, 2010.

Rothschild, Emma. "What Is Security?" *Daedalus* 124 (Summer 1995): 53–98.

Sagan, Scott D. *Moving Targets: Nuclear Strategy and National Security.* Princeton, NJ: Princeton University Press, 1990.

———. *The Limits of Safety: Organizations, Accidents, and Nuclear Weapons.* Princeton, NJ: Princeton University Press, 1993.

Sagan, Scott D., and Kenneth N. Waltz. *The Spread of Nuclear Weapons: A Debate Renewed.* New York: W. W. Norton, 2003.

Sageman, Marc. *Understanding Terror Networks.* Philadelphia: University of Pennsylvania Press, 2004.

———. *Leaderless Jihad: Terror Networks in the Twenty-First Century.* Philadelphia: University of Pennsylvania Press, 2008.

Schelling, Thomas C. *The Strategy of Conflict.* Oxford: Oxford University Press, 1960.

———. *Arms and Influence.* New Haven, CT: Yale University Press, 1966.

Schelling, Thomas C., and Morton Halperin. *Strategy and Arms Control.* New York: Twentieth Century Fund, 1961.

Sheehan, Michael. *International Security: An Analytical Survey.* Boulder, CO: Lynne Rienner, 2005.

Shelley, Louise. *Human Trafficking: A Global Perspective.* Cambridge: Cambridge University Press, 2010.

Singer, J. David. *Deterrence, Arms Control and Disarmament: Toward a Synthesis in National Security Policy.* Columbus: Ohio State University Press, 1962.

Singer, P. W. *Corporate Warriors: The Rise of the Privatized Military Industry.* Ithaca, NY: Cornell University Press, 2003.

———. *Wired for War: The Robotic Revolution and Conflict in the 21st Century.* New York: Penguin Books, 2009.

Singer, Peter W., and Allan Friedman. *Cybersecurity and Cyberwar: What Everyone Needs to Know.* New York: Oxford University Press, 2014.

Sjoberg, Laura, ed. *Gender and International Security: Feminist Perspectives.* New York: Routledge, 2010.

Smith, Michael E. *International Security: Politics, Policy, Prospects.* New York: Palgrave Macmillan, 2010.

Smoke, Richard. *Paths to Peace: Exploring the Feasibility of Sustainable Peace.* Boulder, CO: Westview, 1987.

———. *National Security and the Nuclear Dilemma: An Introduction to the American Experience in the Cold War.* 3rd ed. New York: McGraw-Hill, 1993.

Spiers, Edward M. *A History of Chemical and Biological Weapons*. London: Reaktion Books, 2010.

Steinbruner, John D. *Principles of Global Security*. Washington, DC: Brookings Institution, 2000.

Stern, Jessica. *The Ultimate Terrorists*. Cambridge, MA: Harvard University Press, 1999.

Suhrke, Astri. "Human Security and the Interest of States." *Security Dialogue* 30, no. 3 (September 1999): 265–76.

Terriff, Terry, Stuart Croft, Lucy James, and Patrick M. Morgan. *Security Studies Today*. Cambridge: Polity, 1999.

Toffler, Alvin, and Heidi Toffler. *War and Anti-War: Survival at the Dawn of the 21st Century*. Boston: Little, Brown, 1993.

Tucker, Jonathan. *War of Nerves: Chemical Warfare from World War I to Al-Qaeda*. New York: Anchor, 2007.

Ullman, Richard. "Redefining Security." *International Security* 8, no. 1 (Summer 1983): 129–53.

United Nations. *Optional Protocol to the UN Convention on the Rights of the Child on the Involvement of Children in Armed Conflicts*. New York: United Nations, 2000.

———. *Summary Report of the Expert Panel on the Use of Private Military and Security Companies by the United Nations*. New York: United Nations, July 31, 2013.

United States. The 9/11 Commission. *Final Report of the National Commission on Terrorist Attacks upon the United States*. New York: W. W. Norton, 2004.

———. National Intelligence Council. *Mapping the Global Future: Report on the 2020 Project*. Washington, DC: Government Printing Office, 2004.

———. National Intelligence Council. *Global Trends 2025: A Transformed World*. Washington, DC: Government Printing Office, 2008.

———. National Intelligence Council. *Global Trends 2030: Alternative Worlds*. Washington, DC: Government Printing Office, 2012.

———. The White House. *National Security Strategy of the United States*. Regularly published. Available at www.whitehouse.gov.

Van Creveld, Martin. *On Future War*. New York: Free Press, 1991.

———. *The Transformation of War*. New York: Free Press, 1991.

———. *Nuclear Proliferation and the Future of Conflict*. New York: Free Press, 1993.

Vinci, Anthony. "The Strategic Use of Fear by the Lord's Resistance Army." *Small Wars and Insurgencies* 16 (2005): 360–81.

Walker, William. *Weapons of Mass Destruction and International Order*. Adelphi Paper 370. London: International Institute for Strategic Studies, 2004.

Walt, Stephen M. "The Renaissance of Security Studies." *International Studies Quarterly* 35, no. 2 (June 1991): 211–40.

Walter, Barbara, and Jack Snyder, eds. *Civil Wars, Insecurity, and Intervention*. New York: Columbia University Press, 1999.

Waltz, Kenneth N. *The Spread of Nuclear Weapons: More May Be Better*. Adelphi Paper 171. London: International Institute for Strategic Studies, 1981.

Weiner, Myron. "Security, Stability, and International Migration." *International Security* 21 (1992): 91–126.

Williams, Robert E., Jr., and Paul R. Viotti, eds. *Arms Control: History, Theory, and Policy*. 2 vols. Santa Barbara, CA: Praeger Security International, 2012.

Wriston, Walter B. *The Twilight of Sovereignty: How the Information Revolution Is Transforming Our World*. New York: Charles Scribner's Sons, 1992.

Wyn Jones, R. *Security, Strategy and Critical Theory*. Boulder, CO: Lynne Rienner, 1999.

Yergin, Daniel H. *The Prize: The Epic Quest for Oil, Money and Power*. New York: Simon & Schuster, 1991.

———. *The Quest: Energy, Security, and the Remaking of the Modern World*. New York: Penguin, 2012.

Index

9/11 Commission, 106, 107, 108, 204, 212, 250
9/11 terrorist attacks, 115, 116, 247, 248

Abdulmutallab, Omar Farouk ("underwear bomber"), 102
An Abrupt Climate Change Scenario and Implications for United States Security (Office of Net Assessment), 241, 243
Abu Nidal (terrorist organization), 170
Acheson, Dean, 55
Acheson-Lilienthal Report, 55, 56
Afghanistan, 73, 87, 92, 93, 94, 97, 148, 151, 171, 172, 193, 199, 207, 212, 216, 236, 237; costs of war in, 36, 213; depleted uranium in, 229; drone use in, 32–33, 163; drug trafficking in, 89, 140, 148, 149, 153; and *mujahidin*, 151, 199, 237; Al Qaeda in, 92, 98, 108, 194, 237, 253; Taliban in, 31, 111, 161, 194; U.S. aid to, 5, 254; war in, vii, 2, 4, 5, 25, 28, 31, 35, 42, 85, 95, 98, 162, 190, 197, 246, 253
Agent Orange (defoliant), 73
Agreed Framework, 110
AIDS. *See* HIV/AIDS

AK-47 (Kalashnikov assault rifle), 43, 153
Albania, 80, 112
Algeria, 28, 103, 192
Alibek, Ken, 79
Amherst, Sir Jeffrey, 77
Ancheta, Jean, 164
Angola, 41, 45, 132, 194, 198, 216, 233
Annan, Kofi, 197, 203, 258
anthrax, 67–68, 75, 77–78, 79, 80, 81
Anti-Ballistic Missile (ABM) Treaty, 60, 61, 98
Arab Spring, 26, 74, 196, 223
Arctic National Wildlife Refuge, 237
Ardita, Julio Cesar, 165
Argentina, 117
Arkin, William, 41
Arms and Influence (Schelling), 27
Arms Control Association, 80
Arms Trade Treaty, 39–40
arms trafficking, 139, 141, 143, 144, 145, 148, 150–154, 220, 251, 258
Arquilla, John, 92, 160
The Art of War (Sun Tzu), 35
Asahara, Shoko, 75
al-Assad, Bashar, 74, 196–97, 253–54
assassination, 76, 86, 102, 141, 157, 172, 202. *See also* targeted killings
Assassins (Shia sect), 94

311

About the Authors

Dan Caldwell is distinguished professor of political science at Pepperdine University. He earned his AB, MA, and PhD degrees at Stanford University and a master's degree from the Fletcher School of Law and Diplomacy. He has held visiting appointments at the University of Southern California, UCLA, and Brown University. Dr. Caldwell has received a number of awards, including Professor of the Year and the Howard A. White Excellence in Teaching Award at Pepperdine University, the Pew Faculty Fellowship in International Affairs at Harvard University, a NATO Fellowship, and a United States Institute of Peace Fellowship. Professor Caldwell served on active duty as an officer in the U.S. Naval Reserve and during that time held positions at the Naval Postgraduate School and in the Executive Office of the President. He is the editor of four books and the author of five, most recently *Vortex of Conflict: U.S. Policy toward Afghanistan, Pakistan, and Iraq*.

Robert E. Williams Jr. is professor of political science at Pepperdine University. After graduating summa cum laude with a BA in history from Abilene Christian University, he earned an MA from the Johns Hopkins University School of Advanced International Studies and a PhD from the University of Virginia. Before joining the Pepperdine faculty, Dr. Williams taught at Southwest Missouri State University (now Missouri State University) in Springfield, Missouri, and at Abilene Christian University in Abilene, Texas. He is the coeditor (with Paul R. Viotti) of a two-volume work titled *Arms Control: History, Theory, and Policy*. He has published articles and book chapters on just war theory, human rights, corruption in Equatorial Guinea, and American theologian Reinhold Niebuhr.